THE
collection building
READER

Edited by
Betty-Carol Sellen and Arthur C⊔

Neal-Schuman Publishers, Inc.
New York   London

Published by Neal-Schuman Publishers, Inc.
100 Varick Street
New York, NY 10013

Printed and bound in the United States of America

Library of Congress Cataloging-in-Publication Data

The Collection Building Reader / edited by Betty-Carol Sellen and
    Arthur Curley.
        p.   cm.
    Articles selected from issues of Collection building.
    Includes index.
    ISBN 1-55570-092-6
    1. Collection development (Libraries)   I. Sellen, Betty-Carol.
II. Curley, Arthur.   III. Collection building.
Z687.C63   1992
    025.2 ' 1--dc20   91-48221
                                                                      CIP

CONTENTS

Section III: Evaluation

Section IV: Resource Sharing

PREFACE

All libraries, whether built to satisfy the needs of a research community or to supply information and entertainment to the public, are evaluated by the size and quality of their collections.

Excellent collections don't just happen, even when there are magnificent endowments, gifts, and bequests, or generous tax payers and public authorities. Excellent collections result from the work of librarians—librarians who select, acquire, arrange, and provide access.

The primary element in determining excellence, of course, is the relevance and adequacy of the collection in meeting the needs of its users, including anticipation of the future needs of a scholarly researcher or a recreational reader.

Librarians who build excellent collections are knowledgeable, educated, thinking people. They learn about their constituencies and anticipate their intellectual, informational, and recreational needs. They know about the various forms of knowledge and information and are familiar with the publishing industry as well. Librarians must cultivate a "universal view" of what is needed in a collection rather than relying on the view any one person or school of thought; collection development

is one of the most important professional responsibilities of the librarian—it cannot be left to others.

Collection development in libraries is nearly always done in an environment that requires complex and competitive needs to be met: there is not enough space to house all that is wanted, there is not enough money to buy everything requested, and there is a population that may have strong differences of opinion about what is desirable and necessary.

In response to the need for ongoing professional education in this complex area, the journal *Collection Building* was begun by Neal-Schuman in 1978. Editorial guidance of the journal has been provided by Arthur Curley, director of the Boston Public Library, since its inception. Now in its fifteenth year, the journal has published, and continues to publish articles on all aspects of collection development.

The *Collection Building Reader* brings together some of the most useful and informative articles published in the journal—in a practical one-volume resource for librarians. The articles selected were grouped together around three central issues in collection development.

The first section of the book, "Management Issues," contains articles about collection standards, about the importance of developing written policy statements, and about specific problems in some of the components of collection development.

"Selection/Deselection," the second section, is about what factors influence choices made in choosing materials for collections. It also contains two articles on the more challenging topic of deselection, or the weeding of library collections.

Finally, there is the need to periodically step back and look at what one is doing—to test premises and assess selection decisions. The articles that consider this aspect of collection development—"Evaluation"—make up the third and final solution of this reader.

Since this is a retrospective reader, there is little here on the effects of technology upon the contents of a library. Also, the authorship of the articles is weighted toward academic librarians; this is a reflection of publishing activity and not a selection bias on the part of this editor.

Representing the best of *Collection Building,* the editor believes this Reader will be a valuable asset in the work of the library's greatest resource — the librarian.

Betty-Carol Sellen

INTRODUCTION

From its inception a decade and a half ago, *Collection Building* has been a journal with a mission. Collection development, the central focus of librarianship for most of the profession's history, had by the mid-seventies been ignominiously dethroned—or so it seemed to *Collection Building*'s founders, at least—by such trendier obsessions as automation, networking, resource-sharing, and whatever particular management fad was in vogue that season.

A renewed attention to collections as the foundation of any library, no matter how glitzy or "politically correct" its services and programs, was our principal hope for the journal. The term "building" was deliberately chosen to stress the dynamic nature of resource development.

In the very first issue, Betty-Carol Sellen, a member of the founding editorial board, stressed that while a respectable number of collection development studies could be found in any search of *Library Literature*, the focus of such studies was almost exclusively the large university-research library.

Our goal has been not just to correct that imbalance by publishing more diverse studies, but to attack the underlying attitude responsible for the lack of research data on which to base collection development policies in public, school, college, and community college libraries: namely, a defeatist assumption that excellence in resource development is an appropriate goal only in large research institutions. Today, even some of our greatest libraries have lowered their collection building sights in the name of resource-sharing or "access over ownership."

The publishers and editors of *Collection Building* firmly believe that collection development is an essential responsibility in libraries of *every* size and category, and that building effective library resources requires skillful analysis of community needs, aggressive search strategies, discovery as well as selection, and an extensive body of research on which to base collection planning.

To achieve these goals, as stated in the inaugural issue of *Collection Building*, we have sought to:

- stimulate and publish studies on diverse aspects of collection development
- broaden the traditional scope of collection development studies to include *all* types and sizes of libraries
- reflect the increasing diversity of informational formats which librarians must learn to evaluate

- stress the importance of user (and non-user) studies to effective resources development
- enhance the professional expertise of the practicing librarian
- promote excellence in the development and evaluation of library collections.

The selections in this volume are ones which we believe have been especially pertinent to the mission of *Collection Building,* and we hope that together they will prove continually useful to both the student and practitioner of collection development.

Arthur Curley, Editor
Collection Building

SECTION I

Management Issues

Information Policies for Collection Development Librarians

by Joseph J. Branin

Beware of "Info-Smoke" warns Art Plotnick in a recent *American Libraries* editorial. It clouds the meaning and purpose of libraries by embroiling them in the "world's hottest commodity"—information.[1] "The information age" or "the information society" are clichés used with abandon by many librarians. "Information" is the buzzword for grant applications, articles, and new names for libraries and library schools. As Plotnick rhetorically asks, "Who *isn't* in the information business?"

Underlying the current preoccupation with information, whether couched in terms of "information handling," "information storage and retrieval," "information centers," or "information policy," is a legitimate need for a better definition and broader understanding of how the content of knowledge is organized, preserved, and communicated. In libraries this means expanding responsibility beyond the traditional information boundaries of published print or print-derived materials into new formats of electronic data, images, and sounds. Therefore it means a change in the way libraries deliver information to users. Collections of material that are housed on-site and owned by libraries are being supplemented by information sources that are remote but rapidly accessed using new delivery systems.

Collection development librarians are vitally involved in many aspects of the information business. They are responsible for building and managing the library's resource base, and their activities should be guided by a written collection development policy. This document also serves as an information policy for the library, describing collection strengths and weaknesses, and formats and subjects emphasized or avoided. However, an examination of most libraries' collection development policies would show that bibliographers are asked to focus almost exclusively on collections of owned print and print-derived resources. Such materials now make up the bulk of library collections, certainly in research libraries, and will for years to come. But in this new information age, collection development librarians must look beyond their traditional shelving to a world of computer screens and databases. They must link their collection development policies with campus-wide and national information policy.

Barbara Moran in *Academic Libraries: The Changing Knowledge Centers of Colleges and Universities* predicts a shift away from collections toward information access. According to Moran, "As time goes on, print sources will constitute a diminished proportion of the total information available for scholarly purposes, and as this trend progresses, librarians will deal more with 'information' than with books."[2]

To date, however, the introduction of computer technology has not diminished the output of print resources. As Irving Horowitz points out in *Communicating Ideas: The Crisis of Publishing in a Post-Industrial Society,* "There is nothing in the evidence to suggest that the flow of print has contracted under the impact of the new technology."[3] Book production figures and book publishing revenues continue to rise. For example, book publishing revenues have steadily grown from less than $500 million in 1950, to more than $2.9 billion in 1970, and over $7.0 billion in 1980.[4]

> ... collection development librarians must help create a system that organizes and links all information sources, whether traditional or new, print or electronic

Electronic information is not replacing print formats, it is sustaining and expanding the information explosion of post-industrial society. Not only is there more print information available, but other formats are emerging as effective and popular carriers of information as well. Collection development librarians have been trying for some time to contend with the print information explosion. Even the largest research libraries cannot hope to be self-sufficient. No single library can provide all the research material its clientele may need. To overcome this limitation, libraries have banded together on a local, regional, or national level to form cooperative networks for resource sharing and document delivery. Membership in the Research Libraries Group, OCLC, the Center for Research Libraries, or any number of regional or local consortia is an important element in a library's information capacity.

However, the challenge of managing information services today extends beyond cooperative collection development and interlibrary loan programs. As Patricia Battin states in "The Library: Center of the Restructured University," librarians now face a dual challenge: "we must provide new structures of access to knowledge in an increasing variety of formats and, at the same time, continue to preserve, manage, and make available scholarly information in the traditional printed formats with appropriate links between all formats."[5] Collection development librarians cannot abandon their commitment to the book, the journal, and the microform, but they must extend their range to include computer software and access to local and remote databases. Most important, collection development librarians must help create a system or infrastructure that organizes and links all information sources, whether traditional or new, print or electronic.

AN INFORMATION POLICY

An information policy is essential to define information sources and means of access to them throughout an organization or community, just as a collection development policy is meant to guide the selection and management of library material. Advances in technology have created a decentralized and fragmented information environment. In addition to libraries, computer centers, commercial database vendors, and individual researchers now have the ability to compile and retrieve vast stores of information.

What role can or should collection development librarians play in this new information-rich environment? One important part is to identify and organize various formats and sources of infor-

mation important to a specific discipline. For example, at the University of Georgia, the library's Social Sciences Bibliographer, James Kuhlman, found that databases needed by his faculty were available on campus but often inaccessible. Writing in *American Libraries,* Kuhlman describes a situation commonly found on campuses: "Research libraries have left it up to computer centers to deal with the machine-readable materials. Computer centers in turn left it to users to find, purchase, and maintain their own materials. Data sets were viewed as the personal possessions of individuals; cataloging of data sets was ignored. Faculty in the same department and different state agencies often bought the same, expensive tapes, only to lose and forget about them."[6]

CENTRALIZED SERVICES

Kuhlman, working with social science faculty and computer center staff, changed this fragmented situation by centralizing services in the library. Control of local membership in the Interuniversity Consortium for Political and Social Research, which collects and makes available a variety of numeric databases, was moved from the Political Science Department to the library. The University's Computer Center transferred staff and responsibility for the servicing of census data tapes to the library, and plans were made to move the Business School's database operations to the library. In this example, the library took responsibility for the acquisition and cataloging of social sciences databases and for patron assistance in using them, while the Computer Center handled storage and technical servicing of the tapes.

On a larger scale, Columbia University is planning to integrate all information services on its campus. According to Columbia's former Vice President and University Librarian, Patricia Battin, "The very diversity of scholarly inquiry and information needs requires in the electronic age an unprecedented degree of centralized, coordinated linkages and compatibilities to serve that diversity and permit the autonomy necessary for productive and creative scholarship."[7] Information services at Columbia will be centralized in a "Scholarly Information Center" which will merge the library and the Computer Center. Such centralization and integration will, according to Battin, "provide one-stop shopping for the University community as well as a stabilizing planning mechanism for effective and flexible response to rapidly changing technologies."[8]

Formulating an information policy need not imply any particular organization of information services. Centralized services is just one of many options available. Richard Dougherty, Director of Libraries at the University of Michigan, cautions librarians about their fascination with merging libraries and computer centers. According to Dougherty, the organization of libraries and computer centers differs greatly and "models that rely on coordination and collaboration are more likely to predominate in the near term than models that subordinate one unit to another."[9] Instead of merging the two units, Dougherty recommends careful cooperation between the library and computer center through the use of joint working groups.[10]

Developing a strategy for coordinating or integrating diverse information sources, whether in a single institution or among a group of libraries, is an important policy issue, but not the only one that collection development librarians will have to address. If information has become "the world's hottest commodity," one can be certain that questions of costs, ownership, and access will also be at the forefront of consideration.

INFORMATION: WHO PAYS?

Information has never really been free, but new technology makes the question of who pays more difficult to answer. Should information sources and services be funded centrally and then distributed to users free of charge? Or should users be assessed per-item fees for their access to information, an option that is readily available with computerized information retrieval?[11] Ideally the traditional library model should prevail, where a communal policy allows free access to collections and reference services. In reality, however, more and more costs associated with access to information are being passed on directly to users. Most libraries are charging for computerized search services, either to recover costs or to control demand, and most computer centers have always found it necessary to charge users for their services.

According to Donald Dunn, "One of the driving forces for change in information technology has been the evolutionary, steady reduction in cost in the computer and communication industries."[12] The availability of pocket calculators and inexpensive home computers is evidence of this trend. But the costs of introducing new information technology systems can still be quite high. As Richard Dougherty points out, "It is not unusual to hear of price tags approaching $50 million (or more for large campuses) when planning a fully computerized campus linked together by a telecommunications network."[13] Also, equipment must be maintained and upgraded, and software developed or purchased. For collection development librarians, who already are strapped for book and

journal funds, the prospect of adding new formats and in some cases paying for access to rather than ownership of information may not be encouraging.

There are no easy solutions to this situation. Collection development librarians must become involved in planning the economics of information services at their institutions. Computer software and electronic access to databases are not replacing the need for published print material. One should not be sacrificed for the other. Also, direct charges to users for certain types of information services should be examined carefully. What are the criteria for determining when a user should pay and when have free access to information? A policy that addresses these difficult economic issues will help avoid discrimination against a particular user group or against a certain information format.

INFORMATION: WHO OWNS IT?

Another important issue is that of ownership; information is a valuable market commodity. This issue is complex and can involve questions of censorship and intellectual freedom as well as property rights and privacy. It is both a national and local policy issue. Is information a "public good," that is, "a good that one user can consume without diminishing its availability or usefulness to another user"?[14] Or is it an "economic good," a commodity whose value will be lessened by free, unrestricted access? According to Donald Dunn, "Patents and copyrights create property rights in information and ideas with the objective of making investments in the creation of intellectual property more attractive, relative to investment in goods not subject to copying. Patents and copyrights not only protect the creator of new information from 'piracy' by others seeking to make copies, but also create transferable pieces of property that can be sold in the market, thus enhancing the value of new information by making it more like other goods."[15]

Collection development librarians are accustomed to purchasing books, journals, and microforms that then become the property of their libraries. These materials can be used freely and repeatedly by patrons, usually at no charge. Only copying significant portions of their content, not use, is restricted or controlled by copyright law. Some of the new information formats, however, do have more restrictions or controls over their use. Often the purchaser of a computer software package must agree to limit its use to a particular individual or location. Access to an online, full text database usually involves a fee for each use, and this practice may spread to traditional formats. Looking to

Information has never really been free, but new technology makes the question of who pays more difficult to answer

... librarians must play a vital role in forming a new structure that assures fair and open access to a great variety of information sources

Western Europe and to the control database vendors exercise over their products, authors and publishers of print material in the United States are lobbying for Public Lending Right legislation. If enacted, such legislation would mean an end to the tradition of free access to information in American libraries. The user or the library would be required to pay a fee each time an item is borrowed.[16]

The U.S. Federal government, the largest producer of information in the world, is also turning to a marketplace concept to control and reduce its data output. As part of its agenda to shrink the Federal government, the Reagan Administration tried to assign what were once public responsibilities to the private sector, a phenomenon labeled "privatization." The Office of Management and Budget's Circular A-130, issued in December 1985 after much criticism by librarians, directs government agencies to rely whenever possible on the private sector for the dissemination of government information and to follow an "only-disseminate-it-if-you-must" policy.[17] Examples of information programs of government agencies turned over to private contractors can be found in the Department of Agriculture, the Patent and Trademark Office, and the Environmental Protection Agency.[18] Librarians fear that such practice will restrict access to public, government information, because ownership is being transferred to the private sector where economic and property right controls will be exerted.

On the local level, questions of information ownership may result more from organizational turf or individual privacy issues then from political or economic considerations. Will university departments or individual researchers give up control of a database which they may have purchased with grant funds or compiled themselves? Is the database so idiosyncratic or personal that it does not belong in the public domain? Universities that have begun to prepare directories or catalogs of their campus databases face such questions. Collection development librarians must help their institutions construct policies regarding what are and are not appropriate public information sources.

Restricted access to information because of organizational inefficiencies, pricing, licensing agreements, privatization or parochialism goes against the grain of librarians' basic professional ethic of protecting intellectual freedom. The Council on Library Resources in 1985 issued a statement on Scholarship, Research, and Access to Information with the following introduction:

Those who are concerned with libraries and books have long recognized and often strongly asserted the need for unconstrained access to information as a condition essential to every democratic society. The computer, telecommunications, and text storage technologies that now play a prominent and at times dominant role in many aspects of library service and information systems have created a very different and complicated new environment. The established structure is changing and powerful economic forces are having a profound influence on all aspects of scholarly communication, libraries, and information services generally. While technology is powerful and brings a promise of unmatched opportunities, it is essential to remember that ready access to information is not automatically assured. That goal must be constantly and aggressively pursued.[19]

SELECTION VS. CENSORSHIP

Collection development librarians know there is a fine line between selection and censorship. In fact, too much concentration on the selection activity of a collection development program can lead to censorship. Eric Moon made this point in *Book Selection and Censorship in the Sixties.* According to Moon "the principal reason why shelf collections are so frequently inadequate in meeting readers needs is that the book selection process stops too early, operates too much in limbo. Rare is the library where trained personnel are assigned fulltime to the care and study of the book collection and its usage."[20] To avoid one's own prejudices in the selection process, the collection development librarian must put that process in the context of a complete, well-organized collection management program. Collection development librarians must know their collections, must know their users, and they must follow a carefully prepared collection policy, if they are to select the best and most useful material for their libraries.

Much has changed in the 25 years since Moon wrote about selection and censorship. As the Council on Library Resources statement points out, the new information technology has "created a very different and complicated new environment." Just as collection development librarians must put their selection activities within the context of a broader management program, so too must they relate their library's traditional collections to the larger information environment. The established structure is changing, and collection development librarians must play a vital role in forming a new structure that assures fair and open access to a great variety of information sources. They can do this by actively participating in formulation of information policy on both the local and national levels, and keeping their eyes clear of "info smoke."

References

1. Art Plotnick, "Info-Smoke Gets in Your Eyes," *American Libraries,* 17 (Oct. 1986): 656.
2. Barbara Moran, *Academic Libraries: The Changing Knowledge Centers of Colleges and Universities* (Washington, D.C.: Association for the Study of Higher Education, 1984), 75.
3. Irving Louis Horowitz, *Communicating Ideas: The Crisis of Publishing in a Post-Industrial Society* (New York: Oxford University Press, 1986), 15.
4. Dan Lacey, "Publishing and the New Technology," *Books, Libraries and Electronics: Essays on the Future of Written Communications* (White Plains, N.Y.: Knowledge Industry Publications, 1982), 85.
5. Patricia Battin, "The Library: Center of the Restructured University," *College and Research Libraries,* 45 (May 1984): 172.
6. James R. Kuhlman and Everett S. Lee, "Data-Power to the People," *American Libraries,* 17 (Nov. 1986): 758.
7. Patricia Battin, "The Electronic Library - A Vision for the Future," *EDUCOM Bulletin,* 19 (Summer 1984): 13.
8. Ibid., 16–17.
9. Richard M. Dougherty, "Libraries and Computing Centers: A Blueprint for Collaboration," *College and Research Libraries,* 48 (July 1987): 290.
10. Ibid., 295.
11. Rowland Lorimer, "Implications of the New Technologies of Information," *Scholarly Publishing,* 16 (April 1985): 200.
12. Donald A. Dunn, "Information resources and the New Information Technologies: Implications for Public Policy," *Information Reports and Bibliographies,* 13 (1984): 7.
13. Dougherty, "Libraries and Computer Centers," 293.
14. Dunn, "Information Resources and the New Information Technologies," 8.
15. Ibid.
16. Horowitz, *Communicating ideas,* 80.
17. Task Force on Government Information in Electronic Formats, "Report No. 2" (Association of Research Libraries, Washington, D.C. 21 April 1987), 30.
18. Jeffrey L. Fox, "EPA Dumps Chemical Data System," *Science,* 226 (Nov. 16, 1984) 816.
19. Board of Directors, Council on Library Resources, "Scholarship, Research, and Access to Information: A Statement from the Council on Library Resources" (Council on Library Resources, Inc., Washington, D.C., January 1985).
20. Eric Moon, ed., *Book Selection and Censorship in the Sixties* (New York: R.R. Bowker Company, 1969), 11.

Collection Development and the College Library: A State-of-the-Art Review

by Mickey Moskowitz

ollection development literature has burgeoned over the past decade, yet the complaint is still heard that college libraries are not engaged in meaningful collection development activities. College librarians often consider methods described in published research as too time-consuming, technologically dependent, or statistically complex to apply to their own situations. How relevant is the literature to the practical needs of the collection developer? In addressing this question, a theoretical overview of collection development is presented, and recent publications reviewed, in terms of their relevance to collection planning, implementation, and evaluation in the small college library.

Hannaford points out that collection development must be defined as more than just the sum of its parts—e.g., selecting, acquiring, budgeting, allocating, deselecting, evaluating; a library can do all these and yet do no collection development.[1] Collection development is the systematic building of a library collection based on meaningful data rather than subjective choice or chance. It directly relates to Lancaster's observation that "all libraries have one overriding objective that is practical, that to a certain extent is measurable, and that may be used as a basis for evaluation...the library exists as an interface between the universe of bibliographic resources and a particular user population.[2]

In building the collection, the librarian relies on two essential sources of information: published knowledge and user needs.[3] Published knowledge is dependent upon the subject literature, the collection of which takes into account the college's curriculum and institutional goals. Each subject has its

own heavily used types of information and core literatures through which it records, displays, stores, and transmits pertinent states of knowledge at a given point in time.[4] Each has its own publishing characteristics as well. Some, like the physical sciences, rely heavily on journals; others, like literature and fine arts, on monographs and mixed media. In addition, each has its own associated subject areas in relationship to specific user groups. Aware of these differences, the collection developer must know the most essential publishers in the field, as well as the reviewing channels to trust in building the collection.

Use relates to demand—both the current and potential demands of patrons. Which of these demands should have more influence on the building of the collection is a constant theme throughout the literature. It is obvious that the college library cannot collect in response to unqualified potential use. However, in building collections largely focused on current academic demands, the librarian may become vulnerable to unexpected queries or unanticipated changes in the curriculum and/or student body. In response, college librarians have recognized the integral role of resource-sharing in the collection development process. Through such cooperative efforts, librarians can share that part of their holdings not in current demand and rely on other institutions for resources they cannot acquire or maintain within their own collections.

With this framework in mind, the professional literature since 1975 is reviewed selectively from the perspective of the collection developer at a small college library and discussed in relationship to the three basic components of the collection development process: planning, implementation, and evaluation.[5] In assessing the usefulness of the published research, the following questions are considered: Are the data reported relevant to the needs of a college library? Is the effort involved in implementing the methodology realistic, given staff and time constraints? Is the literature surveyed one of consensus or contradiction?

COLLECTION PLANNING

Collection Development Policy: There is widespread agreement in the literature that an academic library should have a written policy that states collection objectives and provides guidelines for day-to-day decision making. There is also consensus on the elements to be included in such a policy. The model provided by the RTSD "Guidelines on Collection Development" is endorsed in chapters of texts by Evans, Gardner, Katz, and Rader,[6] articles by Bryant, Buzzard, Coleman, Dowd, Feng, Koenig, Osburn, and others;[7] in addition, numerous sample policies have been published in Spec Kit No. 38 and by Futas.[8] Their message is clear: begin the policy with a statement of library goals and objectives; designate responsibility for collection development; define the library's relationship to other institutional holdings; include specific policy on gifts, duplication, deselection.

However, it is the subject-by-subject analysis of the collection that is considered the heart of the document. For academic libraries, this includes division of the collection into Library of Congress or other classification schemes; assignment of guideline codes such as "Comprehensive," "Study," "Basic," to assess the strength of the existing collection in each category; identification of current collection activity and the extent of collection development deemed appropriate to support institutional goals.[9] Emphasis on preplanning and the use of standardized language is echoed throughout the various publications.

In light of this consensus, it is surprising to find that few college libraries have completed collection development policies and that those written are frequently inadequate.[10] According to Bryant, college librarians give subject analysis a low priority because too much time is required to complete the data. She suggests that the weaknesses in collection development policies, and the plans for preparing them, are caused by the failure of academic libraries to have well-tailored information systems.[11]

Collection Needs Assessment: Although sources agree on the need to analyze the library collection when preparing a collection development policy, they are relatively vague on how to go about this. Buzzard recommends that information for the individual subject statements be based on the response of faculty, subject bibliographers, and other librarians. Osburn calls for preceding the drafting of subject statements with a comprehensive evaluation according to a uniform plan, but does not focus on the plan itself. Bryant refers the reader to the "The RTSD Guidelines on Evaluation" for specific techniques; however, this publication provides only an overview of various evaluative methods, and can hardly be considered a comprehensive guide. The standard sources on collection development focus more on *why* to write a policy and what to include than on *how* to gather the data to support decision making.

The large body of research referred to as "use studies" has important implications for assessing collection needs. These studies go beyond input data—how many books in the collection, how many new titles ordered to analyze output—how many library materials actually are used. If use is defined as whether and/or how often a title is borrowed, circulation studies are helpful in assessing collection needs. Based on the earlier work of Fussler and Simons,[12] these studies assume that records of past use over sufficient periods of time can predict future use. The Pittsburgh study, the most publicized use study to appear over the past decade, was designed to show the extent library materials were used over a specified period of time and the full cost of such use. All monographs acquisitions and transactions at the Hillman Library between 1968 and 1975 were recorded through an automated circulation system. Findings showed that 40 percent of these books never circulated during their first six years on the shelf and that any given book purchased had only slilghtly better than one in two chances of ever circulating.[13]

This study has important implications for even the smallest college library. The Pittsburgh syndrome may be observed in most undergraduate collections. For instance, Trueswell's research at Mt. Holyoke College Library found that 40 percent of the holdings had not circulated in the past seven years.[14] Ellelt applied the Pittsburgh methodology to a circulation study in his library of about 20,000 volumes, reporting results compatible with the Pittsburgh findings.[15] Use may be more accurately measured by circulation in a small college library than in a university library where research requires extensive use of noncirculating resources. As Peat points out, the college library is characterized by more intensive use of a small body of material, typically current inprints, and often multiple copies, with a high circulation potential.[16]

The Pittsburgh study is, however, limited in its *practical* application to a small college library: even with an automated circulation system, considerable effort is required in tracking acquisitions and in in-

It is obvious that the college library cannot collect in response to unqualified potential use. However, in building collections largely focused on current academic demands, the librarian may become vulnerable to unexpected queries or unanticipated changes in the curriculum and/or student body.

terpreting and analyzing data. And what would such a study prove? We already know that in the college library selection is largely course-related. Nor would such an investigation determine which new books should be ordered; the data reported are all after-the-fact in terms of book selection. As Massman cautions, such circulation figures may say more about the teaching strengths or weaknesses of various academic departments than the collection needs of the library.[17]

COLLECTION IMPLEMENTATION

Implementation takes place between collection planning and collection evaluation. This review concentrates on two of the most challenging aspects of implementation: which monographs to weed and which journals to retain. The large volume of literature on deselection reflects the rapid growth of most libraries during the 1960s, coupled with the lack of funds to build additional storage space faced from the 1970s on.

Weeding models are usually based on Bradford's Law of Scattering and document obsolescence. Bradford discovered that a comparatively small number of core journals in the scientific fields studied yielded a high proportion of all the relevant papers. Beyond this nucleus of high-yield core journals, he identified zones of less productive journals, each zone provided a reduced yield as increasing numbers of periodicals were added.[18] The Law of Scattering refers to this diminishing returns phenomenon, in which each additional item added satisfies a decreasing numer of demands.

Although developed for journal use, Bradford's theory was applied to monograph collections by Trueswell, whose studies showed about 80 percent of book usage experienced by 20 percent of holdings.[19] The obsolescence factor, described earlier by Fussler and Simon, refers to the decline in use rate as a document ages. Buckland relates these findings to a pattern of diminishing returns observed in the factors determining total library size: number of titles bought and length of time titles are kept.[20]

Building on this research base, Slote's work on deselection attempts to relate theory to practice. He identifies two parts of the book collection—the "core," which satisfies a high percentage of current demands and a "noncore," representing very little use. In distinguishing core from noncore, he considers the most important criterion to be shelf-time period—the length of time a volume remains in the library between successive uses.[21] Although Slote offers a considerable amount of sound, practical advice, academic librarians must question his assumption that shelf-time is a quick and easy approach to

deselection in their libraries. No set period of time can be applied across the various subject literatures contained in the college collection; the shelf-time criterion for books on science will differ markedly from books on humanities. Application of the shelf-time criterion is also highly dependent on the cut-off point selected; many would weed items not used in ten years, but resist doing so if the span were two or three. In addition, distinctions by type of monograph—text, paperback, reference book, thesis—must be carefully considered in setting up a shelf-time standard.

The retention of periodicals is another difficult issue. Buckland's research provides an example for determining how many journal titles to retain for how many years. By analyzing the cost of acquiring, binding, and storing journals versus the cost of attaining them on interlibrary loan, he recommends that heavily used journals be kept till usage drops to the point where it is more expensive to store issues than to borrow them; little-used journals may often be cheaper to borrow than to acquire at all.[22]

The problem, of course, is to identify which journals, and which years of these journals, are actually being used. In academic libraries where journals do not circulate, various methods of inhouse reshelving counts have been attempted. Unfortunately, these tend to be time-consuming and not always reliable; studies have shown that as little as 22 percent of titles consulted in the library in a given area are left on the tables.[23] Nevertheless, a list of all journal titles ranked in order of frequency of inhouse use would be important data to consider in making retention decisions.

COLLECTION EVALUATION

Mosher defines evaluation as the process of determining the utility of the collection or the requirements of the academic program.[24] Evaluation must be based on guidelines and goals provided in the collection development policy. Although time-consuming and demanding in terms of expertise and judgment, evaluation provides the information necessary for effective collection planning and implementation.

There are many different purposes for evaluating a collection and the techniques used should depend on the kind and quality of data required. Checking subject bibliographies, lists of recommended readings, and the catalogs of similar collections is one method commonly used to evaluate college libraries. However, this ignores differences in user needs and the structure of subject literatures.[25] The results of list checking can tell something about a library's holdings relative to the published list; however, the scope of the subject covered on the list may not be an appropriate definition of that subject for a particular library. The problem is to find objective and accurate methods for evaluating the "quality" of a collection. Two possible techniques are the application of standards and the implementation of user surveys.

The "Standards for College Libraries," last published in 1975, has frequently been applied in evaluating undergraduate collections in preparation for accreditation or other self-studies. These standards call for a basic collection of 85,000 volumes, with the addition of specific numbers of volumes for full-time students and faculty members, undergraduate major and minor fields, and graduate programs. For small college libraries, the achievement of these standards would require an enormous increase in collection size and shelving space—improbable to attain given current budgetary constraints.

The use of these standards as a realistic goal for collection evaluation is questioned by Kaser, who points out that the 1977 HEGIS report showed that only a small percentage of American colleges could meet 100 percent of these standards.[26] He warns that there is no clear understanding of the standards within the college library community; some library directors want to use them to prove to their colleagues how good their libraries are; others, to prove to their presidents how poor they are. Evans argues that the standards are wrong for the fundamental reason that they are input measures only and provide no indication of a library's performance.[27] A collection may meet the size recommended in the standards, but be of poor quality and inappropriate in responding to user needs.

User studies are an alternative to checking compliance with standards for collection evaluation. Bonn stresses that finding out what users think comes closest to an evaluation in terms of a library's objectives and mission.[28] By focusing on direct feedback by users, surveys can provide information that use studies cannot, e.g., user failure to find materials, user groups that need to be better served, changing trends or learning interests.[29]

A user survey must be developed with a particular library and a particular purpose in mind. It requires the framing of unambiguous questions and demands considerable time and effort to analyze results. SPEC Kit No. 71 provides several models of user satisfaction surveys.[30] However, these assess a range of library services and do not focus on collection evaluation. "Guidelines for Use and User Studies" states its intention is not to equip librarians to do use or user studies, but to allow them to determine the kind of study best suited to their needs.[31] Librarians must go beyond the collection development literature to learn the survey methods, sampling techniques, and statistics needed to conduct worthwhile self-studies.

CONCLUSION

The current collection development literature is pertinent to the needs of the practicing college librarian in several ways. There are publications which provide a conceptual framework for collection development, analyzing this complex process into its component parts and depicting essential interrelationships. The literature also presents the collection developer with an important mission: the preparation of a written policy statement.

How are data to be gathered and analyzed to support collection development policy planning and decision making? Contemporary literature does not present college librarians with easy solutions. Applications described in the published research require more staff, time, funds, technology, and statistical expertise than available in small college libraries. However, there is an essential connection between the research base of collection development and the everyday needs of the practicing college librarian. To build on this base, librarians must be discriminating in selecting the research pertinent to specific collection development objectives. They must also be imaginative in adapting approaches and techniques given limited resources available to implement them. The challenge is to use the literature to develop an active, ongoing plan for gathering information to support decision making on collection development.

Notes and References

1. William E. Hannaford, "Collection Development in College Libraries," in Robert E. Danford, ed., Library Resources for College Scholars: Transactions of Conference Held at Washington and Lee University (Washington and Lee University, 1980), pp. 13-14.
2. F. Wilfred Lancaster, The Measurement and Evaluation of Library Services (Washington, D.C.: Information Resources Press, 1977), p. 5.
3. James Baughman et al., "A Survey of Attitudes Toward Collection Development in College Libraries," in Robert D. Stueart and George B. Miller Jr., eds., Collection Development in Libraries: A Treatise (Greenwich, Conn.: JAI Press, 1980), p. 92.
4. James Baughman, "Toward a Structural Approach to Collection Development," College & Research Libraries 38 (May 1977), p. 244.
5. Ibid., p. 248.
6. G. Edward Evans, Developing Library Collections (Littleton, Colo.: Libraries Unlimited, 1979); Richard Gardner, Library Collections: Their Origins, Selection and Development (New York: McGraw-Hill, 1981); William Katz, Collection Development: The Selection of Materials for Libraries (New York: Holt, 1980), and Hannelore B. Rader, ed., Collection Development Strategies for Academic and Research Libraries (Lansing, Mich.: Michigan Library Association, 1981)

7. Bonita Bryant, "Collection Development Policies in Medium-Sized Academic Libraries," *Collection Building* 2 (#3,1980); Marion Buzzard, "Writing a Collection Development Policy for an Academic Library," *Collection Management* (Winter 1975); Kathleen Coleman and Pauline Dickinson, "Drafting a Reference Collection Policy," *College & Research Libraries* (May 1977); Sheila Dowd, "The Formulation of a Collection Development Policy Statement," in Robert Stueart and George Miller, eds., *Collection Development in Libraries: A Treatise,* pp. 67-89.; Y.T. Feng, "Necessity for a Collection Development Policy Statement," *Library Resources & Technical Services* 23 (Winter 1979); Dorothy Koenig, "Rushmore at Berkeley: The Dynamics of Developing a Written Collection Development Policy Statement," *Journal of Academic Librarianship* 7 (January 1982); Charles Osburn, "Some Practical Observations on the Writing, Implementation, and Revision of Collection Development Policy," *Library Resources & Technical Services* 23 (Winter 1979).

8. *Collection Development Policies* (SPEC Kit #38), Association of Research Libraries (Washington, D.C.: Office of Management Studies, 1977); Elizabeth Futas, ed., *Library Acquisition Policies and Procedures* (Phoenix: Oryx Press, 1977)

9. Perkins, David (ed), *Guidelines for Collection Development* (Chicago: American Library Association, 1979), pp. 3-8. See also Dowd, p. 75-79.

10. Hannaford, pp. 15-16.; Bryant, pp. 24-293; Futas, pp. xxvii.

11. Bryant, p. 24.

12. Herman H. Fussler and J.L. Simon, *Patterns in the Use of Books in Large Research Libraries* (Chicago: University of Chicago Press, 1969)

13. Allen Kent et al, *Use of Library Materials: The University of Pittsburgh Study* (New York: Marcel Dekker, 1979).

14. Richard Trueswell, "Balancing Library Objectives with Book Circulation (Comment on the Pittsburgh Collection Usage Study)," *Journal of Academic Librarianship* 5 (May 1979), pp. 68-69.

15. Harold Ellelt, "Book Use at a Small (Very) Community College Library," *Library Journal* 103 (November 15, 1978), pp. 2314-15.

16. Leslie Peat, "The Use of Research Libraries: A Comment about the Pittsburgh Study and Its Critics," *Journal of Academic Librarianship* 7 (September 1981), pp. 229-231.

17. Virgil Massman, "There Are No Easy Solutions (Comment on the Pittsburgh Collection Usage Study)," *Journal of Academic Librarianship* (May 1979), pp. 67-68.

18. Samuel Bradford, Documentation (Crosby Lockwood, 1948)

19. Michael Bommer, *Decision Making for Library Management* (White Plains, N.Y.: Knowledge Industry Publications, 1982), p. 36.

20. Michael Buckland, *Book Availability and the Library User* (New York: Pergamon Press, 1975), pp. 6-7.

21. Stanley Slote, *Weeding Library Collections* (Littleton, Colo.: Libraries Unlimited, 1982), p. 46.

22. Buckland, p. 27.

23. Perkins, p. 27.

24. Paul Mosher, "Collection Evaluation in Research Libraries: The Search for Quality, Consistency and System in Collection Development," *Library Resources & Technical Services* 23 (Winter 1979), p. 17.

25. See Baughman's study, "Toward a Structural Approach to Collection Development."

26. David Kaser, "Standards for College Libraries," *Library Trends* 31 (Summer 1982), pp. 14-16.

27. Glyn Evans, "The Cost of Information About Library Acquisition Budgets," *Collection Management* 2 (Spring 1978), pp. 7-9.

28. George Bonn, "Evaluation of the Collection," *Library Trends* 22 (January 1974), pp. 279-281.

29. *Guidelines for Use and User Studies,* Resources and Technical Services Division: Collection Management and Development Committee Working Draft, 3rd Revision, January 1982 (Distributed at RTSD Collection Development Institute in Boston, 1982), p. 6.

30. *User Surveys and Evaluation of Library Services* (SPEC Kit #71). (Association of Research Libraries. Office of Management Studies, 1981).

31. *Guidelines for Use and User Studies,* p. 1.

Recommended Readings and Resources

Theoretical Overview

Baughman, James C. et al. "A Survey of Attitudes Toward Collection Development in College Libraries," in Robert D. Stueart and George Miller, Jr., eds., *Collection Development in Libraries,* (Greenwich, Conn: JAI Press, 1980), pp. 89-138.

Baughman, James C. "Toward a Structuralist Approach to Collection Development." *College & Research Libraries* 38 (May 1977): 241-48

Hannaford, William E. "Collection Development in College Libraries," in Robert E. Danford, ed., *Library Resources for College Scholars: Transactions of Conference Held at Washington and Lee University* (Lexington, Va.: Washington and Lee University, 1980), pp. 13-14.

Hannaford, William E. "Toward a Theory of Collection Development," in Robert D. Stueart and George Miller, Jr., eds., *Collection Development in Libraries* (Greenwich, Conn.: JAI Press, 1980), pp. 573-85.

Miller, William and D. Stephen Rockwood. "Collection Development from a College Perspective." *College & Research Libraries* 40 (July 1979): 318-24.

Osburn, Charles. "Collection Development: The Link Between Scholarship and Library Resources," in Thomas Galvin and Beverly Lynch, eds., *Priorities for Academic Libraries* (San Francisco, Calif.: Jossey Bass, 1982), pp. 45-54.

Collection Planning

Bryant, Bonita. "Collection Development Policies in Medium-sized Academic Libraries." *Collection Building* 2 (#3,1980): 6-28

Buzzard, Marion L. "Writing a Collection Development Policy for an Academic Library." *Collection Management* 2 (Winter 1978): 317-28.

Coleman, Kathleen and Pauline Dickenson. "Drafting a Reference Collection Policy." *College & Research Libraries* 38 (May 1977): 227-33.

Collection Development Policies. SPEC Kit #38. Washington, D.C.: Office of Management Studies, Association of Research Libraries, 1977.)

Collection Description and Assessment in ARL Libraries. SPEC Kit #87. Washington, D.C.: Office of Management Studies, Association of Research Libraries, 1982.)

Dowd, Sheila. "The Formulation of A Colection Development Policy Statement," in Robert D. Stueart and George Miller, Jr., eds., *Collection Development in Libraries* (Greenwich, Conn.: JAI Press, 1980), pp. 67-89.

Ellelt, Harold. "Book Use at a Small (Very) Community College Library." *Library Journal* 103 (November 15, 1978): 2314-15.

Feng, T. Y. "The Necessity for a Written Collection Development Statement." *Library Resources & Technical Services* 23 (Winter 1979): 39-44.

Futas, Elizabeth, ed. *Library Acquisition Policies and Procedures.* (Phoenix, Ariz.: Oryx Press, 1977).

Kent, Allen et al. *Use of Library Materials: The University of Pittsburgh Study.* (New York: Marcel Dekker, 1979).

Koenig, Dorothy A. "Rushmore at Berkeley: The Dynamics of Developing a Written Collection Development Policy Statement." *Journal of Academic Librarianship* 7 (January 1982): 344-350.

Osburn, Charles. "Some Practical Observations on the Writing, Implementation and Revision of Collection Development Policy." *Library Resources & Technical Services* 23 (Winter 1979): 7-15.

"Pittsburgh University Studies of Collection Usage: A Symposium." *Journal of Academic Librarianship* 5 (May 1979): 60-70.

Collection Implementation

Bommer, Michael. "The Collection," in his *Decision Making for Library Management* (White Plains, N.Y.: Knowledge Industry Publications, 1982), pp. 29-39.

Buckland, Michael. *Book Availability and the Library User.* (New York: Pergamon Press, 1975).

Gore, Daniel. "Curbing the Growth of Academic Libraries." *Library Journal* 106 (November 15, 1981): 2183-87.

Gore, Daniel, ed., *Farewell to Alexandria: Solutions to Space, Growth, and Performance Problems of Libraries.* (Westport, Conn.: Greenwood Press, 1976).

Mosher, Paul H. "Managing Library Collections: The Process of Review and Pruning," in Robert D. Stueart and George Miller, Jr., eds., *Collection Development in Libraries* (Greenwich, Conn.: JAI Press, 1980), pp. 159-181.

Slote, Stanley. *Weeding Library Collections.* 2nd rev. ed. (Littleton, Colo.: Libraries Unlimited, 1982).

Spyers-Duran, Peter and Thomas Mann, Jr., eds., *Shaping Library Collections for the 1980s.* (Phoenix, Ariz.: Oryx Press, 1980).

Collection Evaluation

Association of College and Research Libraries. "An Evaluation Checklist for Reviewing a College Library Program." *College & Research Libraries News* 40 (November 1979): 305-316.

Evans, Glyn. The Cost of Information About Library Acquisition Budgets." *Collection Management* 2 (Spring 1978): 3-13.

Guidelines for Use and User Studies. Resources and Technical Services Division Collection Management and Development Committee. 3rd Revised Working Draft, January 1982.

Holt, Mae L. "Collection Evaluation: A Managerial Tool." *Collection Management* 3 (Winter 1979): 279-82.

Kaser, David. "Standards for College Libraries." *Library Trends* 31 (Summer 1982): 7-18.

Lancaster, F. W. "Evaluation of the Collection," in his *The Measurement and Evaluation of Library Services* (Washington, D.C.: Information Resources Press, 1977), pp. 165-206.

Mosher, Paul H. "Collection Evaluation or Analysis: Matching Library Acquisitions to Library Needs," in Robert D. Stueart and George B. Miller, Jr., eds., *Collection Development in Libraries* (Greenwich, Conn.: JAI Press, 1980), pp. 527-45.

Nisonger, Thomas E. "An Annotated Bibliography of Items Relating to Collection Evaluation in Academic Libraries, 1969-1981." *College & Research Libraries* 43 (July 1982): 300-11.

User Surveys and the Evaluation of Library Services. SPEC Kit #71. (Washington, D.C.: Office of Management Studies, Association of Research Libraries, 1981).

General Works

Bonk, Wallace J. and Rose Mary Magrill. *Building Library Collections.* 5th ed. (Metuchen, N.J.: Scarecrow, 1979).

Cline, Hugh F. and Loraine T. Sinnott. *Building Library Collections: Policies and Practices in Academic Libraries.* (Lexington, Mass.: Lexington Books, 1981).

Evans, G. Edward. *Developing Library Collections.* (Littleton, Colo.: Libraries Unlimited, 1979).

Gardner, Richard. *Library Collections: Their Origin, Selection and Development.* (New York: McGraw-Hill, 1981).

Godden, Irene, Karen Fachan, and Patricia Smith. *Collection Development and Acquisitions, 1970-80: An Annotated, Critical Bibliography.* (Metuchen, N.J.: Scarecrow, 1982).

Katz, William. *Collection Development: The Selection of Materials for Libraries.* (New York: Holt, Rinehart and Winston, 1980).

Orden, Phyllis Van and Edith B. Phillips, eds., *Background Readings in Building Library Collections.* (Metuchen, N.J.: Scarecrow, 1979).

Perkins, David L. ed., *Guidelines for Collection Development.* (Chicago: American Library Association, 1979).

Rader, Hannelore B., ed., *Collection Development Strategies for Academic and Research Libraries.* (Lansing, Mich.: Michigan Library Association, 1981).

Stueart, Robert and George Miller, Jr., eds., *Collection Development in Libraries.* (Greenwich, Conn.: JAI Press, 1980).

Organization of Collection Development and Management In Academic Libraries

by Carolyn Bucknall

Academic librarians are being bombarded with an accelerating stream of *news: new* services, *new* public relations, *new* information formats, *new* technologies and *new* catalogs have been introduced during the past 10 to 15 years. Innovations are not always successfully assimilated by large academic libraries and dislocations associated with change in one department often affect the entire library. Coping strategies have been envisioned and even implemented, but usually are grafted onto existing, traditional organizational structures. Therefore, collection development and management in academic libraries is most sensibly addressed in terms of the larger library organization.

THE LARGER FRAMEWORK

Organizational structures have not yet responded effectively to new directions opened as the knowledge base undergoes profound changes. We understand the notion that the printed word is not the only useful medium of intellectual exchange, although we don't always accept it. A limited legitimacy is accorded to sound recordings, nonprint visual materials (slides, photographs, microfilms, video and motion pictures), and now to numerical and textual databases in electronic format (online, ontape, disk or CD-ROM). Multimedia constructs yet undeveloped are the subjects of intense speculation. As potential for fast document delivery is realized, and as electronic networks truly become the academic *via franca*, the very character of libraries will be significantly altered. This assumes, of course, that academic libraries wish to embrace these new systems. Here is a monumental challenge for our profession.

We have been thoroughly warned to expect organizational consequences of change. We have been less successful in anticipating the precise nature of those consequences. New functions have been added, but very little formal restructuring has been undertaken to reflect new relationships that cut across organizational lines.

When the formal organization chart is not relevant to actual needs, alternate routes and interrelationships are developed by the staff. Actual needs and *new worker*[1] interests are officially acknowledged by creating standing committees, councils, and taskforces with librarywide membership, to gather and analyze information and make decisions. These bodies, while now a staple in academic library administration, are rarely shown on organization charts, perhaps because it is difficult to map their relationships as traditional hierarchies. Multiple reporting lines, a relatively new phenomenon,[2] are another—potentially more significant—departure from the norm.

A functionally interdependent and changeable library environment is the larger context in which this complex, dynamic system operates. Some of the components relevant to current academic library administration are selectively identified in the following paragraphs as: dislocation, communication, imitation, and automation.

Frequently what we have in academic libraries is a case of too much, too soon. Too much to absorb in the way of new ideas, too soon to adequately prepare staff for the change. Too much for staff to accomplish, given their existing duties. Too soon because traditional organizational structures cannot absorb so many simultaneous changes. Often, organizational dislocation results. Pressures are unevenly distributed. Developments in one area may be totally unknown or unfelt in another. A nascent *esprit* may transcend organizational lines when certain functions are shared, for example online searching or collection development. But sometimes the sharing becomes a source of discord. ("How come *they* don't serve at the Reference Desk too?") By and large the branch librarian is still ignorant of the difficulties and issues in contemporary cataloging, and the cataloger is still suspicious of the collection developer's right to assign cataloging priorities. Administrators can also be caught in the same knowledge gap, and for the same reasons. Indeed, administrators are perhaps the foremost among overworked librarians pressured by simultaneous changes and the need to respond to several clamorous constituencies at once. Organizational health is at risk, with the threat that stressed relationships will predominate.

Learning basic library functions was simpler when nothing ever changed. Now, education and communication is more difficult and more important than ever. Communication paths can be blazed through the organizational structure, whether informing one area about the functions of another, whether encouraging the director to reevaluate a particular library area, or whether educating the university administration on the importance of funding the online catalog. But effective communication also hinges on good leadership, management style, and imaginative use of a variety of communication devices.

With rapid change in society as well as in libraries, has come a degree of sophistication that no one could have foretold 30 years ago. Public relations is a case in point. Slick, intelligently written publications are effective public relations tools for furthering the library's objectives with the university administration, the library user, the potential donor, and even the library staff.

Another dynamic at work in library administration is the drive to imitate. We librarians may not know everything about our own libraries, but we are very sensitive to what is going on at others. When they *get ahead,* we are quick to follow. We must stay at the cutting edge. This is the "monkey see, monkey do" syndrome. Worthy programs apparently successful at other libraries are frequently imitated without adequate attention to staffing requirements or to dislocations produced in ongoing programs.

A rash of user-instruction programs introduced in the '70s raised people's expectations to an impossibly high level, given limited staff. But user instruction was nothing compared to the demands generated by the *new technology.* The point is not that user instruction is unworthy or that online databases are somehow wrong; the point is that staff (and budget, too) can support only so many add-ons. Somewhere along the line we become too stretched, edgy, resentful, prone to blame someone—perhaps colleagues whose workloads we have misunderstood—for our plight. Where is the leader who will bravely cut a program to relieve resources overload? Then the rest of us monkeys can follow with lightened burdens and refreshed spirits.

Mention should be made of two elements well-recognized as prime movers in any dynamic system of organization. First, is the *new worker,*[3] an employee whose values and expectations of the workplace are different from those of his predecessors. This worker likes to help determine the procedures and policies that shape his work and values a congenial work situation over higher salaries. Second is automation as an agent for organizational change. As automation impacts all areas of library activity, we gain insights into changes underway, even when their ultimate outcome is not perfectly clear. Most agree, however, that automated systems promote greater interdependence and reduce centralized processes and controls.[4] When the latter have grown beyond their capacity to operate efficiently, this process is accelerated.

Many other considerations could be mentioned. An extensive range of economic factors, for example, is not addressed here, political forces are dealt with only indirectly and limitations of physical facilities and logistics must be considered. Such factors, interacting in dynamic systems, are being explored increasingly in strategic planning and ultimately must be thoroughly analyzed in order to build effective organizational structures.

In summary, libraries are undergoing numerous changes, many simultaneously. Most profound, the character of the knowledge base itself is changing, and many of us foresee that the library will emerge from its metamorphosis with a form as yet unknown. Immense staffing pressures have been generated by increasing user expectations and add-on programs, while automation has produced, is producing, and will continue to produce more decentralized functions. At the same time, a greater interdependence is not accommodated by traditional organizational structures. Even when the organization chart appears the same, interrelationships in fact are much more complex. It is in this context that the organization

We librarians may not know everything about our own libraries, but we are very sensitive to what is going on at others

of the collection development function must be considered.

CURRENT PATTERNS

Current concepts of collection development and management were introduced into academic libraries only during the last 20 to 25 years. We have come to identify the components of this function as selection, faculty liaison, collection management (including preservation), collection evaluation, fund management, and library use instruction—or collection interpretation.[5] Even as we have done so, we recognize that we are describing the past better than the future.

Collection development was not born in that simpler period when library functions could be learned only once. It is, from the perspective of many professionals, another add-on program. It does not often enjoy an entrenched constituency within the library, though support from faculty has been typically strong. However, the importance of collection development is increasingly being recognized. Thirteen years ago, only three ARL (Association for Research Libraries) member libraries showed a dedicated staff position for an assistant director or coordinator for collection development. In 1986 at least 34 of 61 organization charts in the ARL Office of Management Studies SPEC Kit no. 129 noted such a position.[6] The same survey showed 52 percent of collection development officers report to the director, and Jeanne Sohn recently cited 74 percent.[7]

The type of organization likely to have a collection development function is determined by several factors, most of which relate to size: size of the collection, size of the book budget, and size of professional and support staff. Generally, the smaller the library, the smaller the collection development program. In evolutionary phases, responsibility may migrate from the director to the head of acquisitions or reference, to a collection development coordinator or head of a collection development department, and finally to an assistant or associate director. Bonita Bryant[8] describes the process very well. Only when a library has evolved to naming one person responsible for overseeing the collection development and management function can it be placed on an organization chart.

No consensus is apparent on where, organizationally, the collection management and development program belongs. It can be solely a staff function reporting to the director. It can be a line function, or a coordinated function attached to technical services, public services, or a department within these areas, it can be dismembered and scattered among the various departments. Conversely, according to Sohn,[9] other functions can be subsumed by the collection development and management programs, the most common being acquisitions and preservation.

A centralized *vs.* a coordinated model for collection development organization has been debated for the past two decades. Centralized collection development in its purest form, staffed by bibliographers[10] whose sole responsibility is collection development, and whose reporting line leads to only one box on the organization chart, exists in few academic libraries. It confers certain obvious advantages:

- individual bibliographer workloads can be monitored to assure adequate time for successful performance
- individual bibliographer performance can be evaluated more easily
- projects can be undertaken more easily because of greater staff flexibility
- strong *esprit* develops within the unit, and there is greater opportunity for prestige as a group
- individual bibliographers are subject only to their own limitations: professional abilities, knowledge of subject specialty, organizational skills, and personal attributes (e.g. initiative, interpersonal skills, etc.)
- excellent opportunity for intellectual accomplishment and job satisfaction.

Offsetting these advantages is one serious difficulty: a troublesome tendency to insulate bibliographers from the *new technology* and from the rest of the staff.[11] This can be exacerbated by competitive hierarchical structures that discourage exploration of shared interests and efforts toward functional integration. When any librarian loses touch with recent and ongoing advances in the field, the entire organization suffers a loss. When a whole group loses touch, its effectiveness is considerably diminished and unless the underlying causes are dealt with, further decline may occur.

A coordinated collection development and management organization, in which bibliographers spend only a portion of their time on this function and the remainder on primary responsibilities in another department, has its drawbacks:

- without line responsibility the coordinator may lack authority necessary to manage the program
- the coordinator may not have control over the time bibliographers spend on collection development and management
- the coordinator may not have a role in bibliographer performance evaluation
- the coordinator's position may be perceived as less prestigious than one who sits on top of a pyramid
- the coordinated program will not have built-in communication linkages

- a coordinated program lacks the flexibility of staff dedicated, full time, to collection development
- individual bibliographers may be frustrated due to conflicting demands on worktime by primary and collection development responsibilities.

Most of these disadvantages can be mitigated by various strategems. For example, having the coordinator report to the director can boost prestige, as can positioning the job at a relatively high level on the organization chart. Of course, the power of the purse is a wonderful authority enhancer; when the coordinator controls fund allocation, many obstacles dwindle.

Some advantages of a coordinated model are:

- part time bibliographers, especially in smaller libraries, may be the only staff available to make a collection development and management program possible
- bibliographers with primary responsibilities are more likely to be aware of the latest advances in their field
- bibliographer responsibilities enhance job satisfaction and the possibility for intellectual accomplishment in subject areas.

Lack of a single, predominant organizational model for collection management and development has been noted in library literature. Sohn has sketched a composite of a typical ARL collection development and management unit. It is composed of a group of bibliographers with multiple subject assignments who report to the collection development officer or to someone else with dedicated collection development responsibilities. This group is complemented by other bibliographers with more limited subject responsibilities, whose primary assignment is in another functional area of the library.[12] Individuals in the second group may have dual reporting lines: to their department heads in their primary capacity and to the collection development head in their capacity as bibliographers. Presumably the collection development officer would have more control over such critical matters as time spent on collection management and development and performance evaluation. A composite model might require coordination, rather than actual line responsibility, on the part of the collection development officer. Apart from this distinction the composite model shares in the best and worst features of the centralized and the coordinated models.

Whether the object is to restructure the collection development and management function or to improve its management within an existing structure, several helpful administrative tools are noteworthy. Compiling a bibliographer's manual can clarify expectations and is extremely beneficial for both process and product.[13] A formal

training program using the manual as a primary tool and including an extended mentor-protege relationship, is an effective introduction to the program.[14] Groups of bibliographers working in their disciplines with similar characteristics, each headed by a coordinator, can achieve a more integrated approach to collection development and management in a large, dispersed organization. When a central core of full-time bibliographers is maintained, their duties often relate to publications from (and sometimes about) a particular geographical area. Typically such a group is expanded by bibliographers who are also catalogers, a natural union of language and area expertise.

Whatever organization form is chosen, a clear understanding of administrative relationships is essential. The best qualified bibliographers must be recruited—whether people already on the staff or from outside the library. They must have enough time to do what bibliographers are supposed to do, as well as adequate support staff, and a good training program. An excellent system of communication that is reciprocal in every possible direction is one of the tools that will help accomplish these things.

More than one organizational pattern can be effective. The ultimate test of any organization is whether it works. In order to pass this test the structure must first be appropriate to its context, with due consideration of the organization's health, traditions and prestige, as well as the management style of the director and other members of the library administration. Internal political factors will also determine where and how collection development and management fits into the structure; for example, the nature of competing programs, their public visibility, the immediacy of the needs they serve, etc. Add to these the director's own agenda and perceptions, tempered perhaps by special interest groups such as library administrators, other staff members, vocal faculty, and certain influential members of the university administration.

Making an organizational structure work is essentially a political process involving education, statesmanship, diplomacy, and an arsenal of other positive attributes. We all have a role in that process.

FUTURE DIRECTIONS

Jeanne Sohn reports that, despite improvements in status, almost one-third of the collection development officers responding to her survey were dissatisfied with the way their libraries have organized collection development; those who ex-

No consensus is apparent on where, organizationally, the collection management and development program belongs

pressed satisfaction but also made negative comments brought the total to almost 50 percent. And this although 81 percent of Sohn's 93 respondents indicated that a change in structure or organizational placement of the collection development unit had already occurred in the past ten years.[15]

Possibly collection developers' dissatisfaction with current organizational structures has less to do with collection development than with the total library context.

Take a hypothetical model of a composite collection development organization: an amalgam of full-time bibliographers in a collection development department and part-time bibliographers in a reference department. Overload has spurred reference librarians and allies to campaign for drawing full-time bibliographer colleagues into reference service, not for *online information* retrieval but for *reference desk* duty. Full-time bibliographers, of course, respond with indignant resistance. Polarities between the two groups are expressed as elitism and populism, and the argument proceeds as follows:

> *Full-time Bibliographers:* Given that reference has more work than it can do—much of it self-imposed—why should full-time bibliographers be made to share in the misery by serving time at the general reference desk where predominantly undergraduate students ask repetitive and nonchallenging questions? It may be populist to reduce the intellectual level at which all staff must serve to the lowest common denominator, but is it sensible? Why not undertake to raise the general intellectual environment of all librarians?
>
> *Part-time Bibliographers/Reference Librarians:* Reference desk service will give full-time bibliographers meaningful (and currently lacking) contact with library users, on which collection development decisions can be based. This will be tremendously helpful to the bibliographer and will at the same time permit broader contribution of his/her subject expertise. Also, it seems unfair that full-time bibliographers have more time to evaluate collections, establish meaningful communication with faculty, and undertake extensive projects related to preservation. *Why should full-time bibliographers be free to come and go as they choose?*

The dynamics of the larger organizational context are at work, with a complex array of opposing pressures and interests. Do we take this marriage proposal seriously? Is a wedding inevitable? Does service at the reference desk really enhance bibliographers' performance? Is a new elite (those possessing the keys to online information) in the making?

Considering the situation in current organizational terms, the following points might be raised.

The proposal, which is symptomatic of some degree of dislocation, must be given serious attention, with diagnosis pending further examination. Routine reference desk service as an aid to collection development and management seems an unsubstantiated claim developed to reduce reference workloads. As such, it may be a further indicator of stress, or, when advocated by nonbibliographer staff, ignorance of the collection development and management function. It would seem more appropriate to examine reference workloads, programs, and constituencies to identify changes needed for reference, not collection development.

Other rationales for joining the collection development function with the reference department might be more compelling. If such a union were to occur, collection development would undoubtedly lose some of its clout, some of its activities would be curtailed, and some of its goals ignored. On the other hand, full-time bibliographers might benefit by swimming into the library mainstream and connecting with current technological advances. The collection development and management program (along with reference) might derive at least limited benefits from such a recasting of the library organization.

Reasoning of this sort helps us to understand underlying organizational forces and sometimes improves operations, but essentially it perpetuates traditional organizational concepts. Thus, while six ARL libraries have recently moved from the centralized to the composite organizational model, five have moved in the opposite direction.[16] The dissatisfactions noted by Sohn are likely to continue until we rethink the basis for our organizational structures.

The case of overworked reference librarians who want to tap collection development staff could have led to an entirely different approach to organization. Had a more integrated role for all librarians been sought, with individual performance at the highest level possible, reorganization of public services, collection development, *and* other functions would have been considered. Charles Osburn has theorized that collection development and management is central to library operations and pivotal in library-community relations.[17] This strong voice on its behalf coming from the Research Libraries Group has done much to underscore its value to library services in general and to cooperative ventures in preservation and resource sharing in particular. If collection development is indeed central, it is in a good position to help restructure traditional library functions into more effective organizational patterns.

Osburn, noting the decreasing importance of

resources ownership in most libraries, suggests that future directions will be characterized by looking outward to community needs, rather than inward to the collection as traditionally conceived. The role of information and service broker remains to be assumed by collection development librarians, for if not, "it will be by other professions, and librarians will continue to be responsible only for maintenance of an intellectual utility, subordinate to the other group."[18] He further asserts that "the shift of emphasis from collection-oriented goals, eventually to process-oriented goals . . . will permit collection development to function most successfully in the future."[19]

As we begin to make this transition, we can be informed by two existing models, each representing an evolutionary step toward a new kind of structure. Branch libraries in large academic systems have typically been quick to explore new relationships with clientele as the knowledge base has evolved. Insights into the *new collection development* are emerging in these academic library settings. A more mature model, the medical library, delivers highly sophisticated and constantly changing information services. Among characteristics shared by the two models are: a focused environment with well defined subject scope, a readily identified library user community, library subject specialists who offer integrated information services with a high degree of involvement in the research process, and relatively small organizational units that exemplify integrated rather than centralized functions. The advantages of small teams as a basic unit of organization have been noted in industry as particularly suited to both the demands of the new worker and functional integration resulting from automation.[20]

A function as reconceptualized might, for example, be the provision of integrated information services for those engaged in advanced research. In the press of public services activity begun in the '60s and continuing into the future, services to researchers in particular have been sometimes neglected and frequently fragmented. Today—at least in the central or research library—most bibliographers select and manage print and audiovisual research materials, and reference librarians select and administer electronic databases useful in research, while individual researchers are often assisted in an uncoordinated fashion, primarily in response to specific queries. Looking at new scholarly systems we are struck by the need to maintain a core of subject specialists who are also experts on available library resources in all formats, cognizant of research trends and methods, conversant with hardware, software, and scholarly networks, and interested in being more involved in the research process. Bibliographers and other specialists could join together in libraries organized to give in-depth support services for advanced research.

Organizational experimentation is one of the lesser-used tools available to us. While librarians are generally not regarded as risk-takers, several organizational innovations have now come to represent the norm. Using such tools as multiple reporting lines, councils, clusters, teams, tribes, etc., we can create different organizational structures that more realistically reflect existing and emerging relationships; structures that facilitate rather than impede communication. Significant organizational regrouping has been rare among large academic libraries, with the notable exception of the University of Illinois.[21] We need to know more about the lessons of such ventures. Still, the organizational response to tomorrow's environment may be largely independent of the past.

Ironically, libraries may run the greatest risk by avoiding risk. Hazards are real, but potential gains are great.

References

1. Robert W. Goddard, "Motivating the Modern Employee," *Management World* 12 (Sept. 1983), p. 8.
2. *Organization Charts in ARL Libraries*, SPEC Kit, no. 129. (Washington: Systems and Procedures Exchange Center, Association of Research Libraries, Office of Management Studies, Nov.–Dec. 1986).
3. Goddard, "Motivating," p. 8.
4. Richard E. Walton and Gerald I. Susman, "People Policies for the New Machines," *Harvard Business Review* 87 (March–Apr. 1987), p. 98–99.
5. University of Texas at Austin, General Libraries, *Bibliographer's Manual: a Guide to the General Libraries Collection Development Program* (Austin: 1982), p. 7.
6. *Organization Charts in ARL Libraries*, SPEC Kit no. 129.
7. Jeanne Sohn, "Collection Development Organizational Patterns in ARL Libraries," *Library Resources and Technical Services* 31 (April/June 1987), p. 125.
8. Bonita Bryant, "The Organizational Structure of Collection Development," *Library Resources and Technical Services* 31 (April/June 1987), p. 113–114.
9. Sohn, "Organizational Patterns," p. 131
10. The term *bibliographer* is applied throughout this paper to "a library staff member, typically possessing superior knowledge of a discipline, whose responsibilities include aspects of development and management of the library's information resources in the subject field(s) of his or her specialization; also referred to as a selector, subject specialist, or collection developer." This definition is

taken from *Guide for Writing a Bibliographer's Manual* (Chicago: Resources and Technical Services Division, American Library Association) [in press].

11. This trend toward "maintaining a professional preserve evolved into a mechanism of defense against questioning from outside the designated collection development area . . . In some libraries . . . the trajectory of this professionally inspired movement led dangerously close to stasis in a function that should be the most dynamic of enterprises," according to Charles B. Osburn, "Toward a Reconceptualization of Collection Development," in *Advances in Library Administration and Organization* (Greenwood, Conn: JAI Press. 1983), v. 2, p. 180.

12. Sohn, "Organizational Patterns," p. 131.

13. University of Texas at Austin, General Libraries, *Bibliographer's Manual*, p. 2.

14. Scott R. Bullard, "Educating Rita—Part II: Training For Collection Development," *Library Acquisitions: Practice and Theory* 8 (1984), p. 244–245.

15. Sohn, "Organizational Patterns," p. 130.

16. *Collection Development Organization and Staffing*, SPEC Kit no. 131. (Washington: Systems and Procedures Exchange Center, Association of Research Libraries, Office of Management Studies, Feb. 1987).

17. Charles B. Osburn, "Toward a Reconceptualization of Collection Development," in *Advances in Library Administration and Organization* (Greenwood, Conn: JAI Press, 1983), v. 2, p. 183.

18. Osburn, "Reconceptualization," p. 183.

19. *Ibid.*

20. Walton and Susman. "People Policies," *Harvard Business Review* 87 (March–Apr. 1987), p. 99–100.

21. The University of Illinois Libraries has recently regrouped on the basis of subject rather than function. As related to a particular subject, the total range of current library activities—collection development and management, acquisition, cataloging and interpretive services—are performed by a single individual.

Collection Development in School Library Media Centers: National Recommendation and Reality

Marilyn L. Miller

The school library media center materials collection has evolved dramatically in the past 60 years from book-centered collections of "the best reference books and...literature that has a natural appeal to young people"[1] to "media collection(s) which represent the essential informational base of the instructional program."[2] The purposes of this discussion are: to trace the evolution of four specific aspects of collection development as found in national standards for school library media programs, 1918-1975; to review some of the research of the sixties and seventies that indicates some of the successes, problems, and trends involved in implementing professional guidelines on collection development; and to provide two case studies of organized evaluation and selection programs that serve as examples of an organized cooperative approach to collection development.

National Standards 1918-1975

An examination of National Standards from the 1918 Certain Report[3] to *Media Programs: District and School*[4] (1975) reveals substantive changes in the statements of the rationale for a school materials collection, the physical composition of the collection, recommended size of collection, and the collection development process.

Rationale for School Library (Media Center) Collections

The Certain Report appeared in 1915 and was the first comprehensive effort to standardize the emerging high school library movement. Although it noted the absence of many good high school libraries in the United States, it did report that "for the first time administrators see that the library is the very heart of the high school."[5]

In 1925 the Certain Committee issued standards for elementary school libraries built upon a more precise rationale:

> Modern demands upon the public school presuppose adequate library service. Significant changes in methods of teaching require that the school library supplement the single textbook course of instruction and provide for the enrichment of the school curriculum. Children in the school are actively engaged in interests which make it necessary for them to have the use of

The author wishes to acknowledge the assistance of David Bender, Administrator, Office of School Media Services, Division of Library Development and Services, Maryland State Department of Education, in providing advance copies of several articles to be published in forthcoming issues of School Media Quarterly; detailed information on the Anne Arundel County, Md.—Maryland State Department of Education Review and Evaluation Center; and reactions to parts of this paper.

many books and a wide variety of materials, such as pictures and lantern slides.[6]

In 1945, the American Library Association, looking ahead to postwar changes and developments in elementary and secondary education, published *School Libraries for Today and Tomorrow*.[7] Building upon the philosophy first expressed in the Certain Report, this statement moved ahead by reviewing contemporary educational philosophy and carefully articulating the school library's role in assisting in the implementation of educational objectives. Stated succinctly, the rationale for the materials collection was to allow the school library "to serve as an instructional agency without regard to grade levels or to subject fields."[8]

American education entered one of its most exciting decades in the sixties. Innovation in curriculum, organization for teaching, and teaching strategies enjoyed wide acceptance in the public schools. Budgets were heavily infused with millions of federal dollars, much of it earmarked for instructional materials to be placed in materials centers. The proliferation and broader acceptance of communication media for instructional purposes encouraged educators to hope that individual needs and learning styles could be matched with appropriate teaching styles, methods, and materials.

The 1960 *Standards for School Library Programs*[9] recognized the imminence of these educational changes and emphases. They reaffirmed the necessity of a broad and varied materials collection:

> In the education of all youth, from the slowest learner in kindergarten to the most intelligent senior in high school, an abundance of printed and audio-visual materials is essential. These resources are the basic tools needed for the purposes of effective teaching and learning. That the achievement of the objectives of a good school program requires the resources and services of a school library has been recognized and demonstrated for many years by school board members, administrators, teachers, parents, and other people in communities having such schools. These individuals, too, have long realized that the school library program contributes something more to the over-all education of youth than materials and services geared to curricular needs. The scope of knowledge has become too vast to be covered extensively within the boundaries of classroom instruction, superior though that instruction may be. Through the school library, these boundaries can be extended immeasurably in all areas of knowledge and in all forms of crea-

tive expression, and the means provided to meet and to stimulate the many interests, appreciations, and curiosities of youth. The school library thus stands as a symbol for the truthful expression of man's knowledge and experiences. The extent to which many children and young people of today will be creative, informed, knowledgeable, and within their own years, wise, will be shaped by the boundaries of the content of the library resources available within their schools.[10]

Specifically, the 1960 *Standards* ask for collections which enable students to "derive the fullest benefit from their classroom instruction," "extend the boundaries of their knowledge," "pursue self-directed learning," "explore and satisfy," "find enjoyment," "learn how to use." These same collections will permit teachers and counselors to "achieve their instructional objectives," "enrich course content," "prepare assignments...that provide for the needs and abilities of individual students," "motivate directly with students," "teach students how to use materials and libraries," "keep abreast with the best ideas and practices in education," and "use materials" for their own purposes.[11]

By the late sixties, the American Association of School Librarians and the Department of Audiovisual Instruction (DAVI) of the National Education Association had decided that a joint statement of national standards for school libraries was imperative, prudent, and timely. *Standards for School Media Programs*[12] appeared in 1969 in response to "needs and requirements of today's educational goals..." and hoped to "coordinate standards for school library and audiovisual programs."[13] In no way did the 1969 *Standards* minimize or negate previous statements of the role and purpose of school libraries. This document's prose is tortured and uninspiring, but the message regarding the materials collection is clear:

> The collection meets the requirements of the various curricular areas and provides for the diverse learning skills of individuals representing all levels and types of ability. Materials are also included that inspire and meet the independent interests and research needs of students. Therefore the media collection is rich in breadth and depth in the subjects covered, the types of material included, and the forms of expression represented.[14]

Media Programs: District and School, the second joint effort of the same two national associations (although by this time DAVI had become the Association for Educational Communications and Technology), appeared in 1975.

This statement is avowedly a replacement for the 1969 *Standards*. Stressing its "continuing concern...for establishing and maintaining standards of excellence in media programs in schools throughout the nation,"[15] the latest *Standards* (or *Guidelines*) recommend planning to meet unique school characteristics. Although quality education, qualitative goals, and excellence in educational experiences are called for, the professional creativity of this document lies in its recognition and support of the need to plan media programs to implement the goals and objectives of an individual school. By supplying a media program planning model, all types and qualities of schools can have a methodology for building media collections to support individual teaching and learning programs.

The rationale for the school media collection as traced through national standards is clear: the school media collection exists to support, extend, and enrich the curriculum/instructional program and to meet the needs of students and teachers for interesting and personally satisfying materials.

Breadth of Recommended Collections

The diversity of materials recommended for the central school library media center (school library) has never been in doubt, from the Certain Report of 1918 to the 1975 Guidelines, *Media Programs: District and School*. But, an understanding of the educational role of the various communication media is not supported with equal fervor throughout the documents. The 1918 Certain Report does recommend the centralized administration of audiovisual materials:

> The Library should serve as the center and coordinating agency for all material used in the school for visual instruction, such as stereopticons, portable motion picture machines, stereopticon slides, moving picture films, pictures, maps, globes, bulletin board material, museum loans, etc.[16]

Print material, especially books, receive the most attention throughout the discussions of administrative procedures, collection development, and budgeting.

The same imbalance, slighting the role of audiovisual media for information, curricular support, and personal use, continues in the 1945 *Standards*. Centralization of a wide variety of materials is advised, and specifically noted are:

> ...the challenging new materials (such as) new audiovisual aids for learning...16mm. films, filmstrips, slides, museum objects, radio

programs, recordings and transcriptions, as well as flat pictures, maps, and other nonbook materials which are essential in a good learning situation.[17]

While listed as important, only films are mentioned as budget items and comparably little information is given regarding selection, quantitative requirements, and space allocations for use of audiovisual materials.

The contribution of the 1960 *Standards* in recommending breadth of collections for school programs lies in the acceptance of the integrity of the multimedia character of the modern school library media center. Although the document equivocates and tolerates the existence of two separate materials programs and services operations already available in many schools, there is narrative and budgetary recognition of the values and uses of a variety of audiovisual media in quality educational programs.

> Films and filmstrips are without peer for conveying many types of information and creative expressions.[18]

> Slides...furnish the only material available on many topics and details. They form an important reference tool in the library.[19]

> Realia represent a unique and vital source of information and appreciation for students, and they are frequently primary sources for teaching and learning.[20]

The 1960 *Standards* also specify that the collection should include a breadth of other kinds of materials: inflatable globes, indexes of community resources, trip and lecturer files, materials on local history, collections of college catalogs, and vocational information services. Detailed recommendations are provided, for the first time, for the administration of supplementary collections and professional materials collections. Supplementary collections are defined as:

> ...books, magazines, and other printed materials that are not shelved with the main school library collections: sets of supplementary text books, dictionaries, and encyclopedias for classrooms, magazines and newspapers for classroom use, and similar materials.[21]

Professional collections are to be centrally located and are to include books, magazines, and instructional materials for administrators and teachers.[22]

Graphic materials such as art prints, pictures and study prints, posters, photographs, charts, diagrams, and graphs, a category of special maps, micro-forms, transparencies, programmed instructional materials, kits, videotape recordings, and remote access programs are added to the recommended media collections in the 1969 *Standards*. Equally important, all media are given appropriate budgetary, selection, and utilization attention, and finally an integrated, or unified, materials collection and program is recommended for school media centers.

The 1975 *Guidelines* recognize the full complement of instructional materials, formats, and equipment available today for instruction, personal interests, and aesthetic satisfaction. In a carefully outlined section which provides recommendations for base level collections, the reader also finds selection guidelines for all materials from books, tapes, and microforms to tactile formats such as games and toys, models and sculpture, and specimens. The resources section also notes the cooperative approaches to collection development through interlibrary loan and photocopying procedures.

Recommended Size of Collection

The failure to recognize the integrity of the informational content and potential curricular use of the audiovisual materials, and thus library responsibility for their collection and organization, can be quickly seen in those sections of the *Standards* published prior to 1960 dealing with recommended size of collection.

In the early standards, size of school determined the quantity of volumes to be provided. The 1918 *Standards* had a wide range of school populations for whom books were recommended: from those schools with fewer than 200 students up to those with enrollments in excess of 1,000.[23] In addition, schools were advised to "subscribe to several good magazines, some for teachers, others for students."[24] No quantitative recommendations were made for audiovisual materials.

The same types of recommendations were provided again in 1945: book collections which provide specified numbers of volumes according to enrollment and "percentage distributions by subjects that vary with the needs of the individual schools."[25] This document did put a ceiling on the size of the collection: "active book collections for the largest school library should probably not exceed 10,000 titles,"[26] and noted the differences between volumes and titles and the need for adequate provision of duplicate titles. A recommended quantity of periodicals was provided and any school of 200 was advised to subscribe to two newspapers, "one local paper" and one "presenting news on a state and national level." No quantitative recommendations were provided for audiovisual materials.

As noted earlier, the 1960 *Standards for School Library Programs* finally recognized the integrity of the intellectual content and curricular contribution of audiovisual materials, but there was still reluctance to make specific quantitative recommendations:

> ...a film used six or more times a year is purchased by the school...it is advantageous for the school to have its own collection of filmstrips and recordings that will be used more than once during the school year.[27]

While budgetary recommendations continued to reflect the importance of print, the 1960 *Standards* did suggest that an "annual budget for the acquisition of audiovisual materials, exclusive of equipment, should not be less than 1% of the total per pupil instructional cost...[which] ranges at the present time from $2.00 to $6.00 per student."[28]

It should also be noted that in the 1960 *Standards* school librarians were beginning to emphasize the need for school district materials collections which would supplement building-level collections with expensive, less-often used materials. This philosophy received continued support in the 1969 *Standards*, which also confronted the then perceived need to recommend purchase of and access to minimum quantities of specific audiovisual materials as well as print materials for schools. Recommendations such as the following attempted to put integrated media collections into a quantitative framework:

Books	At least 6,000–10,000 titles representing 10,000 volumes or 20 volumes per student, whichever is greater
8mm films	1 1/2 films per student with at least 500 titles supplemented by duplicates
Tape and disc recordings	1,000–2,000 titles representing 3,000 records or tapes or 6 per student, whichever is greater (the number of titles to be increased in larger collections)
Filmstrips	500–1,000 titles, representing 1,500 prints or 3 prints per pupil, whichever is greater (the number of titles to be increased in larger collections)[29]

Underscoring the emphasis on integrated media collections, budgetary recommendations requested that not less than 6% of the national average for per pupil operational cost be spent per year per student to purchase materials for both the individual school and the system media center. While the document continued to note the need for flexibility to meet integrated, balanced collections and to meet quantitative recommendations for the breadth of collection, this philosophy was compromised with the suggestion that "half of the annual appropriation should be spent on printed materials and half on audiovisual materials."[30]

In compatibility with the planning model described in *Media Programs: District and School*, the media collection in that document is described as "based on program goals and characteristics of the school and reflects needs, prior action, and resources."[31] Although a single, quantitative model is not provided, base quantities of software and associated hardware are identified "to insure adequate provisions for content coverage, range in levels, and choice of media formats, responding to general information needs and personal interests and preferences."[32] The base collection for a contemporary school with 500 or fewer students is 20,000 items or 40 per student. "An item is defined as a book (casebound or paperback), film, videotape, filmstrip, transparency, slide, periodical subscription, kit, any other form of material, or associate equipment."[33] Cooperative arrangements for use of interlibrary loans, community resources, public libraries, school district, or multidistrict resources that "guarantee a high degree of satisfaction of users' needs" are also urged.

Budgetary recommendations in the current national *Guidelines* are specific: ten percent of the national per pupil operational cost as computed by the United States Office of Education. This figure includes equipment for software and production, retrospective purchasing as well as newly published or produced materials, duplicates, and materials preprocessing costs. The integrity of a planning model used to meet needs and to be flexible is maintained with the recommendation that "all allocated funds are expended for the district program and individual school programs on the basis of program needs."[34]

The Selection Process

The main issues in collection development for school media centers are: Who plans the collection? Who implements the plan? How does it get done? In contemporary schools, the role of the school library media specialist in collection development is as designer, coordinator, and facilitator. Effective collection design and subsequent development call into play many skills and abilities: evaluative, managerial, interpersonal, cooperative, instructional, and interpretative.

The Certain Committee recognized that the school librarian is a coordinator of selection in the recommendation that selection "must be based upon recommendation by heads of departments and teachers"[35] and that she/he only has authority as delegated by the principal.[36] Basic approved standard lists were recommended for intelligent collection development. In the 1945 standards these same recommendations and descriptions were still acceptable except that "films and allied materials be previewed so that intelligent acquisitions can be assured."[37] In addition, students, as well as teachers, were urged as participants in the selection process.

As the array of media for instruction and personal use and attendant problems of selection grew, so did the recommendations for the physical process of collection development. *Standards for School Library Programs* (1960) recommended attention to the "School Library Bill of Rights," the development of well-balanced and well-rounded collections to cover all subjects, a variety of types of materials, evaluation before purchase, and continuous purchase.

The 1969 *Standards for School Media Programs* confronted additional pressures on collection development: the "avalanche of materials in all formats and different degrees of quality which are appearing on the market";[38] increased pressure of commercialism in the sale of media; and the availability of increased funds. To help meet the pressures, school media specialists were urged to develop written selection policies, and reminded that selection, distribution, and use of media should reflect current trends in education and communication, and that responsibility for paperbacks as well as instructional design and computer programs were now all part of media programs. Because of the development of more sophisticated media, increased research, and curricular innovations, media specialists were urged to add other materials specialists and curriculum specialists to the circle of personnel evaluating materials. Collection development, or selection, was viewed by this time as a process of competent evaluation by qualified media specialists at local, state, regional, and national levels.[39]

The 1975 *Guidelines* recognize school library collection development for the complex process it is. This document refers to selection policy shaped and implemented in a cooperative process that includes students and concerned citizens as well as media staff, curriculum consultants, and teachers.[40] It also recommends that collection development be concerned with prior-to-purchase evaluation by reliable tools, and by first-hand examination wherever possible.[41]

The modern school library media collection, as developed philosophically through the national standards, consists of all forms of communication essential for instruction and personal growth in quantities demanded by the specified needs of the instructional program, supported by a specified percentage of the recognized national per pupil operational cost, and selected by a process that involves reviewing, field testing, and school and local community involvement.

The Reality, 1960—Problems and Concerns

Professional literature that interprets, supports, and extends the statements on collection development found in all versions of the *Standards* exists in great quantity. There are also how-to-do-it guides and serious essays that identify and evaluate the problems of collection development. One suspects, however, that in hundreds of schools there is no collection development. There is a great deal of acquisition; there is selection to a degree; and there is collection. But, how much systematic collection development is actually done?

A contributing factor to this suspicion is knowledge of current staffing patterns in school media centers. School media facilities have been improved and enlarged throughout the country, but staffing has not kept pace. The number of professional staff is inadequate. Good collection development takes time, and staff time is in short supply. Coupled with inadequate staff time is the changing quality of personnel, specifically in the elementary schools. There is an alarming increase in the loss of elementary school media positions and a corresponding increase in the employment of unqualified aides for those positions. Also increasing is the number of qualified elementary media staff assigned to administrative responsibilities for several elementary buildings. Collection development can but suffer.

Probing further, it is necessary to comment that "knowing the curriculum"—often defined as knowing what is taught to whom and when—is not quite adequate for responsible collection development. If the collection is to undergird and help implement the curriculum, the media specialist must analyze teacher intent, selection of content, and strategies. Last but not least, she/he

must have solid information about the kinds of materials needed and available that teach effectively or can be used effectively in specific ways by specific teachers to help specific students learn. Even with the present array of reviewing media, we still do not have resources which will adequately and conveniently inform us of the availability and potential effectiveness of the broad range of materials needed for today's instructional programs. It is one thing to select for enrichment, aesthetic pleasure, and/or personal growth and development. It is another to develop collections to meet specified teaching and learning objectives.

In the recent American Library Association (ALA)/American Association of Publishers (AAP) Survey of 516 school library media specialists,[42] the most highly ranked factor in the selection of materials was not personal knowledge (2.44 on a scale of 1-5, 1 being the highest) or teacher requests (2.84), but favorable reviews (1.99). When asked what information would be of most importance in publishers' and distributors' catalogs, applicability to curriculum, grade level, reading level, and source of reviews were ranked—in that order—as most desirable. Of seven factors, learner verification/validation was considered last in importance. Granted, the data relating to curriculum and grade levels is helpful, especially since only 37 percent of the respondents reported access to book examination centers and 24 percent reported access to an examination center for audiovisual materials. However, applicability to curriculum and grade level designation made by publishers and producers can be no more than superficial. The responsibility for these determinations rests with the media and teaching staffs. Higher expectations for learner verification/validation for instructional materials might, on the other hand, lead to more useful instructional materials.

Threats posed by censors, real or imagined, growing problems with out-of-print books, and lack of opportunities to preview materials, combined with changing staffing provisions, shrinking budgets, and an inadequate bibliographic information system pose serious problems for young people who seek good materials collections in school library media centers.

A Review of Selected Research

Although there is an extensive body of professional writing on the subject of collection development, there is a shortage of significant research that either describes the process of collection development as it exists in the schools throughout the nation or supports what many ardently believe about the process of good selection.

This shortage is not just a research oversight. Research on the entire field of school librarianship is limited, and most of what is done is in the form of doctoral dissertations and master's theses. While this work is significant, it does not provide the focus the field needs. Additionally, bibliographic control of completed studies is not yet adequate, and the difficulties involved in identification of pertinent work are extreme.

Lowrie,[43] Aaron,[44] and Freeman[45] have provided the most comprehensive surveys of research in school librarianship to date. Lowrie identified 69 doctoral dissertations and masters' theses and 27 serious articles and books, completed between 1950 and 1967. Several of the latter reported results of studies. Aaron reviewed the research in school librarianship from 1967 to 1972 and identified 58 doctoral dissertations and 23 studies completed by a variety of individuals, professional associations, and the U.S. Office of Education. Freeman identified 368 studies completed in the United States between 1960 and 1974 about, or directly concerned with, school library media centers. These surveys of the research literature and an incomplete review of research reported beyond the Freeman compilation, make it possible to identify fewer than 50 studies in the past 25 years related directly to school library media collection development. Fewer still emerge which are related to the areas of collection development discussed here. Although a significant body of research related to collection development does not exist, there are several studies worth discussing for their historical value and for comparative purposes.

Lohrer[46] conducted a status study of emerging school library media centers in 1963. This study is important as a base line in considering contemporary practices and trends in collection development. Hoping to discover the extent of the impact of the 1960 *Standards*, Lehrer identified a total of 731 schools that exhibited a broad range of services based on good collections of a wide variety of resources. Most of her data was collected from 472 schools in 28 states. She concluded that 82 percent of the states had made progress in developing school libraries as multimedia resource centers in all types of communities and in all sizes and levels of schools. She also found that district level programs were developing as valuable back-up resource collections of expensive materials and important programs for cooperative services. Her findings are further substantiated by Gaver's[47] 1969 study of data supplied in the 1960s by school

districts applying for the Encyclopedia Britannica Elementary School Library Award Program. This data also revealed the existence of many districts in the process of developing broad elementary school media programs based on integrated materials collections.

Several studies verify the need for school materials collections to support the curriculum. Lohrer found outstanding curricular support programs in 41 schools in 17 states, based on rich collections of books (42 percent contained six to 10,00 titles; 83 percent subscribed to between three to six newspapers). These collections also contained extensive periodicals, pictures, and professional collections; half of the schools had holdings in from 10 to 16 of the possible 32 categories of audiovisual materials, including filmstrips, globes, wall maps, disc recordings, films, letter sets, charts, slides, tape recordings, study print sets, posters, models, framed pictures and realia.[48] Lewis[49] (1967) studied the uses of instructional materials in art programs and the responsibilities of the school library media center for art programs and concluded that all types of materials should be housed in the materials center, and that learning in the art curriculum would be enhanced by a wide variety of instructional media. Hardaway[50] (1969) reported that teachers who used media stated that it improved their teaching. Gaver[51] (1963) studied the effectiveness of centralized elementary school library service and found that type of organized program to be educationally superior in a number of ways.

Even though Lohrer's study was optimistic about the availability and ongoing development of multimedia resource centers, research in the sixties also revealed shortages in the breadth and size of collections. Prostano,[52] for instance, found that a low percentage of Connecticut schools met the national standards for school library media programs, and that a low percentage were providing the recommended resources. Two studies completed by Jones[53] and Schmitz[54] of selected Michigan high school science and math collections revealed that while funds from the National Defense Education Act were beginning to have an effect on school library media collections, there was no great impact apparent at the time of the study. There was evidence that some biology teachers were using teaching strategies that required library media collection use by students.

Recent research and marketing data reveal both positive and negative information about the availability, breadth, and size of collections. There is little concern that multimedia collections are still not being developed. It should be stressed again, however, that budgets are decreasing, and consequently expenditures for resources are dropping. The Association of Media Producers[55] reports for 1976 a seven percent (approximately $21,000,000) decline in spending for non-textbook instructional materials by school districts and institutions of higher education. A recent study conducted by the Educational Products Information Exchange (EPIE)[56] reports sobering figures on the use of library media collections. EPIE surveyed 471 teachers at all grade levels and learned that 55 percent of them have their students use library media only "occasionally"; nine percent reported students as using library materials daily, but 19 percent reported that they had no library media centers in their buildings.

The *National Inventory of Library Needs*[57] (1975), a monograph submitted to the National Commission on Library and Information Science (NCLIS), reports that shortfalls in all types of materials are "discouragingly pervasive" throughout the United States. The document reports specifically that: "In 1974 school library media centers held 520 million volumes of books and 100 million items of nonprint audiovisual materials including such materials as games, kits, and specimen." The document continues by stating that "acquisitions [of print materials] are still only about 40 percent of indicated need," and that "while 100 million items of nonprint items were owned by school library media centers, guidelines would indicate the *need for one billion* [emphasis mine] such items ."[58]

The ALA/AAP survey of the marketing, selection, and acquisition of materials for school library media programs[59] provides another dimension to the current scene. This cooperative study surveyed 135 book publishers and producers of audiovisual materials, 112 wholesalers and distributors, and 516 school library media personnel. Data provide information about the effects of changing budgets and a wide variety of marketing, selection, and acquisition procedures. Responses from school library media personnel indicate that the most often selected items besides books are kits, filmstrips, and cassette tapes. From reported expenditures on audiovisual materials, it appears that limited funds are being expended on audiovisual materials such as microfilms, models, reel-to-reel tapes (undoubtedly reflecting changing technology), 8mm film, sound loops, and transparencies (which may reflect trends in local production of materials). Although 20 percent of the respondents felt that their overall budgets would decrease, 49 percent believed their audiovisual budgets would increase; only 40 percent felt their book budgets would increase. A startling finding relating to breadth of collection relates to the purchase of paperbacks. In a time when interest in and use of paperbacks by the young are so well documented, 88 percent of the school library media specialists responded that they would normally buy titles in hardcover before buying titles in paperback–even when available in that format.

One of the most important questions to be considered in any discussion of collection development is how materials get into the collection. Who does the selection? What sources do selectors use to inform themselves? What determines what is finally selected? There are a few studies which provide some interesting insights into these concerns.

Green[60] (1970) concluded that purchasing and selection constitutes one of the nine important problem areas facing administrators of educational media programs. Sheriff[61] (1965) found that the quality of library book selection in Pennsylvania elementary schools is higher in schools using centralized libraries that have a full-time certified librarian. Galloway[62] (1965) called for more descriptive, helpful, and critical reviews of juvenile books by reviewers who are more aware of the increasingly vast and diverse audience which relies on the assessments provided by reviews. Two of the most interesting studies substantiate the belief that high school media collections are actually quite diverse. In a study of 31 high school collections, Altman[63] (1971) found that unique titles comprised nearly 50 percent of the non-core titles in all 31 schools. In a subsequent study directed by Gaver (1974), the collections of six schools were analyzed. It determined that "of the 85,197 book titles held by the six high schools, 52,000 (61 percent) are unique titles."[64]

Collection development in school media centers as a logical systematic decision-making process has not been well documented. The most complete description thus far has been provided by the Lohrer study. She identified 19 tools of significance for those schools developing multimedia collections, and subsequently found that all but six of the tools were checked by a majority of school media personnel.[65]

Specifically, the top five selection tools in the 162 elementary schools were *Children's Catalog* (checked regularly by 76 percent of the library media specialists), *Educators' Guide to Free Tapes, Scripts and Transcriptions* (73 percent), *Educators' Guide to Free Curriculum Materials* (31 percent), *Standard Catalog for High School Libraries* (31 percent), and *Filmstrip Guide* (28 percent). Library media specialists in the 75 junior high schools checked most consistently: *Basic Book Collection for Junior High Schools* (81 percent), *Standard*

Catalog for High School Libraries (76 percent), *Children's Catalog* (74 percent), *Gateways to Readable Books* (61 percent), and special bibliographies (65 percent). In the 103 senior high schools, the five top ranked tools were *Basic Book Collection for High Schools* (75 percent), *Booklist* (71 percent), special bibliographies (60 percent), *Paperbound Books in Print* (52 percent), and *Gateways to Readable Books* (50 percent). Lohrer also described the growing role of the district materials center in the selection process.[66]

A 1972 study of collection development of science materials for elementary schools by Pool[67] (1972) reports some sobering information about the collection development process in two school districts. Pool hypothesized that teachers and librarians who have freedom to select from a wide range of bibliographies, exhibits, and professional journals are more actively involved in building adequate collections for their particular school's needs than are personnel limited to selection from a local buying list. She did find that the data collected about selection criteria, selection aids, selection activities, and the quality and adequacy of collections revealed appreciable differences between the city which had a list and the city which did not in only four aspects.

> First, the schools in the city which uses a local buying list held larger percentages of the books recommended for correlation with the fourth grade science textbooks. Second, their holdings were, on the average, a year more recent than the District I holdings. Third, their 1968-1969 orders contained books with more recent publication dates. However, District I libraries received their orders quicker. There appeared to be no basis for support of the general hypothesis that autonomous selection by librarians and teachers produces better selected and more recent library collections in elementary schools because selectors who are given more freedom (that is, they do not use a local buying list) are more involved and adept at selection.[68]

The ALA/AAP survey reveals interesting shifts in the use of selection tools. The most noticeable is the shift from the use of basic, comprehensive retrospective tools to those which review current materials. In this survey the *Junior High School Library Catalog* is considered unimportant by 44 percent of the respondents. The *Senior High School Library Catalog* is considered unimportant by 45 percent of the respondents. Current reviewing tools are esteemed much more highly in 1977 than they were in 1963. For instance, in Lohrer's study, *Booklist* was used in only two elementary schools although it was obtained through the dis-

trict center and checked regularly by six percent of the elementary librarians. It was used consistently by 61 percent of the junior high school librarians and 71 percent of the senior high school librarians. In the ALA/AAP survey, 90 percent of the respondents reported it as an important tool. *School Library Journal*, not selected by Lohrer as one of the 19 significant tools, is rated as important by 98 percent of those questioned in the ALA/AAP survey. This survey also reveals the use of the tools that have been developed to review audiovisual materials. With the exception of producers and distributors catalogs, which are considered valuable by 82 percent of the respondents, those tools considered of value for selection of audiovisual materials are *Previews* (95 percent), *Audiovisual Instruction* (65 percent), *Booklist* (81 percent), and *Elementary School Library Collection* (56 percent).

Further study of this shift would be helpful. Does it reflect the fact that fewer new schools are being built, requiring fewer new collections and thus reducing the need for retrospective collection development? Is it curriculum change which demands recency, or emphasis on multimedia which the secondary level retrospective tools do not reflect? Do decreasing budgets make selectors want to be sure they have current material first?

An even more basic rationale could be constructed from the changing patterns in publishers' warehousing that are resulting in serious problems with out-of-print titles. Gaver noted in early 1976 that in the course of checking for the forthcoming edition of the *Elementary School Library Collection*, it was learned that 1,200 titles formerly listed in the 9th edition (1974) and its *Supplement* (1975) had been declared out-of-print by publishers.[69] She also pointed out that:

> The effect on ESLC 10th edition (October, 1976) has been considerably greater than in previous editions. Not only are there many more 'drops' than normal, but also these drops have caused real holes in the bibliographic coverage of a number of important subject areas. It should be noted that this is particularly serious in the case of ESLC because one criterion has always been the availability for purchase of 99 percent of the titles recommended.[70]

An analysis of the 1975 *Junior High School Library Catalog* was made to determine the number of out-of-print titles in a stratified sample of 413 titles, representing slightly more than ten percent of the collection (see Table I). When titles were checked against the 1976 *Books in Print*, a range of from 3 percent of the short story collection

TABLE 1

OP Analysis of Junior High School Library Catalog

Class no.	No. of titles in class	%	Sample No. of titles	%	Out-of-Print Total no. of titles OP
000	121	15%	18	5%	6
100	34	30%	11	9%	3.6
200	53	30%	17	35%	18.5
300	348	10%	35	5%	17
400	45	30%	15	22%	10
500	433	10%	43	13.9%	60
600	306	10%	30	10%	30
700	404	10%	40	20%	80
800	205	10%	21	9.5%	20
900	1117	10%	112	16.8%	188
F	525	10%	53	7.5%	39
SC	121	15%	18	3.3%	4

to 35 percent of the "200s" was found to be out-of-print. These figures are of concern, particularly when one assumes that some titles listed in *Books in Print* were already unavailable. Added to this is the year-by-year attrition expected before the 1980 edition of the *Catalog*.

Gerhardt reports that "acquisitions librarians in every region of the country can show that between 25 and 40 percent of their book orders are not being filled for books that are, year after year, listed in publishers' backlist catalogs as in print."[71] It may be that school media personnel simply cannot afford the time to do retrospective purchasing (the orders, the correspondence, the cancellation and reordering process), because the entire procedure is financially prohibitive.

The provisions of selection policies, the involvement of the school community, and prior-to-purchase evaluation are important considerations in the selection process. Again, we know little. The ALA/AAP survey reveals that 71 percent of the respondents operate within the outlines of a selection policy. The quality, effectiveness, and application of the policy is not covered in the survey. The Lohrer study revealed a small percentage of teachers consistently involved in the use of tools in the selection process. The ALA/AAP survey indicates a more

encouraging picture of teacher involvement. While 63 percent of the respondents indicated they had final responsibility for selecting materials, responses also indicated substantial involvement of teachers who make requests (92 percent), attend previewing exhibits (42 percent), participate in subject area development of the collection (39 percent), and attend demonstrations of new materials by publishers and distributors (35 percent). Only 17 percent reported teacher involvement in selection committees. It should be added that we learn nothing from this survey about how the decision is made to select; nothing about the application of criteria for evaluation or selection. Neither do we have data about the involvement of the community or other school staff. In addition, when respondents ranked in priority order the most important factors in the selection of materials, they ranked student requests at 3.89 on a scale of five (one being high).

Many school library media leaders have looked to the educational media examination center as a source to improve the selection process. A well organized center could provide a helpful blend of reviewing tools, new materials for preview, and selectors. Henne[72] called for national and regional bibliographical centers which would provide reviewing access to a wide variety of materials.

Rowell said in the introduction to the comprehensive study of existing educational media selection centers carried out by the National Book Committee, "one component in the instructional landscape of the 1970s, and we believe it to be an important one, is the educational media selection center function."[73]

The dimensions of what these centers should be were subsequently described in *Guide to the Development of Educational Media Selection Centers*.[74] These centers, if implemented, would provide access to materials for preview, staff development programs for teachers and media personnel, consultant service and opportunities for research related to the evaluation, selection, and use of media, as well as policies and procedures for administering media services.

Two Case Studies

KALAMAZOO PUBLIC SCHOOLS EXAMINATION CENTER

The Kalamazoo School System, located in southwestern Michigan, consists of 31 schools. In 1974, the system established the Examination Center as part of the Instructional Media Department's efforts to be accountable to policies and goals established by the School Board and general administrative system policies and procedures. Rather than establish a fixed examination collection, the district has chosen to utilize ongoing approval plans for current materials and the existing 31 school media centers, with their working collections selected from the materials that have gone through the Examination Center.

Four Board and Administrative Policies govern the overall philosophy of the Examination Center and guide the implementation of its policies and procedures.

Board Policy 6521

School Media Center materials shall be selected and withdrawn on the basis of the concepts set forth in the School Library Bill of Rights, approved by the American Association of School Librarians, endorsed by the Council of the American Library Association, which are reflected in the accepted procedures for selection and withdrawal of School Media Center materials.[75]

Administrative Procedures Bulletin No. 6521

Under the supervision of the Coordinator of Instructional Media, media specialists/assistants of Kalamazoo Public Schools shall select and withdraw school media center materials in consultation with teachers, administrators, and students in accordance with the criteria reflected in "Guidelines for the Evaluation of Print and Nonprint Materials" published by the Department of Instructional Media.[76]

Board Policy 6110

It is the policy of the Board of Education of the School District of Kalamazoo to continue to implement affirmatively equal educational opportunities for all students without regard to race, creed, color, age, sex or national origin and positive action shall continue to be taken to insure the fulfillment of this policy.[77]

Administrative Procedures Bulletin No. 3320

In the interest of saving the time of professional personnel, the visits of salespersons or other company representatives to individual buildings and/or individual staff members shall be governed by the following regulation:

The salesperson or other company representative shall first contact the appropriate administrator who is responsible for the selection of equipment or material...[78]

The center has in its short existence attracted a large number of users. In 1976, 3,000 people used the center, including members of the immediate educational community: teachers, library media specialists, students, administrators and parents, and university teachers and students from the area's four colleges and university. In the fall of 1977, a neighboring district with 16 schools entered into a cooperative previewing program with the Examination Center. In addition, media personnel in two neighboring counties come monthly to the Examination Center, and bimonthly listings of previewed materials are shared with local educational and library institutions and 32 school districts throughout a five county area of southwestern Michigan.

The Examination Center previews from 2,000 to 4,000 current, K-12, print and audiovisual items a year. Materials include books, microfilm, microfiche, magazines, pamphlets, study prints, slides, filmstrips, films, kits, records, cassettes, transparencies, realia and sometimes textbooks. Three sets of school district evaluative guidelines serve as criteria for approval of materials which then can be selected by building media specialists according to their individual school community criteria for selection and their materials budget. The guidelines provide general evaluative criteria and specific criteria to be applied in evaluation for positive non-stereotyped portrayal of human roles and minority groups.

Guidelines for the Evaluation of Print and Non-print Materials

What is the subject matter and scope? Does it have significant curricular content to justify its cost?

If print, does it have literary quality? If nonprint, is the item attractive and interesting with some aesthetic value of vitality, style and imagination?

Is it well-researched, accurate and authoritative?

Who is the publisher or producer and what is his reputation?

Is it readable or suitable for students of the age or grade levels at which it will be studied?

Is it up to date?

Does it duplicate or add to other material in the Media Center?

What features are included that will increase its usefulness: table of contents, index, bibliographies, maps, charts, thought-provoking captions, clear labeling, summaries, outlines, questions?

What is the need for it in the school? Is it worth the money it costs and the time and effort to use it?

How much does it cost? Is it expensive or inexpensive in relation to the total materials fund available? Would some less expensive item produce similar or better results?

If print, is it well made...good paper and print, large enough margins for easy opening, good illustrations? If nonprint, is it technically satisfactory in respect to photography, sound, color, type size, illustrations...is it physically satisfactory in respect to intended use?

Is it educationally sound for the age group for which it is intended? Does it stimulate thinking and inquiry? Does it suggest or lead to worthwhile learning activities?[79]

Guidelines for a Positive, Nonstereotyped Portrayal of Human Roles In Media Center Materials

Are parents and children of each sex involved in household tasks?

Are fathers shown in roles other than going to work or doing male-type chores? Are there family concerns, community concerns, personal growth concerns?

Are mothers shown in roles other than housework or child rearing? Are there family concerns, community concerns, personal growth concerns?

Does the home look "lived in" by real, human people or is it a "ready for company," sterile home? Are there accurate portrayals of one-parent families?

Are there accurate portrayals of multiple parent (divorce-remarriage) families?

Do the male characters respect the female characters and respond to them as equals?

Are mothers employed outside the home? In a stereotyping or creative job?

Are boys and girls portrayed with a range of human responses—girls adventurous and aggressive as well as sensitive, boys gentle as well as strong?

Are boys and girls participating equally in physical and intellectual activities?

Are girls developing independent lives, independently meeting challenges and finding their own solutions?

Do girls have a variety of choices and aspire to a variety of goals?[80]

Guidelines for Evaluating Minority Group Materials

Appropriate language. If dialect must be used, it should be faithful to the region of the story. Heavy use of words or expressions fraught with connotations of disrespect and contempt is unsuitable.

Illustrations must be true to the people depicted, not caricatures or stereotypes.

Theme. Minority people should be portrayed in all aspects of life—in different living situations, jobs, and professions.

Treatment of characters. Characters should emphasize that "they are people faced with the universal problems of all mankind: earning a living, hating and loving, rejoicing and grieving, experiencing successes and failures, learning to find their way through a complex world of ideas and living with other people.[81]

The Examination Center is operated by a staff of three: the Consultant on Instructional Media, a secretary, and a part-time clerk. It is supervised by the Director of Instructional Media. Seating capacity for 14 is available with adjacent room for large or small groups. Normal channels of local educational information sources publicize the center's availability. The center's active inservice program and curriculum development activities also serve to publicize it to the broader educational community.

Print and audiovisual media are ordered daily on approval. Items ordered for the evaluation process come from a wide variety of professional journals and reviewing tools, from suggestions of teachers, pupils, parents and community groups. As materials are received, they are sent to individual buildings for evaluation and then are placed on display with accompanying evaluations. Just prior to the display period, an annotated bibliography of received items will be prepared. The bibliography provides a K-12 listing, arranged by broad subject area; a one or two sentence description from the local evaluator's review; reading level; grade(s); suggested curricular use and complete ordering information. Multiple copies of this bibliography are sent to the buildings for perusal by media personnel, teachers and administrators. During the display period, building selection personnel/committees may preview the materials specifically desired and plan orders at the center.

Displays are provided every two weeks and also result in 17 printed bibliographies a year. Twice-a-year subject area listings are provided for all of the materials that go through the center. A master file of review cards is kept for future retrospective selection.

The Examination Center permits a constant flow of prime materials, hands-on previewing for teachers and media personnel, centralization of searching and evaluation efforts, broader access to a wide variety of selection tools, and the development of inservice activities. The latter has developed into an important part of the Center's activities. Staff development programs have been implemented for all district staff, students, substitutes, student teachers, college students and neighboring school district personnel. Center staff also feel that the opportunities for their participation in curriculum development are greatly increased as teaching staff becomes more aware of media personnel's knowledge of materials.

ANNE ARUNDEL COUNTY SCHOOLS AND THE MARYLAND STATE DEPARTMENT OF EDUCATION

In 1976, the Review and Evaluation Center, a joint program of the Anne Arundel County, Maryland Schools and the Maryland State Department of Education, began serving school personnel from all parts of the state.

The philosophy of the Review Center is stated in the introduction to the *Guidelines for the Review and Selection of Textbooks and Instructional Materials*: "The selection and adoption of textbooks and instructional materials is the responsibility of each local education agency in Maryland."[82] The state guidelines consistently encourage school staffs to examine and evaluate all materials on a continuous and systematic basis. The specific purpose of the joint reviewing program, then, is to provide a Review and Evaluation Center for media specialists, teachers, administrators, review and evaluation committees, academic personnel involved in teacher-training programs, public library, children's and young adult staff and personnel of the private schools of Maryland.

The center provides an organized collection of current K-12 educational and professional library media, textbooks, 16mm films, and professional reviewing tools. A master file of evaluation data is available for patron use, and special collections of current issue materials can be arranged for meeting patron needs and interests. The services of the center also include: large collections of print and nonprint materials always available for review; requested materials obtained; special subject collections developed as requested; computer listings of holdings; extended preview period; evaluation criteria assistance.

The Review and Evaluation Center staff is available to assist patrons in examining and selecting appropriate materials which will meet their instructional objectives and needs. The following selection considerations are recommended for use by persons using the center:

. Is the material important enough to the curriculum to be considered for purchase?

. Is the material accurate, impartial, free from sexism, racism, or religious discrimination, and up to date?

. Is the presentation interesting? Are the instructional objectives clearly definable?

. Is the concept, vocabulary, or format too easy or difficult for use with the level intended?

. Can the concept be better developed by another method of presentation? Does it present information other materials do not?

. Is it difficult to follow the print, visuals, or sound?

. Are the notes and guides a useful and integral part of the material?

. Is the material designed for ease of use and storage?

. Is the material durable, or worthy of repair or replacement costs? Could the concept be presented as well by a less expensive satisfactory substitute?

Materials are shelved by subject. Within each subject, shelving is by publisher or producer. Materials do remain in the center, but field testing is available. Facilities permit patrons to work independently or in groups. Since the complete collection is computerized, printouts on specific subjects can be made available as well as complete listings of the holdings for those who desire to have this information prior to visiting the center. The availability of staff encourages evaluation workshops and/or staff development programs.

The center is manned by one media specialist, one secretary, one media secretary-clerk, and a part-time clerk. Located at the Anne Arundel County Board of Education building, it occupies part of the professional media center facilities there. Services of the Review and Evaluation Center are published in a variety of organizational newsletters and promotional brochures. A survey of users periodically analyzes the degree of participation by the educational community and the application each patron makes of the service.

Since its opening in 1976, library media specialists, teachers, and administrators from all parts of the state have used the center. Curriculum and evaluation committee members and inservice workshop participants from public and nonpublic schools have reviewed materials in the center. Patrons have also included public librarians, student teachers, college students, and interested citizens.

Both Kalamazoo and Anne Arundel provide examples of school district efforts to refine the collection development process, to build upon existing research, and to increase the evaluation and selection expertise of the school community.

Notes

1. Committee on Library Organization and Equipment of the National Education Association and the North Central Association of Colleges and Secondary Schools. *Standard Library Organization and Equipment for Secondary Schools of Different Sizes.* (Chicago: American Library Association, 1920):21.

2. American Association of School Librarians and Association for Educational Communications and Technology. *Media programs: District and School.* (Chicago: American Library Association, Washington, D.C.: Association for Educational Communications and Technology, 1975):62.

3. Committee on Library Organization and Equipment, *Standard Library.*

4. American Association of School Librarians and Association for Educational Communications and Technology, *Media Programs:*62.

5. Committee on Library Organization and Equipment, *Standard Library*, p. 7.

6. The National Education Association and the American Library Association. *Elementary School Library Standards.* (Chicago: American Library Association, 1925).

7. The Committee on Post-War Planning of the American Association of School Librarians of the Division of Librarians for Children and Young People of the American Library Association. *School Libraries for Today and Tomorrow.* (Chicago: American Library Association, 1945).

8. Ibid., p. 11.

9. American Association of School Librarians. *Standards for School Library Programs.* (Chicago: American Library Association, 1960).

10. Ibid., pp. 3-4.

11. Ibid., p. 22.

12. American Library Association and National Education Association. *Standards for School Media Programs.* (Chicago: American Library Association, 1969).

13. Ibid., p. x.

14. Ibid., p. 20.

15. American Association of School Librarians and Association for Educational Communications and Technology, *Media Programs*, p. vii.

16. Committee on Library Organization and Equipment, *Standard Library*, p. 21.

17. Committee on Post-War Planning, *School Libraries*, p. 23.

18. America Association of School Librarians, *Standards for School Library*, p. 80.

19. Ibid.

20. Ibid., p. 81.

21. Ibid., p.84.

22. Ibid., p. 85.

23. Committee on Library Organization and Equipment, *Standard Library*, p. 30.

24. Ibid.

25. Committee on Post-War Planning, *School Libraries*, p. 21.

26. Ibid.

27. American Association of School Librarians, *Standards for School Library*, pp. 80-81.

28. Ibid., p.84.

29. Ibid., pp. 30-31.

30. Ibid., p.35.

31. American Association of School Librarians and Association for Educational Communications and Technology, *Media Programs*, p. 69.

32. Ibid., p. 68.

33. Ibid., p. 69.

34. Ibid., p. 41.

35. Committee on Library Organization. and Equipment, *Standard Library*, p. 21.
36. Ibid.
37. Committee on Post-War Planning, *School Libraries*, p. 24.
38. American Association of School Librarians, *Standards for School Library*, p. 20.
39. American Association of School Librarians and Association for Educational Communications and Technology, *Media Programs*, p. 62.
40. Ibid.
41. Ibid.
42. American Library Association and Association of American Publishers. "Marketing, Selection, and Acquisition of Materials for School Media Programs." *Numerical Results from Three Surveys Prepared for Detroit Conference Program...18 June 1977*. (Chicago: RTSD Office, American Library Association, 1977).
43. Jean E. Lowrie. "A Review of Research in School Librarianship," in *Research Methods in Librarianship: Measurement and Evaluation*, ed. Herbert Goldhor. (Urbana, Ill.: University of Illinois Graduate School of Library Science, 1968):51-69.
44. Shirley Louise Aaron. "A Review of Selected Research Studies in School Librarianship 1967-1971" Part I in *School Libraries* (Summer 1972):296; Part II in *School Media Quarterly* 1 (Fall 1972):41-48.
45. Patricia Freeman. *Index to Research in School Librarianship, 1960–1974*. (Stanford, Ca.: ERIC Clearinghouse on Information Resources, 1976).
46. Alice Lohrer. "Identification and Role of School Libraries which Function as Instructional Materials Centers with Implications for Training " (Urbana, Ill.: NDEA Title VII, Part B. Contract B-144, July 1961-June 1962, 1963).
47. Mary Virginia Gaver. *Patterns of Development in Elementary School Libraries Today*. A Five Year Report on Emerging Media Centers. 3rd ed. (Chicago: Encyclopaedia Britannica, Inc., 1969).
48. Lohrer, "Identification and Role " p. 25.
49. Patricia Tandrow Lewis. "Educational Media Administered through the School Library—Instructional Materials Center and Their Contribution to the Art Education Program." (Ed.D. dissertation, University of New Mexico, 1967).
50. Gaiuz Norwood Hardaway. "The Administration and Utilization of Audiovisual Media in the Public Elementary and Secondary Schools in Bossier Parish, Louisiana " (Ed.D. dissertation, University of Mississippi, 1969).
51. Mary Virginia Gaver. The *Effectiveness of Centralized Library Service in Elementary Schools*. 2nd. ed. (New Brunswick, N.J.: Rutgers University Press, 1963).
52. Emanuel Theodore Prostano. "An Analysis of School Library Resources in Connecticut as Compared to National Standards, 1960-61." (Ph.D. dissertation, University of Connecticut, 1962).
53. Norma Louise Jones. "A Study of the Library Book Collection in the Biological Sciences in Fifty-Four Michigan High Schools Accredited by the North Central Association of Colleges and Secondary Schools." (Ph.D. dissertation, University of Michigan, 1965).
54. Eugenia E. Schmitz. "A Study of the Library Book Collections in Mathematics and the Physical Sciences in Fifty-Four Michigan High Schools Accredited by the North Central Association of Colleges and Secondary Schools." (Ph.D. dissertation, University of Michigan, 1966).
55. "Newsfronts." *Education, U.S.A.* (May 2, 1977):266.
56. *Report on a National Study of the Nature and Quality of Instructional Materials Most Used by Teachers and Learners*. (New York: EPIE Institute, 1977):8.
57. Boyd Ladd. *National Inventory of Library Needs, 1975: Resources Needed for Public and Academic Libraries and Public School Library Media Centers*. (Washington, D.C.: National Commission on Libraries and Information Science, 1977):110-1 11.
58. Ibid.
59. American Library Association and Association of American Publishers. "Marketing, Selection."
60. Leroy Adelbert Green. "Case Studies of Key Educational Media Administration Problems." (Ed.D. dissertation, University of Northern Colorado, 1970).
61. Ralph William Sheriff. "A Study of the Level of Quality Used in Selecting Library Books in Elementary Schools in Pennsylvania." (Ph.D. dissertation, Pennsylvania State University, 1965).
62. Mabel Louise Galloway. "An Analytical Study of the Extent and Mature of the Reviewing of Juvenile Books in Eight Journals and Newspapers with Special Regard to Their Usefulness as Selection Aids for School Libraries." (Ph.D. dissertation, Columbia University, 1965).
63. Ellen O. Altman. "The Resource Capacity of Public Secondary School Librarians to Support Interlibrary Loan: A Systems Approach to Title Diversity and Collection Overlap " (Ph.D. dissertation, Rutgers University, 1971).
64. Gale Sypher Jacob. The *High School Library Collection: An Introductory Study of Six High School Libraries*. (Williamsport, Pa.: Bro-Dart Inc., 1974):3.
65. Lohrer, "Identification and Role," p. 184.
66. Ibid., pp. 180-188.
67. Jane Pool. "An Analysis of Book Selection Processes for Elementary School Libraries." Final Report, Project No. 9-G-076, Grant No. OEG-7-9-530076-0136-(095). (Washington, D.C.: Office of Education. Bureau of Research, 1972).
68. Ibid., p. 208.
69. Mary Virginia Gaver. Memo. "Attack of the Backlist." (Rev. 8/17/76).
70. Ibid.
71. Lillian Gerhardt. "Out of Control—Indefinitely." *School Library Journal* 24 (Oct. 1977):63.
72. Frances Henne. "Standards for School Library Services at the District Level." *Library Trends* XVI (April 1968):510-511.
73. John Rowell and M. Ann Heidbreder. *Educational Media Selection Centers: Identification and Analysis of Current Practices*. (Chicago: American Library Association, 1971):viii.
74. Cora Paul Bomar. *Guide to the Development of Educational Media Selection Centers*. (Chicago: American Library Association, 1973).
75. Kalamazoo (Michigan) Board of Education. Board Policy 6521.

76. Kalamazoo (Michigan) Administrative Procedures & Bulletin No. 6521.
77. Kalamazoo, Board Policy 6110.
78. Kalamazoo, Administrative Procedures, No. 3320.
79. Kalamazoo, Public Schools Instructional Media Department. "Guidelines for the Evaluation of Print and Nonprint Materials," 1973.
80. Ibid.
81. Ibid.
82. *Guidelines for the Review and Selection of Textbooks and Instructional Materials.* (Maryland State Department of Education, 1976), n.p.

BIBLIOGRAPHY

Van Orden, Phyllis. "Promotion, Review, and Examination of Materials," *School Library Media Quarterly.* Unpublished.

Vandergrift, Kay E. "Selection: A Reexamination and Reassessment," *School Library Media Quarterly.* Unpublished.

Youth Services Collection Development Issues

by Pat Feehan

Harriet G. Long in 1953 wrote about public library service to children in her book *Rich The Treasure*.

In building book collections, the public library has a responsibility to the child as a whole.[1]

The foundation of public library service to children continues to be the development of a materials collection for children of all ages and, today also includes an increasing number of adults.

Traditionally children's librarians attempted to provide the best collection possible. "Best" meant emphasizing the aesthetic qualities of books. Book or materials selection, however, is not synonymous with collection development. The evaluation and selection of materials is only one element of a dynamic collection development policy. Other elements include acquisition and maintenance.

Today, children's librarians place more emphasis on the community when thinking of collection development. The *Public Library Mission Statement and Its Imperatives for Service* states that:

> Society needs an agency that can actively bring every person regardless of age, education, language, religion, ethnic and cultural background and mental and physical health into effective contact with the human record.[2]

Public librarians when following this service imperative are meeting the needs of the public as a whole, as children's librarians are meeting the needs of the child as a whole. Yet, standards for Children's Services still include the "best" as in the *Standards for Youth Services in Public Libraries of New York State* which declares that:

Children's materials collections should preserve the best of the past, offer the best of the current, and reflect changes in children's interests as well as changes in society.[3]

COLLECTION DEVELOPMENT POLICY

Collection development begins with an analysis of the community in which the library resides, and a definition of its users and nonusers.

A thoughtfully written collection development policy should reflect a knowledge of children's interests and needs, their capabilities and limitations. This policy, in stating its philosophy, should include what resources the library will make accessible in meeting the educational, personal, cultural, recreational, and informational needs of its clientele.

Also to be defined is the materials selection policy. This describes the library's policy on gifts, content by subject areas, depth of coverage, duplication, evaluation criteria, and selection. The policy should describe how books will be obtained and how they will be discarded, replaced, and repaired. Another important element to consider is the availability, if not the acquisition of materials. Stating clearly the policies of interlibrary loans, networking, and relationships to other libraries, the policy also determines the accessibility of materials. The collection development policy should also include statements on intellectual freedom. Another accessibility issue to consider is the concept of user education. Provisions should be made by the library to ensure that patrons know about materials and how they are accessed.

There are several philosophies that have been dividing rooms of children's librarians for quite some time. "We buy only the *best* books!" phi-

Collection development policy begins with an analysis of the community in which the library resides and a definition of both its users and its nonusers

losophy. "Best" for whom? Paraphrasing W. F. Poole, there are as many kinds of "best" as there are readers. There is the "patron-driven" collection based on demand and the cost-conscious librarian who only looks for a bargain. It would seem that a balance of all three philosophies would be a good approach. In spite of the constant fear of falling over into someone's philosophical backyard, I have managed to fence-sit on this issue for quite some time. I love filling a patron's request and I enjoy a good bargain and I feel like a very fine children's librarian when I survey my "domain" of the creme de la creme of children's book publishing. I highly recommend the balance theory, a "harmonious arrangement."

STAYING ON TOP OF THINGS

It's not easy to stay "on top of things" these days. You have the space problem with an ever-growing print collection and back issues of periodicals, even though ideally you try to weed at least 15 percent of the collection annually. There is the problem of resource sharing. Your library belongs to an OCLC network and you made the mistake of cataloging the "choose your own adventures" and "sweet dreams" series and everyone in the state wants to borrow them because they 1) don't purchase ephemera or, 2) don't have the money to purchase ephemera.

There is the problem of trying to take a dispassionate view and very uncensored approach to book reviewing. And of course the biggest problem of all is trying to keep up with all materials of all types for all ages with a limited budget. It takes knowing what is popular, what will be popular, a willingness to experiment, and a continuous re-evaluation of circulation procedures. It also takes the financial and moral support of the administration, a retrospective knowledge of children's literature, and time to actively review current material using selection aids, workshops, meetings, trips to bookstores, and whatever else it takes. I will tell you now, and probably again later, that it's a lot of fun, a great challenge, and leads to most satisfying feedback.

CHANGES IN THE FAMILY

Although satisfying, it isn't easy to stay afloat in the ebb and flow of societal change. Our society is witnessing especially dramatic changes in contemporary family life. The nuclear family consisting of the mythical "2.3 children" living with two married parents of the opposite sex is only one of many possibilities. Psychologist Urie Bronfenbrenner has cited four specific factors changing the family:

1) the increase in working mothers, 2) fewer adults in the home, 3) more single-parent families, and 4) more children of unwed mothers.[4] The family today is analogous to an erector set; all the parts are interchangeable and can be taken apart and put together again in several traditional or nontraditional forms.

The Single-Parent Family

Because of death or divorce, desertion, birth out of wedlock, or adoption, many children live with only one parent and that parent usually is female. With this family structure there tends to be an increase of working mothers, and fewer adults in the home. A single-parent family can be found in any social class. Death, divorce, and unwed motherhood cross all socioeconomic lines, and single adults are able to adopt children. It happens more often in poor families that a parent deserts the home to get economic relief or because they cannot or will not support the family. However, mothers in middle or working class families have deserted the home to seek career opportunities or simply because they no longer wish to be "tied down."

Economic Status

The income of the single-parent unit may be cut in half or nonexistent, depending on the situation. The amount of this income and other economic resources have an impact on the education, health, and life style of the children.

It is the single mother who appears to be having the most difficulty reentering the job market. Often untrained or unskilled, these women take jobs at wages inadequate to support a family. About one in three female-headed families lives in poverty as compared to one in eighteen households with two parents. In 1984, of the 7.3 million families living below the poverty line, 3.8 million were single-parent families and 3.5 million of these were families headed by a female.[5] With more single parents, and working mothers, children are being separated from parents at an earlier age. Child care has become a major issue for our society.

IMPLICATIONS FOR LIBRARIES

In my personal experience, the public library is the informal community education and recreation center (and I emphasize the word *center*), a place of concentrated activity and influence. Libraries as social agencies working with young people must be aware of the factors affecting them. Children's services in public libraries need development based not only on the needs and interests of children, but their families as well.

Taking this into account, planning can then be done—planning for services, programs, and collection development. One of the major considerations in serving the single-parent family or the woman in the work force is the little time these parents have to participate in the life of the community and in the life of the child. I know a single father who felt free to tell me exactly what improvements I could make in the Children's Department. He wanted a "supermarket" atmosphere, a place where he could hurry in, grab all the colorful and inviting books we would place out on top of bookshelves and tables and leave quickly. He was always in a hurry, between leaving his job and going out to his farm and his daughter. He would like to have had books stacked like cereal boxes and "impulse buying" racks all carefully chosen and thoughtfully arranged to save him time. Food for thought! Materials in the library should represent alternative social and personal lifestyles, provide help in basic survival skills, and offer support for educational and career aspirations. These resources should also provide enrichment for parents with limited time and satisfy the needs and interests of their children.

The library is a place where family members can be economically entertained, self-educated, and informed. Resources and activities may add to the choices these families have when spending their limited time together. They can read a book, watch a film or filmstrip, play a game, listen to a recording or cassette, put on a puppet show, or talk with other families.

The library literature documents several good efforts by public libraries on behalf of families, and a number of studies have now been done on the positive effects of library activities and resources on the development of the "child as a whole."

Parent Education

"Parents as Reading Partners" programs, parent-child workshops, parenting programs, the traditional storytimes for preschoolers and older children, and toddler storytimes are all creating an atmosphere of "family services" in public libraries. The world of young children today is surrounded by an abundance of imaginative playthings (mirrors, hats, puppets, doll houses), educational toys and games, and special books and materials (bath books, board books, cloth books, tactile books, novelty books). Librarians use the resources in planning activities for children, and because follow-up at home or in the library is important,

these materials, often in duplicate, circulate. Materials for toddlers and preschoolers will also include flannelboard stories, records and cassettes, filmstrips, 16mm films, and videocassettes. Research documents the dramatic rapidity of infants' and toddlers' developing abilities. The important task of parent interaction should be undertaken with the aid of adequate resources. Suitable materials and the accessibility of visual aids is still a problem for many libraries who are involved in these activities.

Providing services for parents also has an impact on the collection. Parents are in need of information on childrearing, child development, and early education. They need information on health, nutrition, safety, and intellectual stimulation and they need a place where they can meet other parents, exchange ideas, and become better informed. Children's librarians may develop small collections of materials on these subjects, but they must also be very aware of all the resources the library has to offer, promote them, and provide ease of access. This can be difficult in public libraries where children's departments are often geographically isolated from the adult collection. A parenting resource area should contain circulating materials, free handouts from community organizations, magazines on parenting and family issues, newsletters, bulletins, and a vertical file.

Services to the Disabled

Public libraries may also have a toy and game area containing educational and recreational materials for all age and capability levels, designed to enhance child development. By "capability levels" I also mean that children with disabilities must be considered when selecting materials. Services to the visually handicapped can include electronic aids, tape recorders, books in large print and braille, books and music on cassette tapes and records, and rear screen projection equipment to allow children with poor sight to get close to a film or filmstrip. Materials and aids for the mentally and physically disabled might include special equipment, magazines, records, cassettes, games, and collections of low-level vocabulary books.

Child Care Concerns

Because of single-parenthood and more women working outside of the home, increasing numbers of children are placed in custodial and educational agencies during the weekday. Licensed day care centers, which are attempting to accommodate an increasing number of children, have encouraged a closer relationship between libraries and community agencies licensing such facilities and caring for children. ALA has put out a brochure called *Libraries and Day Care* which encourages parents and day care workers to seek sources of help through the local library or library system or the state library. Now child care workers, as well as parents, need assistance in locating materials which supplement the resources in their own agencies.

When child care is too expensive or unavailable, the library's resources again come into play. Storytimes, self-help books for effective parenting, games and crafts ideas, books on interaction activities for all age levels, and a place where parents in similar circumstances can communicate and children can play with a variety of materials chosen specifically to enhance their development. (Children's librarians were doing it for years. Once we learned there was a "method to the madness," accountability for budgeting became easier.)

The Latchkey Child

Another issue that has implications for libraries is what to do about the "latchkey" child. Latchkey children have their own key to let themselves into the home after school. The national PTA estimates that 5 to 12 million American children are at home without adults for some period of time every day.[5] Libraries are developing programs for children who need information, encouragement, and support. More multiple copies of materials on first aid and safety, dental care, preparation of easy meals, pet care, and babysitting will be needed to circulate.

Resource Sharing

All of these materials, resources, and equipment cost money. At the same time the number of working parents and single-parent families is increasing, federal, state, and local governments are cutting back funds for libraries, recreation centers, schools, and other institutions that have traditionally provided services to children. Attempting to meet the needs of single-parent families, indeed, of all families, is straining public library budgets. It's been my experience that public library budgets are not usually at the top of the scale when determining allocations to city and county deparments. Children's services departments don't seem to fare much better when cutting up the budget "pie" within the library structure. I have often given my "miracle of the loaves and fishes" speech to children's librarians—how to make a little go a long way. Resourcefulness is a "must" for any proactive, outreaching children's librarian. We can learn all there is to learn about budgeting and politics, accountability and management, but when the time comes to sit down in a meeting room with the head of Adult Services, Technical Services, Extension Services, and Administration and divvy up the budget, resourcefulness will still definitely help. There is just so much money to go around and even in the most socially aware, unselfish, team-oriented libraries, there will simply never be enough money for everything that needs to get done. Resourcefulness will help and *resource sharing* will help even more.

Children's librarians must learn to cooperate with other concerned child advocate agencies and institutions. These agencies and institutions include: governmental departments, including city and county-wide committees on family issues, and parks and recreation departments; educational agencies, including PTAs, day care centers, child care organizations, higher education institutions who offer parent education, child development, children's literature, etc.; community agencies such as health services, social services, hospitals, museums, and police and fire departments. All of these have funds, personnel, and resources that can be shared to cut down overhead, acquisition, maintenance, and dissemination expense. The library, too, is more than an agency that offers books. It offers programs and activities to help families learn new skills and information and to have fun together and it offers materials to help learn to apply those skills. It is a genuinely concerned and integrally vital part of the community and society. It will take some "vitamin C"—cooperation, communication, collaboration, coordination, and commitment, all the components of a healthy, helping community.[6]

CHANGING POPULATIONS AND ILLITERACY

Two more social and demographic conditions that I would like to look at in tandem are changing populations and the rate of illiteracy in America. I believe that one has a great impact on the other and both have implications for public library collections.

According to the U.S. Census Bureau, 13 percent of all U.S. adults are illiterate in English. Of these about 37 percent speak a language other than English at home, 82 percent are immigrants, and 21 percent entered the United States in the last six years. Some of the repercussions we have seen recently include California's Proposition 63, which voters approved in November, 1986.[7] The proposition makes English the official language of California. A similar measure has been introduced in Dade County in Florida, where Cubans and Haitians make up a large segment of the population.

Communities that have proudly declared their multilingual and multicultural heritage and communities who have not taken sides on the issue will also have an impact on library collections. Multilingual books of fiction and nonfiction and reference books in foreign languages will be in demand in some libraries. During a recent trip to Sweden, I found immigrant services through state libraries to be very interesting and impressive. Although locally controversial, the libraries were spending a great deal of money and time providing materials and activities for their immigrant populations. The budget allocations were in response to a very vocal demand on the part of the immigrants themselves. Comparing that to my own experience in Oregon, where most of the immigrant population was from Asian countries, I found the foreign clientele to be intellectually curious and great users of the library, but very timid in their demand for materials in their own language. It was for me, therefore, a constituency and a subject area that was overlooked until I hired a Chinese student as a shelver.

My foreign travels aside, I also discovered through my new "interpreter"/shelver that many of her friends and acquaintances were coming into the library's children's department to look for high-interest/low-vocabulary readers and read-along cassette and book collections to help in learning the English language. This discovery had an immediate effect on the materials collection. Word of mouth advertising led to several "English-as-a-second-language" classes scheduling library visits and materials orientations.

These same materials are effective in working with illiterate adults. One in every five adults or 27 million Americans are functionally illiterate; 45 million are only marginally literate. Over half of the adults currently on welfare are functionally illiterate.[8] These adults, finding the library to be a nonthreatening, helpful agency, use the children's department of the public library. The resources are there, all it takes is a shift in perspective as to their use and a sensitivity to the user.

As for the preventive fight against illiteracy, experts in literature for children and young adults have pointed out parenting programs that include the "read aloud together" message and teach parents how to select good and appropriate books and materials. And today's children, who may already be tomorrow's committed adult public library users, can also "read aloud together" with

adults who are in need of help with their fight against illiteracy.

Media Illiteracy: The Impact of Technology

There is another kind of illiteracy, media illiteracy, that is a serious problem for today's children's librarians and also has implications for children's library collections. Librarians, both school and public, seem to be taking advantage of every class, workshop, and in-service training program possible to try to catch up and keep up with today's children who are comfortable with the rapid technological changes in their environment.

It isn't just because of computers anymore that adults look in wonder at today's child. Consider the compact discs, electronic calculators, digital clocks, and video recorders which children seem to master with such ease. (Think of velcro! Children today don't have to learn to tell time by the big hand and little hand and they don't have to learn to tie shoelaces!) Library collections as a result of LSCA funds, special grants, and local gifts now house multimedia centers stocked with compact discs, videotapes, and audiocassettes. Studies in how people learn have shown that we learn not only from the facts presented but from the manner in which they are presented. Not all library users are readers. And a recent Bowker study found that almost 200,000 micros are in use in public, school, academic, and special libraries.[9] Computers are an interactive way of learning and children and adults who are computer literate tend to develop learning attitudes that are participative and exploratory. Children and adults have a few expectations about their libraries nowadays and they are expensive expectations.

On the other hand, my personal experience with the impact of electronic communications technologies has been of another sort. In Oregon, library leaders and representatives met to forge statewide library standards about six or seven years ago. One of the standards was to have a telephone in each public library. The "reality gap" between technological advancement and what is realistically possible in some areas of the United States would make a wonderful study.

Computers, audiocassette players, and even television are now accepted as adjuncts to book collections in children's libraries. Audiovisual materials have pizazz. We must ask ourselves as professionals—what is the major purpose of library service to children? The major purpose is to offer children access to literature, information, and experience which would not be available in everyday life. Young people need to know that all libraries are the source of information and pleasure.

RECOMMENDATIONS

I have read a number of collection development policies. Most libraries are still calling them book selection policies; most libraries do not have a separate policy for services to youth. My obvious recommendations for a start would be to turn this around.

Collection development policies should reflect a *current* awareness of a dynamic society. Last Sunday I read two articles in the morning paper. One was concerned with gifted children and the world's focus on the need to cultivate the best and the brightest. On the next page there was an article entitled, "The U.S. is Losing Invention Status to Japan." In essence it said that last year foreigners accounted for almost half of the patents granted by the U.S. Government with the largest number going to the Japanese. The figures also showed that the United States is losing ground in the development of new technology. With more attention focused on education, the U.S. Patent Office was launching "Project XL," a cooperative program with educators aimed at fostering analytical thinking in classrooms. As a children's librarian in a public library right now, I should find out how to get involved in Project XL. As an "educator" in society I want to be party to tapping the potential. The facilities, resources, and materials in the library are there to aid in tapping that potential. Human information resources in the community should also be considered a part of the library's materials, especially if reciprocal services are being used in lieu of monies to provide these materials. The policy should reflect this as well.

Library collection development policies should define the library's role in society and in the community. I believe in letting people know the "method behind the madness." I enjoy the sound a person makes when realization sets in. For example, libraries just don't buy toys for kids to break and waste taxpayers' money. Parent education specialists have written articles and books about the techniques of introducing toys to children for both education and enjoyment. Libraries can act as agents of consumer education for adults when purchasing toys, games, magazines, records, and books for library collections. The policy should say so. It not only sounds good, but it's true! It's simply a different and more substantive way of looking at things. If libraries are making available a wide variety of media on many different conceptual levels for all ages, the collection development should state this also.

By relating goals for service to thoughtful, creative (current) collections of materials, library service to children should be able to grow and develop with the same enthusiasm, zest, and optimism that characterize the children being served.

References

1. Harriet G. Long, *Rich the Treasure* (Chicago: ALA, 1953).
2. *The Public Library Mission Statement and Its Imperatives for Service* (Chicago: ALA, 1979): 3.
3. Task Force on Standards for Youth Services, *Standards for Youth Services in Public Libraries of New York State* (New York Library Association, 1984): 3.
4. Jill L. Locke, and Margaret Kimmel, "Children of the Information Age: Changes and Challenges" *Library Trends* (Winter 1987): 357.
5. Marguerite Baechtold and Eleanor McKinney, *Library Service for Families* (Hamden, Conn.: Library Professional Publications, 1983): 54.
6. Pat Feehan, "Vitamin C for A Healthier Outlook!" *PNLA Quarterly* 51 (Winter 1987): 39.
7. Bertha Cheatham, "The Year in Review" *School Library Journal* (December 1986): 25.
8. Ibid.: 26.
9. Holly Willett, "Current Issues in Public Library Services for Children" *Public Libraries* (Winter, 1985): 139.

Issues in Collection Building: Why Collection Development Policies

Elizabeth Futas

It has been brought to my attention in recent months that there are still a great many librarians who do not understand the value to a library of a collection development policy or an acquisitions policy. When I discuss policies with students in my classes, or when I speak to groups of practicing librarians, I always mention that there are two distinct and differing reasons for the use of such policies. There are, of course, innumerable reasons why an individual library might use or need such a policy, but in general these policies are used to inform and/or to protect. In this issue's column, I will discuss the latter, and probably more prevalent, reason for writing and adopting a collection development policy, and that is to protect the library, librarian or some other group (trustees, for example) from outside groups or patrons, or outside political forces.

The first part of the collection development policy that might be concerned with protection is the intellectual freedom statement. This is a very important part of most policies and, of the ones that I have read, the least thought out on the part of the individual library staff doing the writing or revising of a policy. For some reason, librarians seem to think that the Library Bill of Rights and the other statements that come from the American Library Association can be mentioned (e.g., "We believe in and follow the Library Bill of Rights") or copied (e.g., "In the appendix you will see the Library Bill of Rights and other intellectual freedom statements to which we subscribe. ")

There is nothing wrong with the ALA statements but merely to mention or copy them in a library's policy is a great mistake. More thought should go into the statement and it should be tailor-made to fit the situation of a particular library. In addition, the exact procedures for handling a complaint against material held by a library should be stated in the policy. This will prevent an emotional response to an attack and will prevent the library, as an institution, from treating any group or individual differently from any other group or individual.

Different types of libraries have different needs in the area of intellectual freedom, and the procedures and statements made in the collection development policy statement should reflect the type of library, the political situation the library is in, and the values of the librarians that run the library. All of these differences cannot be stated in a policy simply by quoting from the official policy of the ALA or any other group. That is not to say that these documents do not belong in a policy. Certainly they may be used, but they should not be the only protection that a library or a librarian has within the community.

Intellectual freedom is not the only statement made in a collection development policy that can be used to protect a library or librarian. Several of the other parts of a policy can be used in the same way; as they are informing, they can also be explaining and protecting. For example, in a public library, patrons often want to know why the books that they want to read are not available right away. If there were a paragraph in the policy on purchases of best-sellers and how many are purchased given the number of reserves, it would explain the library's procedures and at the same time protect the librarian from an angry patron. I believe that most people understand procedures once they are explained. In an academic library, the purchase or nonpurchase of textbooks can be explained in the same way. The same type of explanation can also be useful to school media centers and to special libraries.

Another area where it is becoming increasingly necessary for librarians to protect themselves and their libraries is that of gifts. Since the early 1970s the federal government has become very strict about assessments of tax credits for gifts to libraries. A few libraries use the statement that the ALA committee on manuscripts and rare books developed. Again, it would seem advisable to enlarge on that statement because, although it sets out rules, it does not go into the question of why it has become necessary for a library to protect itself in this way. Again, I believe that too few librarians really think of their own situations when writing up a gift policy and therefore write very general statements. When needed, they may not provide the protection they might have. Address the gift policy to the economic, social, and political situation in which a library finds itself. There are a number of libraries that do not have problems with gifts and therefore the statement need not be long or complicated. For those libraries that have become burdened with unwanted and undisposable items, the policy statement can be invaluable.

A final item on protection— this time concerning the librarian, the library, and the patron—is in the area of confidentiality. In all the collection development policies that I have read, only two ever mentioned the privacy of the reference interview or of circulation records. I have always assumed that this was because these statements were in reference policies or in some other procedural part of the library's documentation. I have since discovered that few libraries have any statement on this at all. In the next decade I see a possible need for having this type of protection written down and prominently displayed or available widely to the library's patrons.

None of the above will absolutely guarantee protection for a librarian or library, but without them there is no means of protection at all. If the policy is passed by a board, a corporate meeting, a principal or president , it carries that much more weight. It might come in handy, perhaps even in court!

Collection Development Policies in Medium-Sized Academic Libraries

Bonita Bryant

Edward Evans defines "collection development as the process of assessing the strengths and weaknesses in a collection, and then creating a plan to correct the weaknesses and maintain the strengths."[1] He goes on to describe the collection development policy as "the written statement of that plan...."[2] Many librarians have acknowledged a responsibility to provide documentation of this process in the libraries they serve, yet few have done so. When the flush days of the sixties' Great Society were followed by the information explosion, inflation, and an era of accountability for service-oriented institutions, the need for collection development policies became more urgent than it had been for decades. While selection of library materials has been of vital professional concern during most of the history of modern librarianship, it is only in the past decade that the preparation of selection or acquisitions policies (the terms have commonly been used interchangeably) and of collection development policies has received concentrated attention in library literature.

Even in the literature available there is little specific treatment of the needs of medium-sized academic libraries for assistance in responding to the problems of collection development documentation. These libraries are neither large nor small, neither committed deeply to research nor free of its demands. They have a unique set of problems in determining what their collecting obligations are, how to spend the funds made available to them, and how best to serve the communities which foster them.

In order to obtain a clear picture of what is happening in this discrete population of libraries, questionnaires were sent to 77 of them in January 1979 to collect information about their collection development policies. Responses were examined to identify any trends in statistical description of these libraries that might relate to their 1) having a completed collection development policy, 2) having one in progress, or 3) lacking a policy document and/or plans for preparing one. Librarians in each category of institution were interviewed to expand the descriptions of institutions at each stage. Policy documentation provided by the libraries surveyed is described in relation to models for policies and recommendations for elements to be included in such documents.

MEDIUM-SIZED ACADEMIC LIBRARIES SURVEYED

Identifying which academic libraries are, indeed, medium-sized was difficult. Library materials expenditures were used as the qualifying factor, for having enough funds to purchase more than the best books, yet not enough to buy comprehensively in any given area, is one of the crucial dilemmas facing the medium-sized academic library. Data from 1974-75 were the most recent published by the National Center for Education Statistics.[3] The researcher prepared a list of 77 libraries whose expenditures for library materials and binding ranged from $325,000 to $465,000 in 1974-75. These were libraries serving universities smaller than the members of the Association of Research Libraries and most major state institutions. The list included 16 institutions designated by NCES as U: universities stressing graduate instruction, conferring advanced and baccalaureate degrees in a variety of liberal arts fields, and having at least two professional schools that are not exclusively technological. The other 61 institutions are designated FG: other four-year institutions with graduate programs, but not classifiable as universities.

Because a comparison of the 1977-78 size of budget, collection, professional library staff, faculty, and students with that of three years before might give clues about the characteristics of institutions most likely to enter into a policy-preparation project, the first part of the survey instrument was constructed to update the NCES data. The remainder of the page asked the following questions:

. Do you have a written collection development policy which is in any way comparable to that recommended by the "Guidelines for the formulation of collection development policies?"[4]
. Do you have a written acquisitions policy in any other form?
. Would you be willing to supply a copy?
. If you don't have a completed policy, do you have one in progress?
. If you have no policy and none in progress, what are the major factors which prohibit this activity in your library?
. Who has overall responsibility for collection development/book selection in your library? (Name, title, and library telephone number, please.)

libraries are at privately-funded schools, the remaining 45 libraries (87 percent) are at state-supported institutions. One-half of the libraries which did not respond were in the lowest quartile of 1974-75 expenditure data; the other half was evenly distributed in the upper three quartiles. Of the respondents, 39 (75 percent) sent finished products or drafts of their policies or said they were working on documentation; 13 libraries (25 percent) did not have and were not preparing policy statements at that time. The high rate of returns can be construed as an indication of the depth of concern within medium-sized academic libraries about how their collections are growing, how their money is being spent, and how to plan for the future of information needs in their institutions. Many survey forms were accompanied by letters expressing interest in the results of this study and affirming the value of written policies as planning tools.

Examination of fiscal data returned revealed a dramatic expansion of the original compact range of library materials expenditure data. The 1977-78 spectrum ranged from $40,000 (described as a temporary crisis) and a second lowest of $139,000 (with no indication that improvement could be expected soon) to a phenomenal high of $1,195,000. Although 17 libraries experienced dollar losses over the three-year span of data, an overall increase of 25 percent was reported, with half of the libraries receiving that increase or more. Estimating inflation at 12 percent per year, a 41 percent increase in budget would have been necessary to maintain 1974-75 spending power, a feat accomplished by only 20 libraries (38 percent). The encroachment of periodicals subscriptions on the total budget illustrates the fiscal problems which are being faced by these libraries:

	Periodicals = less than 25% of total $	Periodicals = 25% to 50% of total $	Periodicals = more than 50% of total $
1974–75	38% of libraries	50% of libraries	12% of libraries
1977–78	15% of libraries	64% of libraries	21% of libraries

Within four weeks of mailing the survey instruments to the directors of the libraries selected, 52 replies were received (67.5 percent). Forty-one of the respondents (79 percent) serve FG institutions and 11 (21 percent) serve NCES-defined universities; seven (13 percent) of the

Statistical studies were conducted to determine whether any one of seven factors might determine the likelihood of a library's decision to prepare a collection development policy. The seven factors were 1) expenditure in either of the survey years, 2) proportions of dollar loss or gain, 3) 1974-75 size of book collection, 4) size of student body, 5) ratio of librarians to students, 6) size of library professional staff, or 7) changes in staff size. None of these factors was found to have a consistent impact on policy status. However, consideration of materials expenditure variations over the three-year period yields the generalization that libraries without policy efforts ("No" libraries, for purposes of this discussion) have been treated less well financially than libraries involved in documenting collection development procedures ("Yes" libraries). The aggregate gain in funds for "Yes" libraries was 27.5 percent, and the gain for the "No" libraries was only 11.1 percent. Average dollars for "Yes" libraries increased from $389,190 to $501,149 (28.8 percent), and the "No" libraries' average of $404,630 increased to $439,639, gaining only 8.7 percent in actual dollars. The "No" libraries' original average higher funding level (3.8 percent above "Yes" libraries) then averaged 12.2 percent less than "Yes" libraries. These facts are probably more a commentary on current educational priorities than on collection development policy status, but there is a possibility that administrations would be more inclined to allocate a larger portion of educational funds to libraries if they provide documented proof of their needs and intentions.

THE "NO" LIBRARIES

Thirteen libraries (25 percent of the 52 responding) had no policy preparation activity and no policy documents in early 1979. Eight of these libraries considered having a policy desirable, but gave reasons for the lack of activity in their institutions. Five of them did not see a need for policy documents. Two libraries, awaiting staff changes, expected the writing of collection development policies to become a higher priority after the staff changes occur.

Two other libraries reported campus politics as the factor preventing preparation of a collection development policy. One of these libraries reported: "We drew up a policy statement several years ago and presented it to the Faculty Library Committee. They objected strongly to certain statements and we put it aside." The other library does not have a policy because any such document "would go through a faculty committee whose members are zealously partisan." These situations are certainly cause for discouragement. Most of the sources which discuss how to go about producing policy statements insist that the process is complete only when a document is approved by the governing bodies of the library's host institution. Many of the libraries interviewed have

faculty library committees and as many or more allocate library materials funds to academic departments, yet none of them reported faculty blockage of professional activity.

Two of the 13 "No" libraries claimed that lack of time is the major factor preventing preparation of a policy. These libraries have 12 and 18 librarians respectively. Statistics from the survey show that libraries with 17 or more librarians are somewhat more likely to be sufficiently staffed to tackle such a project. The library with 18 librarians did cite "more urgent need in other areas; e.g., RECON, on-line cataloging, etc. Then I [sic] should be able to tackle this important task...."

Two additional libraries indicated that funding, as well as lack of staff time, kept the production of a policy from receiving the attention it should. They were visited to obtain a broader perspective than the statistics and brief annotations on the survey form could provide about the situations facing libraries in the "No" category.

The first of these libraries has the largest collection of any institution in the survey, and it includes some distinguished research holdings. Funding was cited as the reason for lack of current involvement in preparation of a collection development policy. As part of a private university, the library has suffered a 45 percent reduction in materials budget during the three years covered by survey data. It has also lost 31 percent of its professional staff. The book budget is controlled by academic departments and is "so starved that little choice is possible—bare-bone necessities of the most obvious kind," and although serials constitute 65 percent of the total budget, they are "frozen." The library has a Collection Development Committee, chaired by the Director, which makes decisions about purchases and allocations. These allocations are based on research conducted in the 1950s and are revised yearly with attention to interest expressed by departments and to endowments and grants, some of which the library does not control. The library has an automated acquisitions records system which is expected to go on-line in the near future; it provides much more data about purchases, and hence collection development, than many libraries have. The Reference Department has recently prepared its *Reference Collection Policy*, modeled on the San Diego State University Library document,[5] so the library has made some progress in the direction of documenting collection development policies.

The second visit was to a state-supported university library. Although the library has recently moved into a new building, its meager six percent increase in materials budget over the three-year period dropped the library from a comfortable twenty-sixth place among survey respondents to a rank of 43. This lack of funding and the Library's high student-to-librarian ratio of 690.9:1 in 1974-75 (the median ratio was 364.3:1) anticipate the response that "the major factors prohibiting us from having a collection development policy are insufficient personnel and a lack of money to finance such an undertaking." In spite of these conditions, the library's Goals and Objectives Committee has pointed out a need for a collection development policy in a memorandum. The Acquisitions Librarian indicated that the absence of a detailed published methodology for reaching this goal is also a factor inhibiting policy preparation. Another possibly limiting factor is that the library has not designated any one person as having responsibility for collection development. Nevertheless, a number of situations in this library could contribute to a policy-preparation project: an approval plan whose profile represents considerable effort at analysis of institutional needs, cooperation between teaching faculty and library subject area representatives, a very satisfactory ten-year-old punched-card acquisitions records system, and prospects for participating in a state-wide, on-line circulation system.

Of the 13 libraries in the "No" category, five indicated that they felt no need to have written collection development policies. A library whose budget decreased by 29 percent and its professional staff by 36 percent in the three years covered by the survey said: "Librarians involved in collection development have each been working in this area for over 20 years, and know what is evolving in curriculum reform on campus." In contrast, a library with a professional staff of 15 (no change in three years) and an increase in budget of 90 percent reported: "current practices in collection development/liaison activities have been sufficient to cover patron/curriculum needs; locally historic laissez faire approach to book budget." Another library with 15 librarians and a budget which increased only 28 percent in three years indicated "we have not felt the need....," while a library with a 40 percent increase in staff (to 21 full-time librarians) and an 89 percent jump in funds stated that it has "no time in which to write a policy and (possibly) it is not needed at the present time." Time and priority are mentioned as factors inhibiting preparation of a policy at another library whose staff situation is not revealed satisfactorily on the survey form, but whose budget has risen 49 percent. The Collection Development Librarian believes that the "experience [of producing a policy] is seldom worth the effort... A page statement of purpose will suffice." However, this librarian recommended using a questionnaire for

faculty and book selectors which solicits much the same information recommended for inclusion in a policy based on the "Guidelines." Compiled for every subject area and edited, the results of this type of survey could form the subject portion of a policy and contribute much to its general statements.

The denial of any need for policy documentation by nearly ten percent of all survey respondents is puzzling. Surely the prospect that older librarians will eventually die and be replaced by less experienced ones is justification enough for at least internal documentation. The need to communicate with users and administration, as well as other libraries, can hardly be expected to diminish with the pressures exerted upon libraries today.

At institutions where the librarian responding expressed regret that no effort was being made to prepare a policy document, priority is the most obvious major factor blocking the process. When a philosophy embracing documentation as a means of solving problems is lacking, little progress is likely to be made. On the other hand, administrative pressure and the assignment of a librarian other than the director to the task of studying and laying the groundwork for a policy project could force the issue on even the smallest staff.

POLICIES IN PROGRESS

Twenty-two libraries (42 percent) reported that they are at various stages in preparing collection development policies short of actually having draft documents available for examination. Interpretation of the phrase "in progress" varies widely. Four survey responses did not comment beyond those cryptic words.

One library reported that "at least efforts to produce an outline of what should be included" are being made by an ad hoc committee which is reviewing available statements. Two more libraries are studying SPEC Kits published by the Association of Research Libraries' Systems and Procedures Exchange Center and the "Guidelines." Several of the institutions have outdated policy statements which they are planning to replace and did not wish to share in response to the survey. One library is working on a selection policy to supersede an older acquisitions policy; when this chore is completed, the library "may begin a more detailed collection development policy per individual subjects," although "the size of our library and methods of selection may not require a detailed policy." This statement comes from a library with a materials budget of $506,900 and a staff of 19 librarians, while a library with a budget of $290,628 and a staff of nine professionals reported that "an intensive evaluation has been made of the collection and provides the foundation for the development of a comprehensive collection policy. It is the policy level work which now has to be done."

Another library considers its approval program profile as its interim document. Still another has established a program of liaisons with faculty in order to learn the strengths and weaknesses of the collection. Two more libraries have policies in nearly completed form; after final approval they will be available for other libraries to study.

Interviews were conducted with librarians from seven other libraries whose policy statements are in preparation. Discussion centered on the planning and writing process and on the data about the institution, the collection, and its use which could contribute to policy preparation.

The first of the seven libraries visited has a Collection Development Committee; a subject-divisional reference organization whose librarians do selection; and active monthly cataloging, circulation, and acquisitions reports (although not all are subject-oriented). It anticipates participation in a state-wide automated circulation system within the next year. The library has not produced documentation for its collection development policy nor established a plan for carrying out the project, but it has completed a Management Review and Analysis Project (MRAP) with a final report dated April 1979. The report emphasizes need for a management information system which could contribute much to collection development decisions and need for increased library participation in curriculum planning. The MRAP report specifically mandates the establishment of a policy for collection development which should include gift acquisitions and processing, faculty involvement, and funding for new and expanded programs.

The second library has a Collection Development Division, headed by the University Bibliographer, with three other part-time team members who perform other library functions as well. Although they have nothing on paper yet, the group plans to use the "Guidelines." The University Bibliographer will do the general/basic portion of the document and each subject bibliographer will do in-depth analyses of subject areas which represent selection assignments. The library allocates its funds in subject categories corresponding to academic departments; according to the Acquisitions Librarian (one of the bibliographers), allocations are "arrived at by a combination of 'ancient formula', FTEs, program

strength, and the respective bibliographer's judgement in addition to faculty input," although faculty does not control use of the funds. The Acquisitions Department maintains records of expenditures, annotating its ledgers with subject codes. Serials data, organized by academic department, are also available.

At the third library, two bibliographers have begun work on a collection development policy "to the extent... of collecting and examining acquisition policy statements from other libraries, and we have considered the makeup of our own institution and its users." However, day-to-day activities (including stints as reference librarians) have impeded any substantial progress. The library has performed some circulation studies in support of its reclassification/weeding project, and it has done a title-availability sample as part of a cooperative project with other libraries in the same region of the state.

A telephone interview with the Acquisitions Librarian at a fourth library revealed a policy in the "talking" stage, pending the arrival of a new library director. Construction of the Library's Baker and Taylor approval profile was based on a study of the college catalog; research needs of the faculty were being polled. Documents for the Reference Collection, Special Collections, and Archives were being written. Although the staff has no subject bibliographers, the Library's management council was considering the need for some redeployment of staff. The library has a collection of credit-hour data and statistics on faculty orders and is hoping to start some circulation use studies soon even though this library operation is not automated. Acknowledging the need for a policy document, the library intends to use the "Guidelines" in preparing one.

At the fifth library, the acting head of the Collection Development Division related that policy preparation was "stalled... because of personnel changes." Change in directorship contributed to this slow-down until mid-1979. The previous Head of Collection Development prepared a memo outlining a plan for faculty/library cooperation in preparing a collection development policy. This program would employ the "Guidelines" as its model. The previous director's annual report and appended five-year "Development Plan" support this effort. An additional goal was identified: development and utilization of a library management information system, which should provide data useful to rational development of the collection.

The Chief of Technical Services at the sixth library is performing a one-person collection development policy project. Interim documents have been prepared as abbreviated descriptions of selection and acquisitions policies which are "so far, more informal than formal, more based on experience and knowledge of the needs of the university than on structured formulae." One document lists priorities for building the collection; the other lists criteria to be applied to selections and limitations on what the library will purchase. More complete documentation will follow the "Guidelines" pattern; the final product will be submitted to the library administration, Faculty Library Committee, and department chairpeople. The policy will be enriched by data being accumulated by an automated circulation system, by participation in OCLC via AMIGOS, which provides multiple services for its members, and by a tradition of not allocating library funds for academic departments' exclusive use. Internal allocations began in 1959 with analysis of enrollment, courses offered, and other data; no formula is applied in updating these funds. The university is fortunate to receive some research support funds for library materials in specific subjects. There are no bibliographers on the staff; the Chief of Technical Services does all non-faculty selection except for items to be added to specific form collections in the library.

The seventh library's Coordinator of Collection Development indicated that selected subject areas have received treatment recommended by the "Guidelines," but no "Analysis of General Institutional Objectives" section has been prepared yet. The approval plan profile for Blackwell North America constitutes a general outline of collecting interests at this library; it was reprogrammed in 1979 and portions were assigned to specific subject librarians for monitoring. In addition to a one-time periodicals re-shelving survey, the Library's in-house automated circulation system, which dovetails with OCLC archival records, is designed to provide extensive use/user information which can be used to influence collection development decisions. This system identifies users by subject area (HEGIS codes for departments/majors) and by level (freshman-sophomore, junior-senior, graduate, continuing education student, and faculty). All data are printed out in subject groupings used by the National Shelflist Count project based on 490 sections of the Library of Congress classification schedules.

POLICY MODELS

Judging from the variety of approaches described by these "in progress" institutions, it would appear that the library profession lacks

common patterns on which to base activities aimed toward the production of collection development policy statements. Perhaps it is true that the two most important and unmentioned reasons that a library has no written statement of its collection development policies are "lack of knowledge about how to prepare one, and lack of confidence in one's abilities to do so."[6] However, in the past decade, four models for selection, materials selection, or collection development policies (depending upon the author's terminology) have been published. The one most often cited by libraries presently at the planning stage is "Guidelines for the Formulation of Collection Development Policies." Libraries which have already prepared documents have often incorporated elements from two of the others, Boyer and Eaton's "Introduction" to *Book Selection in American Libraries* [7] and "Development of a Materials Selection Program" in the ALA *Intellectual Freedom Manual*,[8] as well as elements espoused by the "Guidelines" which originated elsewhere. An added model source, published in 1979, is G. Edward Evans' chapter "Collection Development Policies" in *Developing Library Collections.*[9]

The four model sources consider similar elements to be essential to a policy, although they organize and emphasize them somewhat differently. If the libraries which prepared the documents sent in response to this survey have studied the models and their accompanying texts, they certainly have not used them to produce documents composed of universal elements, varied only by content unique to the library involved. The "Guidelines" emphasize that standardization of form and terminology in policies is vital to the future of collection development in American libraries. They see one of the purposes of a policy to be coordination of one Library's policy with those of appropriate other libraries so that selection and deselection can assist regional and network resources planning. That few medium-sized academic libraries consider this an important purpose of their policies is made obvious by the documents available, even though all but one of them indicate that collection sharing via interlibrary loan is vital to their ability to provide library materials to their patrons.

Most of the libraries surveyed appear to have had other motives for writing their policies. In addition to the profession's insistence that policy documents are essential (originally intended to defend libraries from publics wishing to censor their holdings), it is apparent that many medium-sized academic libraries' policies are designed almost exclusively to inform patrons of answers (usually negative) to recurrent questions posed by their requests for library additions. Few of these policies could be used to inform faculty of the Library's awareness of collection strengths and weaknesses and of librarians' competence to shoulder responsibility for collection building. In addition, they could not provide the administration with a rationale for obtaining additional funding or for supporting librarians' participation in curriculum decision-making.

ESSENTIAL ELEMENTS OF COLLECTION DEVELOPMENT POLICIES

All four models of collection development policies insist upon analysis of the institution and its clientele as well as analysis of the library's collection and its collecting policies for individual subjects. The ALA *Manual* and Evans give explicit instructions on carrying out community analyses. The "Guidelines" provide format, and "Guidelines for the Evaluation of the Effectiveness of Library Collections,"[10] suggests a variety of techniques for obtaining the information needed for the subject portions of a policy. Only a minority of published documents received treats any of these factors in suitable depth. It hardly seems possible that policy can be formulated and written without extensive research of this sort; yet absence of the "givens" in a published policy implies that the work was not done. Libraries have awarded such analyses a low priority because they required too much time and because the purpose for which policies were written did not permit that investment. Perhaps the ARL-sponsored Academic Libraries Program and Collection Analysis Projects will reduce some libraries' resistance to such activities in the future.

Many of the documents received have sections entitled "Obligations" which identify priorities of service to types of users (undergraduates, graduate and special students, faculty, and in one case, the general public). They are complemented by the sections entitled "Limitations" which contain inclusion/exclusion statements, some appropriate, others not. Many items listed under this heading should be included in subject statements, which are absent from most of the documents. Only two of the four models call for general statements on the priorities and limitations which govern selection.

Only two documents fail to describe the location of responsibility, legal and/or delegated, for selection of library materials. Several not only outline library collection development organization, but also describe in detail the participation of users (usually faculty) in the process. All four models recommended that this information appear in a policy, but the "Guidelines" call for annotation of individual subjects with "library unit or selector responsible," instead of a description of staff organization.

All except two of the libraries include statements on duplication in their policies, one even recommending that general content duplication should be avoided. Although the "Guidelines" allow space for a general description of duplication policy, they suggest that a library also have a separate policy document on duplication. The three other models include duplication as a justifiable element because this issue receives much attention from patrons and plays some part in allocation of funds.

Ten of the libraries include statements about gifts (three also mention exchanges) in their policies. The "Guidelines" ignore this issue, but the other models include it. Libraries do need extensive documentation about acceptance and handling of gifts; but because gifts should be accepted only if they reflect emphases in subject specifications for purchase of library materials, the technicalities of gift policy should be treated in separate documents which can be supplied to potential donors.

Four documents also refer to the processes of weeding and discarding library materials. One library sent a separate weeding policy which states that "the criteria for placing a book on the shelf serves [sic] as the basis for its removal" and continues with descriptions of criteria for removal of materials in more than 20 subject areas. Boyer and Eaton and Evans include these processes in their policy models. The "Guidelines" specifically exclude them but recommend that "a library's policy for deselection...should be coordinated with its collection development policy."[11] They refer libraries to "Guidelines for the Review of Library Collections"[12] for aid in making these decisions.

All but four documents disclaim responsibility for collecting materials in languages other than English at least until all needed titles in English have been procured. It is obvious that except for supporting foreign language and area studies programs and obtaining information not available at all in English, medium-sized academic libraries do not see themselves as collectors of materials which will not be understood and used by students or at least by more than a few faculty members. Boyer and Eaton suggest a general statement on language coverage; the "Guidelines" ask for language specifications for each subject and each form of library materials.

The last several decades have seen the introduction of many nonbook formats to library collections; some libraries collect or exclude items that other libraries treat in an opposite manner. Boyer and Eaton constructed a checklist of types of materials which might be found in a library; more forms could now be added. It would be helpful if libraries were to make such a checklist a part of their policy documents, cross-referencing those items which apply only to specific subjects to the appropriate subject portion of the document. The "Guidelines" identify forms of materials only when they are cataloged differently from those classified by subject. Enumeration of nonbook materials should be most helpful when policies are used for resource sharing among libraries of the future.

TRADITIONAL POLICIES

The policy statements submitted by seven libraries can be described as traditional in that they are similar to many of the policies collected by Boyer and Eaton[13] and by Futas.[14] These documents are not based on any specific model, nor do they contain extensive analysis of collections or of library environment. Although they do not provide a logical plan for the future, each has unique facets worth mentioning.

The situation in the first of these seven libraries may be representative of that in many libraries which have abstained from producing written policies. The survey was returned with a statement that it is "long established policy here that faculty selects books and instigate [sic] requests for purchase of library materials. Library staff makes every effort to be of assistance." Nevertheless, the library has prepared a two-page *Acquisitions Policy Statement* which is printed jointly with a procedural document, "Faculty book order requests for the Library." The policy contains a list of seven general guidelines which the library "hopes the faculty will voluntarily adhere to in submitting requests for library materials," the last of which indicates that the library will select materials "needed for the development of the library...as a whole."

The second library has a December 1977 *Collection Policy Statement* in draft form. One section of this policy describes allocation of funds for library materials; rejecting the subject format of many libraries' fund distribution, this library claims continuing flexibility for meeting program needs via allocations by type of materials. No further work has been done on the policy because of staff alterations and reassignment of the position of Coordinator of Collection Development. The draft does not reflect awareness of the "Guidelines," but the newly-assigned Coordinator has expressed interest in considering them before updating the policy for publication.

The Chief Bibliographer of the third library sent a two-page *Acquisitions Policy* of indeterminate age along with a note that "we hope to write a more detailed policy in the near future. Lack of staff has prevented [us] from doing more." This is a valiant statement for a library which suffered one of the grimmest losses of funds among the libraries surveyed and has a professional staff of only 11. The document ultimately to be superseded is of special interest because of the no-nonsense language describing priorities for library purchases: 1) curriculum support, 2) bibliographic aids which help to locate materials held by other libraries, 3) a bald statement that faculty research support is a low priority, although encouragement is given to use of local research libraries' resources, and 4) a commitment to the purchase of microforms whenever possible, especially for periodical backsets. This document states that worth, utility, and accessibility in another local library are the three criteria for evaluation of individual library requests. This document is refreshing in its honesty and lack of vague, flowery language.

A substantial document was received from the fourth library. Revised in May 1976, the *Collection Policy Statement,* prepared by the Library's Collection Policy Committee, indicates that it "is not meant to be a description of the present collection but a guide for future development." Although the document does not fulfill the promise of this statement with the prescribed community and subject analyses, it does contain an emphatic statement that "the Library must be informed in advance of new programs or changes in existing curricula so that materials may be acquired or re-evaluated." This is a critical situation for all academic libraries and one which needs much attention for adequate, professionally responsible collection development. This policy has strong sections on government publications, newspapers, serials, and microforms.

The *Material Selection Policy* sent by the fifth library is undated and does not identify its author(s), but attests to its official status by describing how amendments to it may be made and by mandating periodic review by the Director of the library and the Faculty Library Committee. Its one-page "Purpose" statement is a succinct explanation of why selection policies are needed as tools of communication with users; it is based on paragraphs in Boyer and Eaton's "Introduction." This document has a whole page on censorship, a rarity in the policies received; the others which mention intellectual freedom cite the "Library Bill of Rights" but make little other comment. Specific mention is made of this library's relation to other libraries; the policy indicates that locally there is "careful planning and periodic discussions...to avoid needless duplication of books and insure cooperation and mutual understanding."

The sixth library provided a three-page printed *Acquisitions Policy* which underwent its fifth revision in September 1975. Among the sections characteristic of many other policies are explicit statements on 1) cooperation with other libraries as a means of avoiding purchase of expensive and seldom-used materials, 2) textbooks, and 3) declaration of intent not to collect state historical materials or Americana as special collections nor intentionally to collect rare or "museum" items without demonstrated need. An unusual section describes policy for purchase of collections and blocks of materials, guidelines found in only one of the other documents. Review procedures call for faculty-at-large review of the policy each year, a wider source of approval than any other document describes.

The April 1976 *Acquisitions Policy* of the seventh library contains the second best description of institution and library in the documents received. It is unique in committing the library not only to provide materials for academic programs, but also to "achieve the highest grade possible according to the *Standards for College Libraries.*" This is the only reference made in any of the policies to a norm established by the profession for libraries of its kind. This library may wish to replace this reference, in a later edition of its policy, with one citing "*Standards for University Libraries,*" as approved in January 1979 by the ACRL Board.[15] The document describes the role that cost of materials plays in decisions about additions to the collection. A half-page section provides "Procedures for the purchase of items costing more than $500.00." Among random statements of types of materials to be included or excluded is a paragraph recommending evaluation of the collection by comparing it with standard bibliographies in order to identify additional materials for purchase.

SUBJECT-ORIENTATION IN POLICIES

The policies of seven libraries acknowledge either the need to classify additions to their collections by levels of anticipated use or to combine this approach with identification of specific subjects collected. These two techniques are specific-

ally recommended by all four model sources. The "Guidelines" emphasize that the same level definitions and terminology should be used by all libraries to promote comparability of collections and of collecting policies. This is the only source which specifies that subject lists should coincide with the classification system employed to organize the library's collection of both books and periodicals.

The first university library's Head of Acquisitions indicated that the library's "Resources Development Philosophy" was written by a committee chaired by the Assistant Director for Technical Services. This document is included in *Requesting Material . . . for a Library: a guide for library representatives*, published in November 1978. Some elements in the other sections of the Guide would be appropriate to a collection development policy. The philosophy document is divided into "Mission," "Selection responsibilities," "Priorities," "Limitations," and "Levels of collection intensity." During an interview, the Head of Acquisitions indicated that there are no immediate plans to work on subject or form statements on collection development. Although there has been some turn-over in librarians, which may have impeded or diverted priorities, it is unclear why subject policies are not projected. The levels of collection intensity are those recommended by the "Guidelines," but their application for this library is not explained.

The Faculty Library Advisory Committee at a second university approved the library's *Acquisition Policy* in February 1978. The document repeats the familiar pattern of introduction, objectives, and limitations (again, a miscellany). It continues with a statement about extent of coverage, which includes three categories comparable to the "Guidelines" recommended levels of collection intensity, but excludes "minimal" and "comprehensive." These categories are not related to specific subject areas, but appear to be intended to serve as reasons for or against purchases. In addition to statements about types of materials and selection responsibilities, the document provides a description of fund allocation, request procedures, and a review procedure which provides for policy changes to be made in the library after consultation with the committee which approved the original document.

The third library has prepared all but the subject analysis portion of its *Collection Development Policy* and plans to use the levels of collection intensity recommended by the "Guidelines." The library's Collection Development Group "provides a forum and coordinating function for the subject bibliographers...and Acquisitions librarians." Chaired by an acquisitions librarian, the group is preparing a project which will involve "extensive collection analysis and cooperation on the part of the university faculty." The completed portion of the document follows the established pattern of "premises for collection development," obligations, limitations, and responsibility for selection. It provides for annual review before launching into general statements on gifts and exchanges, duplication, weeding, and a litany of "types of materials."

The *Library Materials Selection Policy* of the fourth library was published in November 1977 by the Library Collection Development Committee. It contains much the same pattern and content as the last three documents described. Although the brief introduction does not describe the community served, as recommended by the models, it is one of two documents received which heeds the "Guidelines" suggestion that the Library of Congress classification schedule be the framework for assignments of levels of collection intensity after consideration of university degree and research programs, both current and projected. The levels used do not conform to any of those in the model sources, but each class is also annotated with the library unit responsible for selection of that subject. Separate policy statements for Special Collections and Government Documents are extensive and explicit.

The fifth library sent a 1976 working draft of its *Acquisitions Policy*, one which has "Neither been finally revised nor officially adopted." Its "General statement of acquisitions objectives" is the closest of any document received to approximating the models' recommendations for institutional and user analysis. Although the Director disclaims that the policy is based on the "Guidelines," it also includes a Library of Congress classification arrangement of subject coverage and levels of intensity coding. Again, the levels used do not correspond with any of the recommended definitions or terminology. Statements about separate collections (documents, serials, reference, and special) follow, each organized in the pattern of the parent document: "Objectives" "Implementation" "Criteria" and "Collection review."

Collection development documentation at the sixth library is a one-person project. A proposed *Collection Development Policy Statement* has been prepared as has a draft of the subject "thesaurus" with assigned collecting intensity levels. This can be characterized as a working document; publication is not anticipated. The two-page introduction describes priorities and limitations as well as the way the levels (four, which again are not exact reflections of any of the models) are to be interpreted. Part II is the subject listing, based on one prepared at the University of Illinois. Part III is titled "Format and non-subject statements" and describes not only form collections, but the usual hodgepodge of specifics treated in other policies. This section contains some unique specifications, many of which might be more appropriately placed in sections on subject literatures more extensive than those simply coded by level.

The *Library Collection Development Program* of a seventh library is an attractive 1977 publication by a seven-person committee, which spent two years preparing it. This is the Library's first written policy on acquisitions. Its "Introduction" identifies the goals of the library and the general responsibilities of bibliographers, faculty, and the Director in the area of collection development. The second section, "Bibliographers," details the roles of 18 librarians (out of a total of 21) who hold both functional positions in the library and parallel positions as subject bibliographers. Their tasks are evaluation and selection, collection maintenance, budget management, and communications as faculty liaisons. Thirty subject areas, general and specific, were identified in consultation with faculty. Each subject page begins with a sentence or two describing academic programs or other subject needs. Cross references to "related subjects" are made. The subjects were originally coded for levels of collection intensity with a homemade set of designations; prior to publication, these were revised to coincide with those levels recommended in the "Guidelines." A revision will divide the "study" level into two categories as the latest edition of the "Guidelines" proposes. The collection is classified by Dewey, and there is no intention of reclassifying the holdings. One could hope that the subject list will be cross-indexed with the classification scheme in its next edition. Identification of the librarian responsible for each subject is not made, either by title or by name. A final section of the document delineates, briefly, gift policies and policies relating to special collections.

The Acquisitions Librarian, who served as chairperson of the committee which wrote this *Program*, expects that eventually the bibliographers will do a coordinated collection evaluation project; work in 1980 will focus on the library's central serials record. Periodicals are selected by subject bibliographers and are not budgeted separately. The library puts no restrictions on the balance of monographs versus periodicals, allowing for proportions pertinent to the individual subject area. Monthly reports from the Acquisitions Department accounting system assist the bibliographers in their budget management responsibilities. Administrative support is evidenced by the approval of the policy document by the Vice President for Academic Affairs and by the backing of the Vice President for Programming for bibliographers' participation in the meetings of the academic departments to which they are assigned as liaisons.

VARIATIONS ON THE POLICY THEME

In contrast to all of the two- to twenty-page documents described so far, one university library has subject librarians who have compiled a two-inch thick *Library Materials Selection Policy Manual*. The two-page excerpt provided with the survey instrument indicates use of general statements comparable to other policies examined and of "degrees" of intensity to be applied to the individual subject areas. The segment on "collection building responsibility" shows that although ultimate responsibility rests with the Director, he has delegated it to the several subject librarians, who have written sections listing major subjects and the assigned codes for collection intensity. The manual is "kept up-to-date, more or less, depending upon the interest of the individual subject librarian," reported the library's Director.

Separate subject libraries are the source of 11 one-page statements sent by another library. Apparently updated as the librarian-in-charge sees need, each statement is brief and follows the "Guidelines" recommendation for format of subject statements, although no level of intensity coding is used. Elements treated in these documents include general purpose, languages, geographical area, chronological period, kinds of material collected and/or excluded; some documents add descriptions of special projects or factors influencing materials collected. The library does not have a general collection development policy of any sort.

A third library states that "we are much more thorough here" than the "Guidelines" and other models suggest. This library sent samples of documents used by its Book Funds Committee; one of these, "Suggested criteria to be used in evaluating school/department needs," prescribes ten factual statements to be made by the committee for each unit on an annual basis. A sample report for a department contains a general report on activity in that department followed by comments on each of the ten criteria. "Every unit is carefully examined for its book needs each year and allocations vary from year to year, sometimes substantially. We avoid rigid formulas and static guidelines," reported the Director. Apparently the library operates on a July to June fiscal year; in February, estimated allocations (probably reflecting current-year allocations) are made by the committee, and in August additional funds are allocated to bring the total to that for the new fiscal year. Allocations for specific departments constitute one-third of available funds; serials, standing orders, replacements and funds for the general collection, the Reference and Documents Collections, and SOLINET costs absorb the remaining funds.

CONCLUSIONS

Policy efforts of most medium-sized academic libraries are not close to the ideal presented by the models. Many of the documents sent in response to the survey contain evidence of wording and content organization based on sample policies such as those found in the Boyer and Eaton and the Futas books. They violate the ALA *Manual* warning against such replication because "it is impossible to borrow a statement based on another institution's goals and needs."[16] All the documents examined lack some of the elements and the structures recommended by the models in the professional literature, but the lack of focus on goals, needs, and subject specifications is likely to yield documents which do not "work." When this happens, librarians who contend that policy production is not worth the time it costs are vindicated.

The analysis of institutions and users and the collections and programs they support has resulted, at best, in brief generalizations. It became clear in interviews with librarians that this weakness both in documents and in plans for preparing them is caused by failure of libraries and their host institutions to have well-tailored management information systems. Synthesis and subsequent use of data is difficult enough when the data are available, but when they must be tracked down from an array of sources and are then found to be insufficient to the needs for which they are sought, librarians may indeed find the cost of knowing enough to write a useful policy greater than the resources (time and expertise) that they have to invest.

In addition to information about local conditions, facts about publishing output and subject literatures are vital to planning collections of the future. Approval plan jobbers are making available much helpful information about the number of titles and their cost published annually in discrete subject categories. Librarians and subject authorities must make a great effort to collaborate to produce descriptions of the natures of subject literatures. They need to answer such questions as 1) what are the proportions of monographic to serial publications in a given subject; 2) what other forms of library materials are appropriate to a collection in a specific subject area; and 3) what kinds of publications are appropriate to the various levels of collection intensity mandated by institutional programs and other user needs.

Even when all this information is available, there is at least a vestige of prejudice in the profession against quantifying what is known about institutions and people, library collections, and subject literatures. Very good collections may have been shaped by librarians with uncanny instinct for matching available library materials with local needs. But the future can be best approached if facts are allowed to assist in defining needs and meeting them. Philosophy of collection building, then, must be scrutinized and sometimes adjusted.

Although medium-sized academic libraries have not reached the ideal for collection development policy documentation, they have done well in comparison with the larger libraries represented by Association of Research Libraries membership. A 1977 survey[17] of 69 ARL libraries found that 20 (29 percent) have written documents. The 52 medium-sized libraries surveyed have ten programs (20 percent) which approximate the subject depth required for a useful planning guide, and an additional seven documents (13.5 percent) which will serve as starting points for more detailed policies. ARL found eight libraries (12 percent) in the process of preparing policies; this status is shared by 22 medium-sized counterparts (41.5 percent). In this context, the medium-sized academic libraries surveyed can claim their fair share of future-conscious professionals and can take pride in their accomplishments and their plans for further pursuit of collection development documentation.

Notes

1. G. Edward Evans, *Developing Library Collections* (Littleton, Colo.: Libraries Unlimited, 1979), p. 122.
2. *Ibid.*
3. National Center for Education Statistics, *Library Statistics of Colleges and Universities, Fall 1975 Institutional Data* (Washington, D.C.: Govt. Print. Off., 1977).
4. "Guidelines for the Formulation of Collection Development Policies," in American Library Association. Collection Development Committee, *Guidelines for Collection Development* (Chicago. American Library Assn., 1979), pp. 1-8 (hereafter cited as "Guidelines").
5. Kathleen Coleman and Pauline Dickinson, "Drafting a Reference Collection Policy," *College and Research Libraries* 38:227-33 (May 1977).
6. "Development of a Materials Selection Program," in American Library Association. Office for Intellectual Freedom, *Intellectual Freedom Manual* (Chicago: American Library Assn., 1974), Part 4, p. 5.
7. Calvin J. Boyer and Nancy L. Eaton, eds., "Introduction," in their *Book Selection Policies in American Libraries: an Anthology of Policies from College, Public and School Libraries* (Austin, Tex.: Armadillo Pr., 1971), pp. iii-vii.
8. "Development of a Materials Selection Program," in American Library Association, *Intellectual Freedom Manual*, Part 4, pp. 5-10 (hereafter cited as ALA *Manual*).
9. Evans, *Developing Library Collections*, pp. 122-136.
10. "Guidelines for the Evaluation of the Effectiveness of Library Collections," in American Library Association. Collection Development Committee, *Guidelines for Collection Development* (Chicago: American Library Assn., 1979), pp. 9-19.
11. "Guidelines," p. 2.
12. "Guidelines for the Review of Library Collections," in American Library Association. Collection Development Committee, *Guidelines for Collection Development* (Chicago: American Library Assn., 1979), pp. 20-30.
13. Boyer and Eaton, eds., *Book Selection Policies.*
14. Elizabeth Futas, ed., *Library Acquisition Policies and Procedures* (Phoenix, Ariz.: Oryx, 1977).
15. "Standards for University Libraries," *College and Research Libraries News*, no. 4: 101-10 (April 1979).
16. ALA *Manual*, Part 4, p. 10.
17. Association of Research Libraries. Systems and Procedures Exchange Center, SPEC FLYER 38: *Collection Development Policies* (Washington, D.C.: Association of Research Libraries, Nov. 1977), p. [1].

Preservation and Collection Management: Some Common Concerns

by Margaret M. Byrnes

Awareness of the integral and necessary relationship between collection management and development and preservation programs has been increasing in recent years. At long last, collection managers and preservation specialists have begun to work together more closely and to identify areas of common concern.

Changes in the organization of library operations are being made, because the connection between collection management and development and preservation programs is more widely understood. In the past, many institutions limited collection development to fund allocation and the selection of new materials. If selectors had any involvement in preservation activities, it was usually only decisions to replace deteriorated materials. Often preservation was regarded as a separate function, mainly book repair and binding. Today it is part of the Collection Management and Development Office and its functions have been integrated with other collection management activities. As selectors' roles have gradually been broadened to include collection evaluation, storage, weeding, and treatment decisions, frequent interaction with preservation staff is necessary. Furthermore, there is new emphasis on maintaining fragile retrospective collections because the high cost of not doing so is now recognized. Temperature and humidity controls, and careful attention to commercial binding methods and materials are essential ingredients of collection management programs.

The relationship between preservation and collection development is obvious in libraries that fund at least some preservation activities from the materials budget; selectors are responsible for administering funds intended for both acquisitions of new materials and replacement of deteriorated titles. Issues related to budget are probably the most important area of common concern. Budgets are seldom large enough to buy everything needed for a collection. Consequently, a healthy tension tends to develop between the need to acquire new materials and the need to maintain what has already been acquired.

Replacement decisionmaking is arguably a form of second selection. Just as no library can afford to buy everything published, no library can hope to replace all of its brittle books. Many of the criteria used in replacement decisionmaking are similar to those used in selection of new materials (e.g., significance of author or edition, relationship of the subject to collection strengths and current research activity, probable demand, availability elsewhere, and cost). Areas of mutual interest include the role of faculty in decisionmaking, user preferences in choice of format, the need to balance both current demand and future needs, local priorities and regional or national collecting obligations, and the impact of new publishing technologies.

The recent literature in both fields reflects a widespread desire to develop viable resource sharing programs. Costs of an increasing volume of important research materials published each year continue to exceed any one institution's ability to acquire all of them. Research libraries must rely more on cooperative acquisitions agreements for less frequently used materials. Within the Research Libraries Group, the assignment of subjects of primary collecting responsibility (PCRs) and

Preservation must be dramatically increased if we are not to lose a substantial portion of the late nineteenth and early twentieth century imprints held by American research libraries

current discussion concerning the desirability of assigning subjects of primary preservation responsibility (PPRs) reflect this trend. For collection managers and preservation specialists alike, such agreements raise difficult issues of access and ownership. They also highlight the close interrelationship between the two fields.

BUDGET IMPACT

In moments of despair over the potential costs, several library directors have been heard to refer to preservation as a "black hole." This is quite understandable when one considers the statistics. In at least one of the country's older research libraries, 37 percent of the collection is dangerously brittle and the total proportion of acidic bookpaper is as high as 83 percent. The Library of Congress estimates that approximately 77,000 volumes in that collection become brittle each year. Another study shows the median cost of preservation microfilming (including all stages from identifying an item to providing a bibliographic record for and storing the completed film) is approximately $50 per volume. Guidelines issued by the Association of Research Libraries call for a minimum of 10 percent of ARL members' materials budgets or four percent of their current operating funds to be devoted to preservation programs. It is clear that many libraries are unable to begin to meet that minimum standard. It is also clear that preservation activity throughout the country must be dramatically increased if we are not to lose a substantial portion of the late nineteenth and early twentieth century imprints held by American research libraries.

Considering the size of the problem and the cost of attempting to solve it, it is hardly surprising that preservation programs are straining most library budgets. It is hard to budget for replacement of deteriorated materials when under pressure to buy more current monographs and pay the increasing costs of serials subscriptions. Selectors are often reluctant to use their limited funds for replacement of older materials that may or may not be needed for future research.

The practice of combining funds for preservation with those for acquisition of new materials has some merit; it makes the selector more directly responsible for the retrospective collection. The need to provide funds for preservation replacements will vary according to the age and condition of different parts of the collection, the amount of use they have received, and research patterns typical of each discipline. In addition, the availability of commercial replacements (whether re-

prints or microforms) varies considerably among subjects. Another critical factor is the amount of time each selector can devote to preservation decisionmaking. Establishing a single replacement fund to be used as needs are identified and opportunities arise can reduce the natural tension between the need to purchase new materials and the need to replace the old; it can also result in a more efficient use of funds and personnel and a net increase in the number of preservation replacements acquired each year.

Many of the libraries which have established new preservation programs in recent years have done so primarily with funds obtained by means of internal reallocation and grants from outside sources. Some of the largest preservation programs in the country have been developed without any permanent budget increases from parent institutions. While they provide a model of resourcefulness and creative budgeting, many have reached their limits in terms of finding new ways to allocate existing monies.

Relying upon grants as a source of program support is inadvisable as it exacerbates the difficulty of maintaining existing operations and planning for needed expansion of preservation activities. Projects funded by grants often do not reflect an institution's top preservation priorities and continuing existing projects or initiating new ones is almost always uncertain. In addition, grant funding is difficult to obtain for costly but essential preventive preservation measures such as security systems and air conditioning and humidity control for stack areas. Use of the materials budget for these measures, or for protective enclosures and nondamaging processing and storage supplies is rarely approved, despite the fact that replacement and repair programs are ineffective unless basic preventive measures are in place.

Results of current research in mass deacidification, paper strengthening, and optical disk technology will affect long term preservation budget planning. If these techniques look feasible and desirable, sources for large amounts of additional funding will have to be found.

University administrators and state legislators must become more aware of preservation needs and costs if libraries are to fund preservation programs adequately. In most cases, this will require a major shift in priorities on the part of budget officers in research libraries' parent institutions and members of state and federal appropriations committees. It is essential that library directors and preservation experts work together to communicate their current and projected preservation needs and to obtain adequate resources to address those needs.

Results of current research in mass deacidification, paper strengthening, and optical disk technology will affect long term preservation budget planning

NATIONAL PRESERVATION PLANNING

The Council on Library Resources' has established a Commission on Preservation and Access to inform legislators and the general public of the magnitude of the preservation problem. There are an estimated 75 million brittle books in American research libraries. To preserve only three million volumes will cost approximately $200 million over the next 10 to 15 years. Figures such as these make it clear that the only hope of accomplishing even a portion of the needed work will be through cooperative preservation activities. Fortunately, a number of recent microfilming projects such as those of the Research Libraries Group, the American Theological Library Association and the American Philological Association have demonstrated that well planned cooperative efforts can be successful. There is, however, a critical need to secure major new funding if efforts are to reach an adequate level.

Selection of materials for inclusion in the national brittle book program is now a topic of fairly intense discussion. Earlier cooperative microfilming projects included item by item review by selectors or faculty members to ensure that only the most important materials would be filmed. Because it is hoped that the national brittle book program will increase the current level of preservation activities by tenfold the wisdom of attempting to decide what will or will not be of research interest in future years is being questioned. Strong arguments are being made for the comprehensive preservation of major subject collections at institutions which have been collecting in a specific discipline at the research level for many years. If funding permits, a second sweep would be conducted by another research library with an equally strong ranking in that subject to ensure that important titles were not missed. Assuming that such an approach is affordable, a number of important issues remain to be addressed:

Choice of Collections

Is the wholesale preservation of distinguished collections appropriate for all disciplines? Such an approach may be justifiable in the humanities, but not in the sciences and technology. While title by title review by selectors or other subject specialists is admittedly expensive, it is still necessary for some disciplines to avoid wasting limited funds on materials of little historical value.

Local vs. National Priorities

In most local preservation programs, materials are identified for treatment or replacement as they are returned from circulation. This method meets immediate needs and avoids the political problems inherent in policy decisions to preserve materials in some disciplines rather than others. Nevertheless, the most important or most endangered parts of the collection may not get needed attention and future research may be compromised.

As the national brittle book program evolves, libraries and their primary users will have to balance local and national priorities. If the program is to succeed, libraries with significant subject collections will be obligated to preserve those materials for the rest of the library community. Since full funding is unlikely to be available for national program participants, library staff will need to work hard to convince local users and budget administrators of the long-term local benefit of this approach.

Format Preferences

How should institutions planning to participate in the national brittle book program respond to user preference for paper copy? While making photocopies may be desirable from the user's point of view, many preservation experts do not consider it appropriate for a national cooperative program. They argue that most libraries can afford to produce only one photocopy before discarding the original, thereby risking total loss of information if the photocopy is lost, mutilated, or damaged by water or fire. Photocopying does not lend itself to producing additional copies as needed by other libraries to replace their brittle volumes since a photocopy of a photocopy generally is not very legible. By contrast, future availability of the information and ease of duplication are ensured in properly conducted preservation microfilming programs since they include the production of master negatives (which, when processed correctly and stored under archival conditions, are expected to last many hundreds of years). These master negatives can then be used to produce reading copies requested by other libraries. Photocopying might be an acceptable preservation measure if multiple copies were made and stored in separate locations. A preferable solution is to film the materials first and then photocopy the originals or produce paper copies from the film. Such an expensive process should be limited to frequently used items or those with illustrations that will not reproduce adequately on microfilm.

Microfilm, it must be admitted, is not the format

of choice for most users. However, until further research has been completed for newer technologies that are potentially less cumbersome (e.g., optical digital disk systems) and they are shown to be both feasible and affordable for collection preservation purposes, microfilm will remain the best solution. Barring the unexpectedly rapid development of alternative technologies, many major subject collections will be converted to film during the next decade. Libraries should be hard at work educating their users about preservation so they may begin to understand that microfilm provides access to information that otherwise would no longer be available.

Access to Preserved Materials

Most libraries will not be able to purchase microfilm copies of all collections filmed under the national brittle book program. More than ever before, their users will have to rely on access to materials owned by other institutions. How should libraries begin to prepare their users for this eventuality? Much remains to be done to inform users about the need for a national brittle book program and to develop a broad perspective on issues of access and ownership. A recent study of selection practices shows that providing remote access to lower use materials may not be as controversial as was once feared, if delivery of those materials is reasonably fast. While efforts are being made to improve the efficiency of interlibrary loan services, other possibilities such as increased use of telefacsimile should be explored. If the national brittle book program is to succeed, prompt access to materials must be a critical component in planning for cooperative preservation activities.

Collection Ratings

Implicit in the national brittle book program is the premise that materials will be preserved only once. If a major subject collection has been preserved by one library, others can discard their original copies when they become too deteriorated for use. What are the implications for current standards of collection evaluation? Reliance on collection size as a major indicator of institutional ranking may become invalid. What will be important is the degree to which libraries are able to provide immediate access to high-demand materials and prompt retrieval from other institutions of less frequently used items.

Faculty and Selector Involvement

The role that faculty members, selectors, and scholarly associations should play in national brittle book program decision making remains to be defined. Assistance in identifying those distinctive collections which should be preserved for the nation will clearly be needed. Also useful will be advice concerning which disciplines do not warrant wholesale preservation. Inviting groups of scholars and bibliographers to develop general guidelines and priorities for selecting materials to be preserved is probably the most practical way to take advantage of needed expertise without unduly imposing on busy work schedules. The conclusion being reached by many who have had experience with other preservation projects is that the large scale of the national brittle book program will probably preclude title by title review.

Collection Assessment

Several studies in recent years have shown that the amount of duplication of titles held by research libraries is not as high as previously thought. There is, therefore, a significant risk that a number of important materials will not be preserved because they were not held in the designated preservation collection of record. The study findings lend credence to the argument that second sweep projects will be essential; they also serve to emphasize the importance of documenting collection strengths and weaknesses through collection assessment and overlap studies. Subject bibliographers and collection managers will be greatly needed to conduct such studies and to contribute their knowledge of the collections to national brittle book program planning so that all important materials eventually are preserved.

Copyright

Nagging questions surrounding copyright restrictions remain unresolved. It seems clear that libraries are free to create reproductions of their own holdings for the purpose of replacing deteriorated materials that are no longer available from publishers. Supplying copies of those reproductions to other institutions for the same purpose is, however, very much in question if they might still be protected by copyright. The need to acquire copyright clearance or permission from the publisher before purchasing microfilm copies of thousands of deteriorated titles published within the past 75 years would be a heavy burden for most libraries. Another problem is distinguishing between preservation replacement copies and those sold for the purposes of collection development. This is a particular problem for serials since libraries request copies of substantial runs on microfilm for the dual purpose of replacing deteriorated holdings and filling in missing volumes. Before the national brittle book program can become truly operational, such questions must be addressed.

Bibliographic Access

Access to records of titles preserved as a result of local preservation programs or as part of the national brittle book program must be easily available. Fortunately, notable progress in this area has already been made: OCLC and RLIN have begun to regularly exchange and load tapes of microfilm records contributed by their members; use of the 583 field in the USMARC format was recently approved for recording detailed preservation information; and titles to be included in preservation projects can now be identified with the help of a shadow file in RLIN which contains records from retrospective conversion projects. Use of this file to identify older materials in need of preservation seems a very sensible approach. In future years there will be little point to having bibliographic access to these materials if they are too deteriorated for use. Efforts should continue to encourage:

- the development of a queuing feature in OCLC (i.e., the ability to indicate the intention to film a specific title)
- the exchange of queued records among the major utilities
- more creative uses of automated records to identify collections of importance
- ways to equably allocate preservation responsibilities among the country's research libraries.

It is imperative that information on what has been filmed and what is being filmed is easily and promptly available if costly duplication of effort is to be avoided.

Sources of Funding

The National Endowment for the Humanities, the Council on Library Resources, the Association of Research Libraries, and the Andrew Mellon Foundation, among others, have contributed generously to preservation efforts over the years. The state legislatures of New York and California have provided good examples to the rest of the country by providing substantial support for library preservation programs. In early 1987 a congressional hearing on brittle books raised hopes for increased federal support. It was held by Representative Pat Williams, chairman of the House Committee on Education and Labor's Subcommittee on Postsecondary Education. Much more lobbying on the federal level remains to be done, however.

Financial commitment from many more institutions and foundations will be required for a successful national program. Libraries without preservation programs or significant brittle book problems must recognize their obligation to share the financial burden. Preserving the country's research materials will ultimately benefit all future users. While only a small number of research libraries may actually preserve materials as part of the national program, many libraries must support the effort.

International Preservation Efforts

Coordination with preservation programs in foreign countries is essential, since American libraries alone cannot afford to preserve all endangered published materials. A program of cooperative planning is needed as well as a system for communicating what is being preserved.

Recently, there have been a number of promising developments. A core program in conservation has been established by the International Federation of Library Associations, headquartered at the Library of Congress. In addition, a few foreign libraries have begun to search the OCLC and RLIN databases for cataloging data and now have access to hundreds of thousands of records of microforms produced in the U.S. The decision by the British Library to load records into RLIN from its Eighteenth Century Short Title Catalog project opens the door to future sharing of bibliographic information produced by that major institution. Plans are under way for national registers of microform masters in the UK, France, and Italy and a feasibility study has been done for a European register. Nonetheless, many difficulties must be overcome in coordinating preservation efforts on the international level, if we are to minimize costly duplication of effort and the risk of losing hundreds of thousands of important research materials.

NEW FORMATS

Magnetic Tape and Disk

In the future, collection managers will find themselves faced with more selection decisions for materials produced in new formats such as CD-ROM, subscriptions to serials published in online form, and information available to researchers only on computer tapes. Preservation specialists must be increasingly concerned with these formats and the longevity of the information they

To preserve only three million of the estimated 75 million brittle books in U.S. research libraries will cost approximately $200 million over the next 10 to 15 years

What is important for the future is the cost involved in the periodic reading and regeneration of digital disks

contain. Research data available only in electronic form will be one of the future's major preservation challenges, particularly for information in science and technology.

The preservation of data stored on magnetic media is an infant field. At present, most information on tape or disk is not intended for permanent retention. For electronic information of more lasting value, some guidelines are available on optimum storage conditions and the frequency with which tapes and diskettes should be copied. However, detailed information on electronic media longevity is sparse, possibly because of the proprietary nature of the results of laboratory studies conducted by the private sector. Longevity can of course be increased by transferring data to computer output microform (COM) which, if produced and stored according to archival standards, should have the same lifespan as any other preservation microfilm. Work is being done on the use of scanners to convert COM data back into a form that can be manipulated on whatever new hardware is available at the time the information is needed. While COM may be one solution to the long term storage of computer data, the advantages and disadvantages of microforms still apply.

Optical Digital Disk Technology

During the past two years, there has been a noticeable increase in the number of titles available in CD-ROM or other optical digital disk formats. Some libraries are beginning to purchase them as a matter of course. To date, however, little thought has been given to the longevity of the data being acquired. As long as information issued in this format is rapidly superseded or of only temporary reference value, image permanence is not of particular concern. However, it is likely that many more titles will appear in CD-ROM or some similar form during the next decade. The question of longevity must soon be addressed by those who acquire such materials for their collections and those responsible for preserving them.

While some longevity studies have been conducted by the Library of Congress, the National Bureau of Standards, and optical disk producers, little information is available in the literature. Estimates of the lifespan of digital data stored on optical disk range from ten to thirty years, depending upon the manufacturer. Fortunately, this is not as critical an issue as it is for other media such as microforms or analog videodiscs, since digital signals can be restored to their original form after the disk deteriorates. What is important for the future, however, is the cost involved in the periodic reading and regeneration of digital disks. Whether

libraries will have the resources for this type of preservation activity remains a major question.

Using optical digital disk technology to preserve information in brittle books and other deteriorated library materials is a strong future possibility. Features which could make it a very attractive alternative to microforms include: extremely condensed data storage; the capacity for image enhancement and more accurate display of graphic material; resistance to wear and tear; and greatly increased ease of access since the images can be linked electronically to citations in bibliographic databases. In addition, because computer networks can be used to provide rapid access to information stored at other locations, optical disk technology may offer solutions to several of the problems associated with cooperative preservation and resource sharing programs.

The feasibility of using optical disk as a preservation medium is being examined in pilot projects at the Library of Congress and the National Archives and Records Administration, and in research under way at the National Library of Medicine. NLM's research and development activities should yield much useful information about document conversion rates, image quality, optimum workflow configurations, quality control strategies, and costs. If it demonstrates that conversion can be accomplished in an efficient and affordable manner and if disk formats and equipment are standardized within the next several years, optical digital disk technology may begin to play a major role in library preservation programs.

Assuming that costs will not be insignificant and that libraries will not have the resources to convert all deteriorated materials, several important questions will need to be addressed in the near future:

- Is the cost of using advanced technology warranted for older materials that receive relatively little use?
- If some materials continue to be microfilmed, what criteria will be used to decide which titles or subjects will be converted to disk and which will be filmed?
- Is conversion of deteriorated materials to disk a process best left to the commercial sector or should libraries attempt inhouse optical disk programs similar to current microfilming operations? How will such programs be staffed? Should regional conversion centers be considered?
- Since information on disk can be accessed from remote locations, should one or only a few libraries become national centers for information preserved in this format? If the materials stored on optical disk are not likely to be used frequently, is there still a legitimate need for multiple copies to be held by a number of libraries? How will the cost of acquiring and staffing local optical disk collections compare with that of providing remote access? Which approach will ensure the best quality of public service?

- What are the copyright implications when libraries producing the original disks send copies to other institutions?
- Since information stored on disk at remote locations can be accessed from home or office, what will be the impact on local library operations? To what extent should users be required to absorb the online cost?
- Who should be responsible for regenerating information on disks purchased from the commercial sector when replacements are no longer available? What are the proprietary rights of producers when images begin to degrade?

While many unknowns cloud the rapidly developing optical disk technology, it seems to offer great possibilities for libraries. As with many other issues in collection management and preservation, the common concerns arising from new developments in electronic media should promote continued communication and cooperative problem solving.

References

1. Ross W. Atkinson, "Selection for preservation: a materialistic approach," *Library Resources and Technical Services* 30 (1986): 341–53.

2. Roger S. Bagnall and C. Harris, "Involving scholars in preservation decisions: the case of the classicists." *Journal of Academic Librarianship* 13 (1987): 140–46.

3. Margaret S. Child, "Further thoughts on Selection for Preservation: a materialistic approach," *Library Resources and Technical Services* 30 (1986): 354–62.

4. "Conoco study sets the stage for shared collecting," *Research Libraries Group News* no. 13 (1987): 4–7.

5. John F. Dean, "Conservation and collection management," *Journal of Library Administration* 7 (1986): 129–42.

6. Patricia A. McClung, "Costs associated with preservation microfilming: results of the Research Libraries Group study," *Library Resources and Technical Services* 30 (1986): 363–74.

7. Nina J. Root, "Decision making for collection management," *Collection Management* 7 (1985): 93–101.

8. G.R. Thoma, S. Suthasinekul, F.L. Walker, J. Cookson, and M. Rashidian, "A prototype system for the electronic storage and retrieval of document images," *ACM Transactions on Office Information Systems* 3 (1985): 279–91.

9. Gay Walker, J. Greenfield, J. Fox, and J.S. Simonoff, "The Yale Survey: a large-scale study of book deterioration in the Yale University Library," *College and Research Libraries* 46 (1985): 111–32.

Developing Serials Collections in the 1990s

by Sara C. Heitshu and J. Travis Leach

Managing the serials portion of collection development in research libraries demands the wisdom of Solomon and the patience of Job. The difficulties presented by variations in format, title, and quality of content; bibliographic control; escalating costs; storage; and preservation, not to mention the shifting teaching and research needs of a large campus, require a combination of bibliographer/subject specialist, economist, cataloger, preservation expert, and bibliographic instructor. The interrelationships among library staff, faculty and the library administration can be tested to their outer limits when making decisions about serials.

While it may be argued that serials have always been difficult, it cannot be denied that recent events in serials publishing, pricing, cataloging, and automation have made the work of librarians far more complex than ever before. The economics of serials—including inflation and pricing—have severely affected research libraries in the past fifteen years and will continue to do so.

Efforts to solve problems of selection, processing, and control have produced an extreme range of organizational structures. At one end of the scale all serials work is performed by a dedicated staff under one manager; and at the other, serials are treated no differently from monographs and are integrated into the general work flow. However, neither of these extremes, nor the variations in between, really addresses the problems of managing serials in a research library unless communication about serials decisions in general, and individual titles in particular, reaches and is understood by all of the library staff and the library users.

Communication about a serial title from the point of selection of the title until it dies or is cancelled must be current, continual, clear and concise. Instead, information about serials usually begins and ends with the decision to add a title to the collection. While this may be an acceptable method of dealing with some library materials, it is clearly insufficient when dealing with a format defined as "a publication in any medium issued in successive parts bearing numerical or chronological designations and intended to be continued indefinitely."[1] Librarians engaged in the business of collection development in research libraries must be prepared to actively monitor serials intellectually, bibliographically, physically, and economically for as long as they continue to be part of a library's collection.

Historically, bibliographic control of serials has not been treated as a collection development issue, but in fact, it is. Collections are only of use if the materials in them can be found. Serials records are easily lost in enormous card catalogs or hidden in special lists. The difficulty of updating any form of control system is enormous; so is the problem of whether to classify or alphabetize titles, and where to shelve journals and other serial continuations.

THE CATALOGING DILEMMA

For many research libraries full cataloging of all serial titles, even the most ephemeral, was and is the norm. Others, caught in the dilemma of the cost of such cataloging versus the necessity of providing public access to their collections, have opted for serials lists of various kinds. And, it is not unusual to find major collections within a research library represented by special finding tools created for the users of specific collections. Data processing provided some relief for the production and maintenance of serials lists. Only recently

Sara C. Heitshu is Assistant University Librarian for Technical Services at the University of Arizona. J. Travis Leach is Acquisitions Librarian at the University of Arizona.

have online interactive systems offered an optimal solution to the management of ever-changing serials records.

The conventions used in traditional cataloging and in serials lists have generally depended upon the cataloging practice of the time. The normal choice of entry was often the issuing body usually represented by multiple part corporate entries which required either elaborate cross references or an instinctive feel for the right order of words on the part of the user. Generations of library users are probably still automatically inverting headings such as the University of Arizona, to: Arizona, University, as they approach the card catalog.

The new *Anglo-American Cataloging Rules* attempted to remedy the situation in 1967, but the Library of Congress refused to fully adopt the rules and the era of superimposition began. Since most research libraries depend upon LC copy for cataloging and since the card catalogs, serials lists, and other bibliographic tools of these libraries had long and elaborate histories based on following LC practice, albeit with local variations, the rules had little effect on serials access. Still, new generations of serials and reference librarians thought there had to be an easier way. Title access was the cry of the seventies When the Library of Congress finally did apply AACR to headings, giving us the era of desuperimposition, a brand new code was already well on its way.

The second edition of the *Anglo-American Cataloging Rules* published in 1978 brought changes of a truly sweeping nature. Titles were most often the choice of entry, and the distinction between the hundreds of reports which a research library might hold was entirely dependent upon the selection of qualifiers. Corporate headings which had mostly escaped during the tenure of AACR now had to be flipped to conform with the new rules. Automation promised to make this easier, but few major research libraries had fully automated databases. Opening a new card catalog helped monograph catalogers, but was a nightmare for serials catalogers. It is not clear that catalog users have been well served in either case.

In addition, the full implementation of the philosophy of successive title cataloging, touted as ideally suited for the automated environment which was just around the corner, occurred in the 1970's. A title change could now create an entirely new bibliographic record to which a discreet holdings statement could be attached. A linking note led the catalog user back to the previous title. The practice of "title varies" notes was no longer acceptable. It is little wonder that public services staff were bewildered about what to tell library users about how to find serial titles.

CONSER PROJECT

The CONSER project made a national serials database more than just a serials librarian's dream. CONSER refers to a cooperative program for on-line serials cataloging that resides in the OCLC system. The CONSER file was built upon brief union list entries upgraded by CONSER libraries, and upon the new cataloging of these libraries, and the Library of Congress. It promised to be a tool for shared cataloging and shared resources. Standards for machine readable records and their content were a major event in the 1970's. They also heralded the resurgence of interest in serials automation. The retrospective conversion of serials records in an online environment was a real possibility, not just a dream, and bibliographic records could be linked with holdings statements and easily up-dated.

Local and federal funds were poured into conversion projects in the 1970's and early 1980's. Unfortunately, funds available were not enough for most large libraries to adequately clean up truly old bibliographic records. Cosmetic changes to headings were easily accomplished, but the piece checks necessary for recataloging each successive title change were not possible in many libraries. In spite of national standards, a national database, and a nationally accepted cataloging code, the variations in serials bibliographic control continued and seemed to multiply since many of the variations were now online for all to see.

Union lists, once simple home grown products, were the new focus of bibliographic control as the 1980's began. If a national database was possible, so were nationally based union lists. Even small libraries with no access to OCLC have become part of regional and state union listing groups. The new products possible are remarkable in both size and scope. Whether they are truly an acceptable substitute for the older, simpler lists remains to be seen.

CONTROLLING SERIALS COLLECTIONS

Despite all the changes during the '60s, '70s, and '80s bibliographic control of serial collections is still expensive, labor intensive, and may not always be effective. To provide adequate access, it is necessary to commit large amounts of high level staff time. Costs have not been lowered by automation or rule changes or national databases. It is also doubtful whether a user seeking a serial title in a major research library collection is any better off as a result of the changes.

A selector/bibliographer must strive to understand the principles underlying serials control, as well as the records in his or her library. When issues related to the identification, classification, or cataloging of serials arise, it is important to consider how national standards may apply. When problems arise over where to classify, when to analyze, or what access points to select, the selector/bibliographer ought to represent the public point of view.

Check-in

Added to the complex issues of bibliographic control is the matter of check-in. Each piece must be recorded in some manner when it is received. Manual systems abound, and some research libraries maintain holdings information in a variety of places—kardexes, shelf lists, circulation systems, and local union lists. Different staff members may be responsible for the various files and different rules and regulations may govern the form and function of the files. Associated with check-in is claiming. The integrity of a serial depends upon the receipt of all of its parts. Claiming must be precise and punctual in order to be effective. At the same time, it cannot be done by rote since all delinquent serial titles in a research collection cannot be claimed on the same rigid schedule, and not all are of equal importance. Selectors must indicate priorities for claiming, and subject specialists, particularly for geographical areas, must be consulted before months are spent claiming third world serials. Thus, the day-to-day maintenance of serials collections is also a major task. Staff may not be at the highest classification level, but they must be well trained in the vagaries of serials and understand the systems of control used in their library. The job is complex but can be boring, and high staff turn-over is not unusual. At the same time, there is a need for continuing rapport and communication between that staff and the librarian/selectors in order to ensure that efforts to maintain the integrity of the collection are suitably directed.

Automation of the check-in function holds some real hope for streamlining serials control. Systems developed in the 1970s which depended upon databases and software maintained outside of the library had significant drawbacks. In the 1980s really effective serials control systems are available either as part of an integrated package or as a separate stand-alone system. With check-in files online, random access to records is possible, check-in itself may be done with one or two key strokes and claiming becomes semi-automatic. The record file is no longer confined to one physical location, but is available through terminals in public areas. Binding information also may be-

come part of the system display, solving a major problem for public service staff and library users. The old excuse of "it must be at the bindery" is no longer possible.

Preservation

The preservation of a serial is another complex issue. Binding standards for serials have undergone a dramatic change in the 1980s. Awareness of preservation issues and new mechanical and chemical processes have made the classic Library Binding Institute Class A binding only one of a number of options available. In addition, pamphlet binding or other in-house binding methods, filming in-house or through a contractor, and the purchase of commercially published film or fiche copies are other options. The matter of a film product is further complicated by the continuing debate over silver halide and diazo film.[2] While the choice between film and paper print may be obvious in the case of a national newspaper or a locally produced small magazine, other cases are not always as clearcut. The selector/bibliographer must think of the use to which a title will be put, the frequency of use, and length of time it can survive in useful condition in a particular format.

Economics

The economics of serials collection development is its most complicated aspect. Traditionally, it has been beyond the control of librarians, watching passively from the sidelines as rising costs devastated their budgets, leaving less and less money to buy books, and consequently endangering the integrity of their collections.

Yearly subscriptions to periodicals, indexing services, and standing orders for other serial continuations have soared during the last 15 years. At the same time, library materials budgets have shrunk due to local, national, and world economic conditions. These events coincided with the proliferation of new serials publications, a large part of the widely experienced information explosion. Throughout the "watershed years," as James[3] calls them, of advances in serials management and control, growing concern about pricing overshadowed the considerable theoretical and technological achievements in making the information in these same publications more accessible to library users.

A glance at the three major annual periodical price indexes—A.L.A., B.H. Blackwell, and Faxon reveals the magnitude of increases. These indexes differ in the core base of titles, and in methodology but the trend they portray is the same: a sixfold increase over 15 years.[4] The causes of rapidly rising subscription prices have been studied but they still remain obscure. They do not seem to be based on costs to publishers in labor and supplies; nor can they be explained by distribution costs in transportation and postage. The price increase ratios far exceed the inflation rates recorded in the U.S. Consumer Price Index. In fact, the prices of monographs have been relatively stable over the same period of time.

Library/publisher relationships have been damaged by ignorance and misunderstanding. Publishers know little about the problems of library administration, materials budgets, and serials collection development. And librarians, even administrators and acquisitions librarians, are generally ignorant of the greater world of business for profit. How a periodical is priced seems to be known only to the publisher. However, librarians know or surmise the following:

- Publishers, having known costs and projecting the expected number of sales, can calculate a subscription price that will bring in the desired profit.
- Publishers charge what the market will bear.
- Publishers differentiate between personal and institutional (multi-reader) price: the "soak the library" syndrome. How they calculate the institutional price is unclear to librarians.
- Learned society publishers have perfected the art of exploiting the nonmember. The library may be precluded from membership as a consequence of membership restrictions, structure, services, or cost. However, the library is eligible to subscribe to the society's publications at the nonmember rate, which is, of course always several times higher than the member rate.
- Some publishers set prices based on the customer's geographical location. For example, many British publishers have a three tier pricing policy: the lowest price for customers in the United Kingdom, the highest price for U.S. customers, and a third price for the rest of the world.
- Scientific publications are more expensive and rise in price at a much greater rate than publications in the humanities and social sciences.

Regardless of how prices are calculated, it is obvious there have been excesses, to the detriment of library budgets. Librarians regard ruthless pricing policies as especially audacious since most authors from whom publishers benefit are not paid for their work. In fact, an author may even pay for the privilege of being published. A further irony is that these same scholars are almost entirely dependent on libraries as sources of information.

How much profit is fair? Are libraries subsidizing prices for individual subscribers and society members? Are U.S. libraries subsidizing foreign libraries? This last question finally goaded librarians into testing their collective influence by vociferously questioning these pricing tactics. On this side of the Atlantic it appears to be a clear case of price gouging using geographically-based dual pricing. Increases have been as much as 40 percent or more per year for subscription renewals to overseas customers, mainly U.S. and Canadian libraries.

Librarians have also accused foreign publishers of pricing based on unrealistic exchange rates. Foreign publishers justified their actions on the relative decrease in the dollar's strength and on the historical deficits they had experienced when the dollar was strong. It is interesting to note that American publishers have been using similar geographically based pricing tactics, although perhaps not to the same extent. All in all, it appears that misunderstandings of a fundamental nature exist between American libraries and publishers, foreign publishers in particular. Some progress has been made to unravel the misunderstandings and to effect a de-escalation in the dual price differential. In the meantime, this situation has profoundly affected serials collection development in U.S. libraries and has helped bring into focus the many factors outside the title selection process.

Publishers employ other strategies that cost libraries more. Smaller publishers shortchange libraries and publish fewer issues than advertised by using the tactic of "delayed" issues which ultimately become "combined" issues without a simultaneous reduction in subscription price or an extension of the paid subscription. The free issue claiming period for expected issues is commonly much shorter for expensive, commercially published titles, than for less expensive titles. Also, to obtain a replacement for a single missing issue of say, a quarterly journal, these same publishers, require the library to buy the entire volume or year, or charge as much as the yearly subscription rate for a single backissue. The latter case extends to certain microform publishers, as in the situation where a volume takes several reels to reprint. Some publishers, particularly of scientific journals, have for many years offered "supplements" and "additional volumes" to subscribers. These issues are published and priced in addition to the established subscription price and announced much later in the subscription term. The rate of occurrence in publication of these additional issues has recently accelerated.

THE COPYRIGHT DILEMMA

Other issues surround serials titles in a research environment. Copyright is one. In the past, librar-

THE COPYRIGHT DILEMMA

Other issues surround serials titles in a research environment. Copyright is one. In the past, libraries have been responsible only for use made by library staff of copyrighted materials, and patrons have been left to be guided by their own consciences prompted by signs to remind them of the law. Recently, however, periodical publishers have been adding charges to invoices for the right to copy.

Gordon & Breach explained the sudden appearance of 10 percent additional charges on renewal invoices as the "photocopy licensing fee," to offset losses in revenue by illegal photocopying. But librarians believe the publisher is already protected under U.S. copyright law. This additional fee, coming on the heels of the British publishers' dual pricing excesses, scandalized librarians. These tactics create unanticipated additional expense to the library. Under pressure, Gordon & Breach partially rescinded the fee, but librarians can expect more extortion from journal publishers.

THE PLANNING DILEMMA

Unlike other areas of serials collection management such as cataloging, automation, indexing/abstracting, and indeed, definition of the published entity,[5] there has been little effort toward economic standardization. There is no standard for predicting library budget needs for serials. There is no standard way for allocating funds to subject areas or to other areas such as location or new study/research programs. There is no standard way of predicting periodical subscription price increases. Few standards exist as guides to format selection and purchase, that is, print vs. microform, or format of microform. There are few standards for binding, claiming, replacing missing parts, preservation and conservation, or sharing of resources between libraries to reduce the expenses for any one library.

Is Cunning Enough?

So, in order to stay afloat and not get soaked too badly, each library relies on its own intellectual resources and cunning to administer the budget. However, there is an underlying principle behind a serials budget: funds must reliably appear each year to cover renewals of the serials each library has selected. Each subscription to a serial implies a commitment by the library to a future outlay of money, space, and time. The source of the renewal funds must be reliable and relatively stable,

such as state funds or the yields of large private endowments. Short term grants or donations to cover any part of the serials renewal budget are not acceptable because they may vanish with little warning.

Serials' steady drain on budgets has become critical and has brought into question the optimal allocation of the budget between serials and monographs. Currently, allocation of from 40 percent to 60 percent of the budget to serials is considered acceptable by university library administrators. Of course, the optimal allocation depends on the local serial title mix. Academic libraries supporting strong science programs may allot as much as 70 to 80 percent of the budget to serials. Early fears that serials would consume the entire budget ignored the fact that this would be in no one's best interest, including the publishers. Librarians have had to learn to make hard choices in cancelling serial titles and adding new titles.

Crystal Ball or Algebra?

Since subscription prices are rising faster than library budgets, trying to predict future renewal costs is necessary. This has been attempted in a number of ways, uncertain at best, since many factors are unknown. Of about equal use are educated guessing based on past performance, or a good crystal ball with which to contemplate inflation. However, since greater confidence and accuracy are urgently desired, a few more promising methods, have been formulated.

Mathematical analysis of trends has at last lent some credence to the "science" in library science. For example: Emery has shown the relationship of periodical price increases to times to be quadratic and that "we may therefore with confidence opt for a forecasting model for periodical subscription costs based on the concept of the geometric mean, since this is the model that provides the best trade-off between costs and benefits.[6] Clark and Williams of the Harvard Widener Library have devised a local periodical price index for titles in the humanities and social sciences and say it correlates very well with the Blackwell Index. They note that "with these results the library feels comfortable in using the linear regression method of least squares to determine the slope of the regression line of the Widener Combined Index on the Blackwell Index for the period 1971 to 1982 and to predict the Widener combined average prices for the next five years," and add that it would be ideal if the Blackwell Index appeared in time for correlation to take place.[7]

cost model study for the National Commission on the New Technological Uses of Copyrighted Works. It proposes the following:

> Many libraries are now facing reduced budgets; the rapidly increasing costs of periodical subscriptions, the new copyright law and the proposed national periodicals system have focused special attention upon periodical acquisitions and potentials for controlling or decreasing expenditures in this area.
>
> To realize these potentials, it is highly desirable to be able to estimate the costs of options associated with acquiring periodicals. This report uses a mathematical model for estimating such costs to address the following question: *Should a library own (i.e., subscribe to) or should it borrow, when needed, a specific periodical?* [8]

USING SUBSCRIPTION AGENTS

However poorly librarians have managed external matters of pricing in their communications with publishers, they have made internal matters work to their best advantage through the use of subscription agents. Approximately 95 percent of American libraries use subscription agents to help reduce staff time and money spent on serials collection development and management.

Theoretically, agencies have agreements with publishers and, as middlemen, collectively submit orders and claims for their clients in an effective, efficient, and organized manner. Cash is sent with the orders, eliminating publisher invoicing. Economies of volume reduce costs to agencies below what a library would pay for the same title. Agencies also earn revenue from short term investments of money prepaid by clients for annual subscription renewals, advertising serial titles, and the sale of software for serials control systems. The services the agent provides to the library are based on these revenues. Historically, whether an agent charged a service fee or extended a discount to the library depended on the above cost margin, competition from other agents or from the publisher, and the cost of the overall services which the library asked the agent to provide. However, since the late 1960's publishers have lowered or deleted discounts to subscription agents and service charges are the norm. This has not significantly altered library/vendor relations except to bring the agent and its performance under greater scrutiny by the library.

Libraries still find agencies highly effective in reducing overt and hidden expenses that would be incurred if the library placed each subscription directly with the publisher. Hidden expenses include cost of writing checks or purchase orders, supplies, telephone service charges, postage, up-dating publisher address files, and staff wages and time. Rigorous cost analysis of this system is difficult, but superficial observations indicate that a library may save as much as 90 percent in clerical work on ordering alone and 50-85 percent on claiming by using a subscription agent.

Some agencies can provide custom management/cost reports to their clients, or they can be accessed online thereby eliminating the cost of letters, postage, forms, and telephone calls. Agencies are also better equipped and experienced in dealing with foreign publishers in their own languages and currencies, and often save time in the process.

Although librarians have questioned the subscription agencies' service charge structures, and have suspected them of contributing to escalation of prices, agents have successfully defended their positions and seem eager to have frank and open relationships with their clients. Indeed, some agents have made efforts to help librarians pay lower prices. As the goals of library collection management change, so will the role of the vendors. They must continue their efforts to serve libraries' increasingly complex needs.

DECISIONS DECISIONS DECISIONS

Adding a serial title to a research library collection creates external and internal issues that go beyond traditional questions of content, indexing, price, paper quality, and appropriateness. The decision to buy should include a careful assessment of what type of access should be made available, frequency and urgency of claiming, retention, and physical preservation or merely content preservation. The matter does not end with these decisions. The economics must be carefully monitored year by year, while watching the quality of the title. Editors change, content and subject matter may shift for better or for worse. Teaching and research emphasis on a campus may change dramatically. The decision to cancel a particular title may come up at any time.

Just as there is no perfect formula for budget allocation to serials, there is no perfect organizational structure for optimum serial collection management. Each research library seeks ideal answers. Even if the present arrangement works, the future is very much in question.

Electronic data processing is a powerful influence dissolving old concepts of what a research library is. Electronic formats for serial index and abstracting services have already changed the role of libraries and librarians. Serials in electronic format bring new challenges, with internal control problems as yet unknown. The external factors of

The problems of bibliographic control, preservation, and economics will continue to be paramount in the electronic tomorrow just as they are today

price and format are fluid. As we have seen with traditional serials, the decision to subscribe is only the beginning. Bibliographers, selectors, collection developers, whatever they are called, must now become collection managers whose duties are no longer confined to the selection of printed materials. New demands on the collection manager's expertise will emerge: how to provide access to information through electronic networks? what hardware/software systems are appropriate? how to balance costs for acquisition and storage of information, with convenience and confidence of access to this information?

Will the library ever stop receiving traditional paper-format pieces? Will the cost of online access make that option prohibitive for all but the grant-funded researcher, while students and less well-connected faculty continue to manually search printed sources? Striking a balance between the cost of information and access to information will be difficult. If access only is bought, who will be responsible for backfiles? How will they be accessed? Copyright becomes an even more complex issue when dealing with online access to information. Not only is it feasible to copy electronic data but also to manipulate it in a variety of ways. How will the library user know what is available or even what is an appropriate source for information sought? If traditional serials records have presented problems in the past, imagine the challenge in an electronic future. The problems of bibliographic control, preservation

and economics will continue to be paramount in the electronic tomorrow just as they are today.

References

1. *Anglo-American Cataloguing Rules,* 2nd. ed., edited by Michael Gorman and Paul W. Winkler, (Chicago: American Library Association, 1978), 570.
2. See articles by Jerry Dupont and Suzanne Cates Dodson in *Library Resources and Technical Services,* 30 (January/March 1986), 79-90.
3. John R. James, "Developments in Serials: 1977." *Library Resources and Technical Services,* 22 (Summer 1978): 294–309.
4. For a fuller discussion of periodical pricing, see: Ann Okerson, Periodical Prices: a History and Discussion," *Advances in Serials Management* I (1986): 101–134.
5. See American National Standards Committee Z39, Draft Revision of Standard Z39. 1–77 "American National Standard for Periodicals: Format and Arrangement", Washington, D.C., 1983. The ANSC Z39 is now called National Information Standards Organization Z39 (NISO Z39).
6. Charles D. Emery, "Forecasting Models and the Prediction of Periodical Subscription Costs," *Serials Librarian* 9 (1985): 4–22.
7. Sally Williams and Mary E. Clark, "Using Locally and Nationally Produced Periodical Price Indexes in Budget Preparation," *Library Resources and Technical Services* 27 (1983): 345–356.
8. Vernon E. Palmour, Marcia C. Bellassin and Robert R. V. Wiederkehn, *Costs of Owning, Borrowing, and Disposing of Periodical Publications* (Arlington, Va., Center for Naval Analyses, 1977) CRC 342.

SECTION II

Selection/Deselection

Libraries and Alternatives: An Essay

Patricia Glass Schuman

The library is the only social institution whose main ethical underpinning is the collection, preservation, and dissemination of all manner of information. This, at any rate, is the library's avowed goal. It rarely becomes a reality, and for good and sundry reasons: budget constraints, space limitations, personnel shortages. The danger is not so much that the library often falls short of its heady and laudable goal, but that librarians are sometimes seized by an almost pathological smugness. In short, they come to believe that the goal is actually being realized.

Professionals are always limited by their cultural and educational biases. Most librarians, for example, think of information in fairly narrow terms: the written word, usually contained in the pages of books, magazines, and newspapers. Similarly, the publishing industry tends to be perceived as several thousand corporations whose works and authors are listed or indexed in the standard reference works, whose publications are reviewed and advertised in the major media and displayed and distributed nationwide. These are the visible publishers. It is simple to deal with them, to learn about their products, to purchase and handle their output. There is a good reason for this ease and simplicity: some 3.3 per cent of 6,000 plus companies control about 70 per cent of the publishing industry's volume, and they make it their business to put their books on library shelves.[1] .

Of course librarians' professional training and experience have taught them to deal with other types of publishers as well: government agencies, research centers, university presses, trade or labor associations, and organizations which are not publishers per se but rather producers of information as a by-product of another major purpose. They are often non-commercial or nonprofit; they produce not only books and periodicals, but also pamphlets, flyers, films, microfiche, videotapes, phonograph records, data bases, and other non-print formats.

The larger of these information producers are sometimes encompassed in bibliographic and reference works; in some cases, special tools have been developed to access their products. Many libraries have designed procedures to deal with them, and wholesalers will stock their publications if there is sufficient demand.

But there is another category of publisher with which few librarians are prepared to deal, either by training, experience, or orientation. This mixed bag of publishers is variously referred to as alternative, small, or independent. While none of these labels is entirely satisfactory, alternative probably fits best, because such publishers do indeed provide alternatives to the more traditional publishing and information networks.

By definition, all are small and independently owned, though of course not all small publishers can be considered alternative. Alternative publishers purposely present information with a particular point of view: political, cultural, or literary. By choice, as well as definition, their publications fall outside the mainstream of commercial publishing. This may also put alternative publishers outside the mainstream of traditional bibliographic tools, review media, and distribution channels. Further, it means that they are often outside the peripheral vision of librarians who buy 25,000 copies of *Books in Print* but less than 4,000 of *Alternatives in Print*.

Most alternative presses, limited by size and capital resources, cannot afford to give away masses of review copies, hire sales people, utilize staff to fill out bibliographic forms, mail promotional materials to libraries, bill in triplicate, wait ninety days for payment, etc. Moreover, alternative publishers are sometimes unaware of the potential for selling to libraries and the special kinds of library requirements. Frequently, they are one-or-two-person operations that never find time to develop this expertise. This is unfortunate, because alternative publishers are on the cutting edge of important issues.

TWENTIETH CENTURY PAMPHLETEERS

The role of the pamphleteer in America has been well established at least since the days of Thomas Paine. In the realm of political and social concerns, the alternative press—in whatever format—is our modern pamphleteer. Much of its publishing output arises from the need for activists to communicate with each other rapidly. Standard information sources cannot cope with emerging issues: abortion, feminism, rape, alternative energy, nuclear dangers, gay rights, senior citizen power, alternative lifestyles, vitamins and organic foods, the excesses of government and its intelligence agencies; the list is nearly endless. None of these issues is new, though many are relatively unfamiliar to libraries because they were not dealt with earlier by the major publishing houses. The alternative press has been publishing material on such topics for almost two decades.

An excellent example is the development of information concerning rape as a social issue. The first rape crisis center, established in 1971 in Washington, D.C., was inundated with requests for information, and published a pamphlet "How to Start a Rape Crisis Center." The first feminist article on rape, "Rape: The American Crime," by Susan Griffin, was published in *Ramparts* in September, 1971. Few libraries then subscribed to *Ramparts*, and even fewer had ever heard of the original pamphlet, "How to Start a Rape Crisis Center." At the same time, groups like the New York Radical Feminists were publishing statements on the politics of rape.

Not for several years did the standard periodical literature begin to catch up with the issue of rape as a social, rather than an individual, issue. *Newsweek* and the *New York Times* carried articles in 1972; *Time* in 1973. The *New York Times Index* still only accesses the subject under "sex crimes." The peak year for the topic in standard periodical literature was 1975. Thus it was not until almost half a decade after materials from alternative press services were available that books treating rape as a socio-political issue were available from major publishing houses—for example Susan Brownmiller's *Against Our Will: Men, Women and Rape* (Simon & Schuster, 1975).

In a similar vein, how many libraries bought *Rubyfruit Jungle* when it was published by the small feminist press Daughters instead of Bantam? How many subscribed to the *Whole Earth Catalog* from Portola Institute before buying the *Last Whole Earth Catalog* from Random House? *Our Bodies, Ourselves* was available for years for 35¢ from the New England Press before it was taken over by Simon & Schuster and reissued at $4.95.

Remarkably parallel histories can be traced for many other issues. Energy is probably the most current example. While part of this problem results from the structure of the publishing industry, the phenomenon also stems from the ways in which knowledge is communicated. Activists tend to communicate with other activists, researchers with other researchers, and so forth, until an issue is brought to the public's attention. Then there is a concomitant time lag until material can be synthesized, written, and published in a popular format. If libraries are to collect and access information on issues which have the potential to change the fabric of our society, they must get it directly from those who are creating it. The information produced by alternative publishers is not always neatly packaged, reflective, or even necessarily scholarly. But it is timely, and it is the raw material from which societal transformations are forged.

The alternative media do more than play a vital socio-political role. They also make an important cultural and literary contribution. The publishing outlets for fiction, essays, and poetry have shrunk dramatically in the last twenty years. The alternative press, particularly through its literary magazines, chapbooks, and pamphlets, is one of the only outlets for these genres open to new, and sometimes, even more published writers. As librarians, we should take seriously our responsibility to develop, as well as preserve, the written word. Libraries play a significant role in what gets published, as well as in what information gets distributed to whom. Our plain duty is to make sure that all voices have an opportunity to be heard.

THE MARKETPLACE

We live in a society in which access to information is fast becoming essential to survival. Libraries are central institutions in the information arena. Certainly they are key in the marketplace of information, part of the underpinnings of the communications industry. Libraries are key collectors, indexers, and distributors of information. Their role becomes even more important as a small group of powerful interlocking conglomerates takes over more and more publishing houses and bookstore chains. An excellent discussion of this phenomenon is found in Celeste West's *Booklegger's Guide to: the Passionate Perils of Publishing,* Booklegger, 1978.

The terms of the marketplace may seem commercial, but they represent reality. Libraries are a market, and an important one. The latest *Publishers Weekly* statistics, compiled basically from the traditional publishing industry's sales, show that in 1977 libraries spent close to $500 million on books alone. Libraries are the major buyers of nonfiction hardcover books, and of children's books. A good review in *Library Journal* can account for 2,000 sales, while an average nonfiction hardcover sale is about 5,000 copies and novels are often less.

Libraries are quiet and steady customers. Library sales are a base, but they do not generate the volume from which bestsellers are made. Since most libraries order books through wholesalers, they are not particularly visible to the larger publishers. They are even less visible to the smaller publishers, who are frequently unfamiliar with library ordering and selection procedures. This, coupled with some very real procedural problems, makes it difficult for libraries to collect the alternative press. But the bureaucratic arrogance which underlies many selection criteria and

acquisitions procedures should not prevent librarians from collecting and making available material that represents different points of view. The economic power of libraries is large enough as a total market that libraries can keep the alternative press alive and healthy.

Ways must be developed to overcome the sometimes almost obsessive methodologies by which librarians handle new or different materials—as experimental appendages, or so-called extra services. Some academic and research libraries collect the alternative press, but the majority of these treat it as a special collection. This sort of labeling can create barriers that an integrated approach will avoid. The alternative press is not an artifact; it is vital and important. The problem is not simply to acquire alternative information, but to make it known, and accessible, to the library's users. Procedural difficulties can be eliminated; librarians are limited only by their failure to recognize their own power. We are the major buyers of indexes, reference books, and bibliographic tools; the major customers of several wholesalers; and if we buy alternative publications in sufficient numbers, alternative publishers will eventually be stocked by these wholesalers. Librarians can help by initiating and maintaining meaningful contact with a broad spectrum of alternative publishers.

Footnotes

1. Celeste West and Valerie Wheat, *The Passionate Perils of Publishing* (San Francisco: Booklegger, 1978), p. 1.

Thoughts on Selection

Is selection censorship? That old conundrum will haunt libraries until the countryside is littered with angels. In a 1983 issue of *Top of the News*, the editor claims that "Lately, the topic seems to be fading, and we can all relax for a while and prepare ourselves for the next crisis."[1] And with that ten questions are offered to test if the librarian is selecting or censoring.

The queries are the usual: What is racism? What is sexism? What is obscene? Are there certain elements (such as these) that reduce the literary value of the work? The correct reply indicates whether or not the librarian is controllable. If, for example, the librarian believes there is a scientifically knowable answer to any of these, he or she has either suffered from a lobotomy or is the victim of fundamentalism.

The joker in this type of test/answer approach to selection/censorship is that there are no answers, at least to the degree that every human will be satisfied. At the same time, one must avoid neurotic twitches by coming to some half-way understanding of definitions, of authentic methods of action when the library is under siege.

The *Top of the News* editor appreciates the alarming facts of life, for the conclusion: "I could go on, but I'm getting tired of hittng the question mark key on my typewriter. In the end, that's what it boils down to: one great big question mark. I wish I had some answers." This hardly satisfies a scientific enquiry, but it does measure up to Bertrand Russell's assertion that all science is dominated by the idea of approximation. At best, and humanly speaking, the librarian can only approximate an answer to the question of censorship/selection.

It's a banal fact that few are so objective, so wise as to take a direct action, such as selection of a book, without on occasion making an error. In another sense, rejection (for bad literary quality, of limited interest to readers, sexist, etc.) is open to the same practical doubt. The librarian's treatment of selection should conform to the notion that one must be capable of knowing one is capable of making mistakes.

The paradox is that every librarian must hold some set of beliefs or other, some rules the public knows and understands which temper and control the selection of materials. Without this type of philosophical approach, a formal policy statement, call it what you will, the library will suffer. By now there are numerous writers, policies, programs, and suggestions to assist the librarian in formulating formal policies against censorship—just glance through a recent copy of *Library Literature*, or for that matter, *Library Journal* or *American Libraries*. The profession attaches major importance to intellectual freedom, and it is not unexplored country.

With that, let's return to the *Top of the News* questions, which are as applicable to public and academic librarians as to those in schools. The point of the queries is to try to explain the difference between selection and censorship. Actually, it is the realm of the rhetorical traps and exquisite arguments which pass each other in a wilderness of misunderstanding. The real question is one of the moment: "Am I rejecting this book because I don't approve of it, or am I rejecting it because it does not fit into the vision I have of the library, its purpose, its objective, and its audience?" It is a commonplace question, yet one with so many holes and patches as to gradually develop into a nightmare of polemic proportions. So, let's keep it simple and direct.

The librarian must ask: "Am I censoring or selecting?" This may be more than can be expected from those who are passionately and genuinely committed to an ideal. For example, a feminist may take exception to that chaotic vision of the world offered by Leo Buscaglia. An auto fan is unlikely to be charmed by *Christine*, a novel about an unruly car; and Victorians will not appreciate Jonathan Miller's illustrated *The Human Body*. Just to limit the choices to the bestseller list published in *The New York Times Book Review*, one may discover genuine points of disagreement with every title. Add to this a librarian's vision of the world which sees these assertions in print as immoral or evil, and the principle of selection gives way to censorship.

When one is in passion it is hard to be objective. Granted, but there is an efficient and clear way of skirting this danger. It seems wise for the outraged librarian to divorce self from the parts of the selection process. Not, mind you, from selection entirely, but from books which shock the sensibility. For example, while I firmly believe the average public library should routinely order books on the best-seller lists, I would find it difficult to do anything but groan or dash from the room when it came to ordering Robert Schuller's *Tough Times Never Last, But Tough People Do.* The title is so oppressively lacking in taste, and so arrogantly practical that it immediately sets off an attack of nervous murderous gestures. My purely instinctive reaction is not in the best and most authentic tradition of selection.

If the phenomenon of aesthetic taste is foreign to most who make the bestseller list, it is one thing to call attention to this contemptuous treatment of readers, quite another to then eliminate the popular titles from the library. If one can't take this objective stand, then one should not be selecting—or at least drop out when such titles are being considered.

Much of America is made-up of one-person professional libraries, and here dropping out is to distort the collection beyond belief. Here the librarian must have the strength of a potential and obsessed genius who completely appreciates the need for honest objectivity. In practice what happens is that the one-person library is not so incorruptible, and the result is a view of the world which imparts the theories and ideas of the individual librarian. Actually, this tends to work out pretty well because, from a practical point of view, the small libraries do reflect the limited (or expansive) intellectual and silly interests of the small community served. The librarian really is a part of the community, not a gesture.

In larger libraries the committees, subject experts, and strong-willed administrators allow the artistic privilege of dropping out when censorship and not selection is likely to dominate. Also, there is the buffer of the approval plan.

Approval plans dominate in larger libraries today, and with good reason. Most of them make much sense, and have built-in benefits too well-known to belabor here. The problem, though, is that they tend to have a finality and a perfection which conveys the idea that the individual librarian need no longer select, let alone censor. Once the rhythm of the paper is in motion, it is difficult to break the perfect symmetry with suggestions that this or that book might be added or deleted. The motion of the approval plan is in one direction, and that direction is away from selection of the specific in order to construct the general. The usual succession of individual decisions is not then necessary, and the chronicle of censorship vs. selection is more academic than real.

If approval plans solve the censorship/selection relationship, the same is true of most professional book reviews. It may be vexatious that these reviews today are limited to favorable notices, but it solves two problems. First, the librarian is almost sure that anything mentioned in *Library Journal, Choice, Booklist,* etc., is acceptable to the audiences considered by the library—always, of course, with modifications. Second, the cyclical process of good following the good eliminates the need to consider the bad. The reviews have eliminated evil from the world of books—if not entirely, at least 80 to 90 percent of the time.[2]

Not all librarians, either, are convinced that censorship is a bad thing. The convention adopted in articles and books seems to be that the title "librarian" immediately presupposes a recognizable place on the front line fighting the censor. This is not always the case, for even librarians who conscientiously believe in intellectual freedom are sometimes puzzled and troubled by books which challenge their individual moral values. Others simply let the subconscious run wild and using extremely odd methods label censorship as selection. Doomed to this peculiar and horrid fate, there is not much help available. It is difficult to feel compassion for such people, but they are out there.

Between downright censors, approval plans, and highly selective reviews, one can well appreciate the frustration of the exaggerated and not too typical reader, who wonders why the library does not have a copy of, say *Totally Gross Jokes* or a technical book on the poetaster's guide to politics. The librarian may honestly report that the book(s) is not in the library because it was not reviewed or not received.

Now let's shift into the dreaded consideration of what to do when someone asks to have a book added to the collection. The hunger for freedom and dignity is such that few librarians these days will automatically take a book off the shelf when confronted by some well-meaning idiot, even when backed by political-religious-money machinery. No, the real problem is when one wants to add a book to the collection. Why won't the librarian buy a book when requested by someone who may be slightly more than a gypsy.

Whether it be a group or a single, passionate individual who makes the request, there is only one answer: yes. The only qualification is numbers. The library, or so the less than extremely hard explanation might go, has limited space, limited budget, and limited personnel. The library might like to take your whole collection of timeless masterpieces on the moments of motion in the social milieu, but simply can't handle it. Allow us to shelve two or three of the most precious, most typical titles. And once or twice a year the library will be glad to replace these with newer titles you suggest.

If possible, one should request gifts and not be required to buy—not an unreasonable demand. This engages the problem full on, avoids the endless discussions which occur over literary merit, elements of racism, nonobjectivity, lack of research, lack of knowledge of the field, etc.

If this seems outrageous, consider those numerous studies which demonstrate that less than 10 to 50 percent of the collection is ever read. One does not have to lack convictions to realize that the esoteric, obscure titles often suggested for inclusion will not be measured in circulation figures. This may be trying to find a path that avoids decisions, but it is a decision in itself that seems more direct and honest than skipping among approval plans, book reviews, and madcap rationalizations about elusive quality.

One of the first questions in that *Top of the News* editorial is "On what basis should selection decisions be made?" Well, that depends. If the library is a large research unit, or a small one-person outlet for popular reading, the replies will differ. The larger library traditionally swallows any censorship problem by simply converting everything in view to its collection. *The National Enquirer*, for example, may be taboo in a small library, but it becomes an important part of the popular culture section in a large institution. The irony is not lost on those who remember when pornography was readily available in large libraries, yet always in Latin. Size alone seems to make the measured sin moralistic.

Between the two extremes is the routine answer. The basis of selection is on the reader's needs and wants. Neat, but the obvious problem is to lay down a scheme to verbally organize the profile or portrait of the user in such a way that it can be adapted to selection decisions. This may be done with a formal policy statement, or intuitively, or simply not at all. The latter is rarely admitted, yet in the day-to-day operation of the average public or academic library one had the strong suspicion that despite what may be written in free verse, despite the meetings without past or future, the selection policies follow a strictly measured beat of the reviews or the approval plans or the doggerel of memoranda. This may not be entirely a defect, although to avoid human contact with the public in favor of organized notions of that public can be less than useful in selection. It's not hard to say: "This kind of

book is preferable to that" when one has no clear notion of the reader. (See, for example, the common sense plea for better understanding of the small press in Grant Burns' fine article.)[3]

Finally, this gets back to the beginning in that selection presupposes a sense of literary value in the broadest way. The editor of *Top of the News* asks "What is literary value?" The question just as well might be: "What is truth?" Yet, both replies are used to justify selection, censorship, and numerous defects arbitrarily called up at any selection meeting.

The partial answer to the problem of defining literary value—whether it be applied to science, sociology, or fiction—is education and reading. One, for example, may memorize the rules set down by George Sarton or Robert Penn Warren and be able to distinguish between Buscaglia and Dostoyevsky, both of whom deal with human nature and love. At the same time, one must read both of these writers. If by then one can't distinguish the difference, one should give up the library and go on the television late news program.

How does a librarian become an expert in selection? At the risk of shattering Parnassus, the truth is simple and less than bewildering: read, read, read. This may be in literature, science, or on a computer screen. The form is not important. It's the content. One soon learns that there is no answer to censorship vs. selection, that the universe is not that well-governed or understood to make such answers possible. All one may do is to have no fixed laws, have no fixed techniques, but a lasting faith in one's own ability to admit error and to have childish convictions, if you will, that quality, when given the opportunity, will out. The value of selection is the value of probability—no more. Probably you will select and not censor if you are aware of that value. At the very least you will be a more effective foe against those who follow a stricter and uncorrupted-by-doubt belief in the goldfinch of certainty.

Footnotes

1. "Editor's Note," *Top of the News* (summer 1983), pp. 303–304.
2. Beth Macleod, "Library Journal and Choice: A Review of Reviews," *The Journal of Academic Librarianship* (March 1981), pp. 23–28. There are, of course, critical review media; but not much in the professional, general press. For an exception, and the results, see: Grant Burns, "Like Dreamers Do...," *Collection Building* (summer 1983), pp. 50–54.
3. *Ibid.*

The convention adopted in articles and books seems to be that the title "librarian" immediately presupposes a recognizable place on the front line fighting the censor. This is not always the case, for even librarians who conscientiously believe in intellectual freedom are sometimes puzzled and troubled by books which challenge their individual moral values.

An Analysis of the Relationship Between Book Reviews and the Inclusion of Potentially Controversial Books in Public Libraries

Judith Serebnick

The policies of the American Library Association (ALA) concerning the concept of intellectual freedom are embodied in the *Library Bill of Rights*, the association's official statement on free access to libraries and library materials. The *Library Bill of Rights* is a brief, deceptively simple document that has provoked constant debate and reinterpretation since its adoption by ALA almost 40 years ago.

Selection policy statements of libraries throughout the United States now incorporate the *Library Bill of Rights* to signify the commitment of librarians to intellectual freedom. This commitment is constantly put to the test when librarians select library materials, especially potentially controversial materials.

According to the *Library Bill of Rights*, librarians should judge materials "for values of interest, information and enlightenment of all the people in a community," with "all points of view concerning the problems and issues of our times" represented in collections. No materials should be excluded "because of the race or nationality or the social, political, or religious views of the authors" or "because of partisan or doctrinal disapproval....Censorship should be challenged by libraries in the maintenance of their responsibility to provide public information and enlightenment." The line between selection and censorship is drawn when the librarian ceases to judge materials by professional criteria and instead, for example,

rejects materials because the librarian considers them personally offensive, subversive, or too critical of existing mores.

How do we determine when the line has been drawn, when selection is no longer selection, but censorship? The library profession has not developed generally recognized criteria for differentiating selection from censorship. In addition, censorship in libraries is defined variously, depending on who is formulating the definition.

DIFFERENTIATING SELECTION FROM CENSORSHIP

One reason for the difficulty in distinguishing selection from censorship is that the process of selecting materials in libraries is often subjective, not easy to analyze systematically. For example, if we consider book selection, what objective measures do we have to indicate which of the approximately 40,000 books published yearly in the United States are most appropriate, according to professional criteria, for selection by librarians serving particular communities? Which books are most "interesting," "informative," and "enlightening" for "all the people in a community"? If a potentially controversial book is not found in a library's collection is it because it was lost among the thousands of books competing for the librarian's attention, because it has been judged according to professional criteria and found wanting, or because the librarian has judged it from a biased viewpoint and decided it is inappropriate for the collection?

We can, of course, ask the librarian why a particular book is not included in a collection. In previous studies, answers to this question have elicited varied responses, including: the librarian was not aware of the book's publication; reviews of the book were unfavorable; the book was not in demand by the library's public; the library does not purchase books of "that type"; and the budget did not allow purchase of the book. Rarely have responses been analyzed and verified. In two limited attempts, it was found that books rejected because of "poor reviews" or "not familiar with that title" had actually received a surplus of favorable reviews in widely used selection sources.[1]

PURPOSE OF THIS STUDY

In a broad sense, this study is concerned with both the problem of differentiating selection from censorship and with the investigation of variables that influence selection of potentially controversial books. Specifically, the purpose of the study is to investigate the relationship between book reviews and the inclusion of potentially controversial books in public libraries. It is hoped that the study's methodology and findings will contribute to systematic attempts to differentiate selection from censorship and to analyze variables affecting censorship in libraries.

Book reviews are used by librarians both as guides for selection and as resources to support selection decisions once they are made. In the selection and defense of potentially controversial books, reviews are of paramount importance. Moon's study of problem fiction, in which he surveyed 113 public libraries nationwide, found that published reviews were "the preeminent factor" influencing purchase of controversial books.[2] Other studies indicate that potentially controversial books require more favorable reviews before purchase than do noncontroversial books,[3] and favorable reviews are often the main defense of controversial books once they encounter patron disapproval. That is, when patrons object to books in libraries, librarians usually counter the objections by showing the patrons favorable reviews of the books in the professional journals.

In public libraries, which are the focus of this study, published reviews are major sources for book selection. This dependence on the review media is dictated by several considerations. Public libraries purchase primarily current books, and reviews are one of the few sources for critical evaluations of new publications. Public libraries rarely have the financial resources to purchase books indiscriminately, and therefore guidance is needed to select what is most necessary. In addition, public libraries usually lack sufficient trained staff to read and evaluate each new book, and published reviews provide guidance on the worthwhileness of large numbers of new titles.

If books for libraries are selected according to professional criteria, including, for example, accuracy of information, literary style, and authoritativeness, then reviews often serve as the librarian's guide to how well or how poorly some books are meeting professional criteria. Given the importance of book reviews in the selection process, a number of obvious questions come to mind:

> How widely are potentially controversial books reviewed in the journals consulted frequently by librarians? Do some journals predominate in the number of potentially controversial books reviewed?

> How are potentially controversial books reviewed? Favorably, unfavorably, neutrally? With controversial aspects mentioned, emphasized, ignored?

> How many and which of the potentially controversial books reviewed or not reviewed are found in library collections? Is number of reviews a book receives related to number of libraries owning that book? Is number of reviews more or less significant than where the reviews appear, i.e., in which journals?

In addition, other questions can be asked. For example:

> How does the reviewing of potentially controversial books relate to alleged censorship by librarians? Surveys of censorship in libraries indicate that librarians often say some potentially controversial books are absent from their collections because they are "unknown" to the librarians, rather than because they have been censored.[4] Are those potentially controversial books also "unknown" to the review journals? Or are the books "known" to the journals and still absent from libraries, perhaps because the reviews indicate that the books are controversial?

> Are potentially controversial books which are widely, and favorably, reviewed purchased in greater numbers than potentially controversial books seldom, or unfavorably, reviewed? Or does the controversiality of some books militate against their purchase by librarians despite pro-

nounced favorable comment from critics? Are potentially controversial books which are widely, and favorably, reviewed purchased by librarians in numbers comparable to the numbers of other books receiving similar reviewed? Or do potentially controversial books usually require a greater number of favorable reviews before they are purchased?

These are the questions which have led the investigator to consider examining the relationship between book reviews and the inclusion of potentially controversial books in public libraries. It is the purpose of this study to answer a number of the questions. In particular, the questions of most concern are the last two specified above, namely, are potentially controversial books which are widely, and favorably, reviewed purchased by librarians in numbers comparable to the numbers of other books receiving similar reviews? Or do potentially controversial books usually require a greater number of favorable reviews before they are purchased?

If librarians select books from reviews, and if potentially controversial books and other books are bought in comparable numbers when reviews of both groups are similar, then *in relation to reviews*—which are an example of the application of professional criteria for judging books—librarians are selecting potentially controversial books and other books by similar professional standards.

However, if librarians select books from reviews, and if potentially controversial books are bought in significantly lower numbers than other books when reviews of both groups are similar, then *in relation to reviews* librarians are not selecting potentially controversial books by the same professional standards applied to other books. If a double standard is applied to potentially controversial books, then, in the opinion of some, librarians may be practicing a form of censorship. In particular, librarians are open to this charge when there is demonstrated demand for the potentially controversial books.

DEFINITIONS

For the purposes of this study, *books* are cataloged monographs in the English language published in the United States as new titles. Excluded are reprints, revised editions, annuals, society journals, proceedings, and bound volumes of periodicals and newspapers. Also excluded are original paperbacks under $1.00 and under 100 pages, since such paperbacks may not be cataloged in some libraries surveyed in this study.

Potentially controversial books are those books which have a probability of being restricted in public libraries because, as indicated in previous research, books of their type have been restricted in libraries, and/or have been censored by law. Research indicates that books are censored primarily because they are considered obscene, heretical, or seditious.[5] In addition to sex, morals, religion, and politics, race, sexist and ethnic stereotypes, drugs, and violence have recently proved controversial aspects of books considered for library purchase.[6] In this study, *potentially controversial books* are limited to those books which treat some aspect of sex.

Book reviews are critical descriptions, evaluations, and analyses of books. This study will examine book reviews in six journals consulted by librarians.

As used in the literature of censorship, and in this study, restrictiveness is a limitation on access to potentially controversial materials. An example of restrictiveness is placing potentially controversial books in a library on shelves closed to the public while other books are placed on shelves open to the public.

Censorship has diverse meanings when applied to book selection in libraries. Unfortunately, there is no generally accepted definition. To some, selection and censorship are synonymous, since selection of one book for a library always means rejection of another book due in part to financial and space constraints, and rejection is equated with censorship. To most investigators selection is different from censorship. They believe that although selection necessitates choosing for a library only a portion of what is published, still selection is governed by professional considerations, for example, needs of people in the community, representation of differing viewpoints in a collection, accuracy of information offered, clarity of presentation, literary style, authoritativeness, and so forth. On the other hand, censoring entails rejecting or restricting use of materials for reasons other than those encompassed in normal selection and circulation procedures. Employing this definition, an example of censorship is the refusal to purchase a well-written, clearly presented, authoritative description of birth control measures requested by patrons because the librarian is personally opposed to birth control, or because some persons in the community are opposed to birth control, or because the subject of birth control is considered too controversial to be represented in a library collection. Although the line between selection and censorship is sometimes difficult to draw, this study recognizes the distinction as noted above.

OBJECTIVES AND SCOPE OF THIS STUDY

Primarily, this study asks two questions. First, given checklists of potentially controversial books and randomly selected books published within a designated time frame, how many and which of these books are owned by selected public libraries? Second, what relationship is there between the reviews the books received, or did not receive, and how many and which of these books are owned by the libraries? The answers to these questions are explored in an *ex post facto* correlational study which investigates relationships between specified dependent and independent variables.

Three hypotheses were developed for the study and tested at the .05 level of significance. They are:

> There is no significant relationship between the number of reviews a book receives and the inclusion of that book in libraries.

> There is no significant relationship between the direction of reviews (favorable, unfavorable, or neutral) a book receives and the inclusion of that book in libraries.

> There is no significant difference in the number of potentially controversial versus number of randomly selected books included in libraries if one controls for number and direction of reviews.

To test hypotheses, checklists of potentially controversial and randomly selected books were compiled. The study was limited to new adult non-fiction, published between 1972 and 1974 in the United States. The list of potentially controversial books included cataloged titles that had one or more subject headings related to sex. The checklist of randomly selected books was compiled from six review journals most frequently used by public libraries: *Booklist, Choice, Kirkus Reviews, Library Journal, Publishers Weekly,* and the *New York Times Book Review.*

The libraries initially surveyed were the 30 medium-sized municipal and joint public libraries in New Jersey with average annual total expenditures 1972–1974 of $200,000–$750,000. In those libraries, book reviews were the predominant method for selection of adult nonfiction. The 10 libraries in the final survey used all six journals, and consequently all reviews used to test hypotheses could have been read by librarians in each library.

The study assumes that librarians must be aware of the existence of books before they can select or reject titles for their libraries. While it can be argued that censorship of a book can occur before librarians are aware of the book's publication—for example, censorship can occur when librarians refuse to consult sources that review potentially controversial books—this study is solely concerned with the type of censorship that may occur when librarians have had the opportunity to become aware of a book's publication.

CONCEPTUAL FRAME FOR THIS STUDY

By extrapolating from systematic research and descriptive surveys (in particular, Eakin,[7] Fiske,[8] Farley,[9] Busha,[10] Pope,[11] England[12]), it is possible to conjecture that selection and censorship of potentially controversial books in libraries are influenced by at least six main classes of independent variables. The six classes and their subclasses are:

Class I. *LIBRARIAN VARIABLES*
  a. Librarians' Attitudes Toward Censorship and Intellectual Freedom
  b. Demographic Variables (for example, age, education)
  c. Perceived Role of Library and Librarians in the Community

Class II. *LIBRARY VARIABLES*
  a. Organizational, Administrative, and Legal Structure of the Library
  b. Selection Policies
  c. Budget

Class III. *COMMUNITY LEADER VARIABLES*
  a. Community Leaders' Attitudes Toward Censorship and Intellectual Freedom
  b. Community Leaders' Interest In and Influence Over the Library

Class IV. *COMMUNITY AND COMMUNITY ACTION VARIABLES*
  a. Census Data (for example, size and density of population served, educational levels)
  b. Pressure Groups in the Community
  c. Nature, Number, and Resolution of Censorial Actions in the Community

Class V. *MASS MEDIA VARIABLES*
  a. Coverage of Censorship and Intellectual Freedom in Mass Media (for example, book review media, newspapers)
  b. Relationship of Mass Media to the Library (for example, which book review journals are read)

Class VI. *JUDICIAL AND LEGAL VARIABLES*
a. Judicial Decisions Regarding Censorship and Intellectual Freedom
b. Federal, State, and Local Legislation Regarding Censorship and Intellectual Freedom

Figure 1 represents the relationship between the six classes of independent variables and the dependent variables of selection and censorship in libraries.

To explain censorship in libraries, it may be necessary to examine and account for all six classes of independent variables. However, previous research has been weighted toward analysis of the relationship of Librarian Variables (Class I) to restrictiveness in libraries. Apparent reasons for this emphasis are that it is librarians, rather than the public, who primarily select books, and the influence of the Fiske study (1959), which has centered attention on the role of the librarian as censor.[13]

Findings in research studies emphasizing Librarian Variables have supported Fiske's conclusions on self-censorship. However, findings in these studies are often divergent. Although librarians' attitudes toward censorship and intellectual freedom, and librarians' ages, educational attainments, and professional positions are shown to correlate positively or negatively with a willingness to censor, specific findings on similar variables differ from one study to another, and rarely have investigators attempted to relate attitudinal and demographic variables to actual practice in selecting potentially controversial books. The findings are often weak in explanatory and predictive power.

To explain censorship in libraries, it may be necessary for researchers to deviate from primary focus on Librarian Variables and, rather, to expand on multivariate models such as the model shown in Figure 1. In a small way, this study intends to build on that model by investigating selection of potentially controversial books in libraries in relation to one group of Mass Media Variables (Class V), namely book reviews. By employing books and libraries, rather than librarians as units of analysis, this study is designed to widen the scope for future research aimed at explaining censorship in libraries.

Also, book reviews have been chosen as the focus of attention because it is the investigator's opinion that their role in the selection process may prove, in later research, to be a key variable affecting restrictiveness in the public libraries.

SELECTION OF POTENTIALLY CONTROVERSIAL BOOKS

A key problem in this study was to compile a checklist of potentially controversial books to serve as the data base for comparison with a checklist of randomly selected books. Since previous research has indicated what kinds of books are considered controversial in libraries, that research was reviewed and it strongly influenced the choice of potentially controversial books for this study.

First, based primarily on previous research, the investigator decided to consider as potentially controversial books those nonfiction titles which treat some aspect of sex. Fiske, Busha, Leon,[14] and others have shown that in public libraries sex is one of the most controversial areas—if not the most controversial area. Also, research has indicated that censorship in libraries is most often directed at materials written about subjects of current controversy in society,[15] and explicit sex and alleged obscenity are such subjects. In particular, recent U.S. Supreme Court obscenity rulings, state and local obscenity legislation, and legal action against adult bookstores and theaters, massage parlors, and prostitution have focused attention on explicit sex and alleged obscenity as matters of current national concern.

While this study recognizes that books dealing with sex are not considered controversial by all people in present-day society, still such books are *potentially* controversial—according to the definition of potentially controversial books adopted in this study—in that research indicates they have a *probability* of being censored in public libraries. Also, since studies show that there is no agreement on which books are "offensive" or "too explicit" in their treatment of sex, in a sense all books dealing with sex have a *probability* of being offensive to someone.

Second, the investigator decided to limit the study to books which had been published recently, specifically from 1972 through 1974. The cutoff date of 1974 was necessary to allow time for review coverage in journals surveyed. This decision was influenced by several considerations: the investigator's interest in contemporary self-censorship in public libraries, the knowledge that public libraries primarily purchase current publications, and the belief that questionnaires from librarians—necessary for this study—would probably prove more reliable and have a higher return rate if questions referred to use of recent reviews rather than to use of reviews published in the distant past.

LIBRARIAN VARIABLES

Attitudes Toward Intellectual Freedom and Censorship

Demographic Variables

Perceived Role of Library & Librarians in the Community

LIBRARY VARIABLES

Organizational, Administrative and Legal Structure of the Library

Selection Policies

Budget

COMMUNITY LEADER VARIABLES

Attitudes Toward Intellectual Freedom and Censorship

Community Leaders' Interest in and Influence over the Library

DEPENDENT

Selection and Censorship in Libraries

VARIABLES

Census Data

Pressure Groups in the Community

Nature, Number and Resolution of Censorial Actions

COMMUNITY AND COMMUNITY ACTION VARIABLES

Coverage of Intellectual Freedom and Censorship

Relationship of Mass Media to Library

Judicial Decisions Regarding Intellectual Freedom and Censorship

Federal, State, and Local Legislation Regarding Intellectual Freedom and Censorship

JUDICIAL AND LEGAL VARIABLES

MASS MEDIA VARIABLES

FIGURE I

Once the decision was made to limit the study to books potentially controversial for their treatment of sex, the problem still remained of selecting particular books and compiling a checklist.

In previous studies, the problem was solved in various ways. Some studies used short checklists, usually of between 20 and 50 titles, of books that actually had been banned by law or censored in public libraries, for example, Miller's *Tropic of Cancer* and Salinger's *Catcher in the Rye*. Others used checklists of potentially controversial best-sellers on the assumption that best-sellers have demonstrated demand and therefore would either be in libraries or would have come up for selection decisions and been rejected. And some studies used checklists including both censored books and best-sellers.

Often the choice of titles for the checklists was arbitrary and, consequently, it was easy to fault findings based on arbitrary lists. For example, one survey noted, "In our judgment the greatest flaw in our survey was the lack of an objective yardstick for determining titles to be included in the checklist."[16]

This study attempts to introduce an objective yardstick for choosing potentially controversial books by compiling a checklist composed exclusively of nonfiction with one or more subject headings related to sex, and including all nonfiction published between 1972 and 1974 with those subject headings which meet the definition of book used in this study.

Although it is acknowledged that subject classification is not exact—that the same book may be assigned different subject headings by different catalogers—still this study's use of almost 100 subject headings and several printed catalogs allows for identification of a body of books generally acknowledged to deal with some aspect of sex. The method of using subject headings and of including all books with specified subject headings is less limiting than using selected best-sellers and banned books.

To select potentially controversial books on the basis of subject headings, several bibliographies were consulted. These were:

The Catalog of the Institute for Sex Research. First, the *Catalog of the Social and Behavioral Sciences Monograph Section of the Library of the Institute for Sex Research, Indiana University, Bloomington, Indiana* (1975) was thoroughly searched. The Institute for Sex Research was founded in 1947 by Dr. Alfred C. Kinsey as a nonprofit corporation devoted to basic research in human sexual behavior. The Institute's collections include a Library and an Archive comprised of three major areas—the social and behavioral

sciences, erotica, and sexual ephemera. The printed catalog the investigator looked at included books in the social and behavioral sciences, the area most likely of the three to include books considered for public library collections.

The printed catalog consists of books cataloged by the Institute through September 1973, volumes consisting of "historical materials relating to human sex behavior, including histories of early sex education, marriage, abortion, contraception, women's rights, sex ethics, religion, sex laws, venereal disease and prostitution, as well as contemporary research in sex behavior and attitudes." Although the printed catalog does not include the Library's holdings in erotic literature and art, bibliographies and censorship studies of such materials are included. The Library's collection emphasizes Western works from the nineteenth and twentieth centuries.

The Institute's catalog basically follows Anglo-American cataloging rules and the subject headings, though developed by the Institute, are traditional in format. However, since the Institute's library is a special library devoted to sex research, the subject headings it gives to books often offer more in-depth information about a book than can be found in the cataloging of other libraries.

The catalog of the Institute for Sex Research was consulted by the investigator for several reasons: the catalog offers evidence of how a major library collecting books on sex defines the subject area (of particular interest were the subject headings assigned to the books), the subject headings used in the catalog offer a fairly objective, consistent measure for locating other cataloged books with the same or similar subject headings which can be assumed to relate to the subject of sex as defined by the Institute's library; and the catalog includes an extensive listing of books published in 1972 and the beginning of 1973 (about one-third the time frame for this study) on the subject of sex, especially as applied to the social and behavioral sciences. In all, 157 books with one or more subject headings related to sex, published 1972-1973, were selected from the Institute's catalog for inclusion in this study's checklist of potentially controversial books.

Library of Congress Guide to Subject Headings. Once the decision had been made to select potentially controversial books on the basis of whether the books had been cataloged and had subject headings related to sex, the latest edition of *Library of Congress Subject Headings* and its supplements were checked in order to note the correspondence between subject headings in the Library of Congress guide and subject headings in the catalog of the Institute for Sex Research, and to compile a list of subject headings related to sex that could be used to locate 1972–1974 publications in *Library of Congress Catalog. Books: Subjects.*

As might be expected, the general areas of sex are defined similarly in the Library of Congress guide to subject headings and in the catalog of the Institute for Sex Research. Sometimes both use the same exact subject headings, for example, both use United States—Sexual Beliefs and Customs, and Homosexuality. Occasionally, only the format differs, for example, the Institute for Sex Research uses the subject heading Sex Psychology, and the Library of Congress uses Sex (Psychology). However, many subject headings differ in terminology, although the subject areas are the same, for example, the Institute uses Sex Education while the Library of Congress uses Sex Instruction.

Since the next stage in this study was to search *Library of Congress Catalog. Books: Subjects* for 1972–1974 books related to sex, a complete list of Library of Congress subject headings related to sex was compiled. The subject headings that proved particularly useful in searching *Library of Congress Catalog. Books: Subject* are the following:

Sex	Women's Liberation Movement
Sex Customs	Men
Sex Instruction	Marriage
Sex (Psychology)	Divorce
Sexual Ethics	Abortion
Sex in Art	Birth Control
Sex Role	Conception-Prevention
Homosexuality	Rape
Lesbianism	Adultery
Women-Sexual	Photography, Erotic
Behavior	Sex in Moving Pictures

Library of Congress Catalog. Books: Subjects. Using the list of subject headings compiled from *Library of Congress Subject Headings*, a thorough search of the *Library of Congress Catalog. Books: Subjects* 1972 through April 1976 was made to identify all books published 1972–1974 cataloged by the Library of Congress that had one or more subject headings related to sex, that met the definition of book adopted in this study, and that had not been found in the catalog of the Institute for Sex Research.

American Book Publishing Record. In addition, the *American Book Publishing Record* for 1972–1975 was searched under appropriate subjects and Dewey Decimal classifications to locate titles not found in *Library of Congress Catalog. Books: Subjects* and the catalog of the Institute for Sex Research. As one might expect, almost all books

located in the *American Book Publishing Record* had previously been found in the other two catalogs. However, use of the *American Book Publishing Record* did enable the investigator to pick up some titles not found in the Library of Congress catalog, in particular paperbacks that met this study's definition of book. Also, *American Book Publishing Record* included some popular and ephemeral titles not included in *Library of Congress Catalog. Books: Subjects.*

As mentioned above, the catalog of the Institute for Sex Research turned up 157 books for this study's checklist of potentially controversial books. In addition, 445 potentially controversial books were identified in *Library of Congress Catalog. Books: Subjects* and the *American Book Publishing Record.* Thus, the total number of books potentially controversial for their treatment of sex, published 1972–1974 and meeting this study's definition of book, is 602 books.

This study's checklist of potentially controversial books includes all 602 titles. No doubt some of the titles on the checklist have a higher probability than others of being censored in libraries—for example, Pope's study indicated that illustrated books on sex are more controversial than non-illustrated books on sex[17]—but all books on the checklist deal with some aspect of sex and thus, according to previous research and definitions adopted for this study, are *potentially* controversial.

SELECTION OF REVIEW JOURNALS

Although the selection of potentially controversial books for this study was at first problematic, the choice of book review journals was never in doubt. Recent surveys, texts on book selection, and reference annuals all indicate that, currently, the general, nonspecialized review journals most widely used by public librarians are:

Booklist, a semi-monthly publication of the American Library Association, used especially by public and school librarians. Each issue contains short reviews of books recommended for library purchase. Although opinions expressed in some reviews are based on the judgments of library subject specialists, the reviews are written by the journal's editorial staff. For 1972–1975, *Booklist* averaged 2500 reviews of adult titles annually.

Choice, a monthly publication of the Association of College and Research Libraries, a division of the American Library Association, is used primarily by college librarians, although many public and special librarians also consult it regularly. Each issue includes short, unsigned reviews written by college faculty members, all subject specialists. *Choice* reviewed about 6500 books annually 1972–1975.

Kirkus Reviews, published by Kirkus Service, a division of the *New York Review of Books*, is a semi-monthly intended for booksellers as well as public librarians. All reviews are staff written from publishers' galley proofs, and they appear approximately six weeks to two months before publication date. About 2700 adult titles were reviewed annually 1972–1975.

Library Journal is published semi-monthly by R. R. Bowker, a division of the Xerox Corporation, for an audience of public, school, special, and college libraries. Reviews are written—and signed—by librarians and academics. *LJ* averaged 6000 reviews annually 1972–1975.

The *New York Times Book Review* is published weekly as part of the Sunday edition of the *New York Times*. Although primarily intended for the general public, it is used extensively for public library book selection since it is an indicator of what books patrons will request. Reviews are both long and short and are written by subject specialists, professional reviewers, and well-known literary figures. About 1625 adult titles were reviewed annually 1972–1975.

Publishers Weekly is also published by R. R. Bowker. Reviews appear in the "Forecasts" section of this weekly and are used by booksellers as well as by public and academic libraries. All reviews are from publishers' galleys, are staff written, and are published several weeks before publication date. Some reviews are based on the opinions of outside readers, others on the opinions of *PW* staff. *PW* averaged 3000 reviews of adult titles annually for 1972–1975.

SELECTION OF PUBLIC LIBRARIES

Early in this study, the decision was made to survey only medium-sized libraries with annual total expenditures for the years 1972–1974 of between $200,000 and $750,000. This decision to control for budget was influenced by several considerations. Research findings have shown that total budget is the best indicator of size of book collection.[18] Since this study intends to compare the sizes of book collections of 1972–1974 publications, the investigator wanted to select libraries that had comparable funds to purchase those books. Libraries with annual total expenditures of $200,000 to $750,000 would have funds sufficient to purchase several thousand new adult nonfiction titles annually; therefore, a number of titles on this study's checklists were

likely to be owned by these libraries. In addition, libraries in this class would have funds to purchase review journals (if they wanted them) and to employ staff to read reviews (if they chose to use reviews for selection). And, the investigator was more familiar with selection procedures in medium-sized libraries than with selection procedures in either small or large libraries.

The total expenditures figures of $200,000 and $750,000 were chosen for this study primarily because these limits correspond to limits used in recent research which stratified libraries by budget[19] and because the figures were appropriate for the public libraries surveyed in this investigation.

Although the investigator originally intended to survey public libraries in several states, a decision was made to limit the survey to libraries in New Jersey. This decision was dictated primarily by the practical consideration that the investigator would have to visit each library to check the public catalog for book holdings. Also, by limiting the study to a single state, chances were enhanced that the statistical data used to compare libraries would be similar from library to library.

In addition to published statistics, this investigator had access to the file of public library statistics kept at the New Jersey State Library, and thus the published statistics could be supplemented when necessary. For example, although the published statistics include only figures for total materials budget, visits to the state library allowed access to figures broken down by book budget (usually adult and juvenile), periodicals budget, and audiovisual materials. The statistics for book budget for adult books were important for one phase of this study.

While there is little doubt that by limiting this investigation to a single state, the possibility for generalizing findings beyond New Jersey is curtailed, still the practical considerations mentioned above were heeded in order to enable the investigator to complete this study within a reasonable time period with financial resources available.

Selection of New Jersey Libraries

The legal basis for library service in New Jersey allows for public library service by a variety of types of libraries: area libraries, association libraries, county libraries, federation, joint libraries, municipal libraries, and regional libraries. Also, New Jersey's statewide plan for library service delineates three levels of library service: the first level or local library service, the second level or area library service, and the third level or research library service.

Given the complexity of the New Jersey public library system, and the differing responsibilities of public libraries within that system, it was difficult to decide which public libraries to include in this study. Thus a pretest in four New Jersey medium-sized public libraries was conducted to obtain data to assist the investigator in deciding which libraries to survey.

A systematic sample of 200 books was drawn from the population of 602 potentially controversial books, and *Book Review Index* was searched to locate all reviews of the 200 books in the six journals. In addition, the investigator learned which review journals were used for selection in the four libraries. Two libraries used six journals and two libraries used all journals with the exception of *Choice.*

A check of the public catalog in each library to determine holdings of the 200 potentially controversial books provided evidence that for the four libraries surveyed, a relationship was apparent between number of reviews a book receives and number of libraries owning that book. In each library, those books that received a higher number of reviews in the six journals were owned in greater percentages than books receiving fewer reviews. Books that were not reviewed in any of the six journals fared poorly; of the 73 books with no reviews, one library owned four titles, one owned three, and two libraries owned one title each.

At this time, the decision was made to limit further investigation to municipal and joint libraries. This decision was dictated primarily by two considerations. First, all municipal and joint libraries in New Jersey function at the first or local level of service, and it seemed reasonable to limit the study to an analysis and comparison of book collections of libraries with similar service responsibilities. Second, these libraries serve communities for which recent census data are readily accessible, and use of these libraries would allow for easy analysis of detailed census data if such analysis proved necessary in a later stage of this study.

In New Jersey, a municipal library is one established by law following a referendum in which a majority of voters vote to establish such a library. It is supported by taxes and is governed by a seven-member board appointed by the mayor. A joint library is one established by law following a referendum in two or more municipalities in which the majority of voters vote to establish such a library. It is governed by a board appointed by the mayors of the participating municipalities.

New Jersey public library statistics show that 30 municipal and joint libraries had average annual total expenditures of between $200,000 and $750,000 for 1972–1974. These 30 libraries constitute the population of public libraries in this study.

The 30 libraries are located in 12 of New Jersey's 21 counties. In 1974, they served 1,324,750 people, 18 percent of the 7,324,365 people (estimated) served by public libraries in New Jersey. Census data show that the communities served by the libraries vary in size, median income, median school years completed by those 25 and over, and median age. Differences among communities are welcome, since they can indicate variables that may relate to differences in public library collections.

Once the 30 public libraries in this study were identified, it was necessary to determine each library's use of review media during the time period when 1972–1974 books were considered for purchase.

The investigator decided to send a short pretested questionnaire to the director of each of the 30 libraries to solicit information on which journals were used for selection of adult nonfiction during the years 1972–1976, which journals were used most heavily and in what relative proportions, which sources other than reviews were used for selection, and who did the selecting in each library.

Analysis of the data collected from the 30 questionnaire responses (27 questionnaires were completely usable and three were partially usable) allows for the following generalizations:

The six journals investigated in this study are widely used in the 30 libraries. *Library Journal* and the *New York Times Book Review* are used by all 30 libraries; *Booklist* by 29 libraries (97 percent); *Publishers Weekly* by 28 libraries (93 percent); *Kirkus* by 27 libraries (90 percent); and *Choice* by 24 libraries (80 percent).

The figures for percent of total book purchases from the six journals also indicate the preeminent position of the six journals among all reviewing journals used in the 30 public libraries. On the average, 86 percent of all book orders of adult nonfiction in the 30 libraries was accounted for by reviews in the six journals. Only three percent of orders from reviews were accounted for by all other reviewing media.

Library Journal and *Kirkus* were the most heavily used of the six journals. Each was ranked the most important selection source by 10 libraries, one-third of all libraries surveyed. *Library Journal* was the first, second, or third choice of 25 libraries (83 percent), and *Kirkus* was the first, second, or third choice of 21 libraries (70 percent). On the other hand, *Choice* was clearly the least used of the six journals, with only five libraries (17 percent) ranking it in first, second, or third position, and six libraries not using it for selection. *Booklist*, the *New York Times Book Review*, and *Publishers Weekly* were each the first, second, or third choices of one-third to one-half of all the libraries. Interestingly, each of the six journals was the first choice in at least one library.

Perhaps the most striking, and potentially important, data are those pertaining to the percent of total book purchases made from reviews. For all 30 libraries, the average was 89 percent, indicating that in the estimate of librarians, 89 percent of all the adult nonfiction selected for purchase by the 30 libraries during the years 1972–1976 was selected on the basis of published reviews. Actually, the figures may even be higher, for informal interviews with librarians in some of the 30 libraries—held later in this investigation—indicated that patron requests are often checked against reviews and the reviews determine whether requests are honored. Clearly, reviews are the major influence on book selection in these 30 libraries.

Data also indicate that in the majority of the 30 libraries, selection was by a variety of methods in each library. Methods most widely used and ranked highest in importance in the selection of adult nonfiction were selection by several librarians subject to final approval by director, chief selector, or selection committee (used by 25 libraries, 83 percent), and selection by director of library (used by 23 libraries, 77 percent). In addition, 17 libraries (57 percent) used selection by several librarians selecting independently, and 16 libraries (58 percent) used selection by a chief selector other than director.

Of all the methods used, selection by several librarians subject to final approval by director, chief selector, or selection committee was most often ranked first in accounting for most books selected—13 libraries (43 percent) ranked that method as most important. Two other methods were each ranked first by seven libraries (23 percent): selection by director of library and selection by a chief selector other than director.

After analyzing the questionnaires, it was necessary to decide which of the 30 libraries would be surveyed for holdings of books on this study's checklists.

Given the objectives of this study, it became apparent that the major consideration in selecting libraries to visit was that the librarians in those libraries could have had an opportunity to become aware of the books on the checklists. Again, this study assumes that selection and censorship of a book cannot occur until there is awareness of a book's publication. In order to ensure that librarians in the study had an opportunity to

become aware of all books on the checklists, the investigator decided to survey only libraries which used all six journals, and to include on the checklists only those books which were reviewed in one or more of the six journals. In that way, one could know that librarians in the survey could have been aware of each book's publication. There was, of course, no way for the investigator to be certain that each review in each journal was read by a selector in each library. Data collected from the questionnaires indicated that while the 30 libraries all used five or six of the journals, 19 libraries definitely used all six journals for selection. Since it was not necessary to survey all 19 libraries to determine statistical validity, it was decided to select 10 of the 19 libraries for the survey of collections.

In selecting the 10 libraries, a stratified random sampling plan was employed. A decision was made to stratify on the basis of book budget, since research does indicate that budget is a key variable influencing size of collection. The sample of 19 libraries was stratified on the basis of average annual book budget for the years 1972–1974, when most of the books on this study's checklists would have been purchased or rejected. On the basis of the data, the 19 libraries can be placed into three main groupings: six libraries with average annual book budgets, 1972–1974, of $27,000–$37,999; six libraries with budgets of $38,000–$48,999; and seven libraries with budgets $50,000–$109,999. These groupings indicate that although all 19 libraries are considered medium-sized libraries, still approximately one-third have comparatively low book budgets, one-third are in the middle-range, and one-third have comparatively high budgets.

In choosing the 10 libraries, it was decided to stratify proportionally according to the annual book budget figures. Thus, the investigator could be certain that at least one-third of the 10 libraries chosen would be in the low-budget group, one third in the middle range, and one-third in the high budget group, and perhaps comparisons among groups could be made during data analysis. Consequently, three libraries were selected randomly from the low-budget group, three from the middle-range group, and four from the high budget group.

Among the 10 libraries, if book budget is a key variable in the selection of books on this study's checklists, one may expect that the libraries with budgets $50,000–$109,999 will own more potentially controversial and randomly selected books than libraries in Group I, with budgets $27,000–$37,999, and that libraries in each group may own comparable numbers of books.

TABLE 1

STATISTICAL DATA FOR 10 LIBRARIES IN FINAL SURVEY OF COLLECTIONS, INCLUDING COMMUNITY DATA

Library	Average Annual Book Budget 1972–1974	Average Annual Total Expenditures 1972–1974	Population Served 1974	Per Capita Local Expenditures 1974	Median School Years Completed by Those 25 and Over	Median Income	Median Age
I	$108,973	$625,367	43,635	$16.07	12.7	$14,498	35.5
II	77,000	478,776	82,555	6.40	11.6	11,947	38.2
III	59,902	546,681	73,365	8.27	11.4	10,542	34.3
IV	54,876	307,764	45,310	7.05	12.7	13,495	19.6
V	49,904	399,425	26,245	16.32	15.1	16,500	27.3
VI	38,748	303,613	24,660	13.14	12.7	13,564	37.9
VII	38,614	240,279	37,775	6.66	13.2	14,792	30.5
VIII	30,333	248,171	23,465	11.22	12.9	17,639	36.7
IX	29,990	266,756	44,495	6.19	10.0	6,395	43.9
X	27,333	215,140	29,645	8.67	12.1	11,693	32.0

TABLE 1a

RELATIVE IMPORTANCE (IN PERCENTAGES) OF REVIEW JOURNALS AND OTHER SOURCES IN ACCOUNTING FOR BOOK ORDERS 1972-1976 IN LIBRARIES SURVEYED (N = 10)

(1)	(2)	(3)	(4)	(5)	(6)	(7)	(8)	(9)	(10)	(11)	(12)
Library	Booklist	Choice	Kirkus	Library Journal	New York Times	Publishers Weekly	Six Journals	Other Journals	All Journals	Patrons	Other
I	15%	3%	50%	15%	2%	5%	90%	0%	90%	10%	0%
II	10	1	10	65	5	4	95	0	95	0	5
III	20	15	25	25	10	5	100	0	100	0	0
IV	25	1	14	30	14	7	91	.5	91.5	6	2.5
V	4	10	35	30	5	2	86	0	86	14	0
VI	8	1	25	37	6	1	78	3	81	8	11
VII	40	3	28	5	10	1	87	3	90	5	5
VIII	20	15	15	10	15	15	90	7	97	3	0
IX	2	1	15	25	20	25	88	0	88	5	7
X	3	1	36	34	2	4	80	5	85	0	15
Mean	15%	5%	25%	28%	9%	7%	86%		90%		
Median	13	2	25	28	8	5	89		90		

TABLE 1b

RANK ORDER OF IMPORTANCE OF SELECTION PROCEDURES IN LIBRARIES SURVEYED
(1972-1976)
(N = 10)

Selection Procedure	Rank Order of Importance						Total Number of Libraries Using Procedure (N = 10)
	First Number of Libraries	Second Number of Libraries	Third Number of Libraries	Fourth Number of Libraries	Fifth Number of Libraries	Sixth Number of libraries	
Selection by several librarians subject to final approval of director, etc.	6	1	1				8 (80%)
Selection by director	1	2	2		1		6 (60%)
Selection by several librarians selecting independently		1	3	1			5 (50%)
Selection by chief selector other than director	3	2		1			6 (60%)
Selection by central selection committee				1		1	2 (20%)
Other					1	1	2 (20%)

Tables 1, 1a, and 1b display statistical data on the 10 libraries whose collections will be surveyed. Table 1 includes information on expenditures and community data, Table 1a provides data on the relative importance of review journals for selection; and Table 1b delineates the rank order of importance of selection procedures in the libraries surveyed.

SAMPLING PLAN FOR POTENTIALLY CONTROVERSIAL BOOKS

The 602 potentially controversial books identified for this study constitute the population of 1972–1974 publications that met this study's definition of book and that had one or more subject headings related to sex.

A thorough search of *Book Review Index* for the years 1971 through April 1976 was made to iden-

tify all reviews of each of the 602 books in the six journals: *Booklist, Choice, Kirkus, Library Journal, New York Times Book Review*, and *Publishers Weekly*. *Book Review Index* indexes all six journals. It was necessary to search the 1971 volume to pick up prepublication reviews of 1972 books; the 1975 and 1976 volumes were searched to locate late reviews of 1973-1974 publications.

As stated above, the decision was made to include on this study's check-lists of potentially controversial and randomly selected books only those titles which had received one or more reviews in the six journals. Since 217 of the 602 potentially controversial books were not reviewed in any of the six journals, those books were eliminated from consideration for inclusion on the checklist of potentially controversial books. The 385 books which had received one or more reviews could be included.

TABLE 2

NUMBER OF REVIEWS RECEIVED BY ALL POTENTIALLY CONTROVERSIAL BOOKS
(N = 602)

	Number of Reviews						
	6	5	4	3	2	1	0
Number of books	13	37	55	83	86	111	217
Percent of books	2.16	6.15	9.14	13.79	14.28	18.44	36.04

At this point in the investigation, several considerations came to the fore and influenced the decision of how many titles to include on the checklist of potentially controversial books. The major consideration was the study's objective of testing three hypotheses, and in particular, the third hypothesis: that there is no significant difference in the number of potentially controversial books versus number of randomly selected books included in libraries if one controls for number and direction of reviews.

Given this hypothesis, it is necessary to pay particular attention to number of reviews received by potentially controversial books. Table 3 shows the number of reviews received by the 385

a random sample of 50 books was selected. Thus, a total of 250 books was chosen.

SAMPLING PLAN FOR RANDOMLY SELECTED BOOKS

The next step in this study was to compile a checklist of randomly selected books to test Hypothesis 3.

Again, the checklist was limited to books reviewed in six journals. The decision was made to select randomly 360 books from the journals, with 60 books selected randomly from each journal. The figure of 360 approximates the figure of

TABLE 3

NUMBER OF REVIEWS RECEIVED BY POTENTIALLY CONTROVERSIAL BOOKS WHICH HAD ONE OR MORE REVIEWS

(N = 385)

Number of Reviews	Number of Books	
6	13 } 50	(13%)
5	37 }	
4	55	(14%)
3	83	(22%)
2	86	(22%)
1	111	(29%)

potentially controversial books which had one or more review. Table 3 indicates that only 13 books received six reviews and only 37 books received five reviews. Since the pretest in four libraries showed that books that receive five or six reviews are owned in significantly higher percentages than books receiving four or fewer reviews, this group of books is important to consider.

Since Table 3 shows that the upper limit on number of potentially controversial books with five and six reviews is 50 books, the investigator decided to accept 50 books as the upper limit for number of books in each of the other review categories as well. That is, the study would begin to control for number of reviews by including on the checklist of potentially controversial books 50 books with five or six reviews, 50 books with four reviews, 50 books with three reviews, 50 books with two reviews, and 50 books with one review. Thus the checklist of potentially controversial books would include 250 titles. The same number of titles, stratified by number of reviews, would constitute the checklist of randomly selected books used to test Hypothesis 3.

To compile the checklist of 250 potentially controversial books, first the population of 385 potentially controversial books was stratified by number of reviews as shown in Table 3. All books with five or six reviews were selected for the checklist. Then, from each of the other four strata,

385, the number of potentially controversial books with one or more reviews. All six journals were sampled equally because all were used for selection in the public libraries surveyed, and potentially each journal might have influenced an unknown number of selection decisions.

Sampling of Review Journals

In sampling from each journal, the journal's author-title indexes of books published 1972–1974 were used. For each journal, all the index pages with listings of reviews of books published 1972–1974 were collected and numbered sequentially. In some journals these indexes included titles and authors of reviews of books published in 1971 as well as 1975. Some of the lists also had to be "cleaned up" to remove duplicate listings.

A table of random numbers was used to determine which page would be searched, and which item on the page would be selected. For each listing, the book review was located. If the review was for a 1972–1974 nonfiction title that met this study's definition of book, the title was selected for inclusion on the checklist of randomly selected books. If not, the next listing on the appropriate index page was searched, until a book was located meeting the necessary requirements. This process was repeated until 60 books had been selected from each journal, and a checklist of 360 titles was compiled. The process was laborious, but it did give the investigator confidence that the checklist had been compiled randomly and systematically.

Each title was checked in the *National Union Catalog* or *American Book Publishing Record*, or another catalog, if necessary, to verify publication date and to establish main entry for checking public library catalogs. This checking was especially necessary in the case of books selected from prepublication reviews, since there was always the possibility the books reviewed had actually never been published.

Checklist of Randomly Selected Books to Test Hypothesis 3

A checklist of 250 randomly selected books was needed to test Hypothesis 3. As noted above, a checklist of 250 potentially controversial books stratified by number of reviews had already been compiled. It was decided that the 250 randomly selected books would be chosen from the population of 360 randomly selected books used to test Hypothesis 1 and Hypothesis 2. All 360 books were checked against *Book Review Index* to determine the number of reviews each had received. Table 4 indicates the number of reviews received.

If Table 4 is compared with Table 3, it can be seen that the percentages of potentially controversial books and randomly selected books stratified by number of reviews are dissimilar (r =.728, which is not significant at the .05 level). Significantly more randomly selected books than potentially controversial books received five or six reviews, and significantly fewer randomly selected books received only one review.

Since the checklist of 250 randomly selected books was going to be compared with the checklist of potentially controversial books, it was necessary to delete from the listing of 360 books those titles with subject headings related to sex. Six titles were deleted, two with five reviews, two with four reviews, and two with one review. The remaining population of 354 books was stratified by number of reviews, and 50 books were selected

randomly from each stratum. Thus, a total of 250 books was selected to comprise the checklist of randomly selected books to test Hypothesis 3.

CODING OF REVIEWS

The next step in this study was to code all reviews for direction. The directional scale has three categories: favorable, unfavorable, and neutral.

FAVORABLE REVIEW: The review is an overall positive evaluation. Although the reviewer may make one or more unfavorable comments about the book (e.g., "sometimes tedious," "occasionally dull"), still the positive comments outweigh the negative. Some reviewers indicate forthrightly that the book is recommended (e.g., "public libraries will have a ready audience for this title," "a valuable contribution to the literature"). Other reviewers make a more cautious judgment, but nevertheless end up giving a positive evaluation (e.g., "if expectations aren't too high, this may prove perfectly satisfying to the audience that enjoys this kind of category fiction," or "the book offers no final definitions of bisexuality but does provide lots of provocative discussion").

UNFAVORABLE REVIEW: The review is an overall negative evaluation. Although the reviewer may make one or more favorable comments about the book (e.g., "sometimes amusing," "occasionally interesting"), still the negative comments outweigh the positive. Some reviewers indicate forthrightly that the book is not recommended (e.g., "unnecessary for your library," "wait for a better treatment of . . . ") Other reviewers express their negative opinions in a more personal manner (e.g., "contributes about as much wisdom, information and entertainment as a daytime TV panel show—not the kind with experts on it, the kind with movie stars masquerading as experts," "when an exhausting book's only memorable scene is sex with a bear, that doesn't say much for the book").

NEUTRAL REVIEW: A review is judged *neutral* for one of two reasons: *the review gives scope of the book but offers no positive or negative evaluation,* or *the review is both positive and negative with no overall positive or negative evaluation.* In neutral reviews it is not possible to decide with assurance whether or

TABLE 4

NUMBER OF REVIEWS RECEIVED BY RANDOMLY SELECTED BOOKS
(N = 360)

5-6	91 (25.28%)
4	70 (19.44%)
3	66 (18.335%)
2	69 (19.17%)
1	64 (17.785%)

not the reviewer recommends the book. Examples of equivocal statements in neutral reviews are: "a competent interviewer, she may strike some as being too freewheeling in some of her interpretations and conjectures," "although she writes objectively...this book does not really penetrate Reuther's character."

A test for inter-coder agreement was conducted to determine whether the investigator's coding of reviews for direction was in sufficient agreement with the coding of several judges. In conducting the reliability test, three judges were each asked to code 12 reviews for direction. Two of the three judges are public librarians familiar with selecting books from the six journals; the third judge was a faculty member at the Graduate School of Library Service, Rutgers—The State University, familiar with reviews in the six journals. The investigator gave each judge instructions on coding, definitions developed for categories, and examples of specific reviews coded in each category.

Based on empirical evidence obtained from use of Holsti's and Scott's formulas,[20] it seemed sufficiently clear that the three judges would agree with the investigator to a sufficiently high degree on which reviews belonged in which of the three categories on the directional scale. In addition, 44 library school students in Collection Development classes at the Rutgers University Graduate School of Library Service each coded the 12 reviews for direction. The great majority of judges agreed with the investigator to a very high degree on which reviews belonged in which directional category.

SURVEY OF PUBLIC LIBRARIES

After the checklists had been compiled, the investigator was ready to visit the 10 public libraries selected for the survey of collections.

The checklist of potentially controversial books included 250 titles. The master checklist of randomly selected books included 360 titles to test Hypothesis 1 and Hypothesis 2, and 250 of the 360 titles would be used to test Hypothesis 3. Thus, in all 610 books were checked in each library's public catalog.

ANALYSIS OF DATA

Analysis of Data Related to the Total Population of Potentially Controversial Books

Data on the 602 books were collected for the number of reviews received by each book in the six journals surveyed, number of books reviewed

by each journal, direction of reviews, and agreement among journals on direction of reviews.

Approximately 64 percent of the potentially controversial books (385 books) received one or more reviews in the six journals. Almost one-third of the books received three to six reviews in the six journals. Since a recent survey (1975) sponsored by the Association of American Publishers and the American Library Association—Resources and Technical Services Division found that "currently fewer than 10% of all books published in the United States each year are reviewed,"[21] the potentially controversial books in this study probably received more reviews than did books in many other subject areas. Also, of course, many of the potentially controversial books were reviewed not only in the six journals, but also in additional journals.

The journals varied widely in the number of potentially controversial books reviewed. *Library Journal* clearly ranked first in the number reviewed (291 books), and the *New York Times Book Review* ranked sixth, or last (73 books). It is interesting, at this point, to consider statistics for the *total number of all adult books* (as distinguished from juvenile books) reviewed by the six journals during 1972–1975—when most of the potentially controversial books in this study would have been considered for review in all six journals.[22]

The data show that *Choice* ranked first in number of adult books reviewed (26,170 books) and the *New York Times Book Review* ranked sixth, or last (6,500 books). There is limited correspondence between journal rankings in regard to potentially controversial books reviewed and all adult books reviewed. *Library Journal* is ranked first or second in both cases, and *Booklist* and the *New York Times Book Review* are ranked fifth and sixth in both cases. However, *Choice*, which ranked first among journals in reviews of all adult titles, ranked only fourth among the six journals in reviewing of potentially controversial books. *Publishers Weekly* and *Kirkus* ranked higher in reviewing potentially controversial books than in reviewing all adult books, and both journals challenged *Library Journal*, the leader. Although *Library Journal* reviewed 50 percent more adult titles than did *Publishers Weekly* and *Kirkus*, it reviewed only 11 percent more potentially controversial books than *Publishers Weekly* and only 13 percent more than *Kirkus*.

Table 5 combines the figures, and shows the percentages of total reviews accounted for by each journal. For example, it can be seen that *Library Journal* accounted for 29 percent of all reviews of potentially controversial books and 29 percent of all reviews of adult titles—similar percentages.

TABLE 5

PERCENTAGES IN EACH JOURNAL OF REVIEWS OF POTENTIALLY CONTROVERSIAL BOOKS AND OF THE TOTAL NUMBER OF 1972-1975 JOURNAL REVIEWS

Review Journal	Percentage of Total Reviews of Potentially Controversial Books (N = 1,015) in Each Journal	Percentage of Total Reviews of 1972-1975 Books (N = 89,882) in Each Journal
Library Journal	29	29
Publishers Weekly	22	13
Kirkus	21	12
Choice	14	29
Booklist	8	11
New York Times Book Review	7	7

TABLE 6

DUPLICATION AMONG JOURNALS IN REVIEWING POTENTIALLY CONTROVERSIAL BOOKS
(N = 385)

Review Media	Number of Titles Reviewed by					
	No Other Medium		One Other Medium		Two or More Other Media	
	Number	Percentage	Number	Percentage	Number	Percentage
Library Journal (n = 291)	47	16.15	67	23.02	177	60.83
Publishers Weekly (n = 222)	27	12.16	34	15.32	161	72.52
Kirkus (n = 208)	6	2.88	36	17.31	166	79.81
Choice (n = 137)	24	17.52	27	19.71	86	62.77
Booklist (n = 84)	5	5.95	5	5.95	74	88.10
New York Times Book Review (n = 73)	2	2.74	3	4.11	68	93.15
Totals	111		172		732	

However, *Choice* accounted for 14 percent of all reviews of potentially controversial books and 29 percent of all reviews of adult titles—dissimilar percentages. There is no significant relationship between the percentage of total reviews of potentially controversial books accounted for by each journal and the percentage of total reviews of all adult titles accounted for by each journal (the correlation coefficient obtained was .53, which is not significant at the .05 level).

Although *Choice* reviewed fewer potentially controversial books in relation to all adult titles than might be expected, *Publishers Weekly* and *Kirkus* reviewed more potentially controversial books than might be expected.

Since reviews in *Publishers Weekly* and *Kirkus* are heavily used by trade booksellers as well as by librarians, that audience of booksellers may account for the journals' comparatively strong attention to books dealing with sex. That is, books about sex may sell better in trade bookstores than do books on many other subjects, and journals that review for booksellers will attempt to inform them of books that have a probability of selling well.

Duplication of Reviews

A question that may arise is how much duplication of titles reviewed was there among the six journals, for example, how many titles were reviewed by only one journal, and how many titles by more than two journals? The question is especially important in relation to what journals are used by librarians for selection. For instance, if one journal is reviewing many unique titles and some librarians are not using that journal, then the chances of the unique titles coming to the attention of those librarians are curtailed.

Table 6 shows the amount of duplication among journals in the reviewing of potentially controversial books. As can be seen from the table, the journals with the greatest incidence of duplication are *Booklist* and the *New York Times Book Review*, the two journals that reviewed the least number of books. Eighty-eight percent of the books reviewed in *Booklist* were also reviewed in two or more other journals, and 93 percent of books reviewed in the *New York Times Book Review* were reviewed in two or more other journals. On the other hand, *Choice* and *Library Jour-*

nal had the lowest percentage of all the books they reviewed also reviewed by two or more other journals, 63 percent and 61 percent respectively. Considering only those books that received one review—111 titles—*Library Journal* reviewed 47 books (42 percent), *Publishers Weekly* reviewed 27 books (24 percent), and *Choice* reviewed 24 books (22 percent). The other three journals reviewed very few unique titles among potentially controversial books. Perhaps most important, Table 6 clearly indicates the extensive duplication in reviewing of potentially controversial books among the six journals. In each journal, more than half of the books reviewed were also reviewed in two or more other journals.

Direction of Reviews

The directional scale for this study has three categories: favorable (+), unfavorable (-), and neutral (0). The total number of reviews received by potentially controversial books in the six journals was 1,015 reviews. Each review was coded for direction by the investigator. Since *Booklist* publishes reviews solely of recommended titles, all *Booklist* reviews were coded as favorable.

Almost 60 percent of the total of 1,015 reviews were favorable; more than 18 percent were unfavorable; and more than 21 percent were neutral. Thus, over 80 percent of all reviews of potentially controversial books were either favorable or neutral, while less than 20 percent were negative. These findings support previous research, which found that a majority of published reviews were favorable, and a small percentage of reviews were unfavorable.[23] At this point in the study, it can be said that reviews of potentially controversial books, as a group, are similar in direction to the reviews of other types of books.

The data collected also show the direction of reviews of potentially controversial books in each of the six journals. After *Booklist*, *Choice* had the highest percentage of favorable reviews; 72 percent of the 137 reviews published in *Choice* were favorable. On the other hand, *Kirkus* had the lowest percentage of favorable reviews; only 39 percent of the 208 reviews in *Kirkus* were favorable. In *Library Journal, Publishers Weekly, Choice* and, of course, *Booklist* the majority of reviews were favorable; in *Kirkus* and the *New York Times Book Review*, a minority of the reviews were favorable.

Agreement Among Journals on Direction of Reviews

Of the 385 potentially controversial books reviewed in the six journals, 274 books received two or more reviews. The data were stratified by a number of reviews. First, within each stratum of number of reviews, the Total Agreement figure was calculated. The Total Agreement figure is the number of times when all reviews for a book had the same identical sign. For example, for the stratum of three reviews, Total Agreement was achieved when all the reviews were +++, ---, or 000. Second, within each stratum, the Near Agreement figure was calculated. The Near Agreement figure is the number of times when the majority of reviews had the same sign—for example, for the stratum of three reviews, when review configurations had either two ++'s two --'s, or two 00's. Third, a Disagreement figure was calculated. The Disagreement figure is the number of times no one sign received a majority in the directional configuration. For example, in the stratum of three reviews, a book which received the directional configuration +-0 would be included in the figure for Disagreement, since no sign appears at least two times to achieve a majority.

Analysis of all reviews for the 274 books shows that there was Total Agreement among the six journals on only 83 books, or 30.3 percent of all books. Near Agreement was reached in the case of 92 books, or 33.6 percent; and Disagreement was accorded 99 books, or 36.1 percent.

ANALYSIS OF DATA RELATED TO TOTAL POPULATION OF RANDOMLY SELECTED BOOKS

As previously explained, a checklist of 360 books randomly selected from the six review media was compiled to test Hypothesis 1 and Hypothesis 2, and to serve as the population for choosing randomly selected books to test Hypothesis 3. Each of the 360 books was searched in *Book Review Index* to determine how many reviews each book received in the six journals. Also, each review was coded for direction by the investigator.

Table 7 shows the number of reviews received by the 360 randomly selected books. Although less than 10 percent of the 360 books received reviews in all six journals (column 3), the distribution of books among the other five review strata is similar, with between 15 and 20 percent of the books falling in each stratum. Table 7 also shows that, in total, the 360 books received 1,169 reviews in the six journals (column 4).

The data collected also indicate the number of randomly selected books reviewed by each journal. It is interesting at this point to compare data for the number of potentially controversial books reviewed by each journal and the number of randomly selected books reviewed by each journal. Table 8 displays the data for percentages of total books reviewed and percentages of total reviews accounted for by each journal.

In comparing the data in Table 8 for each journal's reviewing of potentially controversial books (N = 385) and randomly selected books (N = 360), it can be seen that *Library Journal, Publishers Weekly,* and *Kirkus* each reviewed similar percentages of books in the two groups (columns 2 and 3). For example, *Publishers Weekly* reviewed 58 percent of the potentially controversial books and 53 percent of the randomly selected books. However, *Choice, Booklist,* and the *New York Times Book Review* each reviewed considerably higher percentages of the randomly selected books. For example, *Booklist* reviewed only 22 percent of the potentially controversial books, but 49 percent—more than double—of the randomly selected books. The columns for percentage of total reviews in Table 8 (columns 4 and 5) indicate that *Library Journal, Publishers Weekly,* and *Kirkus* dominate the reviewing of potentially controversial books, but the six journals share more equally in the review-

ing of randomly selected books, though *Library Journal* clearly ranks first and the *New York Times Book Review* last.

Duplication of Reviews

The random sample of 360 books was examined to determine the degree of duplication among books reviewed and whether any journals predominated in reviewing unique titles. As shown in Table 9, *Choice* reviewed more unique titles than the other journals, almost three times as many as *Library Journal,* its nearest competitor. Slightly over half of the 60 books selected randomly from *Choice* were unique titles. At the other extreme, only two of the 60 titles selected randomly from the *New York Times Book Review* were unique titles.

Table 9 indicates the extensive duplication in titles of randomly selected books reviewed in the six journals. Actually, duplication in reviewing randomly selected books is even more extensive than was duplication in reviewing potentially controversial books (see Table 6.) Table 9 shows that in two journals, the *New York Times Book Review* and *Kirkus,* 90 percent or more of the books

TABLE 7

NUMBER OF REVIEWS RECEIVED BY RANDOMLY SELECTED BOOKS
(N = 360)

(1) Number of Journals Reviewing	(2) Number of Books	(3) Percent of Total Books	(4) Total Number of Reviews	(5) Percent of Total Reviews
6	33	9.17	198	16.9
5	58	16.11	290	24.8
4	70	19.44	280	24.0
3	66	18.33	198	16.9
2	70	19.44	140	12.0
1	63	17.50	63	5.4
Total	360	99.99	1,169	100.0

TABLE 8

COMPARISON OF PERCENTAGES OF POTENTIALLY CONTROVERSIAL BOOKS (N = 385)
AND RANDOMLY SELECTED BOOKS (N = 360) REVIEWED BY EACH JOURNAL

(1) Review media	Percentage of Total Books		Percentage of Total Reviews	
	(2) Potentially Controver- sial Books	(3) Randomly Selected Books	(4) Potentially Controver- sial Books	(5) Randomly Selected Books
Library Journal	76	75.0	29	23.18
Publishers Weekly	58	53.0	22	16.42
Kirkus	54	56.4	21	17.37
Choice	36	55.6	14	17.11
Booklist	22	49.0	8	15.06
New York Times Book Review	19	35.0	7	10.86

reviewed in each journal were also reviewed in two or more other journals. More than 80 percent of the books reviewed in *Publishers Weekly* and *Booklist* were reviewed in two or more other journals. Almost 77 percent of the books reviewed in *Library Journal* were also reviewed in two or more other journals, and, 67.5 percent of the books reviewed in *Choice* were reviewed in two or more other journals. Of the 360 randomly selected titles, only 63 books or 17.5 percent were reviewed by only one journal. Clearly, on the evidence in this study, with the possible exception of *Choice*, the journals are reviewing a similar pool of books.

Direction of Reviews

The total number of reviews received by randomly selected books was 1,169 reviews. Each review was coded by the investigator for direction: favorable (+), unfavorable (-), and neutral (0).

Almost 72 percent of reviews of randomly selected books were favorable, 9 percent were unfavorable, and 19 percent were neutral. Thus, almost 91 percent of all reviews of randomly selected books were favorable or neutral, while only about 9 percent were negative. It is interesting to compare these data with the data for direction of reviews of potentially controversial books.

Table 10 indicates that randomly selected books received a higher percentage of favorable reviews than did potentially controversial books: 71.60 percent as against 59.51 percent. Also, randomly selected books received considerably fewer negative reviews. Both groups of books received similar percentages of neutral reviews.

The data collected also show that *Library Journal, Publishers Weekly, Kirkus,* and *New York Times Book Review* each gave a higher percentage of favorable reviews to randomly selected books than to potentially controversial books. For example, of the *Kirkus* reviews, 39 percent of the potentially controversial books were reviewed favorably and 55 percent of the randomly selected books were reviewed favorably. *Choice* rated a slightly higher percentage of potentially controversial books favorably, that is, 72.26 percent of the potentially controversial books reviewed by *Choice* received favorable ratings and 71 percent of the randomly selected books reviewed received favorable ratings.

TABLE 9

DUPLICATION AMONG JOURNALS IN REVIEWING RANDOMLY SELECTED BOOKS
(N = 360)

	Number of Titles Reviewed by					
	No Other Medium		One Other Medium		Two or More Other Media	
Review Media	Number	Percentage	Number	Percentage	Number	Percentage
Library Journal (n = 271)	13	4.8	50	18.45	208	76.75
Kirkus (n = 203)	4	2.0	16	8.00	183	90.00
Choice (n = 200)	31	15.5	34	17.00	135	67.50
Publishers Weekly (n = 192)	8	4.0	14	7.00	170	89.00
Booklist (n = 176)	5	3.0	23	13.00	148	84.00
New York Times Book Review (n = 127)	2	1.5	3	2.40	122	96.10
Totals	63		140		966	

TABLE 10

COMPARISON OF DIRECTION OF REVIEWS OF POTENTIALLY CONTROVERSIAL BOOKS AND RANDOMLY SELECTED BOOKS

	Favorable		Unfavorable		Neutral	
Reviews	Number	Percent	Number	Percent	Number	Percent
Potentially Controversial Books (N = 1,015)	604	59.51	190	18.72	221	21.77
Randomly Selected Books (N = 1,169)	837	71.60	110	9.41	222	18.99

TABLE 11

COMPARISON OF AGREEMENT AMONG JOURNALS ON DIRECTION OF REVIEWS FOR POTENTIALLY CONTROVERSIAL BOOKS AND RANDOMLY SELECTED BOOKS

Reviews	Total Agreement		Near Agreement		Disagreement	
	Number	Percent	Number	Percent	Number	Percent
Potentially Contro-versial Books (N = 274)	83	30.0	92	34.0	99	36.0
Randomly Selected Books (N = 297)	109	36.7	115	38.7	73	25.6

TABLE 12

HOLDINGS OF RANDOMLY SELECTED BOOKS STRATIFIED BY NUMBER OF REVIEWS (N = 360)

Number of Reviews	Number of Libraries										
	10	9	8	7	6	5	4	3	2	1	0
6 (n = 33)	4	7	6	8	2	3	1	2	0	0	0
		52%			42%				6%		0%
5 (n = 58)	5	2	9	8	9	9	11	1	2	1	1
		27.6%			63.8%				6.9%		1.7%
4 (n = 70)	3	4	5	4	8	10	7	10	12	7	0
		17%			41.5%				41.5%		0%
3 (n = 66)	0	3	2	5	5	5	9	13	11	8	5
		8%			36%				49%		8%
2 (n = 70)	0	0	2	1	1	1	5	6	11	20	23
		3%			11%				53%		33%
1 (n = 63)	0	0	0	1	0	3	3	1	4	9	42
		0%			11%				22%		67%

Agreement Among Journals on Direction of Reviews

For the 297 randomly selected books with two or more reviews, data were stratified by number of reviews. As with potentially controversial books, the data were analyzed to determine Total Agreement, Near Agreement, and Disagreement. There was Total Agreement among journals on reviews of 36.7 percent of the 297 books; Near Agreement on 38.7 percent; and Disagreement on 24.6 percent.

At this point in the study, data on agreement among journals for both potentially controversial books and randomly selected books can be compared. Table 11 shows that there was less Total Agreement and less Near Agreement on direction of reviews for potentially controversial books than for randomly selected books. Thus, there was more Disagreement on direction of reviews for potentially controversial books.

ANALYSIS OF DATA RELATED TO THE SURVEY OF PUBLIC LIBRARY COLLECTIONS

Testing Hypothesis I

All 360 titles selected randomly from the six review journals were searched in the public catalogs of the 10 libraries. Table 12 displays the data collected on holdings among the libraries. The data are stratified by number of reviews, and the table indicates the number of books within each stratum owned by the designated number of libraries.

Table 12 indicates the strong relationship between number of reviews books receive and number of libraries owning those books. For books that received six reviews (the maximum number in this study), 52 percent of those books are owned by eight, nine, or ten libraries; 42 percent are owned by four, five, or six libraries; and 6 percent are owned by one, two, or three liberties. All of the books with six reviews are owned by one or more libraries in the survey. On the other hand, for books with one review, none are owned by eight, nine, or ten libraries; 11 percent are owned by four, five, or six libraries; 22 percent by one, two, or three libraries; and 67 percent were not purchased by any of the ten libraries.

A Pearson product-moment correlation coefficient was calculated for the number of reviews received by each of the 360 randomly selected books, and the number of libraries owning that book. A correlation coefficient of .69 was obtained, which is significant at better than the .001 level. Since the .05 level of significance was adopted for this study, H1 can be rejected.

On the evidence presented in this study, there is a strong, positive relationship between the number of reviews a book receives and the inclusion of that book in libraries. Books that received a higher number of reviews are owned by significantly more libraries than are books that received a lower number of reviews.

Testing Hypothesis II

Since this study has found that there is a strong, significant relationship between number of reviews a book receives and the inclusion of that book in libraries, before testing H2, the population of books was stratified by number of reviews in order to control for that variable. If number of reviews were not controlled, it would not be possible to make a valid assessment of the effect of direction of reviews.

The data on direction of reviews were arranged sequentially, according to the degree of favorableness of all reviews of a book, with the most favorable beginning the sequence. In developing the sequence, the investigator accorded each favorable review two points, each neutral review one point, and each unfavorable review zero points. For example, a book with the directional configuration +++++ (five favorable reviews) was accorded 10 points, and preceded a book with the directional configuration ++++ 0 (four favorable and one neutral review), which received 9 points.

In each review stratum, half or almost half of the books received directional configurations consisting of all favorable reviews, or all favorable reviews plus all favorable reviews except for one neutral review. Thus, in the stratum for books with one review, 58.7 percent of the books received a favorable review (+), in the stratum for two reviews, 47 percent received two favorable reviews (++), in the stratum for three reviews, 43 percent received three favorable reviews (+++); in the stratum for four reviews, 58.6 percent received four favorable reviews (++++) or three favorable

and one neutral review (+++0); in the stratum for five reviews, 48.3 percent received five favorable reviews (+++++) or four favorable and one neutral review (++++0); and, lastly, in the stratum for six reviews, 54.6 percent received six favorable reviews (++++++) or five favorable and one neutral review (+++++0).

In testing Hypothesis II, books with either all favorable reviews, or all favorable reviews except for one neutral review, *as designated above*, are considered in the category *High Favorables*. All books with other directional configurations are considered in the category *Low Favorables*. Chi square tests were applied to the data. The purpose of the Chi square tests was to determine statistically whether or not there is a significant difference between books in the *High Favorables* and *Low Favorables* categories, as indicated above, and the number of libraries owning books in each category. Each Chi square test is testing the following hypothesis: that books in the *High Favorables* category do not differ significantly (.05) in numbers included in libraries from books in the *Low Favorables* category. In other words, what is being tested is a hypothesis of independence: that direction of reviews is *not* related to the inclusion of books in libraries, which, in essence, is Hypothesis II in this study.

Since the significance level accepted in this study is .05, the critical value for X^2 in all tests—with one degree of freedom—is 3.84.

The findings of this study are that when one controls for number of reviews, there is no significant relationship between direction of reviews and number of books owned by libraries for books receiving *one* ($X^2 = .1364$), *two* ($X^2 = .08$), or six ($X^2 = 1.46$) reviews, but there is a significant relationship between direction of reviews and number of books owned in libraries for books receiving *three* ($X^2 = 5.1617$), *four* ($X^2 = 6.38$), or *five* ($X^2 = 5.3893$) reviews. Those books with three, four, or five reviews that received a higher number of favorable reviews and an absence of negative reviews are owned by more libraries in this study than are books with a lower number of favorable reviews and one or more negative reviews. In this study, perhaps since all books with one or two reviews are owned by few libraries, and 94 percent of all books with six reviews are owned in four or more of the 10 libraries surveyed, direction of reviews is not a significant variable when one controls for number of reviews.

Testing Hypothesis III

Hypothesis III concerns whether there is a statistically significant difference in the number of potentially controversial books versus number of randomly selected books owned by libraries if one controls for number and direction of reviews. For statistical testing, Hypothesis III was postulated in the null form as follows: there is no significant difference in the number of potentially controversial books versus number of randomly selected books included in libraries if one controls for number and direction of reviews.

To collect data to test Hypothesis III, two checklists were employed: one included 250 randomly selected books and the other 250 potentially controversial books. The books on each checklist were stratified by number of reviews.

Table 13 shows the distribution of reviews by review journal for potentially controversial books, and Table 14 displays similar data for randomly selected books. Comparison of data in the two tables shows that *Booklist, Choice,* and the *New York Times Book Review* reviewed more randomly selected books than potentially controversial

books, and *Kirkus, Library Journal* and *Publishers Weekly* reviewed more potentially controversial books than randomly selected books.

As previously indicated, all 10 libraries surveyed used all six journals to select books during the time period covered by this study. *Library Journal, Kirkus,* and *Booklist* were used most heavily, and *Choice,* the *New York Times Book Review,* and *Publishers Weekly* were used less heavily.

Titles on both checklists were checked against the public catalogs in the 10 libraries. Table 15 shows the number of potentially controversial books owned by libraries stratified by number of reviews. Table 16 shows the number of randomly selected books owned, also stratified by number of reviews. When the data in both tables are compared, similarities are at once apparent. First, the same trend is clear in both tables, that is, books with a higher number of reviews are owned by more libraries, and books with a lower number of reviews are either owned by fewer libraries or are not owned by any libraries. Second, when review

TABLE 13

**NUMBER OF POTENTIALLY CONTROVERSIAL BOOKS REVIEWED BY EACH JOURNAL
STRATIFIED BY NUMBER OF REVIEWS RECEIVED BY EACH BOOK**
(N = 250)

| Number of Reviews Received by Book | Review Media | | | | | |
	Booklist	Choice	Kirkus	Library Journal	New York Times Book Review	Publishers Weekly
5-6	38	39	47	49	40	50
4	17	26	46	47	17	47
3	10	12	41	44	6	37
2	0	15	22	37	2	24
1	2	14	4	15	1	14
Total Number of Books Reviewed	67	106	160	192	66	172
Percent of Total Books Reviewed	27	42	64	77	26	69

TABLE 14

**NUMBER OF RANDOMLY SELECTED BOOKS REVIEWED BY EACH JOURNAL
STRATIFIED BY NUMBER OF REVIEWS RECEIVED BY EACH BOOK**
(N = 250)

| Number of Reviews Received by Book | Review Media | | | | | |
	Booklist	Choice	Kirkus	Library Journal	New York Times Book Review	Publishers Weekly
5-6	44	35	48	46	45	47
4	26	28	40	48	23	35
3	24	25	26	40	12	23
2	20	23	14	35	1	7
1	4	23	3	12	2	6
Total Number of Books Reviewed	118	134	131	181	83	118
Percent of Total Books Reviewed	47	54	52	72	33	47

strata are compared, numbers of books owned by the same numbers of libraries are similar. For example, if one considers books owned by eight, nine, or ten libraries: 20 of the 50 potentially controversial books with five or six reviews, and 20 of the randomly selected books with five or six reviews, are owned; eight potentially controversial books and seven randomly selected books with four reviews are owned; six potentially controversial and four randomly selected books with three reviews are owned; no potentially controversial and two randomly selected books with two reviews are owned; and, lastly, one potentially controversial and no randomly selected books with one review are owned.

To test the strength of the relationship between number of reviews received by books and books owned in libraries, for both potentially controversial and randomly selected books, and to compare the findings, Pearson product-moment correlations were calculated, followed by a test for the significance of the difference between two correlation coefficients, using Fisher's Z_r transformation.

The tests indicated that for both potentially controversial and randomly selected books, there is a significant relationship between the number of reviews a book receives and the inclusion of that book in libraries.

In addition, there is no significant difference between the .63 correlation for potentially controversial books and the .57 correlation coefficient obtained for randomly selected books.

TABLE 15
HOLDINGS OF POTENTIALLY CONTROVERSIAL BOOKS STRATIFIED BY NUMBER OF REVIEWS
(N = 250)

Number of Reviews	Number of Libraries										
	10	9	8	7	6	5	4	3	2	1	0
5-6 (n = 50)	3	5	12	8	6	5	8	1	1	0	1
		40%			54%				4%		2%
4 (n = 50)	2	2	4	2	8	5	7	7	5	5	3
		16%			44%				34%		6%
3 (n = 50)	1	4	1	1	4	7	10	5	6	7	4
		12%			44%				36%		8%
2 (n = 50)	0	0	0	2	1	1	5	7	11	12	11
		0%			18%				60%		22%
1 (n = 50)	0	0	1	0	0	2	3	2	10	6	26
		2%			10%				36%		52%

TABLE 16
HOLDINGS OF RANDOMLY SELECTED BOOKS STRATIFIED BY NUMBER OF REVIEWS
(N = 250)

Number of Reviews	Number of Libraries										
	10	9	8	7	6	5	4	3	2	1	0
5-6 (n = 50)	5	4	11	8	5	5	8	2	1	1	0
		40%			52%				8%		0%
4 (n = 50)	1	1	5	2	6	6	5	9	11	4	0
		14%			38%				48%		0%
3 (n = 50)	0	2	2	4	4	2	5	11	10	5	5
		8%			30%				42%		10%
2 (n = 50)	0	0	2	1	1	0	3	5	10	13	15
		4%			10%				56%		30%
1 (n = 50)	0	0	0	0	0	3	3	1	3	8	32
		0%			12%				24%		64%

Data on direction of reviews of potentially controversial and randomly selected books, stratified by number of reviews, showed that the majority of reviews of both randomly selected and potentially controversial books are favorable. In each review stratum, half or more than half of the books received directional configurations of all favorable reviews, or all favorable reviews or all favorable reviews except for one neutral review. As in testing Hypothesis II, those books are categorized as *High Favorables*. Books with other directional configurations are considered *Low Favorables*. Chi square tests were conduced to determine if there is any significant difference in the number of potentially controversial versus number of randomly selected books owned by libraries if one controls for number and direction of reviews.

The findings are that there is no significant difference in the number of potentially controversial versus number of randomly selected books owned by the 10 libraries surveyed if one controls for number and direction of reviews. At the .05 significance level, no significant differences were found. Thus, Hypothesis III cannot be rejected.

ANALYSIS OF DATA RELATED TO INDIVIDUAL LIBRARIES

Table 17 shows the number of randomly selected books and potentially controversial books owned by each library, stratified by number of reviews received by each book. In the table, Library I has the highest average annual book budget and Library X has the lowest average annual book budget, 1972–1974, and the libraries are numbered from I to X in descending size of budget.

As might be expected, Library I, with the highest budget, has the highest number of both randomly selected and potentially controversial books. However, Library X, with the lowest budget, has neither the lowest number of randomly selected nor the lowest number of potentially controversial books. Among the 10 libraries, some libraries with lower budgets own either more randomly selected or more potentially controversial books than libraries with higher budgets.

With regard to the relationship between number of reviews and books owned by libraries, Table

TABLE 17

NUMBER OF POTENTIALLY CONTROVERSIAL BOOKS AND RANDOMLY SELECTED BOOKS OWNED BY LIBRARIES STRATIFIED BY NUMBER OF REVIEWS RECEIVED BY BOOKS

	Potentially Controversial Books (N = 250)											Randomly Selected Books (N = 250)									
	Library											Library									
Reviews	I	II	III	IV	V	VI	VII	VIII	IX	X	Reviews	I	II	III	IV	V	VI	VII	VIII	IX	X
5-6	47	34	32	27	43	34	33	19	30	28	5-6	49	39	40	38	36	31	37	21	13	22
4	37	31	28	20	30	21	20	9	16	9	4	38	31	25	20	28	19	19	11	12	8
3	35	27	24	13	30	17	20	8	6	15	3	27	23	24	19	22	13	23	9	6	8
2	18	11	17	6	17	9	7	4	2	8	2	13	12	16	11	11	8	11	3	0	4
1	13	7	12	3	8	6	6	1	3	2	1	5	7	6	4	8	4	3	2	3	2
Totals	150	110	113	69	128	87	86	41	57	62	Totals	132	112	111	92	105	75	93	46	34	44

TABLE 18

DIFFERENCES AMONG LIBRARIES IN HOLDINGS OF POTENTIALLY CONTROVERSIAL BOOKS VERSUS RANDOMLY SELECTED BOOKS

Library	Potentially Controversial Books (N = 250)	Randomly Selected Books (N = 250)	Difference
I	150	132	+ 18
II	110	112	− 2
III	113	111	+ 2
IV	69	92	−23
V	128	105	+23
VI	87	75	+ 12
VII	86	93	− 7
VIII	41	46	− 5
IX	57	34	+23
X	62	44	+ 18

17 shows that in each stratum of reviews for each library, those books that received a higher number of reviews were owned in greater numbers than were books with fewer reviews, with very slight exceptions. This finding is not unexpected.

Table 18 arranges the data in Table 17 to show differences between number of potentially controversial books and randomly selected books owned by each library.

Table 18 shows that six libraries owned more potentially controversial books than randomly selected books, and four libraries owned more randomly selected books, but for three of those four libraries the differences amounted to only two, five, and seven books. For the fourth library, the differences amounted to 23 more randomly selected books.

On the basis of the data in Table 18, the investigator finds that each of the ten libraries owned similar numbers of randomly selected and potentially controversial books. Differences are slight and follow no apparent pattern, and further investigation is not warranted in this study.

SUMMARY OF FINDINGS

Although this study's findings cannot be generalized beyond the population of medium-sized New Jersey public libraries surveyed, those libraries are similar in many respects to libraries in other states. For example, the total expenditures figures of the New Jersey libraries are total expenditures figures common to medium-sized libraries elsewhere. Also, the six review journals examined are widely used in many public libraries; and most public librarians in all states depend heavily on published book reviews when selecting adult nonfiction.

Each null hypothesis was tested at the .05 level of significance to determine if it could be rejected. Analysis of the data collected showed that Hypothesis I could be rejected, Hypothesis II could be rejected in part, and Hypothesis III could not be rejected.

In regard to Hypothesis I, the data showed a strong, positive correlation between number of reviews a book receives and the inclusion of the book in libraries. A Pearson product-moment correlation coefficient was calculated between the number of reviews a book receives and the number of libraries owning the book. The correlation coefficient obtained was .69, which is significant at better than the .001 level. The findings clearly indicated that in the libraries surveyed, books with a greater number of reviews were owned by significantly more libraries than were books with a lower number of reviews.

In regard to Hypothesis II, the data showed that when one controlled for number of reviews received by books, there was no significant relationship between direction of reviews and books owned by the libraries surveyed for books receiving one, two, or six reviews. However, there was a significant relationship between direction of reviews and books owned by libraries for books receiving three, four, or five reviews.

In regard to Hypothesis III, the data showed that when one controlled for both number and direction of reviews, there was no significant difference in the number of potentially controversial books versus number of randomly selected books owned in the libraries surveyed.

CONCLUSIONS BASED ON THE FINDINGS

Hypothesis I

The investigator predicted that Hypothesis I would be rejected. Based on previous research, a significant positive correlation between number of reviews a book receives and number of libraries owning that book was expected.

In the study, the investigator was specifically interested in reviews in six journals widely used by public librarians nationwide. All 30 libraries in the study's original sample were found to use either five or six of the journals for selection. As noted above, the 10 libraries selected for the final survey of collections each used all six journals.

Since the 10 libraries surveyed selected books from all six journals and each library used some journals more heavily than others, those books that received a greater number of reviews had a higher probability of coming to the attention of more librarians more times—and so had a better chance of being selected than books receiving fewer reviews. Thus the positive relationship between number of reviews a book receives and number of libraries owning the book was not surprising. However, the strength of the relationship was surprising. That is, the investigator did not expect the dramatic differences between ownership of books with one, two, three, four, or five/six reviews. For example, in this study, approximately 40 to 52 percent of books with five or six reviews were owned in eight, nine, or ten libraries, while only approximately 0 to 4 percent of books with two reviews were owned by eight, nine, or ten libraries. Books with one review fared even more poorly; 67 percent were not owned by any of the libraries in testing Hypotheses I and II.

Perhaps, one may conjecture, few randomly selected books with one review were owned because *Choice*, the least used journal in the 10 libraries, reviewed almost half of the titles with one review used to test Hypotheses I and II, and *Kirkus*, for example, the second most heavily used journal, reviewed only 6 percent of the unique titles. However, among books with two reviews, *Library Journal*, the most heavily used journal, reviewed more books than any other journal, and still books with two reviews were purchased infrequently. Among potentially controversial books used to test Hypothesis III, *Library Journal* reviewed more books with one review than did *Choice*, and *Publishers Weekly* reviewed the same number of unique books as did *Choice*, and still 52 percent of the books with one review were not owned by any library surveyed.

This study's findings regarding the strong, positive relationship between number of reviews a book receives and number of libraries owning that book raise serious questions concerning the development of library collections in the public libraries studied. First, one may ask, are those books with a higher number of reviews the books most needed and wanted by the public library's constituency? Obviously, the libraries in this study are purchasing significantly greater numbers of those books that receive four, five, and six reviews in the six journals, but are those books used in greater numbers than books with fewer reviews? What about the books that don't get reviewed in any of the six journals? Are those unreviewed titles of no potential interest to the library's public? This study's pretest indicated they are rarely purchased.

Second, one may ask, what characteristics, if any, do the widely reviewed books have in common? Data collected in this study show extensive duplication of titles reviewed among the six journals. What variables relate to the extensive duplication? And on the other hand, what variables account for the minimal attention paid to other titles by the review medias?

Hypothesis II

The investigator expected that Hypothesis II would be rejected. That is, the investigator expected that books with all or a majority of favorable reviews would be owned in significantly greater numbers than books with less favorable, negative, and/or neutral reviews.

However, in this study Hypothesis II could be rejected only in part. For the 10 libraries surveyed, when the investigator controlled for number of reviews a book received, direction of reviews was significant in the case of books receiving three, four, or five reviews in the six journals investigated, but direction of reviews was not significant for those books receiving one, two, or six reviews. Perhaps because books receiving one or two reviews were owned by few libraries, and 94 percent of the books receiving six reviews were owned by four or more libraries, direction of reviews was not a significant variable relating to ownership.

In this study, the majority of reviews were favorable reviews. For all randomly selected books, 71.60 percent of the reviews were favorable, 18.99 percent were neutral, and only 9.41 percent were unfavorable. For all potentially controversial books, 59.51 percent were favorable, 21.77 percent were neutral, and 18.72 percent were unfavorable. On the evidence, one can observe not only that the majority of reviews were favorable, but that approximately 80 percent of all reviews were favorable or neutral and only approximately 20 percent of reviews were unfavorable. Findings in other research studies support this study's findings on the high incidence of favorable reviews and the low incidence of unfavorable reviews among all published reviews.

Hypothesis III

When Hypothesis III was postulated, the investigator did not have evidence on hand to predict whether the hypothesis could be rejected. However, since previous studies have showed a high incidence of self-censorship among librarians, particularly with regard to materials potentially controversial for their treatment of sex, the investigator thought it might be possible to reject Hypothesis III. That is, the investigator thought there might be a higher number of randomly selected books owned even if one controlled for number and direction of reviews of both randomly selected and potentially controversial books.

The findings in the study, however, show that Hypothesis III cannot be rejected. When one controlled for number and direction of reviews, there was no significant difference in the number of potentially controversial versus number of randomly selected books owned by libraries surveyed.

On the basis of the evidence, several conclusions can be suggested. First, in the libraries studied, potentially controversial books did not require a significantly higher number of favorable reviews before they were purchased. If potentially controversial and randomly selected books received comparable numbers of favorable, neutral, and unfavorable reviews, they were purchased in comparable numbers. Actually, six of the ten libraries in this study owned more potentially controversial than randomly selected books, and libraries with the lowest budgets did not differ appreciably from libraries with higher budgets in proportions of potentially controversial and randomly selected books owned in each library.

Findings related to Hypothesis III suggest that in the libraries surveyed, in relation to purchases from published reviews in the six journals, self-censorship in selecting potentially controversial books was not in evidence. This study, of course, did not examine possible self-censorship with regard to books not reviewed in the six journals. Also potentially controversial books were limited to adult nonfiction treating some aspect of sex.

Second, findings show that use of the six journals in libraries surveyed may be a key variable relating to inclusion of potentially controversial books in those libraries. The six journals reviewed potentially controversial books in substantial numbers, with *Library Journal, Kirkus,* and *Publishers Weekly* reviewing the most titles. Of the original population of 602 potentially controversial books identified in this study, 64 percent were reviewed in one or more of the six journals, and 46 percent were reviewed in two or more journals. Since public libraries surveyed depended heavily on those journals to select adult nonfiction, and since the journals gave extensive review coverage to potentially controversial books, the review media may be key variables that influenced inclusion of potentially controversial books in the libraries surveyed.

OVERVIEW

This study began by referring to the commitment of librarians to intellectual freedom as embodied in the *Library Bill of Rights,* perhaps the single most important document adopted by the library profession. In spite of this commitment, the profession has evidence that censorship is not uncommon in some libraries (see, for example, the *Newsletter on Intellectual Freedom*). Although the findings in this study suggest that in libraries surveyed restrictiveness may not be as much in evidence as previous research suggests, still findings similar to this study's conclusions are limited in number.

Research is needed to identify those variables that relate most significantly to intellectual freedom and censorship in libraries. Identification of key variables is necessary for an understanding of how and why censorship operates in some libraries.

This study has suggested that there are at least six main classes of independent variables relating to selection and censorship in libraries (see Figure 1), and that future research should identify which of these variables are most significant. On the basis of findings detailed above, the investigator believes that the book review media used by librarians is a variable that warrants particular attention in future research on restrictiveness in public libraries.

Notes

1. Eric Moon, " 'Problem' Fiction." *Library Journal* 87 (February 1, 1962): 484-96; and Raymond B. Agler, " Problem Books Revisited." *Library Journal* 89 (May 15, 1964): 2019-30.
2. Moon, "Problem Fiction," p. 494.
3. Kenneth S. Tisdel. "Staff Reviewing in Library Book Selection." In *Reviews in Library Book Selection* by LeRoy C. Merritt, Martha Boaz and Kenneth S. Tisdel (Detroit: Wayne State University Press, 1958), pp. 133-78; and Judith Serebnick. "The 1973 Court Rulings on Obscenity: Have They Made a Difference?" *Wilson Library Bulletin* 50 (December 1975): 304-10.
4. Moon, "Problem Fiction"; and Agler, "Problem Books Revisited."
5. *Encyclopaedia of the Social Sciences.* 1930 ed. s.v. "Censorship," by Harold D. Lasswell; and *International Encyclopedia of the Social Sciences.* 1968 ed. s.v. "Censorship," by Henry J. Abraham.
6. See *Newsletter on Intellectual Freedom.*
7. Mary Lida Eakin. "Censorship in Public High School Libraries." (Master's thesis, Columbia University, 1948).
8. Marjorie Fiske. *Book Selection and Censorship: A Study of School and Public Libraries in California.* (Berkeley: University of California Press, 1959).
9. John J. Farley. "Book Censorship in the Senior High Libraries of Nassau County, N.Y." (Ph.D. dissertation, New York University, 1965).
10. Charles H. Busha. "The Attitudes of Midwestern Public Librarians Toward Intellectual Freedom and Censorship." (Ph.D. dissertation, Indiana University, 1973).
11. Michael J. Pope. "A Comparative Study of the Opinions of School, College, and Public Librarians, Concerning Certain Categories of Sexually Oriented Literature." (Ph.D. dissertation, Rutgers University, 1973).
12. Claire St. Clere England. "The Climate of Censorship in Ontario: An Investigation into Attitudes Toward Intellectual Freedom and the Perceptual Factors Affecting the Practice of Censorship in Public Libraries Serving Medium-Sized Populations." (Ph.D. dissertation, University of Toronto, 1974).
13. Marjorie Fiske, *Book Selection and Censorship.* (Berkeley: University of California Press, 1959).
14. Solomon J. Leon. "Book Selection in Philadelphia: The Survey of the Handling of Certain Controversial Adult Materials of Philadelphia Area Libraries," *Library Journal* 98 (April 1, 1973): 1081-91.

15. Mary Lida Eakin. "Censorship in Public High School Libraries.", and England, "The Climate of Censorship."

16. "Dissent and Sex: Report of the Committee on Restrictive Library Practices, Adult Services Section, New Jersey Library Association." (May 5, 1966), p. 6.

17. Michael J. Pope. "A Comparative Study."

18. Charles E. Rockwood and Ruth H. Rockwood. "Quantitative Guides to Public Library Operation." *Occasional Papers*, University of Illinois Graduate School of Library Science 89 (November 1967): 1-26; and England, "The Climate of Censorship."

19. Ernest R. De Prospo, Ellen Altman, and Kenneth E. Beasley. *Performance Measures for Public Libraries.* (Chicago: Public Library Association, 1973).

20. Ole R. Holsti. *Content Analyses for the Social Sciences and Humanities.* (Reading, Mass.: Addison-Wesley, 1969), pp. 140, 142.

21. Sandra K. Paul and C. A. Nemeyer. "Book Marketing and Selection: Selected Findings from the Current AAP/ALA Study." *Publishers Weekly* 207 (June 16, 1975), p. 43.

22. *The Bowker Annual of Library and Book Trade Information* (New York: R. R. Bowker).

23. See Tisdel. "Staff Reviewing."; Merritt. "The Pattern of Modern Book Reviewing."; Marco. "An Appraisal of Favorability"; and Chen. "Reviewing the Literature." In "Current Book Reviewing." University of Illinois Graduate School of Library Science *Occasional Papers* 57 (December 1959): 1-20; and Ching-Chih Chen and Thomas J. Galvin. "Reviewing the Literature of Librarianship: A State of the Art Report." In *American Reference Books Annual 1975.* pp. xxxi-xlv. Ed. by Bohdan S. Wymar. Littleton, Colo.: Libraries Unlimited, 1975.

Selected Bibliography

Abelson, H. et al. "Public Attitudes Towards and Experiences with Erotic Materials." In U.S. Commission on Obscenity and Pornography. *Technical Report of the Commission on Obscenity and Pornography*, vol. 6. Washington, D.C., 1971.

Adams, Charles J. and Shepherd, Clayton. "Censorship or Selection? in Hoosier Libraries." *Focus on Indiana Libraries* 22 (June 1968): 58-66.

Agler, Raymond B. " 'Problem' Books Revisited." *Library Journal* 89 (May 15, 1964): 2019-30.

Blalock, Hubert M. *Social Statistics.* 2d ed. New York: McGraw-Hill, 1972.

Boaz, Martha. "The Reviews and Reviewers of Best Sellers." In LeRoy C. Merritt, Martha Boaz and Kenneth S. Tisdel. *Reviews in Library Book Selection*, pp. 41-132. Detroit: Wayne State University Pr., 1958.

Boyer, Calvin and Eaton, Nancy L., eds. *Book Selection Policies of American Libraries: An Anthology of Policies from College, Public and School Libraries.* Austin, Tex.: Armadillo Pr., 1971.

Broderick, Dorothy M. " 'Problem' Nonfiction." *Library Journal* 87 (Oct. 1, 1962): 3373-8.

Busha, Charles H. "The Attitudes of Midwestern Public Librarians Toward Intellectual Freedom and Censorship." Ph.D. dissertation, Indiana University, 1973.

————*Freedom versus Suppression and Censorship: With a Study of the Attitudes of Midwestern Public Librarians and a Bibliography of Censorship.* Littleton, Colo.: Libraries Unlimited, 1972.

————"Intellectual Freedom and Censorship: The Climate of Opinion in Midwestern Public Libraries." *Library Quarterly* 42 (July 1972): 283-301.

Chen, Ching-Chih and Galvin, Thomas J. "Reviewing the Literature of Librarianship: A State of the Art Report." In *American Reference Books Annual 1975*, pp. xxxi-xlv. Ed. by Bohden S. Wynar. Littleton, Colo.: Libraries Unlimited, 1975.

DeProspo, Ernest R., Altmen, Ellen and Beasley, Kenneth E. *Performance Measures for Public Libraries.* Chicago: Public Library Association, 1973.

Eakin, Mery Lida. "Censorship in Public High School Libraries." Master's thesis, Columbia University, 1948.

England, Cleire St. Clere. "The Climate of Censorship in Ontario: An Investigation into Attitudes Toward Intellectual Freedom and the Perceptual Factors Affecting the Practice of Censorship in Public Libraries Serving Medium-Sized Population." Ph.D. dissertation, University of Toronto, 1974.

Farley, John J. "Book Censorship in the Senior High Libraries of Nassau County, N.Y." Ph.D. dissertation, New York University, 1964.

Ferguson, George A. *Statistical Analysis in Psychology & Education.* 3d ed. New York: McGraw-Hill, 1971.

Fiske, Marjorie. *Book Selection and Censorship: A Study of School and Public Libraries in California.* Berkeley: University of California Pr., 1959.

————"Book Selection and Retention in California Public and School Libraries." In *The Climate of Book Selection: Social Influences on School and Public Libraries*, pp. 66-76. Ed. by J. Perriam Danton. Berkeley: University of California School of Librarianship, 1959.

Futas, Elizabeth, ed. *Library Acquisition Policies and Procedures.* Phoenix: Oryx Pr. 1977.

Good, Paul. "Politics of Pornography." *Evergreen Review* 15 (Sept. 1971): 21-3, 54-63.

Guilford, J. P. and Fruchter, Benjamin. *Fundamental Statistics in Psychology and Education.* 5th ed. New York: McGraw-Hill, 1973.

Harvey, John Frederick. "Content Characteristics of Best-Selling Novels." *Public Opinion Quarterly* 17 (Spring 1953): 91-114.

Holsti, Ole R. *Content Analysis for the Social Sciences and Humanities.* Reading, Mass: Addison-Wesley, 1969.

Indiana University Institute for Sex Research. *Catalog of the Social and Behavioral Sciences Monograph Section of the Library of the Institute for*

Sex Research, Indiana University, Bloomington, Indiana. 4 vols. Boston: G. K. Hall, 1974.

Kappel, Joseph W. "Book Clubs and the Evaluation of Books." *Public Opinion Quarterly* 12 (Summer 1948): 243-52.

Krikelas, James. "Library Statistics and the Measurement of Library Services." *ALA Bulletin* 60 (May 1966): 494-9.

Leon, Sotomon J. "Book Selection in Philadelphia: The Survey of the Handling of Certain Controversial Adult Materials of Philadelphia Area Libraries." *Library Journal* 98 (Apr. 1, 1973): 1081-91.

Levine, James Phillip. "The Booksellers and the Law of Obscenity: Toward an Empirical Theory of Free Expression." Ph.D. dissertation, Northwestern University, 1968.

Marco, Guy A. "An Appraisal of Favorability in Current Book Reviewing." University of Illinois Graduate School of Library Science *Occasional Papers* 57 (Dec. 1959): 1-20.

Merritt, LeRoy C. "The Pattern of Modern Book Reviewing." In LeRoy C. Merritt, Martha Boaz and Kenneth S. Tisdel. *Reviews in Library Book Selection,* pp. 1-39. Detroit: Wayne State University Pr., 1958.

Moon, Eric " 'Problem' Fiction." *Library Journal* 87 (February 1, 1962): 484-96.

National Education Association of the United States. *Teacher Rights. Kanawha County, West Virginia: A Textbook Study in Cultural Conflict; Inquiry Report.* Washington, D.C., 1975.

Palmer, Joseph William. "Influence of Published Reviews of 16mm Motion Pictures on Film Selection in Public Libraries With Large Film Col-lections." Ph.D. dissertation, University of Southern California, 1973.

Parsons, Talcott. "Implications of the Study." In *The Climate of Book Selection: Social Influences on School and Public Libraries,* pp. 77-96. Ed. by J. Perriam Danton. Berkeley: University of California School of Librarianship, 1959.

Paul, Sandra K. and Nemeyer, C. A. "Book Marketing and Selection: Selected Findings from the Current AAP/ALA Study." *Publishers Weekly* 207 (June 16, 1975): 42-5.

Pope, Michael J. "A Comparative Study of the Opinions of School, College, and Public Librarians, Concerning Certain Categories of Sexually Oriented Literature." Ph.D. dissertation, Rutgers University, 1973.

Rockwood, Charles E. and Rockwood, Ruth H. "Quantitative Guides to Public Library Operation." University of Illinois Graduate School of Library Science *Occasional Papers* 89 (Nov. 1967): 1-26.

Serebnick, Judith. "The 1973 Court Rulings on Obscenity: Have They Made a Difference?" *Wilson Library Bulletin* 50 (Dec. 1975): 304-10.

Tamblyn, Eldon W. "They Play It Safe." *Library Journal* 90 (June 1, 1965): 2495-8.

Tisdel, Kenneth S. "Staff Reviewing in Library Book Selection." In LeRoy C. Merritt, Martha Boaz and Kenneth S. Tisdel. *Reviews in Library Book Selection,* pp. 133-78. Detroit: Wayne State University Pr., 1958.

Tuckman, Bruce W. *Conducting Educational Research.* New York: Harcourt, 1972.

Wallis, C. Lamar. "Confrontation in Memphis." *Library Journal* 94 (Nov. 15, 1969): 4101-3.

Bibliography and the Beginning Bibliographer

by Charles D'Aniello

This essay is offered as advice to those who contemplate becoming or have recently become bibliographers. I begin with the admonition that neither users' studies, statistical analyses, nor approval plans compensate for a lack of knowledge of disciplinary research interests and bibliographic structure. In the final analysis, the best bibliographers are scholars. They keep current with a discipline's investigations and monitor its evolution. Even if they are unable to engage in detailed discourse on the more esoteric subjects its practitioners study, they understand its topography. That is, they possess a "feel" for what students in a given field find interesting, they understand its epistemology, know its publication trends and favored formats, and have a fine reference librarian's ability to use its bibliographic apparatus.

The advice which follows is for those truly curious about the substance and bibliography of the disciplines for which they are responsible. It is meant to complement the intelligent advice already offered by others.

In his article, "Guide for Beginning Bibliographers," Manuel Lopez discusses the checking of comprehensive or critical bibliographies, becoming acquainted with local resources, assessing the strength of the reference collection, the etiquette and diplomacy of liaison with faculty, establishing collection development policies, and sampling techniques for collection evaluation. But he concludes that the craft aspects of book selection are not a substitute for the qualities and qualifications which are essential for a bibliographer: maturity, experience, critical judgment, scholarship, and subject training.[1]

The neophyte bibliographer can easily be bewildered by the responsibilities of the position. For those who wish for a checklist of activities and goals to help in the definition of their labors, in-house manuals such as the University of Texas at Austin's will be helpful.[2] The manual defines six activity areas (Selection of Materials, Collection Management, Faculty Liaison, Library Use Instruction, Collection Evaluation, and Fund Management), lists three levels of priority, and offers suggestions for implementation. An early draft of the manual also includes a section entitled Continuing Education and Professional Development. Among its first priorities, it recommends a familiarity with disciplinary journal literature, as well as attending conferences and lectures in the discipline. A second priority is enrolling in a disciplinary methods course or reading of relevant literature; a third, the publication of research in the subject area, with an emphasis on bibliography.[2]

David L. Perkins describes the advantages to be gained from a bibliographer's training manual in his article "Writing the Collection Development Manual." He advises that it be sensitive to, or relate information in, six areas: 1. the bibliographic structure of a subject field; 2. the library's holdings—the size of various collection components; 3. the use patrons make of the collection—the results of user's studies or informal observation; 4. the materials budget—how the budget is allocated and spent; 5. the library's collection development policies—an explanation of assumptions and unstated policies necessary for an understanding of published policies; and 6. the library materials market—how the library chooses, uses, and evaluates vendors. Another type of bibliographer's manual may be more concerned with the procedures of selection, ordering, and processing. The bibliographer who begins his or her career at an institution that has developed either tool is indeed fortunate. Cited as examples are those of California State University, Northridge, for the former, and Stanford University, for the latter.[3]

All bibliographers will, of course, benefit from studying *Guidelines for Collection Development*, edited by David L. Perkins, and a product of the Collection Development Committee, Resources and Technical Services Division, American Library Association. Carefully composed outlines, complemented by bibliographies, consider the pros and cons of various approaches to the formulation of collection development policies, the evaluation of collections, the review of collections, and the allocation of budgets.[4]

The textbook *Building Library Collections* is a good introduction to all aspects of collection development. And though outdated, a sixth edition is in progress. It is complemented by the more advanced *Collection Development in Libraries: A Treatise*. Prominent librarians contributed essays on various aspects of collection management, the process of collecting, citation and use studies, development by format, and on new developments in the field. Included among the latter is the article by Charles B. Osburn "Education for Collection Development" (Part B, pp. 559–572).[5]

A work which promises to become a standard aid for beginning bibliographers is currently being prepared by the Collection Management and Development Committee, Resources and Technical Services Division, ALA. Tentatively entitled *Selection of Library Materials: Guide to Sources and Strategies*, it will be organized in five groups of essays considering: general selection sources, disciplines in the humanities, core disciplines in the social sciences, science and technology. Essays will also cover selecting nonprint media, government publications, small press publications, microform, and machine-readable data files. Additional volumes are planned to consider the foreign book trade and area studies, and interdisciplinary studies.[6]

Finally, though articles on collection development may appear to some extent in almost all library journals, two publications are exclusively devoted to the subject. Each focuses on a different aspect of the bibliographer's responsibilities. *Collection Management: A Quarterly Journal Devoted to the Management of Library Collections* (1976–) deals with such topics as weeding library collections, resource sharing, and budget allocation.[7]

Collection Building (1978–), on the other hand, carries many articles and bibliographies designed to guide one in the selection of materials on specific topics, for instance: religious books, Soviet dissident authors, the sociology of religion.[8]

The first intellectual task and responsibility of the beginning bibliographer is to identify and/or understand the substantive and bibliographic structure of the discipline(s) for which he or she is responsible. Thelma Freides, in *Literature and Bibliography of the Social Sciences*, presents a detailed discussion of bibliographic structure which is illustrated by numerous examples from each publication format as well as from the genres of bibliographic and reference sources.[9] Michael Keresztesi explores this topic further in his essay "The Science of Bibliography: Theoretical Implications for Bibliographic Instruction." Keresztesi shows how the various stages of a discipline's development are characterized by certain publication formats and a distinctive bibliographic and reference apparatus. Relating his ideas to collection development, he writes: "Developing collections of subject literature for research and graduate education require[s] that all documentary and literary products emanating from the activities of each component of a discipline be brought together and organized in the library for use. This means all communications organs, reports, journals, monographs, texts, publications of academic departments, research centers, institutes, university presses, proceedings of meetings and conferences, annual reviews, various reports of the regional, national, and international professional associations and bodies, documents of pertinent government agencies, and bibliographic instruments and reference tools in printed and electronic form. In a word, it means every important piece of record through which a discipline as a system manifests itself."[10]

Of course, the importance of each of these formats will vary from discipline to discipline and among libraries of various sizes, but the underlying assumption is that the bibliographer will come to understand how scholars in any given field communicate their research and further, how their research is synthesized in reference sources or identified in bibliographic aids.

Once the various formats and publishers of documentation are recognized, their relative importance within the discipline must be appreciated. Pioneering work in this area has been done by James C. Baughman. Basing his conclusions on the results of citation analyses in the social sciences, he notes the increasing dependence of scholars on the work of practitioners of disciplines other than their own, the primary role of certain publishers, and suggests a varying significance of monographs as compared to serials among social science disciplines; overall he sees nonserial literature as critically important to contemporary social scientists.[11]

The craft aspects of book selection are not a substitute for the qualities and qualifications which are essential for a bibliographer: maturity, experience, critical judgment, scholarship, and subject training.

Fundamental issues with which the beginning bibliographer should become familiar are discussed in two works which deserve special attention. *Scholarly Communications: The Report of the National Enquiry,*[12] explores the economic demands of the current structure of communication; among its recommendations are the establishment of a national bibliographic system and a national periodicals center. Charles Osburn's *Academic Research and Library Resources: Changing Patterns in America,*[13] provides an historical and sociological justification for a national structure for cooperative collection development and resource sharing. By delineating changing research patterns and, correspondingly, a changing reliance on library resources, both in terms of the extent and nature of use and of the types of materials used, Osburn provides a basis for thinking about the nature of past, current, and future collections. He too urges that libraries coordinate their collecting with one another.

On the most basic of levels, each of these works suggests that a good collection need not be comprehensive. But this does not excuse the bibliographer from understanding the bibliographic structure and research interests of the disciplines or fields for which he or she is responsible, as well as of having an appreciation of the materials not acquired. In other words, good bibliographers will need to know as much about resources and the epistemology of disciplines as they always have. But they will also need to know about networking and user studies, weeding, the identification of items for storage, and—most importantly—resource sharing. The rubric is "collection management," and it is succinctly defined by Paul Mosher in his article "Collection Development to Collection Management: Toward Stewardship of Library Resources."[14]

Surely the most important effort to coordinate collection development and resource sharing nationally in the coming decade will be that of the Research Libraries Group (RLG). Its work will be achieved through its evaluation tool, the *RLG Conspectus,* which minutely divides the universe of recorded knowledge into Library of Congress class numbers, to which are assigned standardized assessments of collection strength and current collecting levels. These standardized statements are sometimes modified or elaborated to reflect the nature and needs of specific disciplines or fields.[15]

The levels of collecting strength defined in *Guidelines for Collection Development* and in the *RLG Conspectus* assume that bibliographers will be able to identify the major sources within each format of a discipline's communication structure. But for the beginning bibliographer none of this is simple. In fact, determining precisely how successful collect-

ing has been, even for the most knowledgeable bibliographers, can present a host of difficulties and invariably winds up being a lot of work. The challenge of evaluating a collection, and eventually one's impact on it, can be met in many ways.[16]

But where does one begin? Perhaps the easiest way to become familiar with a field is to read the cumulating or synthesizing literature which serves it. Even if one has advanced training in the discipline for which he or she is responsible, this will prove valuable. For instance, all the social sciences are dealt with in the *International Encyclopedia of the Social Sciences.*[17] It is a fine compendium of epistemological knowledge. Other sources such as the *Dictionary of the History of Ideas*[18] and *Encyclopaedia Britannica*[19] may help as well. In addition to concise discussion, important bibliographies often conclude encyclopedia articles.

One work designed specifically to convey to librarians a basic overview of disciplinary structure is Bert F. Hoselitz, ed., *A Reader's Guide to the Social Sciences.* Although outdated, it can serve as an initial introductory reading. It is concerned with disciplinary epistemology, research interests, and current trends. Each of its chapters is written by an expert and selected representative works in the discipline are cited in discussions which take the form of extended bibliographic essays.[20]

But disciplines and many fields are also served by more specific synthesizing sources, such as essay collections, handbooks, annuals, or as overviews or studies of a field's development. Examples include: *Interrelations of Literature;*[21] *Ordinary People and Everyday Life: Perspectives on the New Social History;*[22] *International Handbook of Historical Studies: Contemporary Research and Theory;*[23] *Historical Studies Today;*[24] *Political Science: The State of the Discipline;*[25] and *New Directions in European Historiography.*[26]

Scanning annual reviews such as the *Annual Bulletin of Historical Literature*[27] and the *Annual Review of Anthropology*[28] is also valuable. JAI Press Inc. publishes a legion of these sources for specific fields and for the interdisciplinary concerns of many social science disciplines, for instance, *Advances in Law and Child Development, Research in Philosophy and Technology,* and *Research in the Interweave of Social Roles.* In addition, some journals are devoted to surveying the state-of-the-art, among them, *Progress in Human Geography*[29] and *Progress in Physical Geography*[30] And, of course, review essays appear as special features in most academic journals.

An appreciation of the sources from which knowledge is created in a given discipline should be one of the immediate by-products of such study,

The underlying assumption is that the bibliographer will come to understand how scholars in any given field communicate their research and further, how their research is synthesized in reference sources or identified in bibliographic aids.

Good bibliographers will need to know as much about resources and the epistemology of disciplines as they always have. But they will also need to know about networking and user studies, weeding, the identification of items for storage, and—most importantly—resource sharing.

for instance, archival and manuscript finding-aids, document collections, collections of tests, and serially issued economic and financial reports. And, of course, once the category of source material needed is defined, specific representatives of it must be targeted for acquisition. For instance, collections supporting extensive work in urban history might contain city directories, fire insurance maps, manuscript census returns, government documents, and local newspapers. Or, some fields may require collections of materials normally perceived as belonging to another discipline; for instance, philosophical and literary works for history, or works of political science and psychology for education.[31]

Even before the study of these sources, the bibliographer should "learn" the basic bibliographic and reference sources specific to the discipline or field. It is also important to determine if one's library includes them. These goals may be achieved by checking against holdings works such as Eugene Sheehy's *Guide to Reference Books*.[32] Many disciplines and fields are served by more specific guides, for example: *Asia, Reference Works: A Select Annotated Guide*;[33] *Research Guide for Psychology*;[34] *The Philosopher's Guide to Sources, Research Tools, Professional Life, and Related Fields*.[35]

An outdated but suggested list of research guides concludes *The Modern Researcher*.[36] A more recent and comprehensive bibliography and brief discussion of such aids is Donald C. Dickinson's "A Guide to the Guides: Literary Maps of the Humanities, Social Sciences, and Sciences."[37] Dickinson limits himself to guides covering an entire discipline rather than sub-disciplines, and to aids which discuss research trends, reference sources, and searching techniques.

Discipline-generated or oriented core bibliographies or bibliographic essays are also instructive. Some well-known examples are: *Harvard Guide*,[38] *Guide to Historical Literature*,[39] *Handbook of Popular Culture*.[40] Less well-known examples are *Sources for American Studies, American Studies: Topics and Sources*[41] and *Women's Studies: A Recommended Core Bibliography*.[42] Such sources need not merely be checked against holdings, but may be read—even if primarily citations—for a sense of a discipline's or field's concerns.

Expanding and keeping current one's knowledge demands a commitment to continual learning which is best realized by the regular scanning and selective reading of appropriate journals. Bulletins, journals, and newsletters hold the scholarly community together. In addition to publishing articles, academic journals generally feature extensive book review sections, lists of recently published bibliographic aids and documents, listings of books re-

ceived, and current awareness bibliographies. The advertisements they carry can also be useful. For historians in particular, studies have shown that of all the avenues available, the historian is most likely to learn about a publication either through a reference in an article or book or through the book review section of an academic journal.[43] The same can be assumed for all scholars.

Journals are not without preference in their choice of books to be reviewed, but their prejudices are usually those of the body of scholars it is their intent to serve. To ensure both depth and scope, a group of journals, rather than a single title, should be chosen for regular review and the checking of book review lists. The bibliographer should tailor his or her stable of journals but the contributions of major or umbrella associations, such as the American Historical Association's *American Historical Review*[44] or the Organization of American Historians' *Journal of American History*,[45] should always be included. Journals that are multi-disciplinary, such as the *Journal of Asian Studies*[46] and *Latin American Research Review*,[47] may be valuable. Also, specialized publications such as the *Journal of Psychohistory*[48] and *Social Science History*[49] may be appropriate. And some areas are served by reviewing journals: *Contemporary Sociology: A Journal of Reviews*,[50] *Reviews in American History*,[51] *Reviews in Anthropology*,[52] and *Philosophical Books*[53] are examples.

A good technique for both initiating conversation and defining a scholar's interests is to ask what journals he or she regularly reads to stay current in fields of interest. These are the scholars' most valued and trusted of bibliographic aids and it doesn't hurt for the bibliographer to show that he or she appreciates their importance. This advice applies to disciplinary overviews or state-of-the-art literature.

There are also some bibliographic aids to consult for identifying journals: *Ulrich's International Periodicals directory*, its companion, *Irregular Serials and Annals*,[54] and *Magazines for Libraries*.[55] *Irregular Serials and Annals* is especially useful for identifying the "advances in," "annual review," and "progress in" serials previously mentioned. *Magazines for Libraries*, far more useful, is now in four editions, which retrospectively complement one another, and has annotations of 75–250 words for each title. There are also sources which have a disciplinary focus, for example, *Historical Periodicals Directory*,[56] *International List of Geographical Serials*, and *Annotated World List of Selected Current Geographical Serials*.[57] Of course, one should also consult the list of journals treated in a discipline's major abstracting and indexing source.

Still other important aids are the acquisition lists

of libraries renowned for their particular subject strengths. To identify such libraries, consult *Subject Collections*,[58] and *Subject Collections in European Libraries*.[59]

The novice bibliographer will also want to develop a menu of book trade and general reviewing sources. As he or she becomes more knowledgeable and comfortable, some of these may be discarded and a reliance on national bibliographies, for instance, may increase. The most frequently consulted and most general purpose reviewing sources are *Choice*,[60] *Library Journal*,[61] and *Publishers Weekly*.[62]

Bibliographers in the humanities and social sciences will want regularly to read such publications as the *New York Review of Books*,[63] the *Times Literary Supplement*[64] and the *New York Times Book Review*.[65] Similar publications with specific relevance to one's collecting responsibilities may also be read, such as the *Chronicle of Higher Education*,[66] the democratic socialist newspaper *In These Times*,[67] or the conservative *National Review*.[68] Reading such publications will help one to develop and maintain a feel for contemporary issues.

It is also critical to identify a discipline's academies and associations. In addition to journals, associations often publish memoirs, proceedings, and transactions. These are critical components of a research collection. Useful in identifying these bodies and their publications are: the *Encyclopedia of Associations*,[69] *World of Learning*,[70] and the *Yearbook of International Organizations*.[71] *Associations' Publications in Print*[72] will also help, especially its Publisher/Title Index, which enables one to identify the titles published by specific associations.

An often perplexing problem is the identification of conference proceedings and unpublished papers. *Irregular Serials and Annuals* is the first source of verification for proceedings. In addition, in the humanities and social sciences, *Proceedings in Print*,[73] *Directory of Published Proceedings*,[74] *Index to Social Sciences and Humanities Proceedings*,[75] and the *Bibliographic Guide to Conference Publications*[76] will help. Unpublished papers are generally only listed in conference programs and normally not acquired. An outstanding exception is in sociology; *Sociological Abstracts* provides ready access to unpublished papers presented at major conferences through complete citations, abstracts, and thorough indexing.[77] Further, it is searchable by computer. ERIC provides much the same service for education, by both selectively accepting as well as soliciting the listing of unpublished papers. It also publishes them, with permission, in microfiche and paper format.[78]

These facts have profound bibliographic implications, for they indicate that some disciplines integrate unpublished work into their bibliographic network. Thus the acquisiton of unpublished work may have more validity in some fields than others. On the other hand, it is assumed that most worthwhile work initially reported as "unpublished" eventually finds its way into publication.

In time, the bibliographer will also want to become familiar with the major monographic series of the discipline, as well as with the quality and characteristics of publishers. This is best achieved by reading reviews, advertisements, and examining representative books. The placement of a continuation order for a monographic series assures the automatic acquisition of books whose quality and focus generally are guaranteed by their mode of publication. Some typical examples are Johns Hopkins University's *Studies in Historical and Political Science* and the various *Contributions in . . .* published by Greenwood Press. The identification and acquisition of monographic series has been significantly facilitated by *Books in Series*.[79]

It should be noted that online catalog services such as the Research Libraries Information network (RLIN) and the Online Computer Library Center, formerly the Ohio College Library Center (OCLC), will help with this work as will an ever broadening array of online services normally thought of only as reference sources. Indeed, the computer has revolutionized bibliographic searching and the beginning bibliographer should immediately learn to use the technology.

Obviously, this is all quite labor-intensive. It demands intellectual curiosity, energy, and time. But it is also the only way one can—even with extensive academic training—learn enough about a discipline to appreciate its concerns and epistemology and practice a collection development sensitive to the needs of scholars and students.

In the realm of self-education, the drafting of a collection development policy, a collection assessment, or a discipline-specific bibliographer's manual is to the bibliographer what the preparation of a reference guide is to the reference librarian or the researching of a book or article is to the scholar. The questions asked by such a document determine the quality of the educational experience—not to mention the utility of the knowledge it will record. Collection development policies should respond to local needs, outline the intended broad characteristics and limitations of collections, and identify the sources useful for evaluating and building collections, while respecting the basic concerns and bibliographic structure of the discipline.

These policies readily answer two needs: they record data which justify a policy decision while

Obviously, this is all quite labor-intensive. It demands intellectual curiosity, and energy, and time. But it is also the only way one can learn enough about a discipline to appreciate its concerns and epistemology and practice a collection development sensitive to the needs of scholars and students.

simultaneously helping to give it definition and focus, and they identify the vehicles—bibliographies, journals, reviewing media—which will facilitate its actualization. Further, in the event of personnel change, they promise a chance for continuity in collection.

Special sections to be included in inhouse collection development policies according to disciplinary divisions and/or subdivisions are:

1. Disciplinary overviews or state-of-the-art literature
2. Guides to the discipline's or field's bibliographic and reference apparatus
3. Major relevant recurrent bibliographies and indexes and abstracts
4. Core journals regularly reviewed for current awareness and to monitor acquisitions
5. Bibliographies for evaluation and retrospective collection development.
6. Special selection aids (acquisition lists, national bibliographies, etc.)
7. Book dealers especially useful in the field
8. Undergraduate courses taught
9. Graduate courses taught
10. Dissertations in progress and completed
11. Faculty research interests
12. Relevant resources in the area or available through agreement

For a complete outline of a policy, the reader should refer to *Guidelines for Collection Development* and the Office of Management Studies, Association of Research Libraries, Systems Procedures Exchange Center (SPEC) Kits 11 and 38.[80] Each is a collection of summary collection development policies and related documentation. Such basic or summary policies are presumably based on the correlation of local needs with a discipline's epistemology and bibliographic structure. That is, on knowledge derived from the sources noted above.

Present strength and current collecting levels, of course, may not be the same. Using the standardized descriptions of collecting quality or level employed either by RLG or suggested in *Guidelines for Collection Development*, the bibliographer should indicate an assessment of the quality of each collection component. But detailed collection assessments should be distinct from the policies.

Library of Congress divisions outlined in *Guidelines for Collection Development*, or the more finely segmented classes from the *RLG Conspectus*, may be used to define areas for treatment in the proposed policies. Some areas, such as history, may require the discussion of classes from philosophy, political science, the humanities, the social sciences, and education. In any case, policies should reflect this interdisciplinary nature in ways which are sensitive to disciplinary as well as local con-

cerns. Another approach is to refer to policies for appropriate LC classes. In short, for inhouse as well as summary purposes, a field such as British history can be treated in one or in many complete policies. For instance, whether to record all of the information noted above for a general division or for subdivisions of the field will vary with the intensity of collecting and interest at a given institution.

During the process of developing a collection development policy, the faculties most affected and knowledgeable should be consulted. The clarification, validation, or drafting of policy is a natural invitation for initial personal contact. To begin, the bibliographer might encourage his or her invitation to speak before a faculty meeting, meet with a departmental library committee, or simply go down the roster and meet with each faculty member individually. Social skills are as invaluable in bibliography as they are in many other professions.

In addition, a survey of faculty instructional and research interests and of corresponding perceptions of collection adequacy can be conducted. Information on faculty reliance on collections outside of the institution and the titles of journals read can also be obtained through a survey; this not only generates titles for collection evaluation or possible purchase, but is a way of defining interests. These data gathering efforts should precede or coincide with the formulation of policy, or at least occur before its final codification.

The proposed policies will both ensure and reflect an understanding of a discipline's interests and bibliographic apparatus apart from a knowledge of library policies and procedures. Their discussion with faculty will help to ensure an awareness and sensitivity to faculty concerns and provide the bibliographer with an opportunity to demonstrate a knowledge of disciplinary and local needs. In a sense, the sharing of policies becomes a credentialling process both with faculty and with one's colleagues.

In 1970, a test to measure the competency of a bibliographer appeared in a letter in *College and Research Libraries*. The scoring of some questions is too rigorous while others will be irrelevant to the situations of most bibliographers, but it's worth glancing at because it assumes as critical the basic knowledge urged in this paper. Among its questions: "List five very prominent scholars in the field"; "Give the name of the most important book which surveys the literature in your field"; "Identify at least two, and more if applicable, 'schools of thought' among scholars in your field"; and "List five principal English language scholarly journals in your field."[81]

References

1. Manuel D. Lopez, "A Guide for Beginning Bibliographers," *Library Resources and Technical Services* 13, no. 4 (Fall 1969): 462–470.

2. University of Texas at Austin, General Libraries, *Bibliographer's Manual: A Guide to the General Libraries Collection Development Program* (Austin: General Libraries, University of Texas at Austin, 1982). The draft referred to is dated 1 July 1981.

3. David L. Perkins, "Writing the Collection Development Manual," *Collection Management* 4, no. 3 (Fall 1982): 37–47.

4. David L. Perkins, ed., Collection Development Committee, Resources and Technical Services Division, American Library Association, *Guidelines for Collection Development* (Chicago: American Library Association, 1979).

5. Wallace John Bonk and Rose Mary Magrill, *Building Library Collections*, 5th ed. (Metuchen, N.J. and London: Scarecrow Press, 1979) and Robert D. Stueart and George B. Miller, Jr., eds., *Collection Development in Libraries: A Treatise*, 2 vols. (Greenwich, Conn.: JAI Press, 1980).

6. Telephone conversation with Patricia McClung, general editor of volume one and Associate Director of Program Coordination, RLG, 7 August 1984.

7. *Collection Management: A Quarterly Journal Devoted to the Management of Library Collections,* 1976–   (New York: Haworth Press).

8. *Collection Building* 1978–   (New York: Neal-Schuman Publishers, Inc.).

9. Thelma Freides, *Literature and Bibliography of the Social Sciences* (Los Angeles: Melville, 1973). See also Carl M. White et al., *Sources of Information in the Social Sciences: A Guide to the Literature*, 2nd ed., (Chicago: American Library Association, 1973).

10. Michael Keresztesi, "The Science of Bibliography: Theoretical Implications for Bibliographic Instruction" pp. 20–21 in *Theories of Bibliographic Education: Designs for Teaching* edited by Cerise Oberman and Katina Strauen (New York: R.R. Bowker, 1982).

11. James C. Baughman, "A Structural Analysis of the Literature of Sociology," *The Library Quarterly* 44, no. 4 (October 1974): 293–308 and "Toward a Structural Approach to Collection Development," *College and Research Libraries* 38, no. 3 (May 1977): 241–248. Another approach to this problem examines the circulation records of a particular library: Paul Metz, *The Landscape of Literature: Use of Subject Collections in a University Library* (Chicago: American Library Association, 1983). Also considered are use patterns among different classes of readers.

12. National Enquiry into Scholarly Communication, Scholarly Communication: The Report of the National Enquiry (Baltimore: The Johns Hopkins University Press, 1979).

13. Charles B. Osburn, *Academic Research and Library Resources: Changing Patterns in America* (Westport, Conn.: Greenwood Press, 1979).

14. Paul H. Mosher, "Collection Development to Collection Management: Toward Stewardship of Library Resources," *Collection Management* 4, no. 4 (Winter 1982): 41–48. See also H. William Axford, "Collection Management: A New Dimension," *Journal of Academic Librarianship* 6, no. 6 (January 1981): 324–329.

15. Nancy E. Gwinn and Paul H. Mosher, "Coordinating Collection Development. The RLG Conspectus," *College and Research Libraries* 44, no. 2 (March 1980): 128–140. See also David H. Stam, "Think Globally–Act Locally: Collection Development and Resource Sharing," *Collection Building* 5, no. 1 (Spring 1983): 18–21. Copies of *Conspectus* worksheets and supporting documentation, and the *Conspectus* itself, are available for purchase from the Research Libraries Group, Inc. (RLG), Jordan Quadrangle, Stanford, CA 94305; 415-328-0920.

16. See Gwinn and Mosher, "Co-ordinating Collection Development...," 136–38, and Paul H. Mosher, "Collection Evaluation in Research Libraries: The Search for Quality, Consistency and System in Collection Development," *Library Resources and Technical Services* 23, no. 1 (Winter 1979): 16–32. On evaluation in general see Procedures Exchange Center (SPEC), *Collection Assessment in ARL Libraries, Kit 41* (Washington, D.C.: Association of Research Libraries, Office of Management Studies, 1978); *Collection Description and Assessment in ARL Libraries, Kit 87* (Washington D.C.: Association of Research Libraries, Office of Management Studies, 1982); *Guidelines for Collection Development*; and Thomas E. Nisonger, "An Annotated Bibliography of Items Relating to Collection Evaluation in Academic Libraries, 1969–1981," *College and Research Libraries* 43, no. 4 (July 1982): 300–311.

17. *International Encyclopedia of Social Sciences*, 17 v., David L. Sills, ed. (New York: Macmillan and the Free Press, 1968).

18. *Dictionary of the History of Ideas: Studies of Selected Pivotal Ideas*, 5 v. (New York: Scribner's, 1973–74).

19. *The New Encyclopaedia Britannica in 30 Volumes* [15th ed.] (Chicago: Encyclopaedia Britannica Educational Corporation, continuous revision, 1974–   ).

20. Bert F. Hoselitz, ed., *A Reader's Guide to the Social Sciences* (New York: The Free Press, 1970).

21. Jean-Pierre Barricelli and Joseph Gibaldi, eds., *Interrelations of Literature* (New York: Modern Language Association of America, 1982).

22. James B. Gardner and George Rollie Adams, eds., *Ordinary People and Everyday Life: Perspectives on the New Social History* (Nashville, Tenn.: The American Association for State and Local History, 1983).

23. Georg G. Iggers and Harold T. Parker, eds., *International Handbook of Historical Studies: Contemporary Research and Theory* (Westport, Conn.: Greenwood Press, 1980).

24. Felix Gilbert and Stephen R. Graubard, eds., *Historical Studies Today* (New York: W.W. Norton, 1972).

25. Ada Finifter, ed., *Political Science: The State of the Discipline* (Washington, D.C.: American Political Science Association, 1983).

26. Georg G. Iggers, *New Directions in European Historiography* (Middletown, Conn.: Wesleyan University Press, 1975).

27. *Annual Bulletin of Historical Literature*, 1911–   (London: The Historical Association).

28. *Annual Review of Anthropology*, 1972–   (Palo Alto: Annual Reviews, Inc.)

29. *Progress in Human Geography*, 1976–   (New York: Cambridge University Press).

30. *Progress in Physical Geography*, 1976–   (New York: Cambridge University Press).

31. For a brief but especially thoughtful discussion of these and other concerns see, Hendrik Edelman, "Se-

lection Methodology in Academic Libraries," *Library Resources and Technical Services* 23, no. 1 (Winter 1979): 33–38.

32. Eugene P. Sheehy, comp., *Guide to Reference Books*, 9th ed. (Chicago: American Library Association, 1976 and Supplements).

33. Godfrey Raymond Nunn, *Asia, Reference Works: A Select Annotated Guide* (London: Mansell, 1980).

34. Raymond G. McInnis, *Research Guide for Psychology* (Westport, Conn.: Greenwood Press, 1982).

35. Richard T. De George, *The Philosopher's Guide to Sources, Research Tools, Professional Life, and Related Fields* (Lawrence, Kan.: Regents Press of Kansas, 1980).

36. Jacques Barzun and Henry F. Graff, *The Modern Researcher*, 3rd ed. (New York: Harcourt Brace Jovanovich, Inc., 1977).

37. Donald C. Dickinson, "A Guide to the Guides: Literary Maps of the Humanities, Social Sciences, and Sciences," *Choice* 21, no. 3 (November 1983): 383–393.

38. Frank Freidel, ed., *Harvard Guide to American History*, 2 v. (Cambridge: Belknap Press of Harvard University Press, 1974).

39. American Historical Association, *Guide to Historical Literature*, George Frederick Howe, Chairman, Board of Editors (New York: Macmillan, 1961).

40. Thomas M. Inge, ed., *Handbook of American Popular Culture* (Westport, Conn.: Greenwood Press, 1978–   ).

41. Jefferson B. Kellogg and Robert W. Walker eds., *Sources for American Studies*, Contributions in American Studies, no. 64 (Westport, Conn.: Greenwood Press, 1983) and Robert H. Walker, ed., *American Studies: Topics and Sources*, Contributions in American Studies, no. 24 (Westport, Conn.: Greenwood Press, 1976).

42. Esther Stineman, *Women's Studies: A Recommended Core Bibliography* (Littleton, Colo.: Libraries Unlimited, Inc., 1979).

43. Margaret F. Stieg, "The Information Needs of Historians," *College and Research Libraries* 42, no. 6 (1981): 549–560.

44. *American Historical Review*, 1895–   (Washington, D.C.: American Historical Association).

45. *Journal of American History* (original title *Mississippi Valley Historical Review*), 1914– (Bloomington, Ind.: Organization of American Historians).

46. *Journal of Asian Studies*, 1941– (Ann Arbor: Association for Asian Studies, Inc.).

47. *Latin American Research Review*, 1965– (Chapel Hill: Latin American Studies Association).

48. *Journal of Psychohistory*, 1973–   (New York: Association for Psychohistory).

49. *Social Science History*, 1976–   (Beverly Hills: Sage Publications, Inc., for the Social Science History Association).

50. *Contemporary Sociology: A Journal of Reviews*, 1972–   (Washington, D.C.: American Sociological Association).

51. *Reviews in American History*, 1973–   (Baltimore: Johns Hopkins University Press).

52. *Reviews in Anthropology*, 1974–   (Pleasantville, N.Y.: Redgrave Publishing Company).

53. *Philosophical Books*, 1960–   (Oxford: Blackwell Publishing, Ltd.).

54. *Ulrich's International Periodicals Directory: A Classified Guide to Current Periodicals Foreign and Domestic, 1932–*   (New York: R.R. Bowker) and *Irregular Serials and Annuals: An International Directory, 1967–*   (New York: R.R. Bowker).

55. William Armstrong Katz and Linda Sternberg Katz, eds., *Magazines for Libraries: For the General Reader and School, Junior College, College, University, and Public Libraries*, 4th ed. (New York: R.R. Bowker, 1982).

56. Eric H. Boehm. Barbara H. Pope, and Marie S. Ensign, eds., *Historical Periodicals Directory*, projected 5v. (Santa Barbara and London: ABC-Clio, 1981–   ).

57. Chauncy Dennison Harris and Jerome D. Fellman, comps., *International List of Geographical Serials*, 3rd ed., University of Chicago, Department of Geography, Research Paper, no. 193 (Chicago: University of Chicago, Department of Geography, 1980) and Chauncy Dennison Harris, *Annotated World List of Selected Current Geographical Serials*, 4th ed., University of Chicago, Department of Geography, Research Paper, no 194 (Chicago: University of Chicago, Department of Geography, 1980).

58. Lee Ash and Denis Lorenz, *Subject Collections: A Guide to Special Book Collections and Subject Emphases as Reported by University, College, Public, and Special Libraries in the United States and Canada*, 3rd ed. (New York: R.R. Bowker, 1967).

59. Richard Casimir Lewanski, *Subject Collections in European Libraries: A Directory and Bibliographical Guide* (New York: R.R. Bowker, 1965).

60. *Choice*, 1964–   (Middleton, Conn.: Association of College and Research Libraries).

61. *Library Journal*, 1876–   (New York: R.R. Bowker).

62. *Publishers Weekly*, 1872–   (New York: R.R. Bowker).

63. *New York Review of Books*, 1963–   (New York: New York Review of Books).

64. *Times Literary Supplement*. 1902–   (London: Times Newspaper Ltd.).

65. *New York Times Book Review*, 1890–   (New York: The New York Times).

66. *Chronicle of Higher Education*, 1966–   (Washington, D.C.: Chronicle of Higher Education, Inc.).

67. *In These Times*, 1976–   (Milwaukee: Institute for Policy Studies).

68. *National Review*, 1955– (New York: National Review, Inc.).

69. *Encyclopedia of Associations*, 1961–   (Detroit: Gale Research).

70. *World of Learning*, 1947–   (London: Europa Publications).

71. *Yearbook of International Organizations*, 1966/67– (Brussels: Union of International Associations).

72. *Associations' Publications in Print*, 1981–   (New York: R.R. Bowker).

73. *Proceedings in Print*, 1964–   (Mattapan, Mass.: Proceedings in Print, Inc.).

74. *Directory of Published Proceedings, Series SSH: Social Sciences/Humanities*, 1968–   (White Plains, N.Y.: InterDok Corp.).

75. *Index to Social Sciences and Humanities Proceedings*, 1979–   (Philadelphia: Institute for Scientific Information, Inc.).

76. *Bibliographic Guide to Conference Publications*, 1975–   (Boston: G.K. Hall and Company).

77. *Sociological Abstracts*, 1952–   (New York: Sociological Abstracts). Searchable online, 1963–

78. *Resources In Education* (original title *Research In Education), 1966–*   (Washington, D.C.: National Institute of Education, Department of Education and published by the Government Printing Office) and *Current Index to Journals In Education*, 1969–   (New York: National Institute of Education, Department of Education and published by Oryx Press). Combined and searchable online as ERIC, 1966–   .

79. *Books in Series: Original, Reprinted, In-Print, and Out-of-Print Books, Published or Distributed in the U.S. in Popular, Scholarly, and Professional Series*, 3 v., 3rd. ed. (New York: R.R. Bowker, 1980).

80. Systems and Procedures Exchange Center (SPEC) *Collection Development in ARL Libraries, Kit 11* (Washington, D.C.: Association of Research Libraries, Office of Management Studies, 1974) and *Collection Development Policies, Kit 38* (Washington, D.C.: Association of Research Libraries, Office of Management Studies, 1977).

81. Guy A. Marco, "The National Book Selection Test," *College and Research Libraries* 31, no. 5 (September 1970): 349–351.

Book Selection in the College Library: The Faculty Perspective

by Mary Sellen

It has been acknowledged in the literature of library administration and book selection that in a college library, the faculty play an important role in the development of the book collection. Lyle, in discussing book selection within the larger context of the administration of a college library, notes that "close cooperation between the librarian and members of the faculty is vital in selecting books."[1] He goes on to state that "in lieu of its own specialist staff, the library leans heavily on the faculty,"[2] and yet "there is very little factual information on the methods by which faculty go about choosing library materials."[3] Carter et al.[4] spent six pages on the role of the faculty in selection. They theorized about the faculty's role from incidents that had been called to their attention. Broadus[5] acknowledged the role of the faculty but offered no theory or conclusions on their role in the selection process.

Some information about the faculty's role has been reported in studies in which circulation patterns of books were traced to their selectors. Evans, in two related studies,[6] examined which selector's books (faculty, librarians, or approval plans) had the highest circulation. He found that librarians selected a greater number of titles that were used. Bingham,[7] replicating Evans, found that books selected by faculty were circulated more frequently than those selected by librarians, except in the humanities. Geyer,[8] however, found

that there was no significant difference in the circulation patterns of books selected by faculty and those selected by librarians.

Two studies were found in which the specific role of the faculty in the selection process was examined. Biskup and Jones[9] sent questionnaires to the faculty at the Australian National University and the Canberra College in order to discover how frequently the faculty selected library materials and what sources they used. They found that a minority of faculty systematically selected materials and that they relied on methods of selection that did not automatically guarantee the quality of the collection. Kim[10] sent questionnaires to faculty in the School of Education at a midwestern university in order to examine selected behavioral factors that were likely to influence the faculty's participation in library book selection. Eleven variables were examined. It was found that years of teaching, publication activity, the amount of professional meetings attended, and the number of professional journals read were significant variables in the faculty's participation. One study was found in which book selection in the college environment was studied. Baughman et al.[11] surveyed a random sample of faculty members at four-year institutions. The librarians and general college administrators of each respective faculty member's institution were also sent surveys. The thrust of the study was to measure the attitudes of these three groups toward collection development policies. They found general agreement on the process of formulating a collection development policy but some disagreement on the issue of an allocation formula. Little information on their selection habits, however, was given.

The following study attempted to add to the literature of college faculty in the book selection process by examining the following questions:

1. What are the attitudes of faculty toward whom should be responsible for selecting books?
2. Is the technical process in ordering books adequate or are there needs that are not being met?
3. What is the role that book selection plays within the larger context of a faculty member's responsibilities of teaching and research?

METHODOLOGY

Each faculty member at the Pennsylvania State University–Behrend College was sent a questionnaire. The research, service, and teaching expectations at this institution were clear enough to elicit adequate responses to the research questions. The first part consisted of two questions in which the respondent was asked to indicate what divisions she/he belonged to. The choices were Business and Social Sciences (BSS), Humanities and Communication (HC), and Science, Engineering and Technology (SET). The faculty were also asked to indicate the number of years spent in an academic teaching position. The second part consisted of ten statements regarding book selection to which the faculty responded to on a Likert-type scale. The statements focused on the three research questions of 1. who should select the books (statements 1, 2, 3); 2. the process of selection (statements 4, 8, 10); and 3. the role book selection played in their academic responsibilities of research, service and teaching (statements 5, 6, 7, 9). The statements were:

1. Book selection should be done by the librarians only.
2. Book selection should be done by the faculty only.
3. Book selection should be done by the librarians and faculty.
4. I could use more help from the library (in terms of book catalogs, bibliographies, etc.) in selecting books for the library.
5. Book selection is not a high priority in my work for the college.
6. Book selection for the library is important for my research.
7. Book selection for the library is important for the courses I teach.
8. The monies that are regularly allotted to my depart-

ment are adequate to support the book needs in my discipline
9. Journals are more important for my work than books.
10. The system for ordering books for the library collection (filling out order cards, waiting for months, etc.) is a deterrent when I order books for the library.

Two final questions asked the faculty member to rate the frequency of times they sent in book orders and to rank important sources they used when ordering books. The questionnaire is reprinted at the end of this article. The SPSS subprograms of frequencies and crosstabs were used to analyze the results.

RESULTS

Table 1 presents a general summary of the responses from 44 or 45 percent of the 97 full-time faculty involved in book selection at the college. The majority of the respondents, 63 percent, rated themselves "regular" selectors. Thirty-two percent rated themselves "occasional" selectors, and five percent never participated. An almost equal number of responses was obtained from all three divisions. The number of years of teaching ranged from 1 to 21 +, with the majority in the category of 1 to 15.

TABLE 1 GENERAL SUMMARY

1. Frequency by Total Percentage:

	Total	Percentage
Regular	28	63%
Occasionally	14	32%
Never	2	5%
TOTAL	44	100%

2. Frequency by Division:

	BSS	HC	SET
Regular	8	9	11
Occasionally	6	6	2
Never	–	–	2
TOTAL	14	15	15

3. Frequency by Years of Teaching:

	1-5	6-10	11-15	16-20	21+
Regular	6	8	7	3	4
Occasionaly	8	2	3	–	1
Never	2	–	–	–	–
TOTAL	16	10	10	3	5

TABLE 2 SELECTOR

Statement 1: Book selection should be done by the librarians only.

TOTAL RESPONSE			YEARS OF TEACHING				DIVISION				FREQUENCY			
A	U	D		A	U	D		A	U	D		A	U	D
2	-	42	1-5	-	-	16	BSS	1	-	13	Regular	1	-	27
(5%)		(95%)	6-10	-	-	10	HC	-	-	15	Occasion	1	-	13
			11-15	-	-	9	SET	1	-	14	Never	-	-	2
			16-20	-	-	3								
			21+	1	-	4								

Statement 2: Book selection should be done by the faculty only.

TOTAL RESPONSE			YEARS OF TEACHING				DIVISION				FREQUENCY			
A	U	D		A	U	D		A	U	D		A	U	D
4	3	37	1-5	-	-	16	BSS	1	1	12	Regular	4	3	21
(9%)	(7%)	(84%)	6-10	1	2	7	HC	1	1	13	Occasion	-	-	14
			11-15	1	1	8	SET	2	1	12	Never	-	-	2
			16-20	1	-	2								
			21+	1	-	4								

Statement 3: Book selection should be done by the librarians and faculty.

TOTAL RESPONSE			YEARS OF TEACHING				DIVISION				FREQUENCY			
A	U	D		A	U	D		A	U	D		A	U	D
37	4	3	1-5	15	1	-	BSS	12	1	1	Regular	21	4	3
(84%)	(9%)	(7%)	6-10	8	2	-	HC	12	3	-	Occasion	14	-	-
			11-15	8	1	1	SET	13	-	2	Never	2	-	-
			16-20	2	-	1								
			21+	4	-	1								

A - Agree   U - Unsure   D - Disagree

Table 2 summarizes the responses in regard to the first research question. Faculty were consistent in their response to choice of selector. The responses to statements 1, 2, and 3 were almost identical in agreeing that selection should be done by a combination of faculty and librarians. There was no uncertainty and almost complete agreement that book selection not be left to the librarian alone. Some uncertainty did occur when selection was left to the faculty only or the combination of faculty and librarians. This concern was apparent in the teaching years of 11 to 25+ and the BSS and SET divisions. The greatest dissent to the faculty/librarian combination came from those with 11 to 15 years of teaching experience and the SET division. Those who were "regular" selectors also favored the faculty/librarians combination.

Table 3 summarizes the responses to the second research question. A large percentage of respondents expressed a need for more help in the selection process (statement 4). The responses to the statements on the allocated monies (statement 8) and technical system used to order materials (statement 10) were generally even among the three possible responses. Although the expressed need for help was large (47 percent), the majority was either unsure or did not express any need for help (a combination percentage of 53 percent). Faculty in the 1 to 10 years of teaching expressed the most need, while older faculty were either unsure or in disagreement. Those faculty in the HC division expressed the greatest desire for help while the SET and BSS divisions were almost evenly split in uncertainty or disagreement. The "occa-

TABLE 3 PROCESS

Statement 4 : I could use more help from the library in selecting books for the library.

TOTAL RESPONSE			YEARS OF TEACHING				DIVISION				FREQUENCY			
A	U	D		A	U	D		A	U	D		A	U	D
21	9	14	1-5	9	3	4	BSS	5	3	6	Regular	11	8	9
(47%)	(21%)	(32%)	6-10	7	2	1	HC	10	3	2	Occasion	8	1	5
			11-15	4	1	5	SET	6	3	6	Never	2	–	–
			16-20	–	2	1								
			21+	1	1	3								

Statement 10: The monies alloted to my department are adequate to support the book needs in my discipline.

TOTAL RESPONSE			YEARS OF TEACHING				DIVISION				FREQUENCY			
A	U	D		A	U	D		A	U	D		A	U	D
16	14	14	1-5	3	7	6	BSS	6	4	4	Regular	10	6	12
(36%)	(32%)	(32%)	6-10	6	2	2	HC	7	2	6	Occasion	6	6	2
			11-15	4	3	3	SET	3	8	4	Never	–	2	–
			16-20	1	–	2								
			21+	2	2	1								

Statement 10: The system for ordering books is a deterrent when I order books for the library.

TOTAL RESPONSE			YEARS OF TEACHING				DIVISION				FREQUENCY			
A	U	D		A	U	D		A	U	D		A	U	D
17	14	13	1-5	6	7	3	BSS	4	6	4	Regular	8	9	11
(38%)	(32%)	(30%)	6-10	5	3	2	HC	9	4	2	Occasion	8	4	2
			11-15	5	2	3	SET	4	4	7	Never	1	1	–
			16-20	1	1	1								
			21+	–	1	4								

A - Agree   U - Unsure   D - Disagree

sional" and "never" selectors did agree that they needed help and the majority of "regular" selectors disagreed or were unsure.

The response to the statement on allotments to the departments (statement 8) was almost evenly divided between the three possible responses with agreement that adequate monies were allotted only two percentage points higher than the responses of unsure or disagree. The greatest satisfaction with the monies occurred in the teaching years of 6 to 15, with the younger faculty in disagreement or unsure. The SET division was more unsure about the money amount than the other two divisions, with BSS and HC almost evenly split between agreement and disagreement. "Regular" selectors were mostly in disagreement or un-

sure about their monies. "Occasional" and "never" were in agreement or unsure.

The majority of respondents, 38 percent, found the system for ordering books (statement 10) a deterrent when selecting. An almost equal number were unsure—32 percent, or in disagreement—30 percent. The dissatisfaction came from those with 1 to 15 years of teaching and faculty in the HC division. "Regular" selectors were in disagreement or unsure. "Occasional" and "never" agreed. Faculty in BSS and SET were more inclined to be unsure or in disagreement about the system being a deterrent.

Table 4 summarizes the responses to the third research question. In general, faculty considered selection a high priority in their work for the college and important for their research and teaching. There was also agreement that journals were important for their work. Most faculty were either in agreement or unsure about the importance of book selection in their research (statement 6). Faculty in all years of teaching considered selection important. The SET division was almost unanimous in ranking selection important. A larger number of respondents in the HC and BSS divisions were uncertain or disagreed about the importance. The "regular" and "occasional" selectors agreed that selection was important. There was, however, more uncertainty or disagreement with the "occasional" selector than the "regular".

A large percentage considered selection important for teaching (statement 7). There was little dis-

TABLE 4   ACADEMIC ROLE

Statement 5 : Book selection is not a high priority in my work for the college.

TOTAL RESPONSE			YEARS OF TEACHING				DIVISION				FREQUENCY			
A	U	D		A	U	D		A	U	D		A	U	D
11	5	28	1-5	2	1	13	BSS	7	2	5	Regular	4	4	20
(25%)	(11%)	(64%)	6-10	2	2	6	HC	4	2	9	Occasion	7	1	6
			11-15	5	1	4	SET	-	1	14	Never	-	-	2
			16-20	-	-	3								
			21+	2	1	2								

Statement 6: Book selection for the library is important for my research.

TOTAL RESPONSE			YEARS OF TEACHING				DIVISION				FREQUENCY			
A	U	D		A	U	D		A	U	D		A	U	D
26	10	7	1-5	10	3	2	BSS	7	3	4	Regular	18	5	4
(59%)	(23%)	(16%)	6-10	5	2	3	HC	6	6	2*	Occasion	6	5	3
			11-15	7	2	1	SET	13	1	1	Never	2	-	-
			16-20	1	2	-								
			21+	3	1	1								

Statement 7: Book selection is important for the courses I teach.

TOTAL RESPONSE			YEARS OF TEACHING				DIVISION				FREQUENCY			
A	U	D		A	U	D		A	U	D		A	U	D
30	9	4	1-5	9	4	2*	BSS	8	3	3	Regular	21	4	2
(68%)	(21%)	(9%)	6-10	7	3	-	HC	11	2	1*	Occasion	9	3	2
			11-15	8	1	1	SET	11	4	-	Never	-	2	-
			16-20	2	1	-								
			21+	4	-	1								

Statement 9: Journals are more inportant for my work than books.

TOTAL RESPONSE			YEARS OF TEACHING				DIVISION				FREQUENCY			
A	U	D		A	U	D		A	U	D		A	U	D
19	14	10	1-5	7	3	6	BSS	9	2	3	Regular	11	11	6
(43%)	(32%)	(23%)	6-10	7	2	1	HC	6	5	3	Occasion	7	3	3
			11-15	4	4	1	SET	7	7	1	Never	1	-	1
			16-20	-	2	1								
			21+	1	3	1								

A - Agree   U - Unsure   D - Disagree

agreement about this but some uncertainty. The uncertainty was strongest in the younger faculty and in the BSS and SET divisions. The most noticeable disagreement came with the younger faculty in the BSS division.

While journals were generally considered important for the faculty member's work (statement 10), a significant percentage were uncertain (32 percent). This occurred throughout all years of teaching and in all three divisions. The BSS division rated journal importance the highest while the SET division was split in agreement and uncertainty.

When ranking sources used when ordering books for the library, publishers' announcements, reviews, and advertisements in professional journals were ranked one most often; references and citations found in books and articles, and *Choice* cards were ranked one less often; conferences and informal sources were not ranked one at all. *Choice* cards were chosen as the second ranking source most often. Publishers' announcements, reviews, and advertisements and references ranked second a number of times also. All choices were ranked almost equally in the third and fourth rankings.

DISCUSSION

The overall response to this survey indicated that there was interest on the part of the faculty in the book-selection process. The characteristics of the faculty selectors covered a large range of characteristics. "Regular" selectors were found in all three divisions and in all years of teaching. In general, the faculty felt that the responsibility for selecting books should be assumed by a combination of faculty and librarians.

Faculty expressed some concerns with the technical process of ordering materials. Help from the library in selecting books was a need expressed by a majority of the respondents. The actual system for ordering was seen as a deterrent by the majority, but the uncertainty and disagreement about this was significant. The same was true when faculty responded to the statement concerning allocated monies. The majority agreed that there was adequate support, with significant numbers unsure or disagreeing.

Book selection was overall viewed as important in the faculty members' work for the college. Se-

lection seemed to be more important for teaching responsibilities than research, although there was more uncertainty in the statement about research than in the responses about teaching.

CONCLUSION

Librarians should not underestimate the interests and concerns of faculty in the book-selection process. This survey indicates that selection plays an important role in the faculty members' various responsibilities for the college, a role librarians may not be fully aware of. The faculty gave indications that they regularly selected books and desired to work with the librarians in this process.

Footnotes

1. Guy R. Lyle, *The Administration of the College Library* 4th ed. (New York: Wilson, 1974), p. 176.
2. Ibid., p. 179.
3. Ibid., p. 177.
4. Mary Duncan Carter, Wallace John Bonk, Rose Mary Magrill, *Building Library Collections* 4th ed. (Metuchen, N.J.: Scarecrow Press, 1974), p. 61-66.
5. Robert N. Broadus, *Selecting Materials for Libraries* 2nd ed. (New York: Wilson, 1981), p. 18-19.
6. G. Edward Evans and Claudia White Argyres, "Approval Plans and Collection Development in Academic Libraries," *Library Resources and Technical Services* 18 (Winter 1974): 35-50 and G. Edward Evans, "Book Selection and Book Collection Usage in Academic Libraries," *Library Quarterly* 40 (July 1970):297-308.
7. Robbie Barnes Bingham, "Collection Development in University Libraries: an Investigation of the Relationship Between Categories of Selectors and Usage of Selected Items," (Ph.D. Thesis, Rutgers University, 1979).
8. John Eldon Geyer, "A Comparative Analysis of Book Selection Agents and Tools with Student Use at the Long Beach Community College Library," (Ed.D. University of Southern California, 1977).
9. Peter Biskup and Catherine A. Jones, "Of Books, Academics and Libraries: Some Facts about the Book Selection Habits of the Teaching Staffs at Two Canberra Institutions of Higher Learning," *Australian Academic and Research Libraries* 7(September 1976):159-70.
10. Ung Chon Kim, "Participation of Teaching Faculty in Library Book Selection," *Collection Management* 3(Winter 1979):333-54.
11. James Baughman et al. "A Survey of Attitudes Toward Collection Development in College Libraries" in *Collection Development in Libraries: A Treatise* ed. Robert Stueart and George B. Miller, Jr. (Greenwich, Conn.: JAI Press, 1980).

QUESTIONNAIRE
FACULTY BOOK SELECTION SURVEY

1. Please indicate what division you are in:
    _____ Business and Social Sciences
    _____ Humanities and Communication
    _____ Science, Engineering and Technology

2. Please indicate how long you have been teaching in a college or university:
    _____ 1-5 years
    _____ 6-10 years
    _____ 11-15 years
    _____ 16-20 years
    _____ 21+ years

PLEASE INDICATE YOUR AGREEMENT OR DISAGREEMENT WITH THE FOLLOWING STATEMENTS. THESE QUESTIONS PERTAIN TO THE SELECTION OF BOOKS, NOT JOURNALS.

1. Book selection should be done by the librarians only.
    _____ AGREE   _____ UNSURE   _____ DISAGREE

2. Book selection should be done by faculty only.
    _____ AGREE   _____ UNSURE   _____ DISAGREE

3. Book selection should be done by the librarians and faculty.
    _____ AGREE   _____ UNSURE   _____ DISAGREE

4. I could use more help from the library (in terms of book catalogs, bibliographies, etc.) in selecting books for the library.
    _____ AGREE   _____ UNSURE   _____ DISAGREE

5. Book selection is not a high priority in my work for the college.
    _____ AGREE   _____ UNSURE   _____ DISAGREE

6. Book selection for the library is important for my research.
    _____ AGREE   _____ UNSURE   _____ DISAGREE

7. Book selection for the library is important for the courses I teach.
    _____ AGREE   _____ UNSURE   _____ DISAGREE

8. The monies that are regularly allotted to my department are adequate to support the book needs in my discipline.
    _____ AGREE   _____ UNSURE   _____ DISAGREE

9. Journals are more important for my work than books.
    _____ AGREE   _____ UNSURE   _____ DISAGREE

10. The system for ordering books for the library collection (filling out cards, waiting for months, etc.) is a deterrent when I order books for the library.
    _____ AGREE   _____ UNSURE   _____ DISAGREE

11. Check one of the following that applies to the frequency with which you send in book orders for the library:
    _____ REGULARLY (meaning when you receive a reference for an appropriate book, you consider ordering it from the library)
    _____ OCCASIONALLY (meaning when you receive a reference for an appropriate book, ordering it for the library is a secondary consideration)
    _____ NEVER

12. Please rank (with 1 being the most important) the sources you use when ordering books for the library:
    _____ Publishers' announcements
    _____ Reviews and advertisements in professional journals
    _____ References and citations found in books and articles
    _____ Informal sources (e.g., conversations, visits to other institutions)
    _____ Conferences
    _____ Choice cards

Duplication in Library Collections: What We Know and What We Need to Know

Paul Metz

The great majority of academic libraries find themselves in a vast and often unmarked territory between two polar sets of goals and aspirations. These two poles could be represented by the model of the great research library, on the one hand, and the discount store, on the other. In choosing the first ideal, the library decides to acquire as broad a selection of research materials as possible, including infrequently used primary materials (census records, publications from limited editions, personal manuscripts, and unpublished pamphlets) in order that researchers may, at least in theory, find the collection all- or nearly all-sufficient. Holders of this view point with pride to the contents of the catalog. At the other pole, the library sets out to be as responsive to demand as possible, to provide more and more of the materials which "move off the shelves" and, like the discount store, to discontinue stock items which are less popular than something more attractive which might replace them. Advocates of this view point with pride to the swarming circulation desk.

These opposing views are set off in their clearest contrast when decisions are made to buy duplicate copies of material in high demand. The purchase of a second copy of one item generally means that a decision not to buy a single copy of another item has been made, if only by default. As with all difficult management decisions, deciding between these philosophies calls for a simulta- neous evaluation of values and facts. The value questions are critical, difficult, and highly debat- able. They require a consideration of institutional goals and a relative weighing of research and teaching as enterprises. The facts that are relevant to the issue are equally important, and are sub- stantially more amenable to an objective review. Fortunately, we know more than we might think, relevant to the copies-titles dilemma, although there is unquestionably a great deal still to be learned. The key points of what we know are outlined below, along with some indication of places where our knowledge is lacking.

WE KNOW WHO OUR USERS ARE AND WHAT THEY WANT

In most academic libraries, the heaviest users are the students; most users are not doing original research on projects which will make a new con- tribution to knowledge; and most of them want highly specific items. These three facts tell us the greater part of what we need to know about our users and their desires, and they deserve careful examination.

A variety of library studies and the experience of most individual libraries show—what should not be surprising—that the majority of users come from the student body. Lipetz, in his interviews of users of the Yale University Library, found that 76.9 percent of those who used the catalog were students of Yale or of some other institution. Only 12.0 percent were faculty, and 11.1 percent were either visitors, staff, retirees, or had some other miscellaneous identity. Among Yale users alone, the ratio of students to faculty was 7.7:1.[1] The student/faculty ratio at Yale is somewhat smaller than this, indicating that, if anything, the individual student is more apt to visit the library than the individual faculty member. Significantly outnumbering the faculty as members of the university community, students outnumber them as library users by at least an equal ratio.

It seems fair to assume that only a small proportion of students are engaged in significant original research. Although this statement would not apply to many graduate students, it is almost universally true of the undergraduates who so heavily populate most college and university communities, and is often true of graduate students up until the final years of their studies.

What about the faculty? Why do they visit the library, and what do they require there? The results of the 1975 Ladd-Lipset survey, reported in the October 14, 1975 issue of *The Chronicle of Higher Education*, indicated that faculty are not so heavily engaged in research as might be expected in view of the pressures for publication they are generally assumed to bear. Ladd and Lipset found that publication of research findings is extraordinarily concentrated among a few high achievers, while the great majority of faculty members were not only not engaged in research (one-half never having written or edited a book, one-third never having written a scholarly article), but actively expressed their identity with the teaching role over that of the scholar.[2]

The first question for future research concerns the crucially important minority of the faculty that is engaged in extensive research. What proportion of faculty users in a typical academic setting try to do research in their home institutions, and how many defer their major research projects for sabbaticals and breaks in the academic year, when they can visit the major research facilities (where "one stop shopping," with all its conveniences, may be a reasonable goal)? Given the choice of microforms, interlibrary loan, or visiting a research library which holds the needed materials in hard copy, what do they prefer? These questions are especially important for those many libraries which, while they have sizable core collections, can never aspire to major research status.

Besides knowing who is coming to the library and why, we know fairly well what they want when they come. The results of several studies indicate that the great majority of users are interested in specific documents. It is apparently the atypical user who comes to the library without knowing quite accurately what documents he or she seeks. Lipetz found that 73 percent of the time a user consulted the catalog, it was in pursuit of a specific document, and an additional five percent of the time it was in pursuit of information about a known document, although not the piece itself. Only 16 percent of his users were seeking materials according to their topics.[3] Similarly, Lancaster reports that only 11 percent of users take a subject approach to the catalog.[4] These findings are of great significance for the titles-versus-copies decision. If users were approaching materials through their subjects, it might seem safe to assume that if the first document identified were not found, a second would do almost as well. But if users go to the library to find a specific item and do not find it, they are more apt to be dissatisfied. The literature seems to indicate that it is at this point that the subject approach is reluctantly taken as a backup strategy.

This conclusion points to a second area where our knowledge is insufficient. Besides taking a subject approach, what does the frustrated user do? In economic terms, how substantial is the disutility or the user's frustration? It may be that students especially are led by desperation to rethink their problems and perhaps discover materials of greater value than the standard texts originally sought, but which were, inevitably, being used by other students. But it may also result in potential research projects, in their fertile but tentative and early stages, being deferred or, worse, abandoned. We simply do not know the answer to Michael Buckland's interesting question about how "substitutable" books are; what we do know, however, suggests that the answer may be, "not very."[5]

WE KNOW THAT USERS TEND TO WANT THE SAME MATERIALS

It is a commonplace to describe book use as a "Bradford" or a "Bradford-Zip hr. " distribution, indicating the extreme skewing of demand for a small subset of the titles in a typical library collection. This phenomenon has been found to apply in a nearly comprehensive range of types and sizes of libraries. Galvin and Kent, for example, found that 40 percent of the University of Pittsburgh's library collection had not circulated in its first seven years on the shelves.[6] A recent review by Robert Almony of the literature on conflicting user demands for materials and on the effectiveness of duplicate acquisitions policies lays out a wealth of empirical findings to support this point.[7]

At the Virginia Polytechnic Institute and State University, a collection of over one million volumes, a "rolling" or "on the fly" conversion to brief machine readable circulation records was in place for only *four-and-a-half months* before the probability that an item being brought to the circulation desk would already have been entered in the system reached .50. Only some 57,000 items had been entered in the system at this halfway point.[8]

The economist who observed this phenomenon would call it a serious case of "demand interference" and (besides wondering why supply is so unresponsive to demand) would want to know how severe the demand interference was. Perhaps by thinking more like economists we can formulate questions which will ultimately lead us nearer to an optimum allocation of our scarce resources. There is a story, perhaps apocryphal, of a librarian at the New York Public Library who decided to buy enough copies of *War and Peace* so that at least one would always be on the shelf. According to the story, he never succeeded, despite numerous reorderings. Our economist would want to know at what point this demand becomes satiated. We need to know how much the satisfaction of initial demands stimulates further demands on library resources, and with what effects. Finally, there is a danger if a library overreacts to demand and enslaves its acquisitions procedures to the results of circulation. Potential use of books which are never purchased will of course go unrecorded, and a regressive or imploding downward spiral might begin. We need to know how large the risk of this might be, though it is probably safe to argue that most libraries are at present quite removed from this danger.

WE KNOW THAT USERS ARE NOT OBTAINING THE MATERIALS THEY SEEK, AND WE HAVE A GOOD IDEA WHY

A spate of recent articles has presented empirical evidence to indicate that the rate of success experienced by users in pursuing the materials they want is shockingly low. Daniel Gore's interesting research on user frustration was prompted by his confidence that, at least at MacAlester College, the failure rate must be lower than the 40 percent figure the literature indicated was true in other settings. To his dismay, he ended up replicating, rather than refuting, this dismal result.[9] An interesting review by Kantor of the growing literature on user satisfaction indicates that the reason for this frustration is only rarely a failure to acquire the desired materials. The failure to collect

frustrates only about 10 percent of searches, while other factors account for the overall incidence of about 40 percent.[10]

Of these, the fact that items are unavailable because they are circulating accounts for the greatest share of the problem. Studies conducted at Case Western Reserve, Oklahoma, the University of Tennessee at Knoxville, and other settings indicate that between nine and 23 percent of the items which are sought and which are held by the library are in the hands of other users. For the well-known study which Buckland and his co-workers performed at the University of Lancaster Library, this figure was 23 percent.[11] These findings give empirical confirmation to the idea that demand interference might be high.

A residual category which Kantor calls "library failure" accounts for much of the remaining problem. Of the causes of library failure, theft has been found to be the most prominent. It seems safe to assume that thieves desire the same items as do more honest patrons, just as previous studies have shown that browsers and active borrowers seek and use the same materials.[12] This, too, is of course a researchable question.

A second component of Kantor's "library failure" is misshelving. It is self-evident that books do not need to be reshelved unless they have been used. The misshelving problem, an inevitable and, beyond some point, irreducible fact of library life, undoubtedly constitutes (along with circulation and theft) another form of demand interference.[13]

WE KNOW THAT DUPLICATION OF POPULAR TITLES DOES HELP TO SATISFY DEMAND

At the University of Lancaster, findings such as those which have been reviewed led to the decision to institute a variable loan policy and to acquire more copies of heavily used materials. As Buckland summarized the philosophy behind this shift, "a variable loan policy ought to be a variable loan *and duplication policy*" (emphasis his).[14] While it is impossible to attribute the results to either strategy primarily, the result was a dramatic increase in user satisfaction. Almony's review of the issue gives other instances where libraries were able to use circulation data as the basis for more responsive collections policies, and to do so without seriously affecting the total number of titles collected.[15]

On a more theoretical plane, Arora and Paul have plotted the relationship between multiple purchases and the probability of user satisfaction. Their conclusion is that there is a decided benefit in user satisfaction for each additional copy, although of course the relationship is not linear, but shows diminishing returns.[16] These diminishing returns need to be considered in the context of diminishing costs, for once the first copy of a book has been cataloged and brought under bibliographic control in a library, the addition of extra physical pieces does not require a full duplication of the original expense. Just how much less it costs to add an extra copy is yet another researchable question.

A final question for research was indicated by Michael Buckland when he noted that, "in practice, selection skills are likely to be less than ideal and this will, of course, affect the quality of service."[17] The reduced costs of added copies notwithstanding, purchasing them does entail sacrifices in the breadth of the collection. We need to know how well, in a real world, we can predict both the most used and the unused materials from the vast array of items we might acquire. An obvious implication of the Pittsburgh study is that if the process of prediction were perfected, we could sacrifice as much as 40 percent of our acquisitions in favor of heavily used materials, but this degree of foresight is unattainable and perhaps unapproachable as well.[18]

We are probably better at predicting heavy use than light use or nonuse of items. In part, this is because for the popular items, we can use circulation data as a basis for the necessary response of duplication, whereas for the items which users ignore, circulation data can only confirm our failures after the damage has been done. This is not to say that our ability to profit from circulation statistics is often used: in view of the increasing popularity of turn-key and home-grown circulation systems which provide valuable management statistics on circulation, it is disheartening that there is not more in the literature on how these data may be used—or better, have been used—to facilitate a more rational use of the library's acquisitions dollar. Of course, if circulation data are to be used in this way, we need to know just how quickly various kinds of materials become obsolete, so that we can determine whether it is possible to respond in time to heavy use early in their histories.

The difficulty of predicting use may in fact call for an entire redirection of the way in which we do studies of collections use. Many use studies have charted the probability of use for volumes according to their age, classification, language, or date of imprint.[19] With the exception of language, these are not generally the most useful characteristics of books from the point of view of the typical acquisitions system. Acquisitions systems are set up in terms of domestic jobbers versus foreign jobbers, of trade books versus scholarly presses, of commercial publishers versus societies which publish only within an area of interest. If feedback from circulation to the acquisitions process is to be useful, it must be phrased at least partially in these same terms. A library which found that the publications of foreign societies were little used might be better able to adjust its collections policies than a library which found that books in the R or T classification schedules were in light demand.

CONCLUSION

Although research efforts in librarianship are often criticized for a failure to be cumulative and progressive in their response to key problems, an overview of what we know about at least some aspects of our users' desires and behavior suggests that this criticism may be excessive. A number of studies converge and support one another in telling us who our users are, what they want, and how they seek it. We know how often they succeed, and we have understood in general terms the various reasons for their frequent failures. The studies which tell us this much raise more questions, which must be pursued if our research efforts are to be truly cumulative and useful.

This overview began with a description of two ideals of service, one based on a certain vision of scholarship and one oriented to a response to client demands. Most academic libraries fall well between these two ideals, and will remain close to the center of the scale despite their best efforts to move towards either end. But by making careful use of the knowledge already available to them, and by following a number of obvious signs for future research, they can at least ensure that their movement, however slight, is in the right direction.

Notes

1. Ben-Ami Lipetz, "Catalog Use in a Large Research Library," *The Library Quarterly* 42:129-39 (1972).
2. Everett Carl Ladd and Seymour Main Lipset, "How Professors Spend Their Time," *The Chronicle of Higher Education*, October 14, 1975, p. 2.
3. Lipetz, "Catalog Use." It should be noted that by measuring use of the catalog, Lipetz failed to count the (presumably small) number of users who take the very practical "subject" approach of simply walking to familiar parts of the stacks and browsing.
4. F. W. Lancaster, *The Measurement and Evaluation of Library Services* (Washington: Information Resources Press, 1977).

5. Michael K. Buckland, *Book Availability and the Library User* (New York: Pergamon Pr., 1975), p. 120.

6. Thomas J. Galvin and Allen Kent, "Use of a University Library Collection," *Library Journal* 102:2317-20 (1977).

7. Robert A. Almony, Jr., "The Concept of Systematic Duplication: A Survey of the Literature," *Collection Management* 2:153-66 (1978); for an overview of the statistical distribution of book use, see Stephen Bulick, "Book Use as a Bradford-Zipf Phenomenon," *College and Research Libraries* 39:215-20 (1978).

8. A. R. Pierce, internal memorandum on rolling conversion, The Newman Library, Virginia Polytechnic Institute and State University, 31 July, 1979.

9. Daniel Gore, "Let Them Eat Cake While Reading Catalog Cards: An Essay on the Availability Problem," *Library Journal* 100: 93-99 (1975).

10. Paul Kantor, "Availability Analysis," *Journal of the American Society for Information Science* 27:311-19 (1976).

11. Buckland, *Book Availability*; Kantor, "Availability Analysis"; Rita Hoyt Smith and Warner Granade, "User and Library Failures in an Undergraduate Library," *College and Research Libraries* 38:467-73 (1977).

12. Galvin and Kent, "Use of a University Library Collection"; William E. McGrath, "Correlating the Subject of Books Taken Out and Books Used Within an Open Stack Library," *College and Research Libraries* 32:280-5 (1971).

13. Kantor, "Availability Analysis."

14. Buckland, *Book Availability*, p. 107.

15. Almony, "The Concept of Systematic Duplication."

16. Sant R. Arora and Rameshwar N. Paul, "Acquisition of Library Materials: A Quantitative Approach," in American Society for Information Science. Conference, 1969. *Proceedings* (San Francisco: Greenwood, 1969), 495-99.

17. Buckland, *Book Availability*, p. 33.

18. Galvin and Kent, "Use of a University Library Collection."

19. Herman H. Fussler and Julian L. Simon, *Patterns in the Use of Books in Large Research Libraries* (Chicago: The University of Chicago Press, 1969); Paul Metz, "The Use of the General Collection at the Library of Congress," *The Library Quarterly* (forthcoming).

Problem Librarians Make Problems for Humanists

by J. Wesley Miller

... the whole problem of collection development, whether ordering or weeding, depends on the level of smarts a librarian must possess in order to make the necessary decisions.

Problem librarianship in weeding book collections has reached epidemic proportions with serious short- and long-range ramifications for everyone, especially for scholars in the humanities. Although a number of books and articles in recent years have set forth eminently sensible rationales for such weeding, deselection, or deaccessioning (as it is variously called), in actual practice pragmatism shaped by funding exigencies and a new business mentality among librarians generally produces disturbing results. The business viewpoint has brought fundamental shifts in how things are done, and as Larry N. Osborne suggests in "Hassling Memorials" (*Library Journal* 662, March 15, 1978), many librarians feel that "strategically the best thing they can do is load the board with young management types." Such trustees, most of whom slid through school without Latin and maybe without French, and without much history, art, music, or literature either, are doubtless akin to many of the young librarians themselves, if you view the MLS as a weak academic credential. For managers, performance is the bottom line, and it is reflected in numbers—numbers of book circulated, numbers of books requested that are available in a given library, numbers of users of one collection of books within a library vis-a-vis other collections, even the cost of keeping a book in the library for a year figured by dividing the library budget by the number of volumes on the shelves. Not many people want to know that it costs $2.47 to keep Athenaeus on the shelves if nobody is reading Athenaeus. Such managers may value an attractive dust jacket over what is inside the book,

preferring a small, easy-to-carry corrupt text over a ponderous definitive edition.

Masquerading as an aspect of the euphemism "collection development," weeding is supposed to take place within the framework of a library's written collection development policy. One is immediately struck by the growing distinction between different kinds of libraries, with especially firm lines drawn between research libraries and public libraries (which are apparently used for something other than research). Weeding can occur in any kind of library. According to William A. Katz in *Collection Development* (New York: Holt, 1980, p. 79), "most of the rules for weeding are subjective and qualitative. They assume that the librarian has a solid working knowledge of the subject fields in which the discarding operation is to take place." On the other hand, Rose Mary Magrill and Doralyn J. Hickey in *Acquisitions Management and Collection Development in Libraries* (Chicago: American Library Association, 1984, p. xi) concede that "Collection development and acquisitions, while not ordinarily perceived by the public as particularly demanding or exciting, contain elements that bring great satisfaction to those whose careers are spent in the library." In fact, the whole problem of collection development, whether ordering or weeding, depends on the level of smarts a librarian must possess in order to make the necessary decisions. Any PhD with the slightest modesty will agree with Socrates that he knows nothing. How much less does an MLS know!

Although weeding goes on—and should go on—in all libraries, the typical setting ripe for real trouble is a medium-sized public library of half a million volumes, with stable funding, rising costs, declining readership eroded by urban decay, an aggressive young director eager to make a mark by effecting computer conversion and modernization in record time, and a staff of librarians who were not star students in library school. If the cost of computer converting each book is $N, then clearly many dollars will be saved by dumping a substantial part of the library's stock before the computer conversion occurs. To do things swiftly, all books worth less than $N go, all books with signs of physical deterioration go, and beyond that the sole bibliometric criterion of whether the item has circulated within the last decade (rather than whether it has intrinsic worth or belongs in a theoretic core collection) will determine the fate of each of the rest of the books. No intelligence has to be brought to bear on individual items. Of course, rare items and local imprints will get away, and items will not be advertised to other libraries—attending to such matters would take time, cost money, and cut into the economies of the project. Similar tragedies sometimes occur in well-endowed small-town public libraries with fabulous Victorian holdings that are seldom used and are deteriorating. Also to be watched in both cases is the probability that what was once a workable research library is quietly redefining itself as a nonresearch or public library.

Booksellers can hardly be expected to complain when choice materials from clean-outs of this sort turn up for a quarter a volume at a Friends of the Library sale; indeed, many booksellers are briefly living off of this sort of merchandise. The public probably won't notice what is going on. The press will keep quiet if asked: Be nice to libraries! And the library trustees and staff will point with pride to the shiny new computer terminals as visible evidence that the library is delivering more when in fact it is delivering much less. If complaints are pressed, the librarians may admit to making a few "little mistakes," and no gentleman would push them further.

This kind of operation ultimately impacts on everybody, but especially humanities scholars, in at least two ways. It always sends to the dump at least some unrecognized rare books that should instead be transferred to some regional repository. And weeding always deprives readers who may be at some distance from a major library of many titles that are otherwise unavailable. The ACLS survey of scholars (*Scholarly Communication* no. 5, Summer 1986, digested in the *MLA Newsletter*, Fall 1986, pp. 8-9) points out that younger scholars at weaker academic institutions were the most frequent to complain of inadequate library facili-

ties. And it is these scholars upon whom there is greatest pressure to publish or perish. Frequently they must wait weeks for interlibrary loan requests to be processed, or they must pay substantial photocopying or database charges, or, if they are extremely lucky, they may find some of their needs by piecing together a group of unweeded area libraries. But once a library collection gets weeded, eccentric books get tossed, and even knowledgeable dealers and collectors may not know enough to snap them up before they reach the dumpster. Every humanities scholar should spend a few hours perusing the immense *Library of Congress Catalog of Pre-1956 Imprints* and pay special attention to the fact that there are thousands of titles that have only one or two locator symbols listed at the bottom of their library card, and copies of some of these very books are cleaned out with every library house cleaning. The humanist can immediately see the paradoxes. The more librarians oppose censorship, the more books they censor by deselection. The more librarians talk of freedom of access to information, the more restricted it becomes. Doubtless the double whammy soon will be that our free public libraries will inform us that users of interlibrary loan services should pay not only for shipping but for clerical services.

Humanists must unite in a vociferous outcry to save our libraries from librarians and to restore to the libraries that measure of public support that their maintenance requires. The great immediate need is for humanists all over the country to begin monitoring goings-on in libraries near them. Become a discreet problem patron. Keep a notebook. Visit the library frequently and observe how staff members spend their time. Ask them questions. Check out important or valuable works that never circulate. Monitor library book sales to see what is being sold; if you see anything that definitely should not be for sale, buy it as evidence. Demand open meetings of the library board, and insist that book people rather than business types have control. Support rational weeding of the library's collections, just as long as subject specialists are consulted. Librarians are fond of programming for children; support library programs for adults featuring professors, professionals, artists, musicians, athletes, drag racers—anyone who is willing to discuss books, especially good ones that don't circulate.

Beyond the immediate need, a national task force of librarians on library needs should be convened; it would see that neither guns nor butter will do. We are a large nation with only one national library and fledgling attempts at deposit libraries. Why shouldn't we have four national

The more librarians oppose censorship, the more books they censor by deselection. The more librarians talk of freedom of access to information, the more restricted it becomes.

I have invented anthropological bibliography, the study of library operations by reflecting on the books libraries discard.

deposit libraries—in Washington, D.C., Jackson, Mississippi, North Platte, Nebraska, and Carson City, Nevada? We should move for a substantial reorientation of national priorities to devote much greater sums to all aspects of the Industry for the Advancement of Learning.

We also need to rethink the academic preparation of librarians. The books on collection development contain excellent rules for weeding library collections; we do not need more studies of how to weed. But we *do* need librarians fit for the demanding and high calling of collection development. *Every* librarian should be a subject specialist with no less than a master's degree in that subject area, in addition to a library degree and a solid undergraduate foundation including four years of one foreign language, differential and integral calculus, computer science, and two laboratory sciences, not to mention courses in the social sciences, history, literature, art, and music. Until we have qualified librarians, unemployed humanists should be hired for library positions. Our libraries are a mess, and unless something is done fast they will never recover. The following anthropological bibliography includes some suggestions for meeting our difficulties, culled from my years as a book lover and library gadfly.

ANTHROPOLOGICAL BIBLIOGRAPHY

Everyone knows about analytical bibliography, enumerative bibliography, historical bibliography, and even kleptobibliography. I have invented anthropological bibliography, the study of library operations by reflecting on the books libraries discard. Its kindred disciplines are garbology—the study of famous people by reviewing the contents of their garbage cans—and one of the fields for which I am known—street literature, the study of culture via posters on telephone poles and the tackily printed handouts of picketers and street people.

As a problem patron of long standing, I have watched with growing dismay the epidemic of library cleanouts engineered by kids who went through library school in high hip days, the "has-it-any-relevance?" generation. In June 1984 I published an essay on the subject in *American Libraries*, and the two replies published in September of that year were characterized by more heat than light. Meanwhile, my extensive diaries and private papers as an adjunct of my collecting have been a matter of public knowledge since my 1977 essay in *Resources for American Literary Study*, although I have not heretofore published anything from those diaries or papers, contenting myself to

issue occasional essays on various topics over the last decade.

Because of my love for learning and hence for books, and because my papers say more than a systematic essay ever could, I am publishing now a selection of documents from my collection as an introduction to anthropological bibliography. Whereas the published treatises and articles on collection development and weeding give splendid rules for doing such things, my documents present an in-depth look at what can and actually does happen at a number of the libraries I visit periodically and about which I have, as an historical particularist, written in my diaries. Rather than resting on raw data, however, these documents are of a slightly higher grade because they were written as letters and memos to library and public officials and rest upon a broader stratum of underlying data. Nevertheless, they fall short of academic writing because I myself am an anti-elitist product of high hip culture, and I wrote them as one hoping to redirect library policy rather than in the expectation that they would be published. As things came out, they tell a sad story of the profanation of learning. To reduce length and to improve clarity, I have edited them somewhat from their original versions. I apologize for occasional autobiographical comments, but I had to establish minimum credentials to speak authoritatively about books in a large number of fields. Again, any specialist will find errors and misstatements in my characterizations of various books. But I am a broad-gauged generalist in an age of specialists, writing about a tragedy in our libraries, the last place we ever thought it would happen.

FALL 1984 LIBRARY BOOK SALE MEMO

Hi! As a followup to previous communications, this is a list of just a few of the books I bought at this year's Friends of the Library book sale, with annotations about why I think the books belong in the library and should not have been sold.

Arthur William à Beckett, *The à Becketts of "Punch"* (Constable, 1903). Although a librarian told me that the book weeders "haven't gotten into the stacks," this was one of a whole table of fine Victorian biographies from the stacks that were let go. Included were a good number of books lovingly wrapped in brown paper and tied with string by an earlier and thriftier generation of librarians. There were the papers of John Quincy Adams and of Benjamin Franklin ("Pig") Butler, both Massachusetts men of distinction who never should have been turned away. As for the above, the à Becketts were lawyers and writers for the

British humor magazine *Punch*, of which you are supposed to have a complete run in the stacks. The art department has the Becketts' *Comic History of Rome* and their *Comic History of England*, both with colored plates. There is also a *Comic Blackstone* with plates. I own all three. Since you have two of the comic histories and the magazine, you should have saved the biography.

Thomas E. Besolow, *From the Darkness of Africa to the Light of America: The Story of an African Prince* (Ripley, 1890). Also on the biography table in with a lot of books about Bishop Brooks was this autobiography of an African who studied at nearby Wilbraham Academy back when there were still Methodist connections. *Pre-1956 Imprints* lists Oberlin as the only location of this first edition, though a second edition is in several libraries. The charge-out register indicates that the book circulated five times since it was bound in 1900. Headmaster Casey of the Academy says they have no copy, though they must have had one once. Local History said they'd like to have it. But the point is, it should never have gotten out of the library in the first place—it has interest for black studies and local historians.

Grace A. Ellis, *A Memoir of Mrs. Anna Laetitia Barbauld*, 2 vols. (Osgood, 1874). In fine condition, as were the above. Barbauld was a major eighteenth-century woman poet, and volume two is a collection of her poems: This is not just a biography. With interest in women's studies picking up, why junk it?

Dictionary of American Biography with Supplements I and II. In good condition. Why did the library dump this? It belongs in *every* library, including mine.

Wilson Flagg, *Mount Auburn: Its Scenes, Its Beauties, and Its Lessons* (Munroe, 1861). Up the street from Harvard, Mt. Auburn is one of America's great Victorian cemeteries, the burial place of many notables and a place now much studied by students of Victorian landscape architecture and funerary art. The plates are great. In an age when the study of attitudes toward death and dying is academically fashionable, this belongs in the library.

William Godwin, *An Enquiry Concerning Political Justice* (Knopf, 1926). Originally published in 1793, this is one of the classics of British liberal political thought. While a valuable antique set remains in the stacks, it is hard to figure out why a nice reading copy in fine, recently rebound condition would be discarded.

The Poetical Writings of Fitz-Greene Halleck, with Extracts from Those of Joseph Rodman Drake, ed. James Grant Wilson (AMS reprint, 1969). This is a brand new reprint on acid-free paper of the standard Victorian edition. When I filled out a postcard, the library got me a copy of the original edition of this from the Forbes in Northampton. While there are snippets of Halleck in other places (Charles Dudley Warner's anthology, for one), Halleck is a member of the "American Pantheon," and we should never throw out a brand new copy.

Dom David Knowles, *The Religious Orders in England* (Cambridge, 1948). In addition to my graduate work in English and Classics at Harvard and Wisconsin, I also have a graduate minor in Reformation history. This work is respected by all Christians as the definitive account of what Henry VIII did to the monasteries.

R. R. Madden, *Historical Notice of Penal Laws Against Roman Catholics* (Richardson, 1865). Very brittle. I was unable to find other Madden books on the shelves, though there are still cards for them in the catalog. Same for O'Reilly's *Moondyne*. Madden was a great Irish radical, and in a city with a large Irish population it is part of the heritage of the community and should not be discarded.

W.P. Strickland, *The Pioneer Bishop, or The Life and Times of Francis Asbury* (Carlton and Porter, 1858). This is the standard Victorian biography of Asbury and mentions his visit to this area. I am sorry to see it go.

Howard D. Weinbrot, *Augustus Caesar in Augustan England: The Decline of a Classical Norm* (Princeton, 1978). I could conclude the argument in one sentence by saying you don't throw away Princeton University books! Anyway, the library's shelves are bare of even major modern criticism, and our high school students really have very little in the way of critical aids to understanding. Weinbrot has produced a major reinterpretation of the period, and for once the library bought a fine piece of criticism. Why toss it? Isn't there space for a perhaps brilliant reinterpretation of the age of Addison, Swift, and Pope?

George Nugent, *Memorials of John Hampden* (Bell, 1889). Although I already have a copy of this, I bought this one for the plates, the frontispiece being of Hampden, after whom the county in which we live is named. The card catalog also lists the 1832 Murray edition, but the librarians could not find it. So all forms of this work are now out of the system, and instead it should be in the local history room.

Charles Wright and C. Ernest Fayle, *A History of Lloyds* (Macmillan, 1928). Springfield, Massachusetts, is an insurance city. Why, therefore, was this lavish book with photogravures and fold-out plates, so rich in historical detail, a classic of insurance history, discarded? In fact, this was one of an immense number of social science books tossed, a great many of which appeared outmod-

Tossing out books because there aren't cultivated readers to call for them today is wasteful if they are good books and if there are likely to be cultivated readers tomorrow.

ed, but I'm not a social scientist: I am a historian, and this book should have been kept. If it wasn't circulating, it should have been transferred to an academic library in the region together with some of the esoteric old things that have scholarly interest, but that are not classics.

The above books, therefore, are just a few from more than four boxes of books that I bought in visits on three separate days to the book sale. I was first in line at the Civic Center the first day. Somebody said there were 25,000 books there; I could believe there were 100,000. Not only were all the tables covered, but there were boxes packed under the tables and in the corners, and some of the boxes were piled so thick that nobody ever got into them the first night of the sale even though activity was frantic, especially in the social science area. The first night of the sale was for members of the Friends of the Library only, but you could join on the spot for a dollar. Attending were the usual array of dealers, scouts (subdealers), collectors, and members of the general public. One dealer passed around a list on which to sign up for catalogs, but I never got one. Competition is fierce at the opening of sales — indeed, at a typical tag sale the action is over in 15 minutes and the dealers are lined up to leave. But this was a gigantic sale, and the action lasted a couple of hours as boxes under the tables were piled where they could be opened and run through. Lots of people looked happy with what they were buying.

In the week following the sale, I was told by a member of the local used-book trade that he understood (I have not verified this) that the library has the equivalent of 18 drawers of cards for discarded books which have not been pulled from the card catalog. In any case, I found the card for every single book that I purchased at the sale still in the Rice Hall card catalog.

Meantime, some of the books from the sale turned up in Johnson's bookstore for used books. I bought the 1901 history of the Fire and Marine, which had been in Rice Hall, for five dollars. Local History has other copies, and the Rice Hall copy was probably appropriately discarded because it was defective, lacking a frontispiece. Johnson's was also asking four dollars for Holden's illustrated history of Yale with a federal aid stamp from back in the halcyon days of federal funding of libraries and subsidization of the publishing industry. It's an awfully nice book, but I haven't checked to determine whether the library has another copy. I was surprised to find in Johnson's two Clifton Johnson "Highways and Byways" volumes which had been in Rice Hall and of which there was no duplicate in Local History, so that their sale deprived the library of its only copies. The story is that some catalog cards show second copies in Local History, but in the case of these other Clifton Johnson books the only copy was the copy in Rice Hall, now discarded and offered for sale at Johnson's.

James Gordon Gilkey

My most impressive piece of juvenilia was my history of the Springfield Symphony Orchestra (1959), of which Gilkey had once been president. A couple of times my parents took me to hear Gilkey, who was famous for his children's sermons, among other things. The point is that I bought no Gilkey books at the sale and I didn't even see any there. I didn't go to look at religion books, although I did ask a fellow going through the religion books if he had seen any Methodist stuff, and he said no. I helped a student find Calvin's letters up in the biography section. But in looking in the Rice Hall catalog I found a lot of cards for Gilkey books. In some cases the cards indicated there was also a copy in Local History, and those books are now there, I am assured. But virtually all the Gilkey volumes once in the Rice Hall balcony are now gone, or "out" as the librarians say, and there is a gaping hole on the shelf where the books once were. And the cards indicate that for many of the Gilkey books once in Rice Hall there is no duplicate in Local History. So at the present time there is uncertainty about the status of maybe ten Gilkey books, with the very real possibility that they have been disposed of. And if so, they should all be repurchased, every single one of them, in the antiquarian market if necessary.

Local History has transferred the works of Blackstone and some other books with Worthington's annotations in them that I called up from the stacks. But two volumes of Coke cannot be found. The memoir of Massachusetts Chief Justice Theophilus Parsons, a most important figure in American legal history, cannot be found, and I recall passing over in the sale a banged-up volume of biographies of prominent British legal figures. How many other books that have real relevance and potential usefulness can no longer be found?

One of the senior librarians told me that after a book has not been checked out for 20 years there is good reason for no longer keeping it around. I have replied to this in my piece in *American Libraries* of December 1984. All books are not created equal. They become obsolete in different ways and at different rates. Some books never become obsolete, for particular reasons. Gilkey, for example, will never be obsolete in Springfield, nor will Clifton Johnson, because they were distinguished local writers. Our library must save the works of such figures forever and ever. Amidst the rhythm of decay and renewal, libraries must be responsive in positive human terms, and they must be centers of stability at the same time. Tossing out books because there aren't cultivated readers to call for them today is wasteful if they are good books and there are likely to be cultivated readers tomorrow.

This memo has an elegiac strain indeed. It is my judgment as a publishing scholar in the humanities that at least some of the book discarding at the library in the last year or so has been cutting into the bones. I could see tossing out a complete file of postage stamp catalogs as long as one from every decade is saved. We need a deposit library in the area to keep complete runs of things. It is also my judgment that the stacks should have been weeded carefully, first. As it is, the balconies were weeded first and some say there will be no weeding in the stacks. So you have in the stacks what's left of a fine 1910 collection, but you have tossed basic items published between 1910 and the present.

FALL 1984 BOOK SALE—LATE BULLETIN

My 80-year-old Aunt Eleanor has a circle of similarly situated old ladies with whom she is good friends. Several years ago Agnes loaned her one of her treasures, Helena Higginbotham's *Rover's Story* (Boston: Lee and Shepard, 1903). It's a dog story about Springfield with references to the city in it, I was told. Aunt Eleanor, who acts as chauffeur for the other ladies, is in a good position to get things out of them and asked me if I would like the book for my collections. I responded that if the book is the treasure of Agnes, then she should keep it; besides, I don't collect dog stories. However, I did check with the city library to make sure they had a copy—they did, so I forgot about it.

On December 19, 1984, I checked all the card catalogs in the city library, and there was and is now no card for the above book. So, in addition to the books I know the library threw out because I own them (more than just the ones listed earlier), and in addition to the ones I suspect they threw out because there are cards for them but they cannot be found (Johnson, Gilkey, Miller, Wagner), and in addition, of course, to books that have been lost or stolen for which there is still a card in the drawer, there are also books such as the Higginbotham. These, because of the Springfield connection, should still be in the library, but they are no longer there, and the cards have been pulled.

Please notice how this deaccessioning defeats the "good works" of public-spirited citizens such

as myself. If the library had not had a copy of the Higginbotham when I first checked, I might have proposed a gift, or I might have been tempted to want the book for myself to place with the library. Librarians get paid for what they do, but nobody pays good citizens, and still we get these results! *Trust* is being damaged. We must have a new basis for trust, and somebody with a PhD in fundraising is not going to win it.

Earlier in the year I laughed when I read about a party who was taken to court for stealing books from the library. I laughed because it seems to me that the library has done more damage to its own collections than a dozen determined crafty book thieves ever could and because it would be so easy to steal a book if anyone wanted to. That is because deaccessioned books are frequently missed by whoever it is that wields the "Discarded by the City Library" stamp. Or a thief could go and have such a stamp made and forge stamps on the books he stole.

MAY 21, 1986 LETTER TO MR. BISAILLON, DIRECTOR, FORBES LIBRARY, NORTHAMPTON, MASSACHUSETTS

I am writing to complain that your library has discarded John Payne's translation of the novels of Matteo Bandello in six volumes (Society of Bibliophiles, 1895). I bought the set in excellent condition for six dollars at the Globe Bookshop. Photocopies of the front endpapers with the discard stamp and the title page of volume one are enclosed.

Payne was a major Victorian translator, Bandello a major Italian writer, and these may be the first English translation of the whole business. You do not have other copies of these in your library. At the least they should have been transferred to some research library in the area rather than sold.

Cutter (whose portrait hangs in your reading room) and the likes of him were learned men such as professional librarianship seldom sees today except in the rare book departments of major university libraries. . . . I certainly hope that the Forbes, which is a national treasure as it is, is not on its way to being emasculated in the way that some libraries have been.

FALL 1986 LIBRARY BOOK SALE MEMO

This is a successor to memorandums about the 1984 book sale, plus scattered sales since then. Someplace I sent a memo saying I was unexcited about the 1985 sale because the Pine Point *Grove's Dictionary*, 5th edition, I bought at $1.50 per volume had been superseded. In recent months I complained of valuable reprint sets surfacing at

Shelf reading is one way books circulate, and where there are no shelf readers there is diminished circulation.

the Globe in Northampton (Nichols's *Literary Anecdotes*) with the federal aid stamp in them, and I noted with particular dismay that John Wesley Powell's *Canyons of the Colorado* in the limited 750-copy reprint on acid-free paper—a treatise on geology, travel, ethnology, and (with all those fabulous woodcuts) Victorian art—had been tossed.

Last year I distinctly recall being depressed at seeing such a vast expanse of what I considered to be nearly worthless books: There's no doubt that some books do deserve to be tossed. This year, on the other hand, the sale was exceptionally good. Even when it came to an end on Saturday at 5 p.m. there were hundreds, possibly thousands, of books I could see on the shelf on a good bookstore in a university town. It's a pity the sale couldn't have continued, but they had to get out, and the workers were left with an immense mess to sweep away.

This year I was first in line. Next to me was a music teacher in the local schools who says he has been buying lots of discarded records at all the libraries around town—I've done pretty well on records at Sixteen Acres, myself. He says he has about 10,000 records, which is the same figure I quote for the size of my library.

First night I bought only $18 worth of $1.50 books and helped a friend who runs a bookstore. Just imagine all the stuff the dealers bought that I didn't! Second day I spent $15 on books reduced to $1. Saturday was my day: I bought eight boxes of books at $2 per box, which came to $16, and I made a freewill donation of $14, for a total of $30. One of the workers told me I might come back Monday and take whatever I wanted to help clear the place out, so Monday I carried off about a dozen more boxes, half of them large-print books. I was amazed to find still on the biography table J. B. Wakeley's *Anecdotes of the Wesleys* (1869), rebound, fine, but brittle. So I said I'd pay a dollar for that, and I made an additional freewill contribution of $10 for a total of $11.

And now for the moment you've been waiting for, the moment when I list the books that shouldn't have been in the sale.

James Gordon Gilkey

The library has tossed a lot of religion books. It's a good thing, and I don't think they're discriminating against any particular group. But it doesn't change the fact that way back in my fall 1984 book sale memo I complained about Gilkey titles missing from the Rice Hall balcony. Maybe the people doing the weeding didn't know that Gilkey (and others) were Springfield authors and stuck them in the boxes to go, and once they had disappeared

from the Rice Hall balcony in 1984 nobody was sure where they were or whether they had been in the 1984 sale or not. But because the cards had not been pulled, it was clear what should be on the shelves in the balcony, and also that many of those titles were not in Local History. Well, I found a whole mess of Gilkey books in this year's sale, and I jotted them down on the spot. I trotted directly up to the library and had a nice chat with one of the staffers and to his credit he went right down and got the Gilkey books. The questions remain, however: Why at this late date after all the complaining I have done hasn't the library developed a procedure for preventing local association items from winding up in the sales? Should the Friends of the Library be sponsoring sales at all until the library cleans up its act?

Other Books

This year's sale was better than former ones, I think, because the library has already thrown out much of the junk and, increasingly, it's good stuff that's getting sold, merely because it doesn't circulate in a city that is just beginning to awaken from the dismals. Is that the proper atmosphere in which to be weeding a library collection so massively that, as one children's librarian remarked to me, in so many words, when I asked for a major children's bibliographical volume, "Well, I know the book and we used to have it, and I thought we still did, but we've thrown out so much maybe it got away!"

A prominent author from around Northampton was buying most of the *Memoirs* of the American Folk-Lore Society and remarked to me, "It looks like they're throwing out their folklore collection."

Has *The United States Pharmacopeia and National Formulary* been terminated as a holding? If so, I think you should have the current number though old ones may go.

The 1964 three-volume Blom reprint of Montrose J. Moses, *Representative Plays by American Dramatists*, is a standard title, now available at $100, a mint-condition copy of which should not have been discarded.

Since she was a leading female writer, why toss Elizabeth Inchbald's *A Simple Story*, the 1967 Oxford English Novels edition, in mint condition? Even if it is not circulating well now, future patrons may well appreciate books like this.

Ditto for the Oxford English Novels edition of Henry Mackenzie's *The Man of Feeling*, a satire on the sentimental novel. I caught both of these OEN books on a book truck in Rice Hall about a year ago when they were in the process of being discarded and took the trouble of telling the supervising librarian why they should be saved. Librarian responded by affirming confidence in the judgment of the staff member who weeded them out. I don't trust that judgment. You should have the entire set of Oxford English Novels, and anything coming along should be on standing order. The two-volume Lucas edition of John Webster's works (1928) is standard and should go nowhere—it's in fine rebound condition. William A. Baker's *The New Mayflower* (1958), with charts of the boat in a pocket, should have been transferred to Local History. Why toss Gerald R. Cragg's *The Cambridge Platonists* (Oxford 1968)? Excellent condition.

Almost a whole set of the Eerdmans blue-cloth edition of Calvin's *Commentaries* in mint condition was let go. The Plantation Edition of the works of Thomas Nelson Page, republished in 18 volumes by Scholarly Press on 300-year paper in library binding, and purchased with federal funds. Why toss the prototypical southerner in mint condition? Edmund Calamy's *The Nonconformist's Memorial, Being an Account of the Lives, Sufferings, and Printed Works of the Two Thousand Ministers Ejected from the Church of England*, 3 vols. (London, 1802). The biography of the first pastor of First Church, Springfield is in here.

Edward Foss, *The Judges of England* (London, 1848), disbound, otherwise good. Lord Campbell, *The Lives of the Chief Justices of England*, 6 vols. (Boston: Estes, 1873). In good shape. Sorry to see these go but glad to have them. Antiquarian legal titles bring superstunningly outrageous prices.

Bobbs-Merrill reprint of Grotius's *The Law of War and Peace*, translated by Kelsey, disbound (I have already rebacked it). I think you have the Carnegie edition in the stacks, and if so you should not discard it. This should have been rebound by you. Grotius must not go. James Grant Wilson, *The Poets and Poetry of Scotland*, 2 vols. (1876). This nice, full Scots anthology is available in reprint for $85. I bought the classic Aussie poetry anthology in the 1984 sale.

F. L. Cross, *The Oxford Dictionary of the Christian Church*. Mint. I'd like to think that this 1957 edition has been superseded. This was a circulating copy that never circulated. How about letting people take home reference books overnight starting at 4 p.m., pay an arm and two legs if they fail to bring them back, plus face suspension of borrowing privileges?

Gibb's *Arabic Literature* (Oxford, 1963). Nice new copy. This reminds me of when the Egyptian mummy exhibit opened in the Smith Museum. I came to Rice Hall to check out books on hieroglyphics. I own Budge's *Egyptian Language* (1910) and found it plus Gardner in the catalog, but they were not on the shelf and have been reordered.

Weeders must be sensitive about what's going on in the museums out behind.

John Lacy's *Dramatic Works* (Edinburgh, 1875). Good, unused, rebound, brittle. Lacy is a minor but not forgotten Restoration dramatist, hard to get. Wilson and two others were published along with this. Some library in the city should be keeping the four books.

The Complete Works of Thomas Lodge Now First Collected, 4 vols. (Hunterian Club, 1883). Lodge is a mighty important Renaissance writer whom Shakespeare drew upon, and this is an elegant type-facsimile reprint Rare Book Department sort of thing that could be used in glass case exhibits in the absence of antique copies. It suffered the final indignity of being a broken set: Somebody else bought volumes one, two, and four at a dollar a book the second day of the sale, and I found the missing third volume tucked away with a lot of novels and bought it with other treasures at two dollars per box the last day of the sale. You have other similar Hunterian publications, and they absolutely should not go. It hurts me to see this one go. When Miss Rose retired as Assistant Library Director and Supervisor of Rice Hall she must have been very proud of the way she had, on limited funds, brought together some kind of research collection that still worked as late as 1980. Now look at what has happened!

Heinrich Heine, *Lyric Poems and Ballads* (Pittsburgh, 1961). Mint, German and English interleaved. Sorry to see it dumped. *The Chief Plays of Corneille* (Princeton, 1957). Ditto. William B. Sprague, *Annals of the American Pulpit*, 9 vols. (Times/Arno, 1967 reprint of the 1865 edition on 300-year paper). Mint. There's a long biography of Orange Scott in here, and doubtless there are biographies of other locals as well. Listed at $236.50.

Catholic Publication Society's edition of John Lingard's *History of England*. One day I found Froude on the shelf but could find Lingard only in the catalog, and I asked a librarian where Lingard was and was told it was being "reclassified." The librarians have an answer for books not on the shelf: "reclassified," or "out," or "cannot be found," but never "we heaved it into the discard pile." And who was Lingard (1771-1851)? He was a Catholic priest who didn't like Froude's Anglican version of the history of England, so he wrote his own. I own both Froude and the 1855 edition of Lingard, which I bought way back in 1967. In a city with a substantial Irish Catholic population, Lingard belongs right on the shelf beside Froude even if it never circulates.

Let me tell you all another story. Recently I was in a branch library and a librarian was weeding medical books. There were two copies of Gray's *Anatomy*, a worn copy of the latest edition from a few years back and a brand new reprint of a long-obsolete edition, which is generally available from discount booksellers. You guessed it: The librarian selected the battered-up newer edition to discard and selected the bright new reprint of the obsolete edition to retain. I asked some questions. Do you have an M.D.? No. A Ph.D.? No. Finally the librarian took both books into the back room to decide. But *who* is discarding these books and *what* do they know? I'm not an elitist snob. The librarian didn't need a fancy degree to make the right decision, but the librarian had made the wrong decision, and the librarians have made too many wrong decisions.

Wieland's *History of Agathon*, 4 vols. (London, 1773). Nice. Hugh James Rose, *A New General Biographical Dictionary* (London, 1857). O. L. Zubar, *Twenty Lessons on Barbering* (1902). Nicely bound pamphlet with tonic recipes. Blair's *Lectures on Rhetoric and Belles Lettres* (Philadelphia, 1851). In lousy condition, but this is a major treatise.

A. B. Grosart, *Miscellanies*, 4 vols. (Fuller Worthies Library). You have other Fuller volumes and other similar reprint sets from the Victorian period. Great numbers of these classic old things tantalizingly hint—much like dinosaur tracks—at what a really fine collection Springfield had back about 1910. What kind of permanent accession records do you have? I'm talking library history.

Simpson & Potter's California edition of Donne's *Sermons*! Macksey's *The Book of Women's Achievements* (Stein and Day, 1976). Mint. A good book that probably belongs in each branch. Harrier's *Jacobean Drama*, 2 vols. (Norton, 1963). Paperbacks placed in hardcovers. Never circulated, but a good set, which I already own—but at two dollars a box I took duplicates.

One of three volumes of Saintsbury's *Caroline Poets*. Some of these odd volumes *may* have been broken sets in the library's collections. But this standard work is a good alternative to buying other editions of the included poets individually, and each volume of the set is more or less freestanding. You've wiped out a period.

Volume one, copy two of Swedenborg's *Arcana Caelesta*. Maybe you still have some of this eighteenth-century mystic, and maybe you don't—his poems were also on the table. There was once a Swedenborgian community here in Springfield, their church still stands, and you shouldn't toss Swedenborg completely.

Samuel Kettell, *Specimens of American Poetry*, 3 vols. (Blom, 1967). Mint. Should never, never,

never have been tossed. Springfield College has a set of the first edition in lousy condition, which they kindly loaned me a couple of years ago, and I decided it was so useful I was getting ready to purchase the reprint at $47.50. Thank you so much at two dollars per box, but this belongs on the shelf for everybody.

John Vicars, *England's Worthies* (London, 1845). A Victorian reprint of a classic. Recently I saw one of the plates used as an illustration in a modern book.

David Dudley Field, *Speeches, Arguments and Miscellaneous Papers*, ed. A. P. Sprague, 3 vols. (Appleton, 1884). Field is a major figure in law reform and legal history, and in mint though slightly browned condition, this set would bring plenty in an antiquarian legal catalog. Springfield has always suffered by having so many books in the stacks, which are closed, because nobody knows you have them and they are rarely borrowed. Shelf reading is one way books circulate, and where there are no shelf readers there is diminished circulation. Instead of having high school students run after books, you should consider stationing them in the stacks so that the general public could go down and see what is available. If lawyers knew these were available, they would borrow them.

1837 Felton edition of Homer's *Iliad*. In Greek, with all of Flaxman's designs. This should have been transferred to the Art Department. Flaxman is major.

1839 Paris edition of *Abailard and Heloise* with engravings on rice paper laid in. In good shape for such an old book—a pity to sell. George Moore on ditto, standard edition, fine shape.

And the following: a poorly rebacked edition of Halevy's *Abbe* with hand-tinted plates. *Lives of Eminent and Illustrious Englishmen* by Cunningham, 8 vols. (1838); *Public Characters* for 1802-03, 1803-04; 1806, 1807, 1808-09; *The Historic Gallery of Portraits and Paintings and Biographical Review* (1807ff., with lots of engravings); Wrangham's *British Plutarch* (1816); and the following, which have fabulous engravings but scanty information on the title page—*Family Secrets or Hints to Those Who Would Make Home Happy*, 3 vols. (circa 1810).

These are some, but not all, of what I got in three successive days amidst at least several dozen serious collectors and dealers and a multitude of members of the general public. It's nice to be invited to steal a book, and then again it's not so nice. Certainly everything shouldn't be saved, but enough important things slipped away this year to merit this comment.

Survival Weeding

by Cathy Carey

Most small to medium-sized public libraries are not depositories, research facilities, or storage places, but rather somewhere between these and a bookstore operation. To best serve patrons' needs it is important to have current, attractive, well-displayed books. Trying to save everything just in case someone, sometime, might want a low-use item is frustrating to both staff and clientele. Buildings can only hold a certain amount, so as long as there are new acquisitions, some of the older material has to go. Jam-packed shelves are not pleasant to browse through and make a page's job more difficult.[1]

Why is weeding important? It's "an opportunity to review the collection for content"[2] and perhaps discover that there's not a single resume or tree book on the shelves. Or perhaps the interest in woodworking has died down, and buying adjustments can be made. It's a way to increase the effectiveness of the library because keeping seldom-used items casts a shadow on the newer, generally more useful titles. Since no one wants to check out damaged books, the process of weeding will allow the decision to mend, discard, or bind blemished items. If the latter is chosen, be sure to save the dust jackets to reattach after binding to make the books look more appealing. This is especially important for fiction, where browsing is more prevalent.

Will a patron ever ask for a book that was just discarded? Count on it happening once in a while. Simply handle the request as if that title was never owned, using reference skills to substitute another similar title or offer interloan service.

One of the best times to weed is when the library is closed. Staff members with flexible schedules will accomplish more on a Friday or Saturday evening, for example, while wearing old, comfortable clothes; there will be no reference questions to answer or patrons wondering what in the world is going to happen to all those books.

How does one decide what to discard and what to keep? A search of the literature will produce numerous formulas, but none of them takes the place of experience. Weeding is not a job to assign to a new librarian. It must go to a person who knows the collection and the community. Ideally, more than one person will do it. Try teaming a seasoned librarian with a subject expert, such as an adult page who has an interest in crafts or philosophy. Or perhaps the local coin or astronomy club would send a volunteer to help with that section. If collection building is done by assigning sections to various librarians, each should weed his or her own section along with a helper.

Certainly one cannot rely totally on circulation statistics to determine what to discard, but they are quite important. One rule of thumb suggests that fewer than six circulations in one year makes a book a good candidate for discarding. According to Marvin Scilken,[3] another idea is to check the price of the book in question. For instance, if it cost $16.95, after 17 uses the money has been well spent, and one should not feel guilty for discarding it when demand dies.

Current bibliographies are also useful for weeding purposes; however, there is no point in keeping a book just because it is listed, if that source is never consulted as a reference or reader's advisory tool. In fact, that bibliography should probably be weeded too. If the decision is made to keep a certain book, it is helpful to note right on the top edge why it is being kept. A small "FC 11" is a reminder that it was found in the *Fiction Catalog*, 11th edition. An "OP 89" would indicate that no replacement was available in 1989, which helps justify keeping a somewhat shabby item.

Another consideration is whether a book is part of a series. There is not much point in keeping volume three if one and two are gone and irreplaceable. A note on the book prevents a librarian from wasting time looking up series information again later.

Although the ideal library will have as comprehensive a plan for weeding as for selecting new materials, with both aspects of collection development coordinated, most situations are not perfect. Thus, the need for survival weeding is created. The main problem is time, an almost nonexistent commodity in today's busy libraries. Adopting a plan, such as the one outlined in the Hennepin County Library's *Collection Maintenance Manual* (see the Notes for publication information on this manual), or the ALA "crew" method, can provide structure, even if it's not realistic to follow it to the letter.

It's helpful to have a few survival techniques to rely on in times of staff shortages or other crises. On finding a typographical error in the card catalog, do not immediately rush to have it fixed. First investigate. Is the book still around, being used, and up to date? If not, why fix the card? Start the withdrawal procedure instead.

If the library receives a recent pamphlet on nutrition that recommends new and/or the most reliable books, go and weed just that section. It's much less overwhelming to complete a small area than to determine grimly that the 600s must be done by the end of the month. Keep in mind that every little bit helps.

When going down an aisle in search of a history of Korea, pull those two tattered books on China. It takes only a second. Then, when you're finished with the patron, decide: weed, bind, or mend. A reference question that takes a librarian to the G.E.D. books may provide a reminder to get those pre-1988 items off the shelf and replace them with new editions that reflect the recently updated test. Taken in small doses, weeding is really easy.

There's one area that demands ruthless weeding—the young adult section. These books must be kept current to reflect rapidly changing trends and interests. Dump those 15-year-old hardbacks. If the title is a "YA classic" it will be available in an attractive paperback edition. Any book more than five years old should be seriously considered for discard. Make a special effort to use face-out display techniques for multiple copies of teen reading materials. Several companies, including Brodart and North American Enterprise, have suitable zig-zag shelving inserts available. Certain kinds of metal shelving can be adapted for face-out display by removing a shelf, turning it upside down, and reattaching it. This allows single-copy display of four to six books.

Some other specific collection development ideas include the following: Ask yourself if the library really needs to keep almanacs for every year. They are nice to have if there is space, but if not, keep only every fifth edition, since it usually has five years' worth of statistics. Or, when weeding travel books, you might ask, "Would I want to use this to plan my trip?" It does pay to hang on to old car and appliance repair manuals until they get too dirty. Also, be sure to keep all city directories, phone books, and maps, which could be transferred to the local history area as they age, if there is sufficient staff time available for reprocessing (although recataloging just to place books in storage is not usually cost-effective).

Frequently check the heavily used sections, such as the dinosaur books, for condition. Yes, replacements are expensive, but think of the library's image rather than just dollars and cents.

If a weeder runs across a book that causes the thought "why in the world did we ever buy this?" he or she may want to get a second opinion before discarding. But don't put it off. Immediate action is the key to weeding on the fly.

Using some or all of the suggestions included here should make the library more attractive and useful to your patrons.

References

1. Joseph P. Segal, *Evaluating and Weeding Collections in Small and Medium-Sized Public Libraries* (Chicago: ALA, 1980), 4.
2. *Collection Maintenance Manual* (Minnetonka, Minn: The Hennepin County Library, 1988), 1.
3. Marvin Scilken, "Book Selection Is People Selection," speech delivered September 29, 1988 in Livonia, Michigan.

Systematic Weeding: A Report on the Weeding Project of the Kenosha Public Library

George C. Hammond and Ginnie Cooper

I f you are a gardener, you know the value of weeding. If you are a librarian, you may not. Utilizing CETA funds, the much-needed systematic weeding of the entire collection of the main branch of the Kenosha Public Library System was undertaken in 1978. Certain values of such a project, and certain systematic procedures to accomplish it, crystallized in our minds during the six months needed to perform the task. This report has been written to share the knowledge we gained with all interested librarians.

Background Information

The main branch of the Kenosha Public Library System is housed in a neoclassical building designed for use by a population of 24,000 (when it was built in 1900, Kenosha's population was 11,600). When it opened, 4,600 books were in the collection. By 1910, the city's population had grown to more than 20,000; the collection had developed even more quickly, having exceeded 22,000 volumes. The library seems to have reached its optimal appropriateness at this time. Since then, the library has been too crowded.

It is still crowded sixty years later, but all unnecessary crowding was recently eliminated by our weeding more than 20,000 books from the core collection. Weeding was also done at each of the three branches of the library and at the children's section of the main branch, but the core collection received the most thorough reevaluation.

Owing to a long history of overcrowding (every ten years more shelves were built), the basement was enlarged to add two extra rooms in 1935, a "drastic weeding" of books was done in 1944, and a "major weeding" of the collection took place in 1961. However, as the 1978 project revealed, the earlier weedings must have been neither systematic nor thorough, as numerous old, unused books survived both cuts. Most weeding projects are designed to eliminate one or two thousand books from a collection. Our project was designed to evaluate every book in the collection with regard to its usefulness to the library, with a goal of eliminating at least 10,000 books. We discovered that we could easily survive without 20,000.

The need for expansion was noted as early as 1925. The children's books were all moved to another building a block away in 1929. Throughout the sixties, proposals for a new library were rejected; in the seventies the story was the same. To dramatize the need for a new library, the collection was weeded only a few times after 1961, and then only in small doses. In 1970, with 65,000 books crowded into a building designed to hold only 17,000 volumes, the library finally gave up. Two thousand books were transferred to a storage area in the City Garage. A year later, they were transferred to the Water Department along with 1,000 more of their friends. In 1974, the library rented a store nearby and transferred all 8,500 books that had congregated at the Water Department over the years to the new facility—which came to house 11,750 books by 1978.

Kenosha's population had grown to exceed 80,000 in the same year, and yet, though inadequate since 1943—when Kenosha's population was under 50,000, the library was still housed in its original building. The attention of the head librarians since the early sixties was focused upon obtaining a new library, and so the weeding of the collection was neglected because of a higher priority, and because of the political leverage that overcrowding provided. In spite of the obvious need, a new library was never approved by the government or by the voters (two referenda were defeated in the early seventies). Kenosha's population consists largely of blue-collar workers; fifty percent of the population have not graduated from high school, and though they enjoy the library and its services, the city's residents are not eager to spend much money on the matter.

Recently, however, a new large branch library was approved. Also, the size of the book budget has grown considerably in the last few years. These factors, combined with continued cooperation among local libraries (especially the University of Wisconsin-Parkside) have influenced our decisions greatly. We wanted the collection to be in very good shape before moving it into the new facility, where every volume will be housed in the open stacks.

We doubt that many librarians are in quite the position we were in one year ago, but we do feel that, taken in the context of our predicament, the information we acquired regarding the systematic weeding of a sizable collection will prove valuable to many.

The Project and Procedures

New books were on a waiting list for shelf space; borrowed books, when returned, might find their places taken; and yet the old, unused books remained placidly in their fortified positions. The overflow (14,000 volumes) from the open stacks had long ago spread throughout the basement and then over to the rented storage facility, which held 11,750 volumes in limbo. To obtain these books, patrons had to ask for them at the desk. If the book was in the basement, it could be readily obtained; if it was in storage, there would be a one-day delay. In order to know that these 25,750 volumes existed, one had to use the card catalog. Yet the card catalog could be misleading. Although most of the cards for the books in storage had plastic covers over them signalling the patron to ask at the desk for those books, not all were thus marked, and the cards for the thousands of books in the basement gave no indication of their special location. Most patrons simply assumed that books not found in the stacks were in circulation.

The result was that most of these books had not seen the light of day, or of a reading lamp, for years—and a few unfortunate ones had lain idle for more than fifty years. The cost of keeping these drones was large; their value was minimal to nonexistent. They had served a political purpose in demonstrating the need for a new library, but that purpose no longer existed. They did add numerical prestige to the size of our collection, but even with their help we fell somewhat short in our competition with Harvard, so it was finally decided to weed the collection of all expendables.

Next, it was necessary to establish criteria for determining which books would be withdrawn and which allowed to remain. We decided to begin by weeding the open stacks. The goal was to take one third of the books off the shelves so that there would be room for the new books that would be arriving later that year. Our major criterion was whether the book had been borrowed within the last year. If not, the book was brought downstairs for further processing. If so, it was granted unconditional reprieve. A few minor considerations (the physical condition of the book, whether it contained outdated information, whether a newer copy was already in the collection) made the decision flexible, but the majority were judged solely on the one-year rule. The result was that nearly 30 percent of the books in the open stacks were brought into the basement. Our accuracy in obtaining the number we desired by using these criteria made us confident to continue—and continue we did.

The 7,500 volumes that had been brought downstairs had to be sorted into three categories: those that were to go into the basement collection, those that were to go into the storage collection, and those that were to be sold (for 25 cents each) to citizens. To help us make these decisions, we used the *Fiction Catalog* and the *Public Library Catalog* (plus their supplements) in order to determine whether the book was well-bred. If so (except in special cases where the book was both in bad physical condition and had been ignored for years in spite of its pedigree), we kept the book. If it had circulated within the last three years, it was placed on the basement collection. If it had not circulated in three years, it was placed in the storage collection (at least we thought it would go there).

Now that the basement corners were full of boxes containing books waiting to be added to either the basement or the storage collections, it became necessary to make some room for them. Establishing criteria for the basement and storage collections was slightly more difficult. These

25,750 volumes had been out of the public's eye for years, so we wanted to be more lenient with them. We did sample studies of a section of fiction, of the 200s and of the 800s, to determine how a three-year grace period would affect the collection. The results showed that about 40 percent of the fiction books had been borrowed within the last three years, about 45 percent of the 200s, and about 25 percent of the 800s. (Foreign Literature is not in demand in Kenosha.)

Based on these figures, we began to imagine the possibility of eliminating the storage collection completely. It was hoped that we could once again have the whole collection contained within one building. To accomplish this, we put the three-year rule into effect, with exceptions again made for all *Catalog* entries. We also utilized a personal sift by a few members of our staff to catch any well-known or important books that the *Catalogs* might have neglected. The result was a success: only 10 percent of the storage collection survived the cut. We began to shelve the books for the sale there, intending to move out of the rented facility when the books were gone (which is exactly what we did).

About 50 percent of the basement collection was also weeded, making room for the select few from storage and for the 4,600 volumes saved from the open stacks collection. The shifting of piles of books from one place to another during the six months of the weeding project was unsettling to some of the staff because some books were temporarily unlocatable; but at the end of the project, the basement collection had been considerably spruced up, with about one fifth of each shelf open for new transfers from upstairs (instead of the usual overflow with attendant frustrations). The open stacks collection was also in much better shape, with one fourth of each shelf open for growth. The cleaner, newer look of the books made the shelves seem more appealing—a browser would be sure to find something interesting on the shelf. We no longer compelled our patrons to hunt through old nuisances.

Lest there be misunderstanding, we do not believe that old means bad. On the contrary, occasionally it means rare and valuable. We did find an 1825 edition of the *History of Boston* among the dead weight, and we also found a thousand books there worth keeping in any collection. We did not simply put up sale signs and let people cart the collection away. Rather, we spent nearly two thousand person-hours carefully giving every volume in our collection a chance to prove its worth. We also weighed each final decision with the factor of whether the book would be valuable to keep. Books in poor physical condition

recommended themselves to the axe, but even these did not all depart. Many old volumes whose contents were valuable in one way or another were rebound. However, as the project progressed, it became more obvious that the physical condition of the book was probably the most important factor in each decision. Still, we were careful; we didn't want to miss any book when the project was over. To date, we haven't missed a single volume of the 20,500 that were weeded—and we now have better access to all the valuable books in our collection. Each rose that had hidden among several thistles now stands in neat rows with all its fellow flowers—the weeding project has given our whole collection a well-tended look.

Besides Table 1, which should give a quick overview of what we accomplished, a few additional remarks may be helpful to any library wishing to undertake such a project. Many readers are probably wondering how a library can weed more than 20 percent of its collection and still not miss anything. To give an idea of how that's possible, a few examples of what was weeded and what was not should suffice.

In the fiction section, we discarded mostly titles from the thirties, forties, fifties, and sixties that had lost their followings years ago. We did keep, however, the works of Wisconsin authors whose books are now out of print. In the 300s, we rejected all out-of-date materials—a significant number in a field that changes so rapidly. (Incidentally, the 300s sold less well than any other section, confirming our decision.) In the 500s, science books that had been supplanted by newer volumes were weeded, but we did keep books on unique subjects. Old art books (700s) were no competition for our newer, more colorful editions, so they went—except the best. In the 800s, three fourths of our anthologies and all of our poetry books by unknowns took a spill, as did many of the foreign literature books (those that weren't classics). For example, an obscure German play was donated to our library in 1911; never borrowed, it will, we hope, hold the all-time record for bench-warming here. However, all the Italian literature books in good physical condition were kept—a bow to the dominant heritage of our community. Most of the old histories and travel books in the 900s were re-moved, with the exception of a few gems—including a 1935 study of Hitler's rise to power whose prophetic utterings were very accurate. In the Biographies, such one-time favorites as Jack Paar are now gone. Any name whose appeal lasted more than fifty years stayed, but those of more transient interest were all rejected. It was fascinating to watch the march of time obliterating anyone not truly significant.

TABLE 1: WEEDING STATISTICS BY CATEGORIES

	Before	Weeded	After
Fiction	12,750	3,050	9,700
000s	1,025	225	800
100s	1,050	275	775
200s	2,100	350	1,750
300s	10,400	3,850	6,500
400s	350	125	225
500s	3,500	1,200	2,300
600s	5,150	1,275	3.875
700s	7,025	2,150	4,875
800s	9,600	3,050	6,550
900s	10,300	2,900	7,400
Biographies	6,500	2,050	4,450
Totals	69,750	20,500	49,200

New and better information is constantly outdating older editions in many subjects. In comparative religion, an important, definitive book is added to the shelves perhaps only every 20 years. In physics, the time span is much smaller. *Everything You Wanted to Know about Atomic Energy*, published in 1939, wouldn't tell you much (we got rid of it and its cousins). However, most of these books were excellent in their time. It is not a mistake for a library to purchase a book just because it will eventually be outdated. It was wise to buy it then; it is wise to discard it now. After all, the main purpose of libraries is to lower the cost of books by allowing many people to share them. Even if a book has been used by only a few people, its purchase has been justified.

Fortunately, Parkside University's library has made it possible for us to feel free from the constraints of saving everything for posterity. That has proved highly advantageous to us—and to posterity: it is hard to imagine that future generations will be interested in *everything* we ever did.

The Book Sale

We sold our weeded volumes in two four-day sales during the summer—one in early July and one in late August (we also have continuing sales at the branches). The main purpose of these sales was to distribute the books to people who might use them rather than to sell them as scrap paper. The sales succeeded in redistributing more than 15,000 books, and they also brought in more than $2,500. We sold the books for 25 cents each, but on the last day of each sale we provided a special "ten dollars-no limit" price, which proved to be an effective method of finding homes for otherwise neglected volumes (including that obscure German play).

The sales are good for our public relations. Buying the books is a great deal for the buyers, and selling them is a great deal for the library. It is not often nowadays that you can please everyone: hold a book sale of your unwanteds sometime and you will discover that it is still possible.

Conclusion

The memory of the fire at Alexandria persists. In this age of print, fears of a fanatic destroying all recorded knowledge should finally be put to rest. Ben Franklin, an early American librarian, supported the concept of new editions replacing old in his self-composed epitaph:

The Body
of
Benjamin Franklin, Printer
(Like the cover of an old book,
Its contents torn out,
And stripped of its lettering and gilding,)
Lies here food for worms.
Yet the work itself shall not be lost,
For it will (as he believes) appear once
more
In a new
And more beautiful Edition
Corrected and Amended
By
The Author

We know from experience that weeding a sizable collection is a very large project, but the rewards, if the collection was in poor shape, are even larger. Inertia is forceful, clutter is its domain;

unnecessary difficulties are its result. We all enjoy living with order, with organization, but we often fail to recognize that such inertia-generated difficulties as dead weight in a library's collection are a source of disorder. They are—but they can be effectively and systematically eliminated.

BIBLIOGRAPHY

Bogart, Gary L., and Fidell, Estelle A., eds. *Public Public Catalog 1973.* 6th ed. and supplements. New York: Wilson, 1974.

Bowler, Roberta, ed. *Local Public Library Administration.* Chicago: The International City Managers' Assn., 1964.

Carter, Mary Duncan; Bonk, Wallace John; and Magrill, Rose Mary. *Building Library Collections.* Metuchen, N.J.: Scarecrow, 1974.

Fidell, Estelle A., ed. *Fiction Catalog 1975.* 9th ed. New York: Wilson, 1976.

Gregory, Ruth W., and Stoffel, Lester L. *Public Libraries in Cooperative Systems.* Chicago: American Library Assn., 1971.

Slote, Stanley J. *Weeding Library Collections.* Littleton, Colo.: Libraries Unlimited, 1975.

Wheeler, Joseph L., and Goldhor, Herbert. *Practical Administration of Public Libraries.* New York: Harper, 1962.

Selection and Acquisition of Library Materials in Languages Other than English: Some Guidelines for Public Libraries

Marie Zielinska and Irena Bell

INTRODUCTION

. . . lists of books in the various languages present another opportunity for cooperation. To the unfortunate librarian who is not a linguist, the selection of these books becomes a nightmare. The ALA publishing board has tried to meet this need but the lists so soon grow out of date.

While the number of published lists by experts has increased in the last few years, the matter of selection of books in most languages still presents great difficulties. In spite of the fact that many libraries attempt to supply a small collection of books for special groups, many more cities have similar groups for whom the public library does not buy books for lack of available help in the matter of selection, ordering and cataloguing.

Depending on the number and range of languages to be covered it is difficult for any one library to get staff who know enough of a language or its literature, for selection purposes . . . There is a lack of adequate selection lists which librarians without knowledge of the language and literature can use. No standards in terms of multilingual holdings have been developed.

These three citations seem to be taken from a recently delivered speech or panel discussion on the acquisition of books in various languages, and certainly touch a chord familiar to many librarians concerned with this area of work in public libraries. All the more surprising then to find that the first quotation is from an article by Flora B. Roberts published in 1912 in *Public Libraries*,[1] the second from a report of the Committee on Inter-Racial Services of the New Jersey Library Association presented in 1933,[2] and the third from the final report of the Multilingual Library Services Committee of the Directors of the Ontario Regional Library Systems dated March 1979![3] It is a stunning and rather disturbing realization that the acquisition of books in various languages from other countries continues to present a serious problem for public libraries, and that despite ardent pleas for help and many efforts on the part of individual librarians, library associations, and other concerned groups, no satisfactory solution to problems connected with the acquisition of books from abroad has been found over almost a century. Even more astonishing is the fact that in a time when cooperation is one of the most important, even vital, guidelines in the library field, no international organization has taken this important issue under its wings for proper development.

It is therefore particularly commendable that *Collection Building* decided to tackle the problem. The purpose of this article is to give public librarians, particularly those who are new to the field, a practical guide to collection building in languages other than English. Our remarks are based on experience acquired at the Multilingual

Biblioservice, on the known practices of many librarians, and on the available literature on the subject.

The Multilingual Biblioservice is a division of the National Library of Canada established in the fall of 1973 as one of the services created by the federal government to implement the official policy of multiculturalism introduced in Canada in October 1971. Its purpose is to help public libraries across the country provide library services to all ethno-cultural communities and assist them in preserving their language and their cultural heritage. Because libraries in Canada fall under provincial jurisdiction, the service is in fact the federal government's contribution to provincial library services. The Multilingual Biblioservice, or MBS as it is called in short, selects, acquires, and processes books in various languages spoken in Canada and sends them on long-term deposit to the Provincial Library Services or designated centers which in turn circulate the books through the network of public libraries according to local needs. The MBS presently has collections in 26 languages and regularly adds new ones in order to attain its ultimate goal: provision of services in all 72 languages spoken in Canada. However, it is not our intention to dwell upon the MBS, but rather to present our credentials.

To delineate more precisely the scope of the linguistic field covered by the MBS, the following explanation is in order. Canada is officially a bilingual country and French-language material is not covered in our collections. French is therefore included in the discussion mainly for the benefit of American librarians who, in turn, may find the coverage of Spanish-language material too restricted for their purposes. But since the scope of this article is only to provide guidelines to selection and acquisition of books in languages other than English, it is hoped that the presented basic ideas will provide the librarians involved in collection building with enough material to help them develop their own body of knowledge needed for the provision of adequate library services for specific communities.

One more area that requires some preliminary discussion is the question of terminology. When speaking about patrons or groups of patrons, we shall use "ethno-cultural groups" or "ethno-cultural communities." These terms have been adopted by the Canadian government as the most appropriate to designate groups which feel that they have a cultural identity of their own or are interested in the preservation of the culture of their forefathers. It is more difficult to agree on a proper term to determine in one word the gamut of languages we shall be talking of and putting it in proper relation to the English language. Since the word "foreign" cannot be used to designate the actual mother tongue or heritage language of the country's legitimate citizens, and the descriptive term "non-official languages" adopted for official usage in Canada does not seem quite appropriate in the American context, we have decided to use the term "languages other than English." Although rather long and unwieldy, it is clear, exact, and acceptable to all ethno-cultural groups.

A REVIEW OF THE LITERATURE

An examination of Library Literature and LISA reveals a disconcerting scarcity of articles dealing with collection building in languages other than English. Aside from selection lists published in Booklist and a few articles of a similar nature, no more than 35 articles published over a period of 50 years can be discovered. Out of these less than half proved to be of some relevance and none examined the subject in all its aspects.

Monographs on the subject of building collections in languages other than English are equally hard to find. There are several handbooks dealing with the acquisition of foreign books for university and research libraries but problems relating to public libraries are consistently overlooked in these works. The best and most relevant work for public librarians is, in our view, Acquisition of Foreign Materials for U.S. Libraries, compiled and edited by R. Samore.[4] This volume covers the major portion of papers presented during a two-week institute organized by the School of Library and Information Science, University of Wisconsin-Milwaukee, in 1971. The first part provides "an overview of development in the collection of foreign materials by U.S. Libraries, including descriptions of various cooperative acquisitions programs such as NPAC, PL480, Farmington Plan, etc."[5] Parts two and three deal with problems connected with acquisition of materials from various parts of the world both from the point of view of the book-dealer and of the librarian. The fourth and last part deals with problems involving the acquisition of such special materials as ephemera, manuscripts, rare books, maps, microforms, and the like. Although the book covers such a wide variety of subjects, many of which are of interest to university libraries only, any librarian involved in collection development of foreign materials will find it a most useful tool. The material is well-arranged and clearly presented. References to various bibliographic tools, agencies, book-dealers, and specific acquisition arrangements applicable to public library practices are included in this volume.

Another reference source of prime value is *Books in Other Languages: How to Select and Where to Order Them* by Leonard Wertheimer.[6] It originated as a checklist of selection aids and book suppliers prepared for an Ontario Library Association workshop in 1971. The publication grew within five years to a full-fledged monographic guide published by the Canadian Library Association in 1976. The fourth edition of the guide became available in June 1979. Co-published by CLA and K. G. Sauer, N.Y., the guide covers 59 languages and language groups including headings such as "African Languages" or "East Indian Languages." Selection aids for various types of library material, as well as suppliers in Canada, the United States and abroad are listed. The entries were selected according to a variety of criteria: their value known by virtue of experience or by recommendation from other libraries or, in the lack of direct information, by critical evaluation of periodicals and trade journals. Recommended titles and addresses usually bear short annotations. Separate entries covering all languages are provided for children's literature, large-print books, and records. An introductory chapter provides valuable information on major problems involved in the acquisition of books in various languages and useful tips concerning cataloguing, processing, and readers' services.

To make the guide easy to use for librarians in other countries, certain characteristic descriptive elements such as frequency, mode of payment, quality of services, etc., have been coded. Translations in French, German, Italian, and Spanish are provided in a table. Although the guide is far from comprehensive and does not relieve the librarian from searching for local ethnic bookstores, it is an invaluable and unique tool which should be on the desk of every acquisition librarian. Most of the selection tools and suppliers mentioned in this article are listed in *Books in Other Languages*.

Another recently published list of suppliers is *Ethnic Library Materials: A Preliminary Vendor List* prepared by the California Ethnic Services Task Force.[7] This edition simply lists suppliers of American Indian, Asian, Black, and Spanish-language materials. The editors hope to provide an evaluative listing in the final version of the list.

BOOK SELECTION

The Community

To properly serve an ethnic group, or any community for that matter, it is necessary to first study that community. Background information on the ethnic groups is important, as is an analysis of the group's requirements. The selection of books will depend on the information acquired.

Some of this information can be gathered from official sources, but information received from local community leaders is even more helpful. Establishing a communication link with the ethnocultural community at the very beginning is of extreme importance, both in ensuring that the collection will suit the needs of patrons and in establishing within the community a sense of trust in the library's efforts. Community leaders, such as school teachers, association presidents, or religious ministers, are suggested as contacts because they are more likely to reflect the attitudes of the community as a whole. Usually they will be only too happy to advise on the characteristics of their community, the kind of material of interest to its members, and often, on sources of books. If the library's credibility is established with them, these community leaders will often become the library's best public relations representatives, spreading the news of available books throughout the ethnic community and encouraging library attendance. This aspect can be of great importance, because some immigrants come from countries where there is no public library tradition or where governmental institutions are by definition suspect. Community leaders could therefore help considerably by publicizing the library's services and encouraging their use by the ethnic community.

One word of caution, though. It may not be wise to accept advice proffered by a patron whose qualifications are unknown. Otherwise, the collection may be built according to the suggestions of someone who is not familiar with the scope of the literature, has extremist or biased views, or is out of touch with the community to be served. It is always preferable to approach the community leaders directly. If they cannot advise the library, they will undoubtedly suggest a reliable contact.

Although the information thus obtained may be varied and unexpected it will always be helpful. It may be found, for example, that it is not enough to identify a community as Yugoslav. It must be known whether the readers expect books in Croatian, Serbian, Slovene, or Macedonian. And, although Serbo-Croatian is officially considered one language, it may be found that Serbian patrons expect only books in the Cyrillic alphabet, and will demand that these be shelved separately from the Croatian collection. It may be found that Estonian patrons do not want any books published in Estonia at all, and will only read Estonian books that are published outside the Soviet Union. It will, of course, be helpful to know whether Spanish-language patrons have come from Cuba, Mexico,

Puerto Rico, Chile, Colombia, or Spain. It may also be useful to find out about special interests—that Italian women in the community have formed a handicrafts club, or that the Portuguese group operates a kindergarten.

A knowledge of the patrons' cultural, political, and religious affiliations, their general level of education and their interests, is important. All this information will help in the creation of an intelligent book selection policy, one that is geared to the readers' needs.

Type of Material

A decision must be made as to the type of material that the library will acquire to serve ethno-cultural groups. If funding is sufficient, as it rarely is, a full range of materials may be acquired: serials, language-study materials, recordings and other audiovisual materials, reference books, English-language works of particular interest to the group, and, of course, foreign language books. A selected number of the best foreign-language newspapers and journals would be much appreciated by the community. Films in various languages could be purchased, or rented. In Canada, for example, films in various languages can be borrowed from the National Film Board free of charge.

Some of these materials will be of interest not only to the specific ethnic groups, but to the general population as well. Recordings of music and songs transcend the barrier of language; they will be popular not only with the ethnic patron but other library patrons too. Language-study materials could be used not only by second- or third-generation Canadians or Americans to brush up on proficiency in their mother tongue, but also by a library patron wishing to learn another language. Dictionaries, grammars, and language-study records or cassettes also fall into this category.

English-language materials of "ethnic" interest would of course also be accessible to the general library user. The selection of English-language material suitable for patrons from ethno-cultural communities does not fall within the scope of this article but it must at least be mentioned when discussing selection policies. It is quite often neglected or simply forgotten by librarians responsible for collection building. English-language materials may include encyclopedic works, reference books, histories, photographic albums presenting the country, travel guides, cookbooks, or translations of literary classics. Books are also being published now on the specific contribution of various ethno-cultural groups. These works recognize the place of ethnic groups in North

American history and civilization. Such books are particularly appropriate for library collections. Three series that come to mind are *A History of Canada's Peoples* series, published by McClelland and Stewart, the *Multicultural Canada* series, published by Van Nostrand-Reinhold, and the *Ethnic Chronology* series, published by Oceana Publications.

English-language children's books which foster an awareness and understanding of other cultures are also valuable. Translations of traditional folk tales can be appealing to all library patrons. Examples of this are some of the publications of *Kids Can Press*.

In making such materials available to its users, libraries can play an important role in reducing prejudice based on ignorance, and in promoting intercultural understanding and tolerance in the community. Two good annotated bibliographies of English-language material of "ethnic" interest are *Resource List for a Multicultural Society*[8] and *Building Ethnic Collections*, by Buttlar and Wynar.[9]

When serving its ethnic communities specifically, however, it is important that the public library stock a good collection of other-language books. A fair percentage of the library's budget should be allocated for this purpose, possibly proportionate to the size of the ethnic group within the community the library is serving. The other-language books should be selected as carefully as books for the main collection. Too often the action in a public library is a dismal assortment of outdated books, irrelevant books received as gifts, and translations of Mark Twain and Charles Dickens. One visit from an ethnic library user to such a collection is enough to discourage the borrower from ever returning, and the librarian is then convinced that there is no demand for books in languages other than English!

As a minimum, a good collection of contemporary fiction, a collection of children's books, and some books of general interest are required. A detailed selection policy, taking into account the ethnic community's needs and interests, should be outlined. Books should be purchased according to this policy.

It may be found when purchasing books from various countries that some books are of little value for North American readers. A Swedish guide to gardening is not of much help to someone living in a different climate; electrical repair manuals published abroad are often based on different specifications. Children's books may be geared to a reading level different from that of North American children of ethnic origin who often do not have a good mastery of their mother tongue.

The advisability of purchasing translations is a moot point. A language collection should consist mainly of books in the national literature if it is to be of cultural value. Translated classics from other literatures, or translations of best-sellers should make up only a small fraction of a collection. Translations of current best-sellers may have some value in that they would allow immigrants who read only in their mother tongue to feel less isolated in their new surroundings. An Italian grandfather can then read *Jaws*, or *Airport*, or another best-seller, and in this way participate in the current interests of the rest of his family. But the choice of too many translations would certainly reflect a selector's poor knowledge of the literature in question and defeat the important cultural purpose of having collections in languages other than English.

In case the size of the group does not warrant a regular acquisition program in a given language, some kind of cooperative acquisition plan should be worked out which would assign to individual libraries the responsibility to develop collections in certain languages only. These collections should then be made available to others in the system through rotating deposits or interlibrary loans.

Methods of Book Selection

There are two main methods used by public libraries to select books in languages other than English: the selecting of individual titles for purchase, and the placing of blanket or approval orders. Each system has its particular merits and its drawbacks.

The selection and ordering of individual titles require far more library resources. Staff knowledgeable in the language and literature of the country must peruse review journals, publishers' catalogues, and national bibliographies. Multi-part purchase-order forms must be filled out for each item; they must be filed and followed up. Often, ordering of individual titles is an exercise in frustration, since the out-of-print rate for even recent foreign publications can exceed 50 percent. New publishers' catalogues and the latest lists of forthcoming books are probably the best selection aids to use to ensure the availability of books. However, there is usually no critical evaluation of the books in these catalogues and acceptance of a publisher's enthusiastic praise can, at times, be risky. Review journals, on the other hand, although helpful in providing evaluations, usually describe books that were published months, if not years, earlier, and are therefore no longer available. National

bibliographies are helpful in the verification of bibliographic information for ordering, but they do not offer selection advice, and are rarely up to date. Such tools as the *Library of Congress Accession List* do not list popular fiction or children's books in most languages, and are therefore also inadequate as selection tools for public libraries. Review journals, however, can still be very useful in evaluating the development of the collection and in checking individual titles.

There are several English-language journals that review books published in other languages, notably *World Literature Today*, a literary quarterly published by the University of Oklahoma, and *Bookbird*, a children's literature review journal issued quarterly by the International Board on Books for Young People. However, because books in many countries go out of print very quickly, the books are often no longer available by the time the reviews appear a year or two later. These journals are therefore recommended not so much as selection tools but rather for their current-awareness value. Reviews in *World Literature Today*, previously titled *Books Abroad*, are also geared more to the scholarly community, and may therefore not be completely suitable for public library selection. A more appropriate review source would be the regular foreign-language acquisitions column found in the *ALA Booklist*.

Publishers' Weekly occasionally has interesting reports on publishing in various countries, including interviews with specific publishers and information on their areas of specialization. Recent reports included coverage of the publishing situation in Spain, Portugal, Japan, and Israel.

A preferred method of selecting individual titles is off-the-shelf selection from a smaller local ethnic book store, if travel funds are limited, or from a larger store further afield, if funds allow. The advantages of this system are many. Newly published books can be examined by the selector personally for their suitability. Staff time is not wasted typing and pursuing orders for out-of-print books. And, since ethnic bookstores are often owned or managed by persons who know the literature well, the library selectors will often benefit from their advice and suggestions.

The alternative to the selection of individual titles is the placing of blanket orders. This method is becoming quite popular with increasingly understaffed libraries because it requires fewer library resources than does the selection and ordering of individual titles. In the case of a blanket order, the dealer does the selection; purchase order forms are unnecessary. Budgets are also better controlled since funds are not left committed for many months for books that are back-ordered or out-of-print. Detractors of the blanket-ordering system consider such ordering to be an abrogation of a librarian's basic duty, that of selecting appropriate books for the library according to professional criteria. However, individual selection of books in languages other than English can be problematic, as stated earlier. Many libraries, therefore, find that acceptable blanket selection according to detailed library specifications can be done by a reliable dealer. More and more dealers are now offering such selection services in response to library demand. The library should, nevertheless, carefully monitor dealer selection to get optimum results.

Probably the best method of collection building in languages other than English would be a combination of a modified blanketorder system and of individual ordering. Under such a system the bulk of the selection would be done by the dealer, but it would be closely monitored by the library. The remaining selection would be done from review journals and other journals on an individual basis to fill the gaps left by the dealer's selection. This combined system would have the advantages of individual selection with only a few of its disadvantages.

When deciding to build a collection in a language other than English, a comprehensive book selection policy should first be prepared, listing in detail the types of books required. A detailed policy will prove valuable to the library as a record, and to the dealer as a guide in selecting. For the library depending upon dealer selection, the "blanket-order" plan would best be modified to an "approval" plan. The approval plan allows the library to approve books selected by the dealer upon delivery and to return those considered unsuitable, normally up to 5 percent of the order.

It is, of course, necessary for the library to have a resource person, on a contract or on a volunteer basis, who knows the foreign language and literature in question. This person should check the dealer selection, advise the selection librarian on what is acceptable and what should be returned, advise the library of possible gaps in its collection, and suggest individual items for ordering. The library, in turn, should subscribe to at least one good review journal to allow the resource person to keep aware of current publishing in the language.

METHODS OF BOOK ACQUISITION

There are several methods of acquiring books for the public library, some more successful than others, some cumbersome and some less so. Normally, no one method is used exclusively in acquiring books for a language collection. The means and ways chosen would differ according to the language in which books are being acquired and would depend on the availability of books and dealers. Suggested methods for individual languages will be discussed in more detail further on in this paper. However, some remarks will be made here regarding the basic methods: purchasing from local versus foreign dealers, receiving books as gifts or on an exchange basis, book-buying trips, and placing blanket or approval orders, and individual orders.

Purchasing books from a local ethnic bookstore can be a very satisfactory method which reduces acquisition paperwork considerably. Requirements and problems can be discussed in person with the dealer and selection done off the shelves by the library selector. Personal contact makes the dealer more aware of the library's needs, and often makes the service more obliging. A small local dealer with a limited stock could probably offer selection advice, and could supply books on approval according to the library's selection policy and budget. The negative aspects, though, are a very limited stock of books and higher prices. Prices from a local dealer would necessarily be higher than those paid abroad, but in comparing prices it is necessary to consider that the services of the local dealer eliminates necessary steps in the acquisition process, such as correspondence in a foreign language, a task cumbersome for small libraries. Foreign dealers also often require payment before the books are sent. This should, for obvious reasons, be avoided if at all possible. Payments may have to be made in foreign currency, lost shipments tracked down, and parcels ushered through customs with appropriate forms filled out, one hopes, by the dealer. Books arriving from tropical countries may have to be fumigated. Buying books from abroad does not always involve such headaches, but when it does, a local dealer's price may well be worth it.

Some countries, however, have a very well-organized book trade and purchasing directly from them does not present major problems. Buying abroad provides a much broader selection base, allowing for the assembling of a better, more varied collection, corresponding to the specific needs of the community to be served to a higher extent. Collections selected from larger and more varied stock will, as a result, differ from library to library and provide more interesting material for inter-library exchange. More details about advantages and disadvantages of buying directly from a given country will be found in the section on specific areas or languages.

Books in languages other than English can also be acquired by the public library as gifts or as part of an official exchange program. Although private collections received as gifts are sometimes of great value to a research library or a large public library, they may not be as useful in a smaller public library. Certainly, no gift should be added to a collection without questioning its value. Despite a sometimes high proportion of inappropriate material, gifts can often be an excellent source for expanding or supplementing library holdings. There is a variety of sources which can be explored and successfully used. Embassies and legations usually receive small stocks of books for publicity purposes and are more than happy to donate them to the library. Ethnic organizations are often willing to purchase and donate a batch of books to commemorate an anniversary, as a gift of a community member or local clubs. Ethnic groups also can be encouraged to appropriate for book purchases a part of the proceeds from bazaars, festivals and similar events. In every case, a gift label with the name of the donor should be placed in the book. Such signs of appreciation very often result in an augmented interest in the library and generate further donations. Exchange programs are more complex. They may be feasible for a research or large public library but rarely for the smaller public library.

An efficient way of purchasing is the book-buying trip. This may be just a trip to a local bookdealer's shop, a trip to a large city close by, or it may be a trip abroad. Budgeting for trips abroad may be financially impossible for the individual public library. However, a cooperative effort by several libraries may be worthwhile, with each library carrying a part of the cost of sending a selector to purchase books in the country of publishing. Book-buying trips are generally an exhausting venture and, to be successful, they must be well planned and prepared. A recent article in *The Unabashed Librarian* provided some useful guidelines for those planning such trips.[10]

Placing blanket or approval orders, as mentioned previously, can be a quite acceptable method if the dealer is reliable, and if the library can check the selection. Dealer selection puts a minimum work load on acquisitions staff because there are no purchase order forms to type, file, and follow up. However, a person knowledgeable in the literature should check the books for suitability when they arrive. A few unsuitable books, returned with an explanation, will serve to let the dealer know that the selection is being closely monitored. They will reduce any temptation to send items from publishers' overstock.

The problem of duplicate items, sent by the dealer in separate shipments, may arise when using the method of blanket ordering. To avoid this, blanket or approval orders should be placed with only one dealer who can then keep track of the books sent earlier. A helpful method is to update the collection only once a year. In this case, the dealer should be instructed to send only books published in that year. This reduces the possibility of duplicates to reprints.

Individual selection of books from review journals is considered by many librarians to be the most professional method of collection building. For the acquisition staff it is a very time-consuming method, especially when dealing with books in languages other than English. Searching bibliographic information for foreign items can present difficulties. Individual purchase-order forms must be typed in the original language, and in the case of nonroman alphabets the romanized form must be given. Orders must be filed, and followed up. At this point, it may be useful to warn against the temptation of sending a dealer a copy of a catalogue with the required items checked, or a marked list of desired titles. Although this procedure may seem an easy way of placing an order, it can quickly become very cumbersome. Since the dealer must order items individually from the publisher, books from one order will arrive at the library at various times, often over a period of several months. Back orders will trickle in often without reference to a purchase-order number, and it is difficult to tell when an order is finally completed. An order cannot be retired until the last item requested has been accounted for. In short, the "list" method of ordering books is the least controllable from the administrative point of view.

Selection and ordering of books in languages other than English by individual titles can however be satisfactory if proper selection tools are available, and if the library's acquisition unit is well-staffed. Some libraries attempt to simplify the purchase of books from abroad by placing their foreign-language orders with one of several large booksellers, most of which are centered in New York. These often offer blanket-order programs in various languages, as does Stechert-Macmillan with its "Popular New Titles from Abroad" program. These services can be useful to the small public library without selection tools and staff. However, many of the foreign language titles proffered by these dealers are translations of current best-sellers; libraries would therefore be well-advised to specify in their order profile the proportion of translations they are willing to accept. If a library's resources permit, it would be preferable to place an order in a particular language with a dealer who specializes in supplying books in that language: the selection will inevitably be superior.

SERIALS ACQUISITIONS

Serials, mentioned only briefly in the previous discussion of selection principles, actually play a very important and often underrated role in collections in languages other than English. In a public library, serials cover newspapers and periodicals of general interest for the use of the patron, as well as working tools for the book selectors, such as review journals and current bibliographies. The latter may also be used by the patrons because review journals often contain articles of general interest about authors, literary trends, and publishing programs. Both categories can cover material published in the country and abroad.

The subject of handling serials in libraries is well-covered in professional literature, to mention only the chapter on serials in Stephen Ford's *The Acquisition of Library Materials'.*[11] Therefore only those aspects of handling serials will be mentioned here which differ from the methods recommended for handling scholarly journals.

As pointed out earlier, newspapers and journals of general interest constitute a very important part of library materials and will attract a number of patrons who are not regular users of the library collection. They provide the best up-to-date overview of political and cultural development in the country, and the language and format of information are attractive to those whose limited knowledge of the particular language makes reading books difficult.

In establishing the list of titles for acquisition the same criteria should be applied as suggested for the selection of monographs. A survey of the communities to be served is essential to determine their field of interest.

Newspapers in particular tend to represent definite political ideologies which may not be acceptable to the local reader. Leading newspapers from countries behind the iron curtain may constitute an exception because they are, despite their clear political attitude, the best sources of information on political and social developments in these countries. The same selection criteria should be applied to publications of the local ethnic press. They should be well-represented in the collection. Concerning subscription methods, using a reputable dealer saves the library a considerable amount of work in the searching of addresses, preparation of individual payments,

and renewal of subscriptions. Use of subscription agents works very well for most Western European countries and should be recommended for libraries with a large volume of subscriptions. It must be remembered however that most agents now add a service charge which can in certain cases be quite considerable. Therefore, for a library which has a small number of subscriptions, it is worth considering the placing of subscriptions directly with the publishers. This has to be done anyway for local ethnic press publications because they are usually too small or difficult to handle to be of interest to any subscription agent. A convenient solution can be found by placing subscriptions through an ethnic bookstore. Many of them also handle newspapers and periodicals and receive discounts from the publisher. They are not obliged to add service charges other than, eventually, postage.

Newspaper and magazine subscriptions usually start in January which makes renewals less tedious. For those magazines which have a different subscription time, the Kardex or administrative card can be tagged in different colors for each month. A quick check each month will prevent the lapse of the subscription. It is worth keeping in mind that even if the library places a standing order, many newspaper and magazine publishers will not send renewal invoices, or will insert them in an issue where it can be easily missed. If that is the case, the librarian should request an invoice in due time. If it does not arrive in time, the best thing to do is to check the current subscription price on the masthead and send a check with a statement of the period the payment covers.

Some magazines have reduced rates for long-term (e.g., 3 years) subscriptions. A library can easily take advantage of such rates without unbalancing the budget by dividing all long-term subscriptions into approximately equal batches and spacing the renewals over the years. It should also be remembered that many magazines can be obtained free through embassies, organizations, or the dealers. Some examples would be *Uber Bucher, Polska* (published in several languages), or *Holland Herald*. The latter can be picked up at every KLM airline office!

SPECIFIC AREAS AND LANGUAGES

Several Western European countries—Denmark, The Netherlands, West Germany, Norway, Sweden, Finland, and Switzerland—have organized national centers for library services with the purpose of promoting the development of their public and school libraries. They are the

Bibliotekscentralen in Denmark; the Einkaufszentrale, or ekz, in West Germany; Kirjastopalvelu Oy in Finland; the Nederlands Bibliotheek en Lektuur Centrum, or NBLC, in the Netherlands; the Biblioteksentralen in Norway; the Bibliotekstjänst in Sweden; and the Schweizer Biblioteksdienst in Switzerland. These centers range from independent commercial companies to state-supported nonprofit organizations; they are all members of IFLA's Round Table of National Centers for Library Services. Their activities include the production of aids for selection and acquisition of library materials, and centralized cataloguing. Most of the centers will export books; North American libraries can therefore take advantage of the services provided by these centers. However, because selection tools provided by these centers usually contain annotations in the language of the country of origin, an American library would need the services of a language resource person to choose books from these lists. Some of the centers will, however, do selection according to submitted specifications if so requested. The centers also produce convenient time-saving order forms which can simply be clipped and sent. Also available are sets of catalogue cards for the books purchased, with the books bound in sturdy library bindings and provided with book pockets and cards.

The centralized library services in the countries mentioned are indeed enviable, and many North American public libraries will want to take advantage of the selection, acquisition, and cataloguing aid offered. Even without these services, however, libraries will find the book trade in these countries well-organized. The larger book-dealers, such as Sautter & Lackmann in West Germany, or Meulenhoff-Bruna in the Netherlands, are experienced in exporting books and will do selection according to library guidelines. Correspondence with them can be conducted in English. Selection tools are also available, such as *Uber Bucher*, an annotated German-language quarterly listing of new publications. For Swedish books, an English-language quarterly review journal called, appropriately, *Swedish Books*, will soon begin publication. For Finnish books, there is the English-language *Books from Finland*.

The countries mentioned have, of course, a well-ordered book trade and publishing industry, and a sophisticated library service. Ordering directly from them offers few problems. The same does not hold true for all Western European countries, however.

The political situation in Portugal in the last several years has affected the publishing industry in that country. The result is that it may be extremely difficult to obtain books. Also, communication with even the large dealers is expected to be in Portuguese. Catalogues can be difficult to come by, and even when orders are placed immediately, there is a large out-of-print rate. There is hope that the situation may be improving with the announcement of a new journal called *Noticias do livro* which will list newly published titles. In the meantime, however, libraries will probably prefer to search out a North American dealer rather than attempt direct purchasing. The dealer may also offer to supply Brazilian books. Considering the difficulties involved in acquiring books from South American countries, most libraries will find such an arrangement highly desirable.

Spanish-language books would have to be obtained from Latin American countries and from Spain, depending on the library's readers. In the United States, Hispanic Americans are a fast-growing minority, currently numbering 19 million. The number of bookstores stocking Spanish-language books is therefore increasing, and libraries should be able to find a reliable dealer in New York, San Francisco, or closer to home. Spanish-language books are also being published in the United States, notably Cuban emigre literature. And at least one large English-language publishing house, J. B. Lippincott, has ventured into Spanish-language publishing with a series especially designed to meet the needs of Hispanic American young readers. Libraries serving Spanish-speaking patrons are undoubtedly aware of the journal *Cartel* which lists and annotates bilingual and bicultural educational materials for several minority groups, but mostly for the Hispanic.

French-language books should cover literature from France and from francophone Canada. Both France and Quebec publish a variety of selection tools, bibliographies, and review journals. Both the French and the French-Canadian book trade are well-organized, although the prices are fairly high and many titles are published in soft cover only. It is quite easy to find a reliable dealer such as Guy Boussac in Paris, or a well-stocked, large bookstore. In Quebec, the best equipped for handling blanket-orders is Librairie-Dussault in Montreal which has a foreign order section and competent staff to select books according to specifications. For those who can afford it, a book-buying trip to Montreal will be most rewarding. The city has a large number of bookstores well stocked with French and Canadian books. Recommended is a trip during the annual Salon du Livre which usually takes place in the late fall. A good number of French publishers is represented at the Salon every year. At the end of the Montreal Book Fair there is usually an opportunity to buy books with a good discount, amounting sometimes to 50 percent.

In purchasing Italian books a North American library's largest problem may be currency fluctuation which tends to make budgeting in this area difficult. Direct buying, however, does not present many other problems. Many good books are published yearly, and a large dealer, such as Casalini Libri, will select books according to the library profile and will conduct correspondence in English. Italian books can be very expensive. It may therefore be wise, when placing orders, to specify a maximum price per book. A good Italian-language selection tool would be *Tuttolibri*, a literary weekly containing book reviews and short annotated book lists. For Italian children's books, an excellent selection and acquisition tool is *Schedario*, a bimonthly publication which contains descriptive and evaluative annotations for recommended books. The information is on 3 x 5 cards on perforated sheets for ease of ordering.

Greek books may be purchased directly from Greece or from North American dealers. Prices from certain North American dealers can be fairly high, but ordering directly from Greece would often involve corresponding in Greek. There are at least two reliable dealers of Greek books in New York: Pagosmion, who will do selection if so requested, and Caratzas Brothers, who also publish beautifully illustrated and expensive volumes on Greek history and civilization.

Icelandic books are among the most expensive, due to the small number of printings and the high quality of the books. These books are probably best obtained directly since there do not seem to be any North American dealers who specialize in Icelandic books.

Maltese books can present a problem. There is very little original literature available. What there is can be obtained from the Klabb Kotba Maltin or Aquilina in Valletta, Malta.

Scottish books in Gaelic that are particularly suitable for public library collections are published by, and available from, the Club Leabhar in Scotland.

The Welsh Books Council publishes *Llais Llyfray/Book News*, a quarterly review of Welsh literature, which lists and annotates in Welsh and English the most recent Welsh publications, including children's books. The books selected can then be ordered from Oriel, the retail bookselling division of the Welsh Arts Council.

Purchasing books from Eastern Europe—Czechoslovakia, Hungary, Poland, Yugoslavia, and the Soviet Union—presents different problems than purchasing from Western Europe. Since every aspect of publishing in communist countries is in the hands of the state, there is of course centralized control over book production and distribution. Every country has a central government export agency and all books must be purchased through it. Printings of books are often very limited and items must be ordered from lists of forthcoming books if they are to be received. However, inclusion of a title in a list of forthcoming books does not mean that it will be published. Sometimes titles are included simply to gauge the degree of interest in such a publication and the title may then be dropped without further notice. Literature is also considered a political tool in these countries, and immigrants who are refugees from these political systems may object very strongly to the contents of books published there. It will be found that most of these immigrant groups have set up publishing outside their native countries, and books published this way will be in demand by many of the library's users.

Books from Czechoslovakia may have to be ordered directly, since there are few dealers in North America who specialize in this area and can give satisfactory service. Orders should be placed with the two government export agencies, Artia for Czech books and Slovart for Slovak books. Libraries should be prepared to pay invoices in advance of receipt of books at least for the first few shipments, or until credit rating is established. Two English-language selection tools are available from these agencies: *Czech Books in Print* and *Slovak Books in Print*. These publications list and give extensive annotations for forthcoming books. Libraries will find, however, that even though orders are placed immediately upon receipt of the catalogues, a large percentage of the orders will not be filled, and others may take a year to arrive. Payment will be requested in U.S. or Canadian dollars, and the verification of conversion rates is practically impossible. Regarding Czech books published abroad, every public library will at least want a complete collection of the publishing output of 68 Publishers in Toronto for its Czech readers. These books are obtainable directly from the publisher.

Hungarian books can be purchased directly from Hungary's central export agency, Kultura. However, there is an excellent Hungarian book dealer in Toronto who will do selection if requested. This dealer, Pannonia Books, stocks books published in Hungary and abroad, and will supply book-lists on request.

Poland has a well-developed publishing trade, although printings are too small and books must therefore be ordered in advance of their publication through the central book export agency, Ars Polona. The selection tool, *Zapowiedzi wydawnicze*, lists forthcoming books in the form of entries that can be clipped and used as order slips. Each entry contains full bibliographic information, the reading level, and content annotation. There are also English-language selection tools, such as *New Polish Publications*, but the time-lag in their appearance makes them less useful than *Zapowiedzi*. While selecting books in Polish, proper attention should be given to emigré and local literature. There are two major publishing centers in Europe for such books, Paris and London. In Paris, the major publishing center is the Polish *Institut littéraire*. In London, the major resource center which carries books published both in Poland and abroad is Orbis Books. Both publish catalogues. A good source for Polonica Americana is the Kosciuszko Foundation Bookstore in New York. There also exist a number of good Polish ethnic bookstores in several other Canadian and American cities.

Books from Yugoslavia are more difficult to obtain from North American sources. Agents in Yugoslavia are Jugoslovenska Knjiga and Prosveta in Belgrade and Mladost in Zagreb. Most books in Serbian, especially those published abroad, are printed in the Cyrillic script; Croatian books use Roman script. Libraries may find that their users prefer that the Serbian and Croatian collections be kept separate. Slovenian and Macedonian books will also warrant separate collections.

Some public libraries will have requests for books in Russian, Ukrainian, Lithuanian, Latvian and Estonian, i.e., languages spoken in countries that now form a part of the Soviet Union. Many of the readers who emmigrated from this part of the world in this century have been political refugees. Since much of the literature published in the U.S.S.R., including even some children's books, has political overtones, it may be unacceptable to library users. The problem is compounded in the case of the non-Russian nationalities. Non-Russian refugees may also object to cultural and linguistic repression in their homelands and will feel that Soviet cultural policies are reflected in books printed in the U.S.S.R. Nevertheless, a collection in any of the above languages could not be deemed representative if it did not include at least some of the works currently being published in the Soviet Union. Libraries will probably want to purchase much of what is published in the West in these languages, and, very selectively, what is published in the Soviet Union as well.

Soviet books are published in very limited quantities and must be acquired immediately upon publication. The central export agency for all Soviet books is Mezhdunarodnaya Kniga in Moscow. Several booksellers abroad who special-

ize in Russian-language publications are also distributing agents for Mezh Kniga, as it is known. Libraries are encouraged by Mezh Kniga to purchase books through these booksellers rather than attempt direct purchasing from Moscow. The service offered by these dealers, however, varies greatly, and libraries may have to try several dealers before finding one that offers the service they require. Two of the larger agents are the Four Continent Book Corp. in New York, and Les Livres Etrangers in Paris which handles the Russian-language blanket-order plan for the Library of Congress. Librarians involved in the purchasing of Russian-language books will find that C. M. Hotimsky's *The Acquisition of Russian Books* gives valuable insights.[12]

Many significant Russian-language books are published yearly in the West, notably by the YMCA Press in Paris. This publisher was the first to publish the Soviet-censored works of Pasternak and Solzhenitsyn. YMCA Press publications and other Russian-language books published abroad are available from Les Editeurs Reunis in Paris. This bookdealer publishes a substantial yearly catalogue which, despite some limitations, is a very good selection tool.

There are several bookdealers in North America who specialize in Ukrainian-language publications. Most limit themselves either to books published in the West, or to books published in the Soviet Union. The Ukrainian Book Store in Edmonton, Alberta, carries both books published in the West and a selection of Soviet publications. This bookstore offers very good service and will do selection for public libraries if requested. It also regularly publishes lists of newly published books as well as catalogues of their book-stock.

Estonian books are published abroad mainly in Sweden. Public libraries will want to acquire all publications of the Eesti Kirjanike Kooperativ in Lund, Sweden, a book club which publishes mainly light novels. Agents for this book club are also found in North America.

Lithuanian books abroad are mainly published in the United States. Many of these are published by, and available from, the Lietuvisku Knygu Klubas in Chicago, a book club which specializes in contemporary Lithuanian fiction. Latvian books can be purchased from the Daugavas Vanagi Bookshop in Toronto, or Gramatu Draugs in New York.

Arabic-language books are published in Egypt, Lebanon, Libya, Iraq, Kuwait, Algeria, and Syria. Books from all these countries can be purchased from Al Ahram, the official government export agency in Cairo, Egypt. Other dealers also exist, but they may have trouble exporting books. In purchasing books directly from Cairo, libraries would be advised to have selection done by their own staff, and to pay invoices only when the books have been received. There are no adequate selection tools in the English language, and selection must be done from Arabic-language catalogues. Unfortunately, there do not seem to be any established North American dealers specializing in the import of Arabic-language books.

Chinese-language books can be acquired directly from Hong Kong or Taiwan, or from North American dealers. Books from Mainland China are most easily obtained either from North American agent-bookdealers, or from Hong Kong dealers. The larger book dealers, such as the Lingnam Book House, and the Chiao Lin Publication Service in Hong Kong, or the Chung Hwa Book Co. in Taiwan can do selection according to library guidelines, will provide catalogues, and will correspond in English. Smaller bookdealers, on the other hand, are also often publishers, and libraries may find them reluctant to provide any publications other than their own. In North America, there are several large suppliers of Chinese books. The Sun Wa Book Shop in Toronto, for example, has a large stock and can do selection for libraries. Libraries wishing to do their own selection can obtain Chinese-language publishers' catalogues and lists from bookdealers. English-language selection tools for public-library materials are not available.

Acquiring books published in India does not present many problems. Libraries that wish to purchase books in Hindi, Punjabi, Urdu, Gujarati, Marathi, Bengali, or any of the other languages spoken in India will find that there are several good dealers both in India and in North America. Star Publications and Sherieff Publications, both in New Delhi, will supply catalogues, and will dispatch books quickly and efficiently. Himalaya Books in Brampton, Ontario, and Far Eastern Books in Toronto will also accept blanket-orders and will do selection upon request. Books from India are generally inexpensive, but libraries must budget for the binding of all books, even those in hard-cover, if they expect them to withstand library use.

The selection and acquisition information given for the above specific languages is necessarily limited, since it is based largely upon our own experiences at the MBS. The above observations are therefore given as a basic, personal guide.

SUMMARY

A survey of the community and the various ethno-cultural groups it encompasses is a pre-requisite to the building of a good collection of books in languages other than English. The aspects to consider when making a survey are the country of origin of the readers, their political and social attitudes, their economic and educational levels, and if possible, the reasons for their interest in specific reading material in a given language, such as reading material for immigrants, for children, students, etc. The latter data can be most helpful in determining the type of books and other library materials best suited for the patrons' needs.

The next step is to establish a written policy concerning the type and ratio of material to be acquired, the subject fields to be covered, and the reading level in the various groups of materials to be acquired. It is also a good idea to spell out what type of material is excluded, what is the purpose of building a specific language collection, what physical characteristics are preferred (e.g., hardcover, illustrated), and which are unacceptable (e.g., loose-leaf format, books with cut-outs). Price limits have to be set and the number of copies to be acquired specified.

Once a firm selection and acquisition policy has been worked out, consideration will be given to the various ways and means of purchasing open to the library in a given situation. Books and other library materials can be acquired from local dealers or from abroad. There are a number of methods which can be used effectively. They are: orders of individual titles, blanket or approval orders, visits to local bookstores, book-buying trips for an off-shelf selection, and collection building by means of gifts and exchanges. Each of these methods has distinctive merits and disadvantages.

The methods of selection and acquisition a library decides to use in building its collection will depend on several considerations: on the publishing output in the language in question, the organization of the book trade in the country of publishing, the availability of selection and acquisition tools in the given language, and on the existence of local ethnic booksellers. The extent of library resources and the availability of resource persons in the language will also affect the choice of method. Depending on these considerations, each language collection may have to be handled somewhat differently. A combination of methods is, without any doubt, the best solution, and is recommended as the most effective way of acquisition.

Building collections in languages other than English requires the librarian in charge to have sensitivity, ingenuity, and flexibility in choosing working methods as well. It also requires an interest in and a willingness to establish contacts with the ethnic communities, and calls for careful monitoring of any changes in community needs. The establishment of cooperative schemes and rotating collections is recommended to ensure a regular flow of new material, especially if the size of the budget or the size of the community to be served does not warrant the development of exclusive collections.

ADDENDUM

In the decade since the preceding article was written, developments have occurred in the area of multilingual collection building. An update to the article follows, with a short review of some of these changes.

The National Library of Canada's Multilingual Biblioservice has grown from 26 languages to 32, and has added large-print books and books-on-cassette to its collections.

Guidelines have been developed in the intervening years in several countries. The first standards were prepared in Victoria, Australia and adopted by the Library Council of Victoria in 1982. These were followed by the "Guidelines for Multicultural Library Services in Canadian Public Libraries" which The Canadian Library Association issued in 1986. Then in 1987 the Section of Library Services to Multicultural Populations of IFLA issued the international "Guidelines for Library Service" which are available in English, French, German, Spanish, Russian and Japanese. In the U.S., the American Library Association published guidelines for services to Spanish-speaking populations.

The establishment of IFLA's Section on Library Services to Multicultural Populations has created a forum for the international exchange of information through its preconference programme and the Journal of Multicultural Librarianship. The Section has also prepared a manual on various aspects of services, with a chapter on collection building and acquisitions, which will be published in late 1991.

Several books have been published on multiculturalism and libraries, and a few specifically on the acquisition of other-language materials. A valuable reader, even for the North American context, is the Australian publication *Buying Books in Other Languages: a Handbook for Australian School and Public Libraries* by Anne Holmes and Derek Whitehead, published in 1983. Another valuable tool is the 1990 publication *Developing Library Collections for California's Emerging Majority; a Manual of Resources for Ethnic Collection Development,* edited by Katharine T. A. Scarborough.

More acquisition tools are now available. The Metropolitan Toronto Library Board in cooperation with the Multilingual Biblioservice of the National Library of Canada produced the 99-page "Multilanguage Vendors List" in 1988. Books-on-cassette, or talking books, have made inroads into libraries, and the Multilingual Biblioservice responded with the 27-page "Guide to Suppliers of Commercially Available Books-on-Cassette in Languages Other than English or French," which is now in its third edition.

Bilingual publications are now available from several publishers of children's books in Canada, the U.S., Britain, and Australia.

Regarding specific areas and languages, the situation has changed in several areas. The political situation in Portugal, mentioned in the preceding article, has since stabilized, and books are again being published in quantity; nevertheless, the book trade is not organized in such a way as to make available single reliable sources for books by various publishers.

Conditions in Eastern Europe, and especially the Soviet Union, are currently in a state of flux. The Soviet Union, until recently, had only Mezh Kniga as a central exporter. Now other Soviet republics are establishing book export agencies; Ukraine recently announced the formation of its Ukrainian Printed Products Exporters Association in Kiev.

The reduction in government controls, and the new freedom in Soviet publishing, will also gradually make the content of books published in the Soviet Union more acceptable to emigre readers. This will undoubtedly also affect the direction and quantity of emigre publishing, which often specialized in publishing works forbidden in the Soviet Union. Various Western dealers, that on principle would not have handled Soviet or East European publications, are beginning to do so. A good new source of both Western and Soviet Russian-language publications is the Erudite bookstore in Toronto.

In other East European countries such as Poland or Czechoslovakia, political censorship has been abolished and many books which could only be published abroad are now being re-issued in the home countries.

New dealers have also appeared in some languages, and other sources have disappeared. In Scottish Gaelic, for example, the best source of books would now be Gairm Publications.

The publishing scene constantly changes and although the principles of multilingual collection building remains the same, it is essential to be in touch with the current situation in every country that the library plans to deal with.

Notes

1. Flora B. Roberts. "The Library and the Foreign Citizen." *Public Libraries* 17 (May 1912):166-69.
2. Maud I. Stull. "Inter-racial Services Needed by Libraries." *The Library Journal* 58, No. 22 (15 December 1933):707.
3. Directors of the Ontario Regional Library Systems. Multilingual Services Committee. *Final Report.* Toronto, 1979.
4. Institute on the Acquisition of Foreign Materials, 1971, University of Wisconsin. *Acquisition of Foreign Materials for U.S. Libraries.* Compiled and edited by T. Samore. Metuchen, N.J.: Scarecrow, 1973. 350 p.
5. Ibid., p. 9.
6. Leonard Wertheimer. *Books in Other Languages: How to Select and Where to Order Them.* Ottawa: Canadian Library Association; N.Y.: K. G. Sauer, (in publication).
7. California Ethnic Services Task Force. *Ethnic Library Materials: A Preliminary Vendor List.* Santa Barbara. University of California, 1978. 27 p.
8. *Resource List for a Multicultural Society: an Experience '76 Project.* Toronto Sponsored by the Ministry of Education and the Ministry of Culture and Recreation, Ontario, 1976. 626 p. Identification No. 76-77/6173.
9. Lois Buttlar and Lubomyr R. Wynar. *Building Ethnic Collections: an Annotated Guide for School Media Centers and Public Libraries.* Littleton, Colo.: Libraries Unlimited, 1977. 434 p.
10. Crystal Capelis. "From Store to Library: Direct Buying of Foreign Languages Materials." *The Unabashed Librarian,* No. 22 (1977): 9.
11. Stephen Ford. *The Acquisition of Library Materials.* Chicago: American Library Association, 1973.
12. C. M. Hotimsky. *The Acquisition of Russian Books.* London: Clive Bingley, 1974. 37 p. ISBN 0-85157-183-2.

SECTION III

Evaluation

Issues in Collection Development: Collection Evaluation

Elizabeth Futas

Building a collection in academic and public libraries entails knowing the publishing market and matching it to the community to be served. This requires a guiding philosophy with goals and statements of objectives, which usually end up as part of a collection development policy. Sometimes such a policy is a formal, written document and sometimes it exists only in the minds of the people in charge of the library. In any case, one of the important aspects of collection building that never makes it into the formal policy is the evaluation of the existing collection, or, after a time, the evaluation of the one which the policy has described. In the former case it is always important to know what it is that you are building on and in the latter case it is a good indication of the success of the policy.

Obviously, before an evaluation takes place, it must be determined who is being served. Whether it is an academic curriculum or the people of a town, the needs and tastes of the patrons are foremost in the evaluation process. Without knowledge of the community, no evaluation can hope to pinpoint where the collection must go. Once the goals and objectives of the library are set, and the community analyzed, then it is time to evaluate the collection.

There are two types of collection evaluations that are currently being done in libraries across the nation: quantitative and qualitative. The more common one is the qualitative analysis. We either use lists of the best books in the field that others have compiled (*Reader's Advisor, Public Library Catalog*, etc.), or we hire subject experts to go through our holdings and to inform us of their strengths and weaknesses. If specialized lists exist of the subject areas which need evaluation, then this type of evaluation can be very useful. There are a number of bibliographies that do list the "best books" in a subject. In addition, there are catalogs of fine collections that one can use to measure one's own. This type of evaluation is subjective but certainly can lead to discovery of real needs in a particular field. There are also scholars with a particular subject expertise who will act as consultants and evaluate a collection.

Although not entirely objective, quantitative evaluations are based far more on numbers and far less on an individual's or even a group's decision on what is important and what isn't. In accomplishing such an analysis, it is necessary to truly understand the importance, to the collection and the people it serves, of a body of literature. This body can consist of textbooks used for class, a fundamental journal in the field, or even the citations used in a dissertation. In a public library, this type of analysis is often connected to circulation figures. The classification schedule is broken down into large subject areas and the monitoring of circulation within the areas is closely kept so that it becomes obvious after a time where the most use is being made of the collection. Use statistics are then equated directly with a collection's value.

This reveals a real shortcoming of the quantitative evaluation. In order to count anything there must be discrete entities. Yet counting items circulating does not do anything but indicate popularity which can ebb and flow with the times. It is the leap from use to value that some in our profession find difficult to make. It would appear that using only this analysis is just as fraught with errors as using only the qualitative approach. A reasonable solution would be to use both approaches on the same collection, thereby getting the qualitative one to validate the quantitative one. In class assignments in the field of collection development I have tried to get my class to use both approaches to see if there are major differences in the results. It is rare that one way will be far removed from the other, but when this happens the students are forced to see if there are any problems with the methodological setup of the project.

There is one thing which students realize no matter how the results turn out: the time-consuming labor intensity of evaluation. These projects, important as they are to the well-being and health of the entire collection, are very expensive to do. Before they are started they should be carefully planned. Time schedules should be made to do the checking and the counting, and the forms to do this must be designed. The more careful the plan, the easier the execution and the more trustworthy the results.

Bill Katz/**Perspective**

By the Numbers: The Fallacy of Formula

The purpose of this and future columns about collection development is to be judiciously critical and mildly constructive.

Too much of library literature is received without comment, although numerous hard working librarians would enjoy firing a rejoinder. You can do it here, and you are invited to suggest topics for future investigation in this section. If you feel strongly about this or that, you are asked to sound off. Your comments (including those in opposition to my point of view) will be printed here from time to time.

With that—on to the matter of evaluating library collections by the numbers.

In the almost manic urge to explain the "science" in "library science" there is an unseemly group of librarians, teachers, and camp followers who insist that collection development may be pretty much reduced to quantitative formulas. They openly scoff at considerations which can't be reduced to a mathematical pattern—a pattern, by the way, that few skilled mathematicians or statisticians would recognize.

Consider Stanley Slote's excellent summary of the situation. Reading his review of the literature in the second edition of his guide to weeding (an unfortunate descriptor, perhaps, but somehow fitting if one considers the library a garden of delights), one finds that there have been over 1,000 use studies. The would-be scientists of the library continue to plow the same field, or as Slote puts it: "It is serious criticism of the literature of librarianship . . . that articles currently appearing could have been written 15 to 75 years ago."[1] What makes it even sadder—librarians seem to avoid paying any attention to the plowboys; or as Slote says somewhat more gently: "The literature has had little impact on the practitioners, teachers, and leaders in the field."[2]

Slote blames such things as bad writing, bad research, and even inadequate access to the literature for the less than massive impact of these studies on librarians. He wisely adds that there is nothing wrong with carefully worked out formulas, but very few fit this category.

I agree with most, yet hardly all of his explanation. A major reason these studies fail is that they smack of infallibility in a library which is a monument to fallibility. In their inexorable rush to impress, lacking any real perspective about themselves or about libraries, the would-be researchers establish laws built upon nothing but air. It seems to me, for example, that any librarian or student with a modicum of common sense who comes across a formula guaranteed to exorcise doubt from selection of materials should be skeptical. It may, like the alchemist's findings, work; but the odds are that the only real work the formula has done is to serve as an entry in the writer's vita.

Another reason for the failure of the formula is its inherent abstruseness. Most explanations are really a panegyric to energetic, dancing numbers which can neither be understood or employed. One may counter with the argument that these people are writing for their peers, not for the average, puzzled librarian; but that is simply to argue that they are writing in a vacuum. The only real peers this group has are of two types: (1) Those who will use the published material to generate more of the same, (2) The baffled and less than secure who must applaud anything they don't understand, rarely guessing there is really nothing to understand.

I strongly suspect that these writers have not only failed to appreciate the audience they are allegedly trying to contact, but have such contempt for that audience that the writing is boiling over with hidden aggression. Yes, it is aggressive (or, in some rare cases, such as Joyce or Einstein, genius) to be vague and difficult. This aggression surfaces in a type of fundamentalism, i.e., *true* collection development discussion must be limited to formulation. Anyone who dares suggest a somewhat wider point of view is not truly a member of the collection development group, but a mere soldier of selection or acquisitions.

The class system is operative, too. Those in academic libraries who have tasted of the *true* collection development formula have little patience with the untouched and unwashed public or school librarian. And within the academic world, the junior college formula expert is certainly to give way to the senior who is parading about the big 100. Fortunately, this jocund viewpoint is shared only by the sportive few who keep the flame of formula sputtering.

A major reason these studies fail is that they smack of infallibility in a library which is a monument to infallibility. In their inexorable rush to impress, lacking any real perspective about themselves or about libraries, the would-be researchers establish laws built upon nothing but air.

A History of Use Studies

Now, let's turn to two or three studies and reports. It is not giving anything away to note that as early as 1902 the president of Harvard, who had some interest in a five (or was it six) foot book shelf venture, happened to mention some books in the library were not used as often as others, and it might be useful to know how to discover which ones are likely to circulate and which ones are likely to gather dust. One would like to say this passing comment is so self-evident as to be a cliche, but almost 80 years later the formula fans are still repeating the same words.

Take, for example, the formula which emphasizes "the frequency distribution of the circulation (of an item) is representative of future circulation."[3] This presupposes a mathematic truth which is much closer to speculation than objective formulation. The University of Pittsburgh Study employed a more involved, yet essentially similar, approach to determine what is or is not useful in a library, and concluded that as "books get older, first time use is reduced . . . and only objective techniques of weeding should be used."[4] The only mystery, of course, about these and scores of similar studies is that anyone should waste so much time reformulating the Harvard president's mumblings. Granted, a hard statistical observation, de rigueur for fastening the otherwise less than apparent Emperor's clothes, is of value in argumentation or preparing an annual report. Still, must thousands be spent to reach such startling facts as 48.37 percent of the University of Pittsburgh Library[5] collection did not circulate in seven years; and that 39.8 percent of the books acquired in 1969 never circulated during the first six years on the library's shelves.[6]

Actually, the Pittsburgh study was done by people whom one respects and, if nothing else, it at least caused a controversy. It did achieve what most of the 1,000 other reports failed to achieve—it was read. Yet, it is quite beyond belief that it had any lasting effect on any library this side of Pittsburgh. One wonders if the time might better have been spent on the tennis courts, and the money to employ a few more librarians.

I am not arguing or suggesting that the Lancasters of the library be cast out, that there is not a quiet corner in library policy formulation for judicious user studies. If wisely done, if fashioned in such a way that the results may be applicable, useful, and easily understood and appreciated (and Lancaster[7] and Slote are two who meet this simple test), then a limited number of studies might be pursued and published each decade or so.

Granted, a hard statistical
observation, de rigueur
for fastening the otherwise
less than apparent Emperor's
clothes, is of value
in argumentation or preparing
an annual report. Still,
must thousands be spent
to reach such startling facts
as 48.37 percent of the
University of Pittsburgh
Library collection did not
circulate in seven years. . . .?

From a practical point of view, I'd insist that *College & Research Libraries*—one of the worst offenders, *Journal of Librarianship, Library Resources & Technical Services,* and *Library Quarterly* limit publications of such studies to one every two years. Lesser read journals might make that one every three years. I am now working out a method of enforcing this rule, although suggestions from readers who might like to serve as enforcers would be welcome.

The verso of the discussion is familiar: well, if you don't use objective formula to evaluate what to buy or what not to buy, what do we do with collection development? The authoritative answer is simplicity itself: you hire, encourage, and support librarians who know more about books, periodicals, AV materials, and readers than they know about the rules of statistical folly.

A perceptive, well-read librarian in a small- to medium-sized library can tell you what type of specific magazines or journals are read or not read, used for reference purposes, or glanced at to determine how to invest an idle dollar—and so on. As the periodical collection grows, the same formula for determining what is or is not used remains. Now, however, the single librarian divides into subject experts or bibliographers or whatever you wish to call them. Mix in a few

readers with their words of advice and you have not an infallible formula, but a good workable formula for determining what is to be retained or dropped, what is to be added or passed over.

The secret in this approach is judgment, knowledge of the public and the magazines, and a definite touch of confidence—confidence not only to make decisions, but to admit from time to time the decison is wrong, that it is a mistake to drop the *Ladies Home Journal* or *Journal of the Mechanics and Physics of Solids.* It seems to me many library schools, perhaps the majority, waste valuable effort on statistical and related courses which might be turned over (or, more correctly back) to the Helen Haines of this age. Experience indicates that most library school students (even if they are now called students of information science), lack subtle understanding of numbers, and, for the most part, go through a superficial course on the subject and come out knowing even less. Ditto a number of other courses which do nothing to educate the would-be librarian in essentials, i.e., books and appreciation of the needs of their fellow citizens. More of that at a later date.

References

1. Stanley Slote. *Weeding Library Collections-II.* 2nd ed. (Littleton, Co.: Libraries Unlimited, 1982), p. 61.

2. *Ibid.* p. 62.

3. Trusewell, Richard. "User Behavioral Patterns. . . ." (Unpublished Ph.D. dissertation, Northwestern University, 1964), p. 105. Quoted in Slote, p. 77.

4. Allen Kent et al. Use of Library Materials: *The University of Pittsburgh Study.* (New York: Dekker, 1979), p. 14, 48. Slote, p. 85.

5. *Ibid.* p. 9.

6. *Ibid.* p. 13.

7. F. W. Lancaster. *The Measurement and Evaluation of Library Services.* (New York: Academic Press, 1978). This is the best work now available on the subject of evaluation, including the several landmark formulas in collection development. One might add other names, such as the late Jesse Shera; but even a charitable list would not contain more than four or five people.

Bibliometrics: A Model for Judging Quality

Richard Bruce Warr

As we librarians complete the transition from the affluence of the 1960s to the austerity of the 1980s, we are facing the most creative and challenging era of collection development in the history of librarianship. Bibliographers will have to face the transition with great optimism and make collection development a "joyful science" if we are to survive such austerity and overcome its resulting bibliographic depression. The bad news is only that we will have to work harder and become sharper bibliographers and administrators.

In these austere times, librarians must add to the collections only titles which patrons will use. A carefully formulated collection policy will help selectors anticipate the level of use of any given title.

The terms "bibliometrics" and "structuralism" have been tossed about in collection development circles for some time now. Surveys have been undertaken and the results have been published in various library journals. One noticeable problem, however, is the lack of qualitative statements regarding high frequency publishers or high frequency citations of books by these publishers.

Baughman[1] and Worthen[2] have applied Bradford's Law[3] to monograph publishers in Sociology and Medicine respectively, by culling citations of nonserial publications from journal articles and then applying the Bradfordian equation. Baughman concludes from these studies that "the most productive publishers on the subject tend to publish the monographs that are most frequently cited."[4]

The major question here is whether or not citation quantification is a valid criterion for evaluating publisher quality. This method does not yield the qualitative information needed to make wise collection development decisions. In order to form a true picture of this quality, we must look to the reviewers, and to the most current reviews, as publishers may tend to lose or gain ground from year to year in their efforts to survive financially. A high quality publisher of the 60s may have compromised his or her quality toward the end of the 70s.

One might question the validity of reviews in evaluating the quality of a publisher, as most reviewers tend towards subjectivity in describing the worth of a book. One the other hand, it is the general pattern of favorability of each publisher that we are observing and not the quality of any individual monograph. There may be a slight margin of error in the statistical analysis of each publisher, but we are concerned with the relative ranking of publishers which should not be greatly affected.

What guarantees the correlation between a publisher's favorability of reviews and the use of his or her books in our libraries? It stands to reason that a monograph by one publisher may receive

Table One

Reviewing journals consulted, 1978-79, total reviews per journal, general favorability index for all reviews in each journal

	# of Reviews	Favorability Index		#of Reviews	Favorability Index
Archivfür Geschichte der Philosophie	14	4.2	Mind	103	2.8
Archives de Philosophie	42	3.8	Nous	26	3.7
Canadian journal of philosophy	23	3.9	Philosophia	31	3.1
Erkenntnis	13	2.3	Philosophical books	136	3.7
Les Etudes philosophiques	24	2.5	Philosophical quarterly	104	2.7
Filosofia	14	3.8	Philosophical review	87	3.3
Journal of philosophy	22	1.5	Philosophy	64	3.1
Journal of the history of philosophy	107	2.9	Revue internationale de philosophie	15	4.0

and bad books exist in equal numbers in our ⟨libraries⟩, we have no control over what our patrons ⟨are rea⟩ding. It is therefore the responsibility of the ⟨subject⟩ specialist to make available the greatest per-⟨centag⟩e of high quality monographs so that ⟨undiscr⟩iminating patrons will not be victims of lower ⟨quality⟩ literature.

favorable reviews but is never consulted in a given library. Conversely, a poorly reviewed book may be consulted several times by users of that library, especially if nothing equivalent is available in the collection. The solution is to eliminate this possibility by adding books by high quality publishers to our collections, and by scrutinizing each title by a less favorable publisher before buying a book. What we want is a high circulation of well-written books and a low number of poorly written ones in our collections. This is the perfect configuration of a library's collections, and I believe that we can approach this ideal if we pursue it empirically.

Goldhor's study[5] of circulation records of favorably reviewed books versus less favorably reviewed ones indicates that the former category is not necessarily used more than the latter in public libraries. The same obviously applies to academic libraries. Some patrons are alerted to quality literature through reviews, while others select books through the subject categories of the card catalog.

If good and bad books exist in equal numbers in our libraries, we have no control over what our patrons are reading. It is therefore the responsibility of the subject specialist to make available the greatest percentage of high quality monographs so that undiscriminating patrons will not be victims of lower quality literature.

The application of this methodology to collection development should be done with caution and opposing schools of scholarship should be considered. In the case of philosophy, an analytical philosopher might be unduly negative in criticizing a monograph written in a synthetic perspective, or conversely. Certain philosophical journals such as *Erkenntnis* publish only analytic philosophy, while others such as *Journal of the History of Philosophy* are synthetic. If the reviewing journals are selected to balance this anomaly, the favorability structures should be quite accurate.

Books selected by a faculty member may sometimes reflect the bias of a particular school of scholarship. For this, as well as other reasons, the primary responsibility for building collections has been delegated to librarians with some knowledge of the subject. Evans[6] submits that librarians are usually better able to anticipate the reception of

Table Two

Total publishers by country and type

UNITED STATES

University Press:

Alabama	Idaho	Penn State
Bucknell	Indiana	Pennsylvania
California	Johns Hopkins	Pittsburgh
Chicago	Kansas	Princeton
Columbia	MIT	SUNY
Cornell	Marquette	So. Carolina
Duke	Minnesota	So. Illinois
Duquesne	Massachusetts	Texas
Florida	No. Carolina	Wayne State
Fordham	Notre Dame	Washington
Georgia	NYU	Wisconsin
Harvard	Ohio	Yale
Hawaii	Oklahoma	

Scholarly Society:

American Philosophical Association
Jewish Publication Society

Private:

Academic Press	Harper and Row	Prometheus
Adams	Hogarth	Putnam
Barnes and Noble	Humanities	Random House
Basic Books	Open Court	Rowman and Littlefield
Bobbs-Merrill	Pathfinder	St. Martins
Crowell	Philosophical Monographs	Simon & Schuster
Dickenson	Precedent	Twayne
Doubleday	Potter	Univ. Press of America
Edwin Mellen	Prentice Hall	Univ. Press of New England
Hackett		

UNITED KINGDOM

University Press:

Cambridge	Manchester	Sheffield
Edinburgh	Oxford	Sussex
Heythrop College	Scottish Academic Pr.	Warwick

Private:

Allen Lane	Edward Arnold	Mouton
Allen and Unwin	Faber and Faber	New Left
Blackwell	Gill and Macmillan	Oriel
Cass	Harvester	Penguin
Chatto and Windus	Longman	Pergamon
Collins	Macmillan	Routledge
Duckworth	Methuen	

CANADA

University Press:

Dalhousie	Pontifical Institute	Toronto
McGill/Queens	Queensland	

Scholarly Society: Canadian Assoc. for Publ. Phil.

HOLLAND

Private:

Brill	North Holland	Van Gorcum
Nijhoif	Reidel	

GERMANY

Private:

Bouvier/Grundman	Karl Albert
Felix Meiner	Springer

NORWAY

University Press:
Universitetsforlaget

Scholarly Society:
Norwegian Research Council

SWEDEN

Private:
Almqvist

ITALY

Private:
Antenore

GREECE

University Press:
Athens University Press

AUSTRALIA

University Press:
Australian National Univ. Pr.

books in library collections than are faculty members or blanket dealer selectors:

> The methods of acquisition are in association with the differences in use in the predicted manner. That is, librarians selected a greater number of titles that were used than did the faculty or than were acquired under the blanket order program.[7]

Similarly, library subject specialists should be the review evaluators in compiling a favorability profile. While faculty specialists have a broader and deeper perspective on their areas of expertise, librarians are disinterested observers, concerned only with the quality and use of the books which they select.

This approach should be seen as a guideline and not as an ultimate solution to the problems of collection development. It places publishers in a perspective which should engender some consideration of those publishers that we depend on to the exclusion of other sources of high quality literature.

METHODOLOGY

This survey collects data from 16 major philosophical journals supplying frequent reviews by scholars from North America, Europe, and elsewhere. Eight hundred and twenty-five reviews were read and the favorability of each was noted. Numerical values were assigned to each review and a profile of each publisher evolved when the values were averaged for all books by each publisher.

The following values were assigned, indicating the degree of favorability (or lack thereof) of each review

-10	exceptionally unfavorable
-5	unfavorable
0	neutral
+2-1/2	remotely favorable
+5	favorable
+10	exceptionally favorable

After assigning values to all reviews, two neutral book selectors with a knowledge of philosophy read a random sample of the reviews and assigned a degree of favorability to each. There were divergences of opinion in only four cases, and these differences were only between the 0 and 2.5 ranges of favorability.

The reviewing journals consulted and the number of reviews supplied by each are listed in Table One. It further indicates a favorability index for all reviews supplied by each journal.

Table Three

Favorability index for each publisher, ranking
by number of reviews and by favorability index

Ranking by # of Reviews	# of Reviews	Publisher	Ranking by Fav. Index	Fav. Index
1	101	Oxford U.P.	9	3.515
2	68	Reidel	16	2.751
3	63	Cambridge U.P.	11	3.373
4	47	Univ. California Press	6	4.412
5	39	Routledge	21	2.179
6	37	Blackwell	20	2.365
7	32	Cornell U.P.	14	2.891
8	21	Princeton U.P.	17	2.620
9	19	Macmillan	19	2.368
10	15	Nijhoif	15	2.833
11	15	Univ. Chicago Pr.	10	3.500
12	12	Harvester	18	2.500
13	10	Yale U.P.	1	5.500
14	9	Humanities	5	4.444
15	8	Allen and Unwin	3	4.687
16	7	Duckworth	7	4.286
17	6	Harvard U.P.	4	4.583
18	6	Notre Dame U.P.	8	3.750
19	6	Univ. of Toronto Pr.	12	3.333
20	6	Mouton	13	3.333
21	6	Edinburgh U.P.	2	5.000

Out of 120 publishers (Table Two), 21 indicated a number of reviews great enough to be included in the universe for ranking. Table Three indicates the publishers ranked by both quality and favorability of reviews (favorability index).

If a publisher received a total of 18 reviews, and the favorability configuration was 10 favorable, 5 unfavorable, 2 exceptionally favorable, and one remotely favorable, the computation would be as follows:

$$
\begin{array}{rl}
10 \times 5 & = 50 \\
5 \times \text{-}5 & = \text{-}25 \\
2 \times 10 & = 20 \\
1 \times 2.5 & = 2.5 \\
\hline
& 47.5
\end{array}
$$

Since there were 18 reviews for this publisher, the 47.5 would be divided by that sum and a favorability index of 2.639 would result. This would indicate that the eighteen reviewers collectively considered the publications to be more than remotely valuable (2.5), but not as substantially valuable as an index of 5.0 would indicate.

Observing Table Three, we see that the publisher receiving the greatest number of reviews in the two-year period in the 16 journals (quantitative ranking), has dropped to the ninth position in the ranking by favorability index (qualitative ranking), whereas number 21 in the quantitative column has risen to the second position in the qualitative ranking. The first ten publishers in the quantitative ranking have all fallen to lower positions in the qualitative ranking, while those with a quantitative ranking of 11 through 21 have gained in the qualitative ranking. The only exception is number 12.

A Spearman rank correlation coefficient was computed on the comparison of the two rankings which indicates a negative relationship between the rankings of the number of reviews and the rankings by favorability index.[8] One would expect these ranks to be very similar, since it is often assumed that higher volume publishers can afford to exercise greater quality control and garner more favorable reviews. This study does not support that assumption.

On the other hand, we cannot assume a direct relationship between number of reviews and number of books released by a given publisher. Another study would have to be done in order to draw conclusions on a frequency correlation between the number of reviews, number of books, and quality of each publisher. It should inspire some thought, however.

APPLICATION

The favorability index and other rankings associated with it can be valuable tools to assist in collection development since these surveys bring out empirical relationships between books, publishers, and reviewers. These relationships are not founded upon the subjective biases of a few reviewers, but upon the judgements of the larger universe of scholars in the international community evaluating a major part of the publishing output in a discipline. By applying the information gained in a favorability study, we may avoid the narrowness of judgement by a few faculty members adhering to a particular school of scholarship. We may likewise avoid the misjudgments made by the overly generalized subject specialist who has too many disciplines to focus on in collection development in today's research libraries.

For publishers indicating a low-to-medium favorability profile, we can scrutinize individual monographs more closely as their books arrive on blanket orders or investigate these when they appear on trade lists. For publishers indicating a high favorability profile, we can instruct our blanket suppliers to deliver all of their monographs within particular disciplines. Blanket profiles can be constructed around favorability profiles as well as subject configurations. This survey does not only indicate that some frequently reviewed publishers receive less favorable reviews, but that some less frequently reviewed publishers indicate

a high review favorability and should be given greater consideration for representation in our collections.

Faculty departments should be made aware of the relative rankings of publishers, as these rankings indicate just how the international reviewing community judges each publisher. A separate list of pertinent remarks culled from the reviews may be kept, documenting the negative criticisms of the monographs. A pattern will emerge, indicating why certain publishers receive less favorable reviews.

To the scholar, this is important information, and knowing which publishers produce consistently well-reviewed books will assist them in their efforts to publish their research. Faculty members will also exercise greater scrutiny in recommending books for collections which they and their students will be using.

If survey results of this type are applied to collection development, the result will be well-balanced core collections of books from reliable publishing houses and containing the quality literature on any topic. Our patrons will make better use of our collections, rely less on interlibrary borrowing, and we will stretch our dwindling book budgets toward optimum utility.

References

1. James C. Baughman, "A Structural Analysis of the Literature of Sociology," *Library Quarterly* 44:1 (1974) 293-308.
2. Dennis B. Worthen, "The Application of Bradford's Law to Monographs," *Journal of Documentation* 31.1 (1975): 19-25.
3. Bradford's Law of Scattering states that when a group of journals in a specific subject area is ranked according to decreasing numbers of useful articles, zones are formed which indicate the quantity of useful articles. The first zone is the nuclear zone, consisting of the most productive journals. The zones decrease according to their yield of useful articles.
4. Baughman, "Toward a Structural Approach to Collection Development," *College and Research Libraries* 38:3 (1977): 248.
5. Herbert Goldhor. "Are the Best Books the Most Read?" *Library Quarterly* 29:4 (1959): 251-255.
6. G. Edward Evans, *The Influence of Book Selection Agents Upon Book Collection Usage in Academic Libraries.* Ph.D. dissertation, (University of Illinois, 1969).
7. Evans, p.46.
8. The Spearman rho needed to reject a null hypothesis of a no relationship is: rr .03 - .440. The correlation obtained here is: rr .05-.46 which indicates a statistically significant relationship between the ranks. Note that this relationship, however, is a negative one.

List-Checking as a Method of Evaluating Library Collections

Cynthia H. Comer

The most widely used method of qualitatively evaluating a library's collections is the list-checking method, a process in which the library's holdings are compared with one or more lists of selected titles. The types of lists commonly used are published, standardized lists representing core or basic collections, catalogs of other libraries, or specialized subject bibliographies. The literature on this method of collection evaluation is extensive, dating back to the 1930s; covering the types of lists used for evaluations, the advantages and disadvantages of using such a method, and the various ways of implementing this type of evaluation.

There are several reasons why a library may decide to perform an evaluation of its collections. The most common are the suspicion of inadequacy in the collection or in certain of its areas; dissatisfaction of the clientele or administrative authority; and the justification of a request for increased appropriations. List-checking is one of the more easily implemented ways to evaluate a collection, and it can be used for examining books, serials, and other materials. It can be used to check the entire collection, or a particular subject area within the collection. The major objective is to arrive at a percentage of the list being checked that is represented in the library's collection—presumably, the higher the percentage, the better and more adequate the collection.

List-checking is generally viewed as an initial step in improving the library's collections, allowing a check on the thoroughness of coverage in certain areas, and the identification not only of what is lacking, but what is available. Both collection gaps and strengths can be identified. What begins, then, as a method for collection evaluation becomes an important tool for collection building; the strengths and weaknesses of the collection are pinpointed and a want-list for filling in the gaps grows.

Of course, checking lists implies two basic assumptions that the librarian should be well aware of in order to intelligently choose a list and to fully understand the results. The first is that a list of certain core titles belongs in any collection or type of library that exists; the second is that such a list represents the composite judgement of many librarians or specialists, and that the titles included are the best and most important in a particular subject area. Since there are no established guidelines regarding the percentage of specific lists that are adequate or appropriate for the collection being evaluated, an evaluator must be careful to choose an effective tool. He or she may want to consult other librarians or subject specialists to be sure the list chosen is adequate for the purposes it will serve, as well as appropriate to both the type of library and community.

STANDARD LISTS

There are so many different lists used in collection evaluations that it would be impossible to cite them all here; in a survey done in the early 1930s at the University of Chicago alone, more than 400 different lists and bibliographies were used to check the collection.[1] Lists have been prepared by academic and professional organizations, by various accrediting bodies, and by surveyors and librarians to meet the needs of a particular library.

Those most frequently checked are the published, readily available, basic lists that are considered to be the core collection for smaller or nonspecialized libraries, or the foundations upon which a research or special collection rests. The following are generally considered to be the standard lists of this kind:

1. American Library Association's lists, *Books for College Libraries, Choice's Opening Day Collection, Books for Junior College Libraries, Basic Book Collection for High Schools, Basic Book Collection for Junior High Schools, Basic Book Collection for Elementary Grades, Books for Children, Picture Books for Children*
2. H. W. Wilson's five catalogs, *Public Library Catalog, Fiction Catalog, Senior High School Library Catalog, Junior High School Library Catalog, Children's Catalog*
3. Bro-dart's two lists, *Junior College Library Collection, Elementary School Library Collection*

Three earlier lists heavily used in the past for evaluation are the *A.L.A. Catalog* and its supplements, which were published through 1949; *A List of Books for College Libraries*, by Charles B. Shaw, the forerunner of *Books for College Libraries*, with its supplement covering through 1958, and *List of Books for Junior College Libraries*, compiled for the Carnegie Corporation of New York and published by A.L.A. in 1937. The published catalogs of several important libraries have also been used as a checklist in collection evaluations. Frequently cited are Harvard's Lamont Library, Princeton's Julian Street Library, and University of Michigan's Undergraduate Library.

Even the Library of Congress catalog was used at the University of Florida in terms of subject distribution in order to balance the book-allocation formula "to favor funds from which substantial retrospective purchasing was desirable."[2]

SPECIALIZED COLLECTIONS AND LISTS

These general lists are most effective for measuring the worth of a basic collection but are inadequate for evaluating special subject collections of larger or more specialized libraries. Authoritative and appropriate subject bibliographies must be carefully chosen for this. A variety of subject lists exists—those published by technical, professional, and learned societies or organizations are often used for collection evaluation, as are the catalogs of specialized library collections, guides to the literature, definitive bibliographies of major authors, and lists prepared by federal, regional, state, or local authorities. Some subject areas have one, or perhaps several, bibliographies that are more or less generally accepted by librarians and specialists in the discipline as the list(s) for that field. This is not the case, unfortunately, for all fields, and much care must be taken to locate or compile a list that will be an effective measure for a particular subject area.

Special attention is often paid to the reference section of the collection. Frequently, it is the only area of the collection checked, the assumption is that reference holdings reflect the holdings of the general collection and that a high correlation exists between the two. In any case, the reference collection should be inspected closely and critically when a library collection is being evaluated. It may be checked against standard subject lists or, more likely, against a special guide just for reference works. Eugene Sheehy's (previously Winchell's) *Guide to Reference Books* and Walford's *Guide to Reference Materials* are the obvious lists. In a study of Kansas City and St. Louis public libraries, the Enoch Pratt Free Library list was used to sample the quality of reference collections,[4] and in a study of public libraries in the Minneapolis-St. Paul metropolitan area, Mary N. Barton's *Reference Books: A Brief Guide for Students and Other Users of the Library* was chosen as a checklist.[5]

The periodicals collection must also be given special attention. Common checklists used in evaluation are lists of periodicals covered by standard or specialized indexing and abstracting services, lists of periodicals most frequently cited (particularly in the area of science), and the periodical collections of other libraries. Bill Katz's *Magazines for Libraries* is an excellent evaluative guide, and Ulrich's *International Periodical Directory* is another comprehensive listing.

Librarians also use contemporary lists in evaluating collections. These include lists of bestsellers and prize-winners, lists of best books of the year, acquisitions lists of other libraries, lists of scholarly journals in a particular subject area, annual subject compilations, and catalogs of selected publishers, such as government agencies, university presses, and professional societies.

These lists are geared to current interests and cover a limited amount of material and/or time span and should be used with even more discrimination than the standard published lists. Current best-sellers, for example, may be of only ephemeral interest, and therefore not suited for every library.

Another type of list sometimes used in evaluations is one that has been specially compiled for a particular library. These "ad hoc" lists, drawn up by the evaluator of a particular library, are designed to measure and evaluate the collection based on that library's particular goals and objectives, as well as community interests. Such lists are considered much more effective than the standardized, published lists, but they are often more difficult and time-consuming to compile. They are especially valuable when comparing different libraries in a particular location to measure their collections relative to each other, and are also effective in evaluating one particular aspect of a single library.

ADVANTAGES AND DISADVANTAGES OF LIST-CHECKING

The list-checking method, regardless of which type of list is eventually chosen, has its definite advantages. The process is relatively simple, especially when compared to other evaluation methods. Numerous comprehensive and specialized lists are available. Most are easy to use, many are systematically and regularly updated; they are usually competently put together by librarians and specialists in the field, and are relatively effective for a rough evaluation of where the collection or certain parts of it stand in terms of adequacy and completeness.

But, list-checking has been frequently criticized as an evaluation tool; it does have its weaknesses. Any list is likely to be somewhat arbitrary, and therefore subject to question. The smaller the list and the fewer the number of people who helped to compile it, the more subjective it may be. What one individual or group deems appropriate or useful may not, in fact, be suited to a particular library's collection. Some lists may have particular emphases that do not apply to a specific library's holdings, or will not evaluate the aspects of a collection a library wishes to check. All titles on a list are not of equal value, and there is generally no way to determine which titles are most important; in fact, many important titles may have been left off the list altogether.

Lists usually do not help identify any outdated or superseded material the library has, nor do they consider the differences between library communities and the special interests and needs of each community. Unless they are systematically revised, lists quickly become dated. Other problems occur if the checklist used for collection evaluation was used in the past as a buying guide; obviously, the results of the study will indicate that a high percentage of the books on the list are held by the library, therefore making the study largely useless. Also, utilization of the same checklist by large numbers of libraries to evaluate their collections and fill in gaps could lead to uniformity, diminishing the uniqueness of different libraries. One of the most frequently voiced criticisms is that this method provides no means for evaluating materials the library does have. The books a library owns which happen to be included in a given list may be only a small percentage of the total books the library has in that area. The other books which the library owns may be just as good—or even better in terms of meeting local needs—than those on the list.

This method presents greater problems for university and research collections. Few truly comprehensive subject bibliographies exist for evaluating scholarly collections; even if they did, they would be too long (and simply too expensive) to check against holdings. Standard lists do not include the special, esoteric materials held by research libraries that make their collections valuable. For example, certain manuscript holdings may be an important strength of a collection, but there is no list for checking them. In addition, checking against standard lists does not fully assess the adequacy of the collection in meeting the existing needs of the university's curriculum and programs. Besides, a large, well-developed collection is likely to have most of the books included on a basic list anyway. When checking against the catalog of another library, the evaluating library must take into account the differences between the programs of the university it supports and those of the university whose library's catalog is being used. Depending on what other resources are locally available, a university may find it needs to buy other materials. Attempting to emulate the collection of a larger, well-established research library will almost certainly present formidable budgetary restrictions for the library undergoing evaluation. Generally, standard lists are less suited for evaluating large, research collections, and more practical for smaller or newer collections, or possibly for looking at one specific area of a larger collection.

Several variations on the standard list-checking method have been designed to overcome these weaknesses. One, developed by Herbert Goldhor, is the "inductive method."[6,7] Most useful for the small college or public library, this method involves taking all the books a library has in a subject area and checking them against several book-reviewing and selection tools. "Presumably, the titles held by the library which are on multiple lists are clearly desirable, those which are included on no list are probably not desirable, and those which are on only one list are of borderline quality."[8] Goldhor recommends using no more than five different lists. He implemented his method in a study of public libraries in the Minneapolis-St. Paul metropolitan area by taking one hundred titles in adult fiction from the letter "W" of each library's catalog and comparing it with four book-reviewing and retrospective book selection tools to see what percentage of the library's holdings were included in one or more of these lists.[9] He did similar studies for titles in American history and for the reference collections in these libraries.[10]

The major fault of this method is the assumption that the best works being published do get reviewed and do get included on lists of recommended titles. The fact often is that it may be nearly impossible to locate certain works at all, much less to find reviews of them. This is particularly true for works published by small or alternative presses, which by no means disproves their worthiness or value. Furthermore, that a work was reviewed does not necessarily mean it received a favorable review—it may have been thoroughly discredited by every reviewer who read it. Therefore, precautions need to be taken before making final decisions about works that do or do not appear on whatever lists are used.

Robert Coale has developed another variation especially useful for large research collections which could be called the "citation method."[11] The idea is to test to see whether recent scholarly works could have been written using the resources and materials at the library being evaluated. This process requires a considerable background and knowledge in the areas being evaluated and basically involves checking against the footnotes or bibliographies from a select number of works that are considered authoritative in their field. Sources for these citations include theses, faculty research publications, journal articles, textbooks, and state-of-the-art reviews. The library is therefore using not a theoretical list of best books on the subject, but a list of sources actually consulted by the authors. This method should not only reveal the weaknesses of the collection "in coverage of particular periods, languages, or types of materials,"[12] but also the adequacy of the collection's holdings of materials tangential to the particular subject being evaluated. Coale used this

method to evaluate the holdings of the Newberry Library in the colonial history of certain areas of Latin America[13,14] by checking the library's holdings against a select group of works by recognized scholars. The bibliographies ranged from 100 to 400 titles and reflected works from the colonial periods as well as current research. He then checked the same lists with libraries having similar collections to compare Newberry's collection with theirs.

Several criticisms of Coale's method should be mentioned. His method assumes that the library being evaluated is an appropriate place for the work or works which are the source(s) of the citations to be written, and that it is similar in size, purpose, and scope to the one where the author was working. Atmosphere, motivations, and emphases on particular aspects of a field vary from place to place, and the author, (or anyone else, for that matter) might *never* have written that particular work at another institution or library, regardless of how strong its collection was. This method does not account for the fact that an author generally uses whatever resources are available, procuring the rest through interlibrary loan.

USEFULNESS OF LIST-CHECKING

Checking bibliographies, catalogs, and other types of lists can reveal the strongest foundations on which the library can build and the obvious gaps that need to be filled. But, lists must either be very carefully chosen by the librarian, or special lists must be drawn up, keeping the library's goals and objectives in mind. For a complete evaluation, the list-checking method should be used in conjunction with other evaluative methods. Careful interpretation of statistics is imperative; a list is valuable "only for estimating the strength of a collection, to the degree that the collection approximates the list."[15] List-checking is time-consuming, expensive, and tiring; it is really only a beginning, offering a rough guide to the kinds of materials available or not available to the library's patrons. The evaluator will have to decide on the next step. Most likely, the evaluation will have created a list of future purchases for further developing the collection—some of those titles may be ordered immediately; others may have to wait. The librarian may decide to examine the titles the library does own to see if they are adequate substitutes, or to call in outside experts for this purpose. If large or undesirable gaps continually turn up, the evaluation may ultimately lead to a reevaluation of selection policies to find out why the gaps occur and to insure that they will not happen again.

Notes

1. M. Llewellyn Raney, *The University Libraries* (Chicago: University of Chicago Press, 1933).
2. Paul B. Kebabian, "The Distance to a Star: Subject Measurement of the Library of Congress and the University of Florida Collections," *College and Research Libraries* 27 (July 1966):267.
3. Edwin E. Williams, "Surveying Library Collections," in *Library Surveys*, ed. Maurice F. Tauber and Irlene Roemer Stephens (New York: Columbia University Press, 1967), p. 31.
4. Singe Ottersen, "A Bibliography on Standards for Evaluating Libraries," *College and Research Libraries* 32 (March 1971):131.
5. Herbert Goldhor, *A Plan for the Development of Public Library Service in the Minneapolis-Saint Paul Metropolitan Area.* St. Paul, Minn.: Library Division, State Department of Education, 1967, p. 88.
6. Herbert Goldhor, "Analysis of an Inductive Method of Evaluating a University Collection," *Libri* 23 (1973): 6-17.
7. Goldhor, *A Plan for Development.*
8. Goldhor, "Analysis of an Inductive Method," p. 6.
9. The lists Goldhor used were *Fiction Catalog*, and supplements for 1961, 1962, 1963, and 1964; Syracuse Public Library, *Gold Star List* for 1966; *Book Review Digest* from 1905-1965, with credit given only for predominantly favorable reviews; *Booklist* from 1905-1965.
10. For more information on these studies and a list of titles used in checking, see Goldhor, *A Plan for Development.*
11. Robert Peerling Coale, "Evaluation of a Research Library Collection: Latin-American Colonial History at the Newberry," *Library Quarterly* 35 (July 1965):173-84.
12. F. W. Lancaster, *The Measurement and Evaluation of Library Services* (Washington, D.C.: Information Resources Press, 1977), p. 176.
13. The areas were Mexico, Peru, Chile, Colombia, and Venezuela.
14. Coale.
15. Mary Duncan Carter, Wallace John Bonk, and Rose Mary McGrill, *Building Library Collections* (Metuchen, N.J.: Scarecrow Press, 1974), p. 166.

Selected Bibliography

Bonn, George S. "Evaluation of the Collection." *Library Trends* 22 (January 1974):265-304.

Carter, Mary Duncan; Bonk, Wallace John; and McGrill, Rose Mary. *Building Library Collections.* Metuchen, N.J.: Scarecrow Press, 1974.

Cassata, Mary B. , and Dewey, Gene L. "The Evaluation of a University Library Collection: Some Guidelines." *Library Resources and Technical Services* 13 (Fall 1969):450-57.

Coale, Robert Peerling. "Evaluation of a Research Library Collection: Latin-American Colonial History at the Newberry." *Library Quarterly* 35 (July 1965):173-84.

Golden, Barbara. "A Method of Quantitatively Evaluating a University Library Collection." *Library Resources and Technical Services* 48 (Summer 1974):268-74.

Goldhor, Herbert. "Analysis of an Inductive Method of Evaluating the Book Collection of a Public Library." *Libri* 23(1973):6-17. *Plan for the Development of Public Library Service in the Minneapolis-Saint Paul Metropolitan Area.* St. Paul, Minn.: Library Division, State Department of Education, 1967.

"Guide to Methods of Library Evaluation." *College and Research Libraries News*, 9(1968):293-99.

Hirsch, Rudolph. "Evaluation of Book Collections." In *Library Evaluation*, ed. Wayse S. Yenawine, pp. 7-20. Syracuse, N.Y.: Syracuse University Press, 1959.

Kebabian, Paul B. "The Distance to a Star: Subject Measurement of the Library of Congress and the University of Florida Collections." *College and Research Libraries* 27(July 1966):267-70.

Lancaster, F. W. *The Measurement and Evaluation of Library Services.* Washington, D.C.: Information Resources Press, 1977.

Ottersen, Signe. "A Bibliography on Standards for Evaluating Libraries." *College and Research Libraries* 32(March 1971):127-44.

Raney, M. Llewellyn. *The University Libraries.* Chicago: University of Chicago Press, 1933.

Tauber, Maurice F. "Survey Method in Approaching Library Problems." *Library Trends* 13(July 1964):15-30.

Webb, William. "Project CoED: A University Library Collection Evaluation and Development Program." *Library Resources and Technical Services* 13 (Fall 1969):457-62.

Williams, Edwin E. "Surveying Library Collections." In *Library Surveys*, ed. Maurice F. Tauber and Irlene Roemer Stephens, pp. 23-45. New York: Columbia University Press, 1967.

Collection Evaluation in the Research Library

by Ferne B. Hyman

Among many unflattering characterizations of librarians is the one that accuses us of wishing to keep *our* collections neat, clean and in proper order on the shelves. That is, not being used. This is a half-true, if exaggerated, statement. As rational professionals, librarians realize that if a collection is well used it is not always in order and available, or else the collection is not as good as it should be. Control—knowing where an item is, who has it—is the goal librarians strive to achieve, rather than maintaining every item in its place.

Knowing the "where" and "who" of the collection is important, but knowing "what" is in the collection and whether it meets the objectives and goals of the institution the library serves is equally important. Evaluating holdings is necessary to ensure that a library is providing useful materials.

The Chronicle of Higher Education reported in August, 1986, that scholars in the humanities and social sciences "have strongly criticized some of the mainstays of their professions—including . . . the availability of research material in college and university libraries."[1] The article continues, "nearly half rate the book collections in their institutions' libraries only fair or poor in meeting their research needs. About one-third make similar evaluations of their libraries' journal collection, as about one-fourth do of newspapers and other references sources."

If half of the college and university faculty rate library collections as only fair to poor it follows that librarians must work toward improving their collections to better serve one of their primary constituents. Regularly evaluating collections is one of the major means of establishing the value of materials to specific users.

In a recent article criticizing the *Chronicle's* reporting of the survey, that publication was faulted for ignoring many of the survey's less negative conclusions.[2] Even so, the least laudatory statements indicate that librarians need to do a better job communicating information about available research and instructional support. Faculty who are unaware of library holdings are certainly not served by the library; it is not surprising that they should criticize the library's collections.

The locus of responsibility and the methods used to collect materials have changed over the years. In the past, faculty of colleges and universities assumed the major responsibility for book selection. Librarians took over much of the selection chores when expansion of university programs and the building of library collections reached a high point during the 1960s. As research in librarianship shows, both the campus programs and library support went beyond traditional acquisitions to the purchasing of large research collections.[3] In the late 1960s and early 1970s when the great expansion was curtailed, librarians continued to develop collections rather than revert to faculty selection.

As collection development became the new approach, the literature on the subject expanded and methods of evaluating collections were discussed. In 1979 the Collections Development Committee of the Resources and Technical Services Division within the American Library Association produced the *Guidelines for Collection Development*.[4] These guidelines were concerned with formulating written collection development policies and the "Evaluations of the Effectiveness of Library Collections." The guidelines included a list of purposes: "research, recreation, community service and development, instruction, support of a

> . . . librarians need to do a better job communicating information about available research and instructional support

179

corporate activity, or a combination of these." Evaluation is a process to determine whether or not the collection meets the objectives and how well it serves users. The guidelines called for more objectivity in evaluation.[5] In making recommendations, the committee relied largely upon publications that still remain valuable standards today: George S. Bonn's article, "Evaluation of the Collection," and F.W. Lancaster's Book, *Measurement and Evaluation of Library Services*.[6] Paul Mosher's compilation of the literature on collection evaluation from earlier decades is another source.[7] Blaine Hall produced a manual for collection evaluation that detailed methodology and suggested answers to specific evaluative questions.[8]

CHOOSING A METHOD

Library administrators must join collection development librarians in choosing the best approach to evaluating their collections. Various costs, including staff time, can make a complete evaluation prohibitively expensive. The first step is deciding which section of the collection to evaluate. Which disciplines are expanding or contracting and how fast; where are budgets consistently inappropriate; in which departments are faculty and students most critical of the library? The answers to these questions will point to areas which cry out for evaluation. Next, a choice must be made between collection-centered or people-centered studies. Qualitative and/or quantitative approaches may be employed.

Collection Centered

A collection-centered study involves counting the number of volumes owned and comparing the numbers with libraries in universities offering comparable programs. The numbers may be checked against minimum standards set by accrediting and other educational agencies. Conventional wisdom is that numbers correlate with excellence: the larger the numbers, the greater the chance of having items users need. Another collection-centered approached is to check, the holding against bibliographic lists from different sources. Lists might include catalogs of published titles considered standard works, extensive bibliographies in a particular subject, specialized lists, as well as shelf lists from other established collections. An advantage of collection-centered approaches is that they provide a firm grasp of both quantitative and qualitative comparative information. The disadvantage is that programs and activities of other institutions, though similar, are not identical—particularly in the area of faculty research. Num-

bers compared and titles listed do not necessarily address the question of users' needs.

User Centered

User-centered studies are more subjective and intuitive. They should be included in an evaluation, but the results will be suggestive rather than definitive. One user-centered method, evaluating circulation statistics, counts which titles are used and, with computerized data, who uses them. These numbers reveal how often some items are used and which are currently vital for instruction, but they do not show which titles have been or will become important for research or instruction. Nor can in-house use be fully established. In some studies in-house and circulation records are similar enough to be used, while other studies do not show a correlation.

Asking users for information on how often and how well a library responds to their needs, gives swift feedback. One important factor in user satisfaction is access: not only ownership of a title, but availability on the shelves. Therefore, evaluation should follow-through to determine accessibility.[9] A successful interlibrary loan program can improve user satisfaction by securing needed titles in a timely manner.

The citation study is one means of evaluating acquisition of journal titles. By checking standard citations indexes, librarians can point to the journals most frequently cited by authors who are publishing in the various fields studied.[10] This is helpful in assessing the value of in-house titles, and deciding which titles to purchase or prune.

The advantages and disadvantages of these collection evaluation techniques are well covered in the literature. In general, they are most useful for evaluating holdings for instructional support, but are not as valuable when assessing research support. Additional evaluation measures are required to assess collections in this area.

DOING RESEARCH

The university has become a vital center for expanding research projects since World War II. Federal government funding, as well as enlarged private foundation support, has accelerated research activity in all disciplines. Universities enrollments expanded, bringing increasing numbers of faculty and projects. The publish or perish environment on the campus has continued to fuel the explosion in research projects. Jacques Barzun, in a recent article, suggests that the academy has, perhaps, gone too far and that it is time to take a long look at "doing research":

The best means of rescuing research in the long run is the steady encouragement of solid, manifestly useful undertakings. In the modern infatuation with "findings" these are at a disadvantage: they look regular, not innovative; they call for sober work, not fancy techniques; they promise utility along recognized lines, not amazing revelations and upside-down revisionism. With common sense in charge, the superstitious regard for "doing research" could be held in check, if not dispelled, and the genuine investigation of great subjects might once more give to research and its products the value and the praise they used to deserve.[11]

The library is affected by the "doing research" frenzy Barzun mentions. Cooperation between researchers and librarians is essential for "encouragement of solid . . . undertakings."

Charles Osburn comments in his study of changing patterns of academic research that the research enterprise between the library and the university community does not function as a system. Library resources are not an immediate part of research fund requests either from federal or private sources. Library materials are often included in overhead figures at the last minute for large grant requests, causing the libraries to react and try to support research rather than having the opportunity for planning in advance with the faculty for the specific project.[12] Libraries are largely unprepared for expanding and changing research techniques. New technologies add to the problems facing librarians.

EXPLORING INNER SPACE

Space is a prominent and persistent problem. During the great expansion of the 1960s, many new facilities appeared but collection requirements outgrew the facilities, and they continue to do so. There was a stabilization of financial support in the 1970s,[13] but the programs and the continued need to support research put strains on available space and budgets. The need for discrimination became evident. Through collection evaluation, librarians have been able to take a more selective approach to collection development, not only to support instruction, but also to support graduate and faculty research.

No one disputes the fact that the cost to support a major research collection is greater than to sustain an undergraduate program. A 1966 study by E.W. Reichard and T. J. Orsagh ". . . noted growth in collection size and expenditures correlated with faculty growth and expansion of graduate programs; [but found] no ascertainable correlation with growth in undergraduate population."[14] It is, therefore, important for librarians to be aware

of planned new graduate programs in order to assess library support. New faculty appointments should also be routinely reported in advance so that collections may be evaluated to determine whether they will accommodate new research interests. In a *New York Times* column about the American Council of Learned Societies survey, Fred Hechinger quotes scholars finding inadequate resources for research in libraries.[15] With space and cost reductions, librarians have to find out whether their collections are adequate for faculty research programs. The budgetary implications for libraries and the impact on faculty careers are too significant to ignore. Libraries provide the knowledge and information needed to further man's understanding and fuel technological innovation.

SHARING COLLECTIONS

In 1974, the Research Libraries Group (RLG) was formed by the chief collection development librarians of Columbia, Yale, New York Public, and Harvard. This cooperative group was created to alleviate some of the problems of rapid expansion. Its members have changed over the years, as it has grown. Now a computer-based bibliographic processing system, RLIN, is used to expedite its cooperative plans.

John Finzi of the Library of Congress presented a paper at the ALA Annual Conference in 1978 suggesting a distribution of collection responsibilities among institutions. His reasoning was that no one library, not even the Library of Congress, could collect in all areas to suit all users.[16] Out of that beginning, the chief collection development officers of institutions from the Research Libraries Group moved forward to establish the RLG Conspectus.

As Guinn and Mosher reported, "the Conspectus is an overview, or summary of existing strengths and future collecting intensities of RLG members."[17] The planners of the Conspectus have encouraged other libraries to subscribe to provide a national cooperative collection development effort. The Conspectus is a long-term effort for cooperating libraries to inventory their collections and to develop institutional policies to support individual and local needs and programs. Cooperating libraries agree to serve as collectors of record for specific, often narrow, subject areas. Access is provided to research material, if not ownership of the titles.

The labor of inventorying collections has been justified by recognition of the need for cooperative effort. The Conspectus is broken down into Library of Congress classification schedules to permit ap-

One user-centered method, evaluating circulation statistics, counts which titles are used and, with computerized data, who uses them

Libraries are largely unprepared for expanding and changing research techniques. New technologies add to the problem

proaching both inventory and collecting responsibilities in workable segments.

Participating libraries have collection development policies to fit local situations, and through the RLG Shared Resources Programs, knowledge of research materials among members. Many libraries in the Association of Research Libraries are participating in an ARL/RLG project, the North American Collection Inventory Project (NCIP), which is an attempt to inventory collections outside the original group. Funding support for this project is from the Council on Library Resources, the Lilly Endowment and the Andrew Mellon Foundation. As reported in *American Libraries,* "[t]he project is meant to strengthen coordinated management of national research collections and help determine shared responsibilities for the resources."[18] The potential benefits as outlined in the ARL proposal are:

1. Availability of a standard tool for collection description and assessment for the identification of North American collection strengths and weaknesses;
2. Development of a mechanism to locate needed research materials more expeditiously;
3. Development of the capacity to relate local collection development policies to collection levels at other institutions and to serve as the basis for cooperative collection development, both nationally and regionally;
4. Development of the capacity to relate collection development strengths to cataloging and preservation needs and to serve as the basis for cooperative cataloging and preservation efforts, again both nationally and regionally;
5. Support for emerging coordinated retrospective conversion projects; and
6. Enhancement of individual libraries' collection management programs. Analysis of Conspectus data will lead to identification of collection strengths and weaknesses, contribute to the preparation of collection development policies, and to improve budget allocation decisions.[19]

Scholars are the final arbiters of what the library must contain to support research. However, without librarians, they have less chance of finding appropriate holdings in any collection. The complaints of researchers about the quantity and quality of library holdings are compounded by the problem of keeping up with growing numbers of publications in most disciplines. Worse, some are of questionable value. Recent scandals caused by falsified reports or premature release of unproven research results, serve to warn both scholars and librarians of the need to evaluate individual titles. The paradox of too much and not enough is hard on the scholar and the librarian.[20]

Evaluation is mostly hindsight. As Oscar Handlin, the Harvard historian/librarian, wrote: "Building collections to satisfy current demands is building them too late, and librarians must anticipate research interests of twenty years hence."[21] A challenge, indeed. In order to make decisions about the future, librarians must work in the present, and study what was needed in the past. Close ties between faculty and librarians are essential to future planning. Techniques specifically for evaluating research materials and researchers' satisfaction levels will help the library find out whether it has successfully supported current research projects.

In 1983, librarians at the University of California at Irvine conducted an "investigation of collection support for doctoral research" on their campuses. They focused on graduate students' requirements for doctoral research. Their method was to examine a sample of bibliographies in dissertations completed at the University against the holdings of the library. The results confirmed that the library had a large portion of the secondary materials required by those users. Nuances within that assessment, however, showed areas that needed additional attention for collection building.

The faculty and students are being well served if the library is able to supply a significant portion of required titles either in-house or through interlibrary loans. If most of the works have been obtained by the faculty without recourse to library facilities, then improvements should be made in the support of research.

Checking bibliographies of published faculty research as well as graduate dissertations broadens the evaluation base. Verifying shelf availability of titles is essential to be sure they are not lost from the collection. At the same time, evaluating the condition of materials can aid preservation/conservation activity.

Recent emphasis on bibliographic instruction, including working with students and faculty on new technologies to enhance research has produced less than spectacular results so far. Some faculty still prefer informal research networks, the so-called "invisible college," to library facilities or librarians' help. It seems easier to telephone a colleague for information than to work through the library/index system and perhaps still not find the title needed. This attitude is gradually changing as technology for database searching becomes more available and sophisticated. CD-ROMs and advancements in other technologies, impress even the reluctant, cautious users.

Planning for these new tools and technologies is essential. Resources are limited and faculty requirements often know no bounds. Knowing what materials are available where they are and who is and will be using them, gives librarians confidence to meet users' demands.

Basic research-centered evaluation techniques are a good way to assess how well the library serves the researcher/user. Quantitative reports from automated circulation and acquisitions systems and the results of the NCIP studies, give librarians the information they need to become effective research colleagues in the academic world. By embracing this labor-intensive work, librarians can strengthen working relationships with faculty. Evaluation enables collection managers to do a better job of developing collections and supplying information needed for the research university library's primary user group—faculty and researchers.

References

1. Jacobson, Robert L., "Scholars Fault Journals and College Libraries in Survey by Council of Learned Societies," *Chronicle of Higher Education,* 33 April 6, 1986, 181.

2. Epp, Ronald, H. and Segal, JoAnn, "The ACLS Survey and Academic Library Service" in *College and Research Libraries News,* 48 (2) February, 1987, 63–69.

3. Bonk, Wallace J. and Magrill, Rose Mary, *Building Library Collections,* N.Y., Scarecrow Press, 1979, 26.

4. American Library Association, *Guidelines for Collection Development,* Chicago, American Library Association, 1979.

5. Ibid, 9.

6. Bonn, George S., "Evaluation of the Collection" Library Trends, 22 (3) (January 1974), 265–304.

7. Lancaster, F.W., *Measurement and Evaluation of Library Services,* Washington, Information Resources Press, 1977.

8. Mosher, Paul H. "Collection Evaluation in Research Libraries: the Search for Quality, Consistency and System in Collecting Development" *Library Resources and Technical Services,* 23 Winter, 1979; 16–32.

9. Hall, Blaine H., *Collection Assessment Manual for College and University Libraries,* Phoenix, Ariz., Oryx Press, 1985.

10. Discussed in Magrill, Rose Mary, "Evaluation by Library Type" *Library Trends,* 33 Winter, 1985, 281.

11. An excellent overview of methods of evaluations in Mosher, Paul H., "Collection Evaluation or Analysis: Matching Library Acquisitions to Library Needs" in Stueart, Robert D. and Miller, George B. Jr., *Collection Development in Libraries: A Treatise,* Greenwich, Conn., JA Press v12, 527–545.

12. Barzun, Jacques, "Doing Research—Should the Sport be Regulated?" *Columbia,* February, 1987, 22.

13. Osburn, Charles B., *Academic Research and Library Resources: Changing Patterns in American,* Westport, Conn., Greenwood Press 1979, 144.

14. Bonk and Magrill, *Building Library Collections,* 26.

15. As quoted in Lancaster, *Measurement and Evaluation of Library Service,* 172.

16. Hechinger, Fred "About Education" *New York Times,* Sept. 30, 1986, 21–22.

17. Described in the article by Gwinn, Nancy E. and Mosher, Paul H., "Coordinating Collection Development: the RLG Conspectus" in *College and Research Libraries,*" 44 March 1983, 128–144.

18. Guinn and Mosher, "Coordinating Collection Development the RLG Conspectus," 129.

19. "In Support of Scholarly Research," *American Libraries,* March 18, 1987, 188.

20. Quoted in Sohn, Jeanne, "Cooperative Collection Development: A Brief Overlay" *Collection Management,* 8 (2) Summer 1986, 7.

21. An example is in the *Chronicle of Higher Education* for December 31, 1986.

22. Handlin, Oscar "Research Library Collection" *College and Research Libraries* May, 1984, 217.

23. Buzzard, Marion L. and New, Doris E. "An Investigation of Collection Support for Doctoral Research," *College and Research Libraries,* 44 Nov. 1983, 469–475.

Quantitative Approaches to Qualitative Collection Assessment

by Mark Sandler

In recent years there has been increased recognition of the need for both descriptive and analytical data about library collections. Coordinated efforts like the RLG Conspectus and ARL's National Collection Inventory Project are attempts to identify collecting strengths among the nation's research libraries. In many cases, however, participation in these programs has raised the consciousness of collection officers to the realization that they know less than they would care to admit about the holdings of their own libraries. What institutions report are often little more than a series of educated guesses which has led to the need for verification studies as a check on the validity of the data being gathered. In other areas, too, the need for more and better data has become apparent as managers within and outside the library are less willing to accept intuitive and impressionistic responses to their questions about acquisition budgets and priorities for preservation, storage, or retrospective conversion. Thus, there is increasing discussion in the literature of the need for, and approaches to, collection assessment and analysis.

For most bibliographers and subject selectors, however, the thought of designing and implementing a collection study remains a frightening prospect. And too often, those who do make efforts in the direction of collection evaluation end up with results that are too insignifi-cant to justify the time required to produce them. It is therefore necessary that librarians begin to share projects that are methodologically sound so that others might benefit from their experiences.

The present article is based upon a 1985 study of sociology holdings at the University of Michigan. In the course of that project, it was possible to identify a number of discrete problems that must be resolved in conducting a collection evaluation. It is likely that others who have undertaken similar studies can add to or modify the list set out in this article. In fact, it is not expected that the seven questions addressed herein will in any way cover all the issues likely to confront a would-be researcher. The approach, however, is intended to give direction and encouragement to those considering an assessment study. The emphasis is primarily on the design of such collection studies although procedural suggestions for data entry and analysis are discussed as well.

RESEARCH DESIGN

What Is To Be Learned?

Generally speaking, when a selector proposes an assessment study it is to judge the "strength" of a collection in a particular area. Strength, however, is a relative term to be judged against some comparative standard. If a list of citations is used as the sole standard it is inevitable that the collection under study will show some deficiencies, leaving the researcher to determine if a hit rate of ninety, or eighty, or fifty percent suggests strength or weakness. Furthermore, these cutoffs will change from study to study depending on both the collection under review and the rigor of the standard being applied. In sum, the common question about strength is probably not the best basis for organizing an assessment study. It is preferable to establish a study design that permits comparison within classes of items; i.e., variables. Useful variables might include date of publication, country of publication, subject, stylistic orientation, or theoretical school. Comparisons within these categories could tell a selector whether, for example, selection appears to be more or less comprehensive over time or if foreign publications are adequately and evenly represented. Information of this sort has much greater utility for analyzing selection than a simple finding showing that the collection holds some percentage of items checked.

What Is the Scope of the Collection to Be Studied?

To a great extent, decisions about the appropriate coverage of a study flow from its stated objectives as determined above. If, for example, a primary objective is to compare the comprehensiveness of psychology selection between the 1970s and present, then obviously the scope of an assessment study would include psychology materials published in that time period. This process, however, is far more complicated than it might at first appear. It remains to be determined if "psychology materials" shall include works written by psychologists, works about psychological issues, or all those of interest to psychologists. Shall "published" be construed to cover reports, proceedings, and dissertations? And, when reference is made to selection "in the 1970s" does that include selection of items published in that decade or selection that actually occurred during that time? If the latter, the nature of searching for designated items would be quite different than if the former definition is used.

In setting out to conduct an assessment study, the researcher must realize that limited resources require limits to the scope of what shall be included. These limitations should be carefully thought through so that their consequences can be anticipated. Such issues as time

period, language, and format are obvious categories for defining scope. So too is the specific subject coverage of a study; it often being preferable to focus on a few key areas than attempting to draw a thin sample of the whole of a field. When selecting such areas for study it is desirable to identify areas of presumed strength as well as areas of presumed weakness, established and new areas, and those falling in the center of a field of study as well as some interdisciplinary topics. Including contrasts of this type is likely to disclose patterns of selection that may or may not be intended.

From Where Should the Citations Be Drawn?

Having determined the scope to be covered in an assessment study, it is then necessary to find an appropriate source or sources from which to draw citations. This particular aspect of collection evaluation has been well covered in several excellent articles in the recent literature and need not be belabored here.[1] Suffice it to say that a list against which to check a collection can be drawn from the catalog of another library; citations from a reviewing source; items in an index or subject bibliography; and/or references from a book, article, state-of-the-art review, or dissertation. The ideal source for collection assessment purposes is comprehensive yet selective and consistently classified over time. Since the perfect list is rarely available to accomplish all the objectives of a planned study, it falls upon the researcher to find a source, or combination of sources, that most closely approximates the ideal. This search can be the most frustrating and time consuming aspect of an evaluation study but care must be taken at this point if the results of the study are to be accepted as credible.

Although obvious perhaps, it seems worth mentioning that the source chosen can have a profound effect on the conclusions reached. Some sources are likely to yield much lower rates of found items than others. For example, sources including a high percentage of foreign citations (e.g., *International Bibliography of Social Science*) will likely present a more difficult standard for comparison than would a list like *Choice* or *Books for College Libraries*. So too lists comprised of citations from articles can be both eclectic and quite esoteric. For assessment of a research collection, it is probably better to employ a more difficult standard if one is really interested in identifying relative strengths and weaknesses in a collection. If the goal,

The need for more and better data has become apparent as managers within and outside the library are less willing to accept intuitive and impressionistic responses to their questions about acquisition budgets and priorities for preservation, storage, or retrospective conversion.

however, is to impress someone with the efficacy of book selection, then it is undoubtedly tempting to seek those sources that are primarily comprised of more standard titles. The point here is that a numerical result does not tell us much about a collection if we do not know the source of the citations being checked.

What Shall Be Included?

As alluded to earlier, decisions related to the scope of materials covered can be among the most difficult that the researcher must face. Dissertations, technical reports, and unpublished papers are often cited in the scholarly literature but generally fall outside the collecting profiles of research libraries. Should these items be included in a study because patrons often come in search of such materials? And what of government publications, including those emanating from foreign or state governments? In some cases these materials may be virtually unobtainable while in others they might be received on 100 percent deposit. In either case the researcher should be aware of the impact of including such items on the outcome of the study. One's decisions should ultimately reflect the goals stated at the outset.

Another decision of this nature is whether a study should include serial publications. Obviously, serials are an important part of any research collection and weaknesses could seriously impair the ability of the collection to support significant scholarship. By definition, however, most serials are not selected anew each year but reflect decisions made many years earlier and which are tacitly accepted to the extent that exceptional measures are not taken to initiate cancellations. Thus, if the thrust of an evaluation is to monitor the adequacy of current selection, including serials might distort the results. On the other hand, if the interest is to assess the ability of the collection to support research, then including serials would seem to be a must.

What Information Will Be Taken From Each Citation?

As was stated at the outset, an assessment study can yield a great deal of detailed information about a collection if the significant elements of a citation are coded and analyzed. In the study of sociology holdings at Michigan, it was possible to determine the relative strength of various foreign language holdings dealing with five different subject areas and written

from two competing theoretical models. Furthermore, such factors as decade of publication, campus libraries holding an item, and the source of sample citations were analyzed. The latter provided interesting information about the effects of drawing citations from one or another source as discussed in question three.

Obvious and readily coded elements of a citation include subject matter, place, and date of publication. Other elements that might be analyzed are format, theoretical orientation, or publisher. And, less commonly, such questions as the sex of an author or the cost of an item could be analyzed. The main point is that such an approach can detect an underlying bias in collection building that might otherwise go unnoticed by a bibliographer.

How Will Specific Citations Be Selected?

The question of sampling, which appears to be a major stumbling block for many undertaking a collection evaluation, is really easier to deal with than most of the decisions discussed above. Sampling involves two major questions: How many total items must be included? and How will these items be selected? The question of sample size can be resolved in several ways. The researcher could apply any of a number of basic statistical formulas available for the determination of appropriate sample size. Or, one could use a table that lists adequate sample size for a given set of assumptions. Formulas and tables aside, it is important that the researcher not lose sight of the fact that determining sample size is an exercise in approximation—there are no absolutes, no right or wrong numbers. In other words, different guesses about the nature of a population under study will yield different cutoffs for sample size.

Furthermore, using one or another formula or table will yield different results, even if identical assumptions are employed. Therefore, it should be understood that there is more latitude in determining an acceptable sample than many textbooks in statistics would lead us to believe. In the final analysis, the prime determinants of sample size are most likely to be the time and money available for carrying out a study rather than any prescribed statistical cutoff.

As for how sample items will be selected, the question is not merely one of ensuring random selection but rather how best to organize the population prior to sampling. One might simply choose to draw a random sample of items from the whole, fully expecting that the resultant sample will accurately reflect the character of the population under study. There are times, however, when the researcher wishes to ensure an adequate number of cases in a particular category, thus leading to a decision to partition or stratify the sampling population and then draw items, either in equal numbers or by some designated proportion, from each of the parts.

For example, if one wants to compare selection of United States and foreign publications from a list that is heavily weighted toward United States titles, it might be necessary to first categorize titles by place of publication and then draw a separate sample from each of the categorized segments. For a hypothetical total sample of 150 items, one might draw 25 titles from each of six countries. If one were further interested in comparing selection by 1970s imprint and 1980s imprint, it might again be wise to cross-cut the language segments by year and draw a sample from the resultant cells. This would ensure that an adequate number of items were included to permit analysis by decade for each of the countries under study.

This process of stratifying a sampling frame has consequences that the researcher should recognize at the outset. First, if one adopts a sampling strategy that gives equal weight to items that are less likely to appear in the population, then the overall results of the study will be unduly skewed toward the minority cases. Thus, in the example above, United States publications represent only one-sixth of the total sample, a fact that does not reflect the collecting practices of American libraries and is bound to result in a rather low rate of found items as compared with a study where United States publications are proportionately represented.

Second, stratifying a population will usually have an effect on the overall size of the sample required—generally (but not always) reducing the prescribed total. The researcher, however, should be aware that adding variables to a matrix will tend to reduce the number of items likely to appear in any one cell. If that number becomes too low, it is impossible to generate meaningful results as more refined analyses are attempted.

What Will Constitute a "Hit" or Determination that the Item Is Held?

Once the sample is drawn and the citations are prepared for searching, it remains to be decided how certain findings will be interpreted. Determining whether an item is held or not held in the collection is more difficult than might first be assumed. Apart from the difficulties of finding anything in a research library, a number of decisions must be made regarding the treatment of editions related but not identical to the citations being searched. The most obvious question involves alternate editions, but translations and microform copies are also problematic. There are no right or wrong answers to these questions but it is advisable to provide some guidelines prior to searching to ensure consistent treatment.

Problems of whether to count an item as a "hit" also arise from where that item is held. For example, on campuses where law, medical, or business libraries are administratively separate it must be decided if their holdings will be counted for the purposes of an assessment study. It must also be determined if items on order but not received will be counted. And finally, there is the question of whether a purchased and cataloged item is actually on the shelves and in usable condition. In brief, the correct response to these questions depends upon what the researcher is hoping to learn from the study. If the focus of the study is related to the adequacy of selection then the decision to purchase is the key factor. If, on the other hand, the focus is on the ability of the collection to meet patron needs then checking the shelf status of an item might be called for.

DATA ANALYSIS

The above suggestions for designing a collection evaluation study have assumed that the results obtained from searching a list of citations would be coded and analyzed by computer. Although not impossible to do an analysis by hand, the speed, convenience, and flexibility of computerized statistical packages make it well worth the effort to learn these systems. If this is impossible, one can turn to the legions of graduate students in most university settings who are familiar with these programs and generally eager for an opportunity to earn a little money while building their resumes.

Depending upon the availability of computer access both campus-wide and at the library, the analysis of assessment data can be carried out on a mainframe or microcomputer. In either case, it is first necessary to set up a coding scheme that accounts for the variables being analyzed and the many decisions about that which will and will not be counted. Each cita-

It seems certain that those who fail to move in the direction of systematic assessment will be unable to cope with the increasingly difficult questions that promise to confront collection officers in years to come.

tion checked should be given a unique identification number that might simply reflect consecutive numbering from $item_1$ thru $item_n$ or might otherwise be coded to indicate the source from which it was drawn. Codes must be established for each of the elements being extracted from the citations, e.g., subject, date, nationality, publication type, etc. Finally, the search results need to be coded in such a way as to indicate first, if an item is held, and then, if appropriate, at what campus library or libraries it can be found.

Perhaps a brief illustrative example would be instructive. Consider the abridged coding instructions in the box for a hypothetical study in education.

Analyzing Results

Those who have followed the discussion to this point might legitimately be wondering what they can expect if they undertake a study of this type. The answer, simply put, is a great deal of descriptive tabular data about the collection under study. Once the data are coded and entered in a datafile, the potential for analysis is almost endless. Tables can be generated, for example, to show the percentage of held items by subject, by decade, or by subject for each decade under consideration. It is this capability to combine and refine elements of analysis that makes this quantitative approach to assess-

Item No. (col. 1-3)	Subject (col. 4)	County of Origin (col. 5)	Pub. Date (col. 6)	Holdings (col. 7)
001-999	School Administration = 1	U.S. = 1	1960-69 = 1	Main Lib. Only = 1
	Teaching Methods = 2	U.K. = 2	1970-79 = 2	Main & Division = 2
	History of Education = 3	France = 3	1980-85 = 3	Division Only = 3
	School Media = 4	Germany = 4		Not Held = 4
		Other = 5		Not Determined = 9

Given these few categories, the citation, Frederick Rudolph, "The American College and University: A History," New York: Knopf, 1962, would be coded as 0013113 to indicate that this was the first item listed, its subject is history of education, it was published in the United States, the date of publication falls between 1960-69, and it is held only at the Education Library.

This brief example calls to mind two cautions. First, it is best to know the particulars of the statistical package to be used prior to coding so that problematic codes can be avoided. Note, for instance, that in the above example zero was not used in the "holdings" category to indicate items not held; this because some statistical programs reserve the zero code to indicate missing data. Such codes can generally be converted at the time of analysis but it is easier to avoid this additional step. Second, assignment of codes to the decade of publication would not, in most cases, be necessary nor desirable since most programs can categorize dates at the time of analysis. Thus it is preferable to enter the specific year of publication and collapse the data at a later time to produce the decade categories. This suggests a very basic principle of data entry: code data with as much detail as possible—it can always be collapsed to more general categories but the converse, of course, is not true.

ment such a powerful collection management tool. One can hone in on very specific aspects of the collection under study. Furthermore, collecting and analyzing data in accord with basic statistical principles permits the researcher to distinguish statistically significant differences from those that are a simple product of chance events.

In other words, use of a simple t-test or the chi-square statistic, can tell the researcher if an observed difference is of sufficient magnitude to be meaningful. For example, if a study reports that 72 percent of United States citations were found in a collection as compared with 65 percent of British citations, it remains to be determined if the 7 percent difference reflects a difference in collecting practice or just an expected degree of variation in sampling. One would never expect identical results in a comparison of this type so the question becomes: How much difference represents a difference? The answer, of course, depends on the size and nature of the sample drawn, although this point is often missed by those undertaking studies which eschew established principles of research design.

As questions about library collections become more complex, library and campus administrators will demand more and better information upon which to base decisions. Collection assessment studies will undoubtedly become part and parcel of the collection management responsibilities of the subject selector or bibliographer. Too, the form of these studies should and will become more methodologically sound so that results can be shared among institutions as well as with the larger scientific community that surrounds the academic library. It seems certain that those who fail to move in the direction of systematic assessment will be unable to cope with the increasingly difficult questions that promise to confront collection officers in years to come. The profession as a whole needs to integrate the basic tools of statistical analysis in its package of librarian (and library) survival skills.

References

1. See Mosher, Paul H., "Quality and Library Collections: New Directions in Research and Practice in Collection Evaluation." In *Advances in Librarianship, 13,* Orlando, Fla.: Academic Press, 1984; Faigel, Martin, "Methods and Issues in Collection Evaluation Today," *Library Acquisitions: Practice and Theory, 9* (1985), pp. 21-35; Hall, Blaine H., *Collection Assessment Manual for College and University Libraries,* Phoenix: Oryx Press, 1985.

Serials Review
in the Humanities:
A Three-Year Project

by Lois Olsrud and Anne Moore

The journal publishing industry has been and remains in a state of flux, reeling under a variety of stresses.

Many libraries have been affected by the proliferation and price inflation of serial publications in recent years. Academic libraries have been especially hard-hit since they are trying to cope with increasing subscription prices while facing budget reductions or very small increases. Although requesting additional funds and freezing new subscriptions help as short-term measures, some libraries have undertaken serials evaluation and cancellation programs as a more permanent solution. Our university library conducted a comprehensive serials review, which is described here. This article explains the justification for the review and describes the methodology used and the problems encountered in canceling serials subscriptions.

JUSTIFICATION

During a ten-year period from 1976 to 1986, the serials budget at the University of Arizona Library increased from roughly 31 to 52 percent of the total materials budget. If the trend continues its upward spiral at this rate, the serials budget will consume the entire budget within about five years. Our overall materials budget has not kept up with the annual increase in book prices and U.S. periodical prices, much less with the prices of foreign subscriptions. A letter from the FAXON Company to its clients in July 1987 stated that book prices were increasing 4-6 percent and U.S. periodical prices 5-7 percent per year.

The causes of this crisis include:

1. Double-digit inflation
2. Rising costs of serial publications (5-30 percent annual increase, double or triple the rate of inflation)
3. Declining value of the American dollar in foreign markets
4. Differential pricing toward American libraries by European publishers

The journal publishing industry has been and remains in a state of flux, reeling under a variety of stresses. Large European and Japanese publishing organizations have bought up smaller publishers, thereby gaining control of much of the scholarly publishing market. They now are in a position to charge whatever they wish. Publishers claim the size of journals has increased while the number of copies printed has decreased, causing a per-unit price increase. Competition to publish everything in a journal's subject area before another journal does and the mushrooming of information in general result in increases in the size of journals. New journals also appear constantly to compete with the established ones. As the costs of paper, typesetting, printing, binding, and postage continue to rise, production costs go up. The intellectual efforts put into journal preparation, including design, selection, and review and editing, cost more now as well. In addition, referees and editors of scholarly journals currently receive more compensation than in the past.

Price discrimination by foreign publishers toward American libraries began in the early 1980s when the dollar was strong and foreign publishers wanted to compensate for the relative weakness of their own currency. But this trend was never reversed and now it compounds the current problems with inflation and the declining value of the dollar. British publishers who took advantage of the U.S.'s awkward position by charging American academic and research libraries four times the British price have been more understanding than most. When confronted with this issue, British publishers merely froze the U.S. price until they brought their prices for others up to the same level. According to a FAXON projection, in 1988 the average periodical subscription price to U.S. buyers increased 7-9 percent in the U.K., 20-23 percent in Germany, 25-31 percent in the rest of Europe including Scandinavia, and 25-30 percent in Japan.

Since libraries are the primary market for scholarly journals and the number of libraries is relatively static, publishers cannot expand their subscription base but must rely on price increases to raise their revenues. If enough libraries drop their subscriptions, it is hoped that publishers will have to respond. Perhaps new means of disseminating scholarly research, such as electronic journals produced at universities or cooperative sharing ventures among libraries, will be the outcome of the current battle between libraries and publishers.

The problem became serious at our institution when the library materials budget was not sufficient to retain its buying power for books and cover the increased cost of serials. The library was forced to suspend ordering new subscriptions to journals and realized it had to take action if it wanted to keep the serials budget at an appropriate fraction of the total materials budget. As a response, the university in 1986 undertook a three-year comprehensive review of its 22,000 periodical subscriptions.

ORGANIZATION

Before the review project began, the library formed a serials review committee with members representing the serials department, central reference department, and science library. The head of the serials department chaired the committee, which was charged with these responsibilities:

1. Outline the procedures to be followed in the review process
2. Set a calendar or timetable of events
3. Provide the criteria to be used in reviewing each serial
4. Serve as a forum for questions and discussions
5. Draft policies regarding reinstatement of canceled titles

The Library of Congress classification was divided so different subjects would be reviewed in each of the three years. The serials in the humanities were to follow a schedule with general (A), religion (BJ-BX) and fine arts (N) reviewed the first year; philosophy (B-BH), music (M), linguistics, classics, and Modern European, Asian, and African languages and literature (P-PL) and Romance and English literature (PQ-PR) the second year; and American Indian languages, literary history and criticism, communication, film and drama (PM-PN), and American and Germanic literature (PS-PT) the third year. (See Table 1 for a complete list of subject areas reviewed.)

Although the main burden for the review would fall on the shoulders of librarians, we felt it essential to inform and consult members of the teaching faculty for their input. The university librarian distributed a letter to all deans, directors, and department heads on campus explaining the necessity for serials cancellations. The letter urged faculty members to participate in the process by responding to the lists they would receive and marking the titles they felt were expendable. Several articles appeared in the campus newspaper describing the need for the review. A Campus Library Council meeting and discussions in the Faculty Senate also brought the topic before the faculty.

Procedure

One of the first tasks for the serials review committee was to outline the process for the year. The serials acquisition librarian would provide INNOVACQ printouts in call-number order of all serial titles to be reviewed. Ten to 15 percent of the titles in each subject area of the Library of Congress classification scheme were to be cut. Each subject area would be examined by librarians who worked with students and faculty or participated in selection for that subject. The teaching and research faculty would be involved through lists sent to appropriate departments for their comments. The final review of cancellations and retentions would be made by the serials review committee before any action would be taken. Cancellation lists would be available in the reserve book room for anyone to see. This process would be examined after the first year to see what improvements should be made before the second-year review took place.

Timetable

The schedule for the project for the first year began in early February 1987 when library selectors received their respective lists. They had three

Table 1
Subjects for Review

Year One: 1987		Year Two: 1988		Year Three: 1989	
A	General	B-BH	Philosophy/	C	History
BJ-BX	Religion		Psychology	D	History
E	North American History	H-HJ	Social Sciences	G-GV	Geography/
F	South American History	J	Political Science		Anthropology/Folk-
K	Law	M	Music		lore/Sports
L	Education	P-PL	Linguistics/	HM-HX	Sociology
N	Fine Arts		Language	PM-PN	Literary History
Q	General Science	PQ	Romance Literature	PS	American Literature
QH-QR	Life Science	PR	English Literature	PT	Germanic Literature
R	Medicine	SF	Animal Culture	QA-QE	Math, Sciences
TS-TX	Manufactures/	U-V	Military Science	S-SD	Agriculture
	Home Economics		Oriental Studies	SH-SK	Fisheries/
Z	Library Science				Hunting

Newspapers
Duplicate Subscriptions

months to review the titles using the prescribed criteria and to annotate each title as they felt necessary. Faculty members in teaching departments received their lists at the same time. Annotated lists from librarians and faculty members were to be returned to the serials department by April 30. Members of the serials review committee would then review the combined lists for each subject and confirm the titles to be canceled. The serials department was to notify the vendors during June 1987 in time to cancel the issues to be received in 1988.

Criteria for Deselection

The criteria used in the deselection process include several important elements. Relevance and support for the programs of our university were major considerations. For this, we followed the collection intensity from the University of Arizona collection development policy. Our policy uses code numbers to indicate strength denominators for the depth to which acquisition is attempted for each subject. The range is from 0 (out of scope) for areas in which we do not collect to 5 (comprehensive level) for those in which we want all significant works in all applicable languages.

Evaluators were expected to note the quality of the articles and language, current level of use, and retrospective usefulness. They also questioned whether to keep materials printed on inferior quality paper, newsletters, broadsides, or ephemeral materials, which can be expensive and difficult to preserve.

Availability was another consideration. We wanted to know if a title was available elsewhere on campus, held by another library in our state, or

obtainable from the Center for Research Libraries. Finally, we wanted to know if a title was covered in major abstracting or indexing services.

METHODOLOGY: FIRST-YEAR REVIEW

For the first year, the aim was to cut 10 to 15 percent of all titles for the subjects under review. The methods for reaching this goal varied since the participating librarians were free to go about the process in any manner they wished as long as they produced the desired results. Some used separate cards or slips with notes for each title while others made their annotations directly on their INNOVACQ printouts.

The review of religion (BJ-BX) is used as an example of the methodology for the first year. Since it is an interdisciplinary subject, lists were sent to several departments including the center for religious studies, Oriental studies department, English department, and history department. Two librarians also reviewed this subject: one in special collections who had an advanced degree in theology and another who was the subject representative in the reference department. All participants were asked to indicate which titles they believed were essential, which were important and should be kept, and which could be canceled.

The reference librarian served as the coordinator for this portion of the serials review and the steps she followed are outlined below. The first step was to examine the current issues in the current periodicals room. This evaluator judged the journal's usefulness, whether it related to the curriculum or filled a particular need not covered by another title. The quality of the articles and the type of user (facility for research or students for class assignments) were considered. Publishers were noted, especially those known for their tendency to inflate prices. Examination of the current issues provided a good opportunity to note problems the library had in receiving the titles. In some cases a title had not been received for up to five years. Serials personnel researched these special problems so that we could eliminate a title if it had ceased arriving or make the decision to keep it despite the receiving delays.

Another step was to examine the bound volumes in the stacks. The evaluator noted the length of the holdings and attempted to determine use (heavy use versus layers of dust or many uncut pages). Annuals and irregular serials were also examined in the stacks since they are not kept in our current periodicals room. The printout lists included reference items, so volumes were checked in central reference as well.

The *Religious Periodicals Directory* (edited by Graham Cornish, ABC-CLIO, Inc., 1986) was consulted as a guide. It provided helpful descriptions for most of the titles under review and listed coverage in leading abstracting and indexing services. The last step was to check the titles in question for holdings in other libraries. Decisions were then made and the suggested cancellations were marked on the INNOVACQ printout.

After the lists for religion were returned to the reference librarian, she made a composite document showing the decisions of each of the six participants who had reviewed this subject. The responses varied depending on the department and the viewpoint of the reviewer. The center for religious studies suggested 14 titles for cancellation; the Oriental studies department, 27; the history department, 26; the English department marked none for cancellation, but wrote question marks for 33 titles; the reference librarian suggested 38; and the special collections librarian, 69.

Altogether there were 245 titles reviewed from BJ-BX, so approximately 35 had to be canceled in order to make a 15 percent cut of the total number. As a general rule, any titles marked *essential* were retained and a title was canceled when there were two or more recommendations to cancel.

A list of 41 titles was submitted for cancellation. However, after all of the first year's subjects were reviewed, not enough titles had been recommended for cancellation to reach a 15 percent cut in dollar value. Since prices were not given on the printouts, some deletions were for gifts and did not help the cause. So an additional seven titles were cut from the religion collection.

METHODOLOGY: SECOND AND THIRD YEAR REVIEWS

During the summer of 1987, the procedures used in the first-year review were evaluated, streamlined, and improved before the second-year review began. Having done it once, the librarians knew what problems awaited them and settled on procedures that would work more efficiently. The procedures used in the second year carried over into the final year.

A significant difference in the second and third years was that faculty members were not asked to deal with unannotated lists early in the process. Instead, they were asked to react to lists already reviewed or screened by the library staff. This required less of their time. Another difference was that many more librarians became involved in the review. Teams of librarians including reference librarians, acquisitions bibliographers, catalogers, and serials librarians were formed for each classification area. Almost all of the more than 75 librarians participated in the review. Each team member added his or her expertise to the task of cutting 15 percent of the dollar value of the subject area.

The printouts now included prices, so evaluators could determine items received free of charge through memberships and could more effectively judge quality versus price. Each team was given a dollar amount to cut. Another improvement was a special fund of $1,400 provided to pay students to assist with routine checking of indexing services, directories, degree program status, titles without price information on the lists, citation values, and price increases reflected in FAXON Scope reports.

The teams still designed their own methods to arrive at suggested cuts. The American literature (PS) review serves as an example of the methodology used in the second and third years. This group went through the list at the first meeting and assigned a *1* (essential) to the titles group members knew were so important they did not require further evaluation. Two members checked indexing coverage through *MLA International Bibliography, Arts & Humanities Citation Index,* and *Ulrich's International Periodicals Directory.* A student was assigned to search for prices not listed on the working printouts. Each librarian then examined all remaining titles in current periodicals and the stacks and assigned each title a tentative ranking of *1* for essential, *2* for important, *3* for useful, and *4* for cancellation.

Subsequent meetings featured comparison on rankings and discussion until the group reached an agreement and met its required goal. Some

Perhaps new means of disseminating scholarly research . . . will be the outcome of the current battle between libraries and publishers.

journals had to be reexamined before the decision could be made. After thorough discussion and evaluation within the group, final rankings were assigned to each title. The chair of the group annotated the list with justifications for eliminating the serials marked 4 and returned the list to the serials acquisition librarian by the beginning of January.

The serials acquisition librarian then sent the annotated lists to appropriate faculty departments designated by the teams. For example, while the PNs went to the English, drama, communications, journalism, media arts, French, and Spanish departments, the PS list went only to the English department.

Faculty members were given one month to respond to the lists. A letter that accompanied the lists asked them to review and annotate the titles with comments, suggestions, and appropriate rankings if those differed from the rankings established by the librarians. If faculty members wished to retain a title targeted for cancellation, they were asked to suggest an alternative title of comparable price from the same category to be canceled instead.

The departments returned their lists to the serials department, and many faculty members wrote individual letters with their comments. Only some faculty members suggested alternative titles for cancellation when they wanted to retain something marked 4. A few faculty members did not want to cancel anything on their list.

The review teams met again to discuss the faculty letters. They tried to accommodate any request to retain a title and made exceptions to the 15 percent goal when there was no other solution. Difficulties arose when faculty members did not agree on whether to cancel or retain a specific title. The teams of librarians used their best judgment to make their decisions. As an example of the impact of the review on the humanities, the P-PT committees cut 164 from a total of 1,330 titles.

After the final recommendations were submitted by the teams, the serials review committee discussed the overall picture. Since some groups were able to cut more than 15 percent, this allowed the retention of most journals for which faculty members made strong cases. The committee tried to be as flexible as possible within the parameters established by the requirements of the review. Its recommendations were passed on to the library's administrative group, which made the ultimate decisions.

Cancellation lists were available on reserve from April onward. The serials acquisition librarian processed the cancellations in May and June.

He had a note added to the INNOVACQ records for canceled titles stating "CANCELED AFTER 12/88 SERIALS REVIEW." He also had a code added to the processing fixed field element on the INNOVACQ records for all reviewed serials designating the serials review ranking assigned to the journal. This element produces a note on future order slips "SER RANK 1." This element could be used to produce lists of titles by rank to assist in subsequent reviews. If we must make additional cuts, we will begin evaluating the 3s and move on from there.

PROBLEMS

The serials review raised several problems; some are of a general nature with respect to procedures, while others pertain more specifically to making cuts in the humanities. Some of these problems are presented here.

Timing

Reference librarians felt the timing of the review was especially difficult the first year. Their part came during the semester when work in the reference department was at its most intense because of a heavy load of bibliographic instruction sessions and students needing help with term paper research. Since the process required many hours, participating librarians needed more time than was originally allotted for it. By the third year, the review was spread over more months and the teams were able to choose when they accomplished their work. This was a definite improvement.

Reaching the Faculty

It is hard to reach every faculty member who might be interested in the review. The Library of Congress classification does not correspond neatly to campus academic departments and many sections of the classification schedule include titles that are interdisciplinary in their coverage. Despite the library's attempts to reach the appropriate departments, some faculty members expressed concern because they did not know a title was being considered for cancellation. And even when a printout was sent to a particular department, not everyone in that department was aware of it. In one case, a faculty member returned from sabbatical only to discover a title he thought was important had been canceled. The lists were available in the reserve book room, but few faculty members consulted them there. A limited number of titles have been reinstated after cancellation when requesters provided supporting documentation and information.

Quality Versus Cost

One of the problems during the first year was the lack of prices on the printouts, so evaluators were not aware of either higher-priced or free journals. However, this changed by the second and third year reviews since the INNOVACQ database, the source of the printouts, was more complete and could provide such data. Once prices were known, there was often a conflict of quality versus cost. Members of a team frequently disagreed when a decision had to be made about whether to keep a very expensive title that was important to the collection. Some librarians feel more strongly than others that a journal should be canceled strictly because of its price. They believe a message must reach publishers that we cannot and will not continue to absorb their high inflation rates.

Undergraduate Versus Graduate and Faculty Scholarly Needs

Several public service librarians were concerned that titles used primarily by undergraduate students would not be considered as necessary as more scholarly ones and would consequently be cut. Undergraduates use titles not linked to a specific curriculum for many of their papers. The journals they use do not necessarily have serious research value. However, the library must have what undergraduates need because there is not enough time for them to benefit from interlibrary loan since their assignments are usually due in a short period of time.

Although undergraduates are often satisfied with ''some'' information on a topic, a scholar needs exact, precise information. The quality of the library's holdings greatly affects the faculty's research, as well as the university's ability to attract the best junior and senior professors. Typically, faculty members are also very concerned about keeping journals in foreign languages. Even though the foreign journals are not used by many individuals, they are read by the most scholarly people on campus.

Indexed Journals

When considering which journals to cancel, librarians tend to put great emphasis on whether or not a journal is covered in abstracting or indexing services. As librarians, we are aware of users' disappointment when the library does not own titles found within our abstract and index sets. This is not as important to some scholars, who believe it is more important to have journals that are not indexed, especially the better ones published in foreign countries. This idea is based on the premise that if you know something exists, you can get it through interlibrary loan. If not, you learn of it by browsing through what is at hand.

Problems in the Humanities

There are some special concerns regarding serials cancellations for the humanities. The works of literature, art, and religion are forever unique and must be experienced and analyzed by each individual. Eliminations from the collection can be felt for a long time.

Journals in the humanities are used for a long period of time. Recency is not the only factor. Once a good article is written, it is important for the future as well as the present. For example, students and scholars in science do not rely on articles that were written in 1945. But in literature, good articles written even in 1925 or earlier can still be useful. In fact, filling in backfiles is beneficial since older material is just as important as current material.

It is difficult to ascertain how many users benefit from journals in this discipline because many are multidisciplinary. Art is one example. The N classification was among the first subjects to be reviewed because the serials collection in art exceeded the level of our current curriculum and the collection development policy. Since our university does not have a PhD program in art, we thought this was an area that could absorb many cancellations. But there were objections because the art section is used by many kinds of students, not just art majors. Art history is interdisciplinary, and its journals are needed by students of history and the classics, who also rely on visual resources.

Some areas of literature will suffer more from serials cuts than others. Material written about early time periods, such as Old English or Middle English, is published more frequently in journals than in books because the nature of the material is article—rather than book—length. This is different from the nineteenth century where a higher percentage of the critical material is in books.

Literature journals are relatively inexpensive and frequently cost $20 or even less per year. If an arbitrary figure or percentage is the goal for cuts, many specialized titles with a narrow focus may have to be canceled. This can undermine the breadth of the literature serials collection. Another approach is to cut only the expensive titles. This can leave a collection full of specialized journals, but lacking in core periodicals. A balance must be struck so that both heavily used and specialized titles remain after the cuts. Some librarians believe ongoing processing costs should be considered along with purchasing costs. It costs the same amount to process each issue of an inexpensive journal as an expensive one.

RESULTS

A variety of benefits arose out of the serials review besides monetary savings and the purchase of new titles. Each review group discovered at least one miscataloged title and initiated recataloging. Problems in publication or receipt of issues surfaced and were passed on to the serials receiving section for resolution. The committees decided to cancel some titles with exceptional receiving lags of four or more years if they were of questionable value.

The review provided the opportunity to evaluate the number and type of journals we are carrying in specialized subject areas, to reduce oversubscribing (too many serials in a narrow subject area), to eliminate coverage of subjects no longer being studied, and to note gaps in the collection.

The teams looked for creative ways to streamline serials purchases. This included transferring some serials to the monograph budget. Some were actually classed-together monographic series which were canceled from the serials list and will be selected, evaluated, and ordered in the same way as other monographs in the future. We dropped some expensive annuals, such as major business directories and science handbooks held in the reference collections. We plan to order them every two or three years.

CONCLUSIONS

After three years of reviewing the serials, the University of Arizona library has canceled 2,600 subscriptions. The review was necessary although those involved believe it was a difficult process and the overall effects will not be known for some time. And even though the process was extremely time-consuming, it helped librarians to know the collection far better than before and brought librarians from throughout the system together through teamwork.

Users will undoubtedly be hurt by some of the cancellations. Our library will suffer more from cuts than many other libraries because of our geographical isolation from other large institutions. In the northeastern and midwestern parts of the country, good libraries are closer together (within convenient driving distance), and students and faculty are able to obtain materials held in other libraries much more easily.

The review may continue as needed depending on the budget, inflation, and publishers' pricing policies. If so, subsequent reviews will be even more challenging for librarians and detrimental to faculty and students since duplicate subscriptions, ephemeral materials, little-used titles, and titles that no longer support the curriculum were eliminated in the first review.

The most positive outcome of the review is that we have been able to begin ordering new titles again. The reaction of the faculty and the persistent efforts of library administrators convinced university officials that the library needed more funds. As a result, an increase was added to the base materials budget. From now on, any request for a new serial will require justification and will follow the prescribed evaluation criteria used in this review.

BIBLIOGRAPHY OF SERIALS REVIEW IN THE 1980s

Methodology

Barnard, Roy S. "A Serials Deselection Method." In *Proceedings from the 1982 Spring Meeting of the Nebraska Library Association, College and University Section (Seward, Nebraska, April 15-16, 1982)*. Ed. Elaine A. Franco. Lincoln: Nebraska Library Association, 1982. ERIC ED 231 359.

Bensman, Stephen J. "Journal Collection Management as a Cumulative Advantage Process." *College & Research Libraries* 46 (January 1985): 13-29.

Blake, Monica. "Journal Cancellations in University Libraries." *Serials Librarian* 10 (Summer 1986): 73-79.

————, and A.J. Meadows. "Journals at Risk." *Journal of Librarianship* 16, no. 3 (April 1984): 118-128.

Bostic, Mary J. "Serials Deselection." *Serials Librarian* 9 (Spring 1985): 85-101.

Bousfield, Wendy. "Boundary Spanners and Serials Deselection." *Serials Librarian* 10 (Spring 1986): 23-31.

Broadus, Robert N. "A Proposed Method for Eliminating Titles from Periodical Subscription Lists." *College & Research Libraries* 46 (January 1985): 30-39.

Carter, Ruth C., and Scott Bruntjen. "Pittsburgh Regional Library Center Serials Cancellation Project." *Library Resources & Technical Services* 28 (October 1984): 299-307.

Dougherty, Richard M., and Nancy E. Barr. "Paying the Piper: ARL Libraries Respond to Skyrocketing Journal Subscription Prices." *Journal of Academic Librarianship* 14, no. 1: 4-9.

Dove, H. Paul, Jr. "Subscription Cost: A Five-Year

Comparison." *South Carolina Librarian* 28 (Spring 1984): 9-11.

Goehner, Donna M. "Core Lists of Periodicals Selected by Faculty Reviewers." *Technical Services Quarterly* 1 (Summer 1984): 17-38.

Grefsheim, Suzanne, Shelley Bader, and Pamela Meredith. "User Involvement in Journal Deselection." *Collection Management* 5 (Spring/Summer 1983): 43-52.

Hanson, Roger K. "Serials Deselection: A Dreadful Dilemma." In *Serials Collection Development: Choices and Strategies.* Ed. Sul H. Lee. Ann Arbor, Mich.: Pierian Press, 1981. 43-59.

Horwill, Cherry, and Peter Lambert. "1 Man—100 Votes: A New Approach to Reviewing Periodicals Subscriptions at the University of Sussex." *ASLIB Proceedings* 39 (January 1987): 7-16.

Johnson, Steve. "Serial Deselection in University Libraries: The Next Step." *Library Acquisitions* 7 (1983): 239-246.

Kaiden, Phyllis. "From Periodicals Budget Cuts to Management Information Systems." *Serials Librarian* 9 (Winter 1984): 83-92.

Logan-Peters, Kay. "Serial Cancellation Programs in Academic Libraries in Missouri." In *Proceedings from the 1982 Spring Meeting of the Nebraska Library Association, College and University Section (Seward, Nebraska, April 15-16, 1982).* Ed. Elaine A. Franco. Lincoln: Nebraska Library Association, 1982. ERIC ED 231 359.

Neame, Laura, "Periodicals Cancellation: Making a Virtue out of Necessity." *Serials Librarian* 10 (Spring 1986): 33-41.

"Nine University Libraries Attack Journal Inflation." *College and Research Library News,* no. 4 (April 1988): 208.

Peters, Andrew. "Evaluating Periodicals." *College & Research Libraries* 43 (1982): 149-151.

Pinzelik, Barbara P. "Serials De-Acquisition." In *Projects and Procedures for Serials Administration.* Ed. Diane Stine. Ann Arbor, Mich.: Pierian Press, 1985. 61-73.

"Rising Cost of Serials Tackled by Midwest University Libraries." *Library Journal* 113 (April 1, 1988): 23.

Segal, Judith A. "Journal Deselection: A Literature Review and an Application." *Science & Technology Libraries* 6 (Spring 1986): 25-42.

"Stanford Cancels Journal Subscriptions." *Wilson Library Bulletin* 63 (September 1988): 8.

Weisheit, Ralph A., and Robert M. Regoli. "Ranking Journals." *Scholarly Publishing* 15 (1984): 313-325.

Welsch, Erwin K. "Price Versus Coverage: Calculating the Impact on Collection Development." *Library Resources & Technical Services* 32, no. 2 (April 1988): 159-163.

White, Herbert S. "Factors in the Decision by Individuals and Libraries to Place or Cancel Subscriptions to Scholarly and Research Journals." *Library Quarterly* 50, no. 3 (July 1980): 287-309.

Williamson, Marilyn L. "Seven Years of Cancellations at Georgia Tech." *Serials Librarian* 9 (Spring 1985): 103-114.

Publishers' Pricing Policies and Librarians' Responses

"ARL Threatens Legal Action Against Differential Pricing." *Library Journal* 111 (August 1986): 27.

Astle, Deana, and Charles Hamaker. "Pricing by Geography: British Journal Pricing: Including Development in Other Countries." *Library Acquisitions* 10, no. 3 (1986): 165-181.

Basch, N.B. "Pricing." *Library Acquisitions* 12, no. 2 (1988): 203-205.

———. "The Scholarly Journal and the Library Market." *Scholarly Publishing* 19 (April 1988): 157-162.

"British Price Gouging Reported Still Going On." *Library Journal* 110 (June 1, 1985): 70-71.

Clack, M.E., and J.F. Riddick. "The Balance Point: Focus on Serials Issues." *Serials Review* 14, no. 3 (1988): 89-95 and 14, no. 4 (1988): 65-68.

Cox, B. "Scholarly Journal Prices." *Serials Librarian* 13 (October-November 1987): 135-138.

Curtis, J. "Publishing Policies, off the Top of My Head." *Library Acquisitions* 12, no. 2 (1988): 221-224.

"Differential Pricing Still Gouging U.S. Libraries." *Library Journal* 111 (November 15, 1986): 28.

Dougherty, Richard M. "Serials Prices: Outrageous or Just the Cost of Doing Business?" Editorial. *Journal of Academic Librarianship* 14, no. 1: 3.

———, and Brenda L. Johnson. "Periodical Price Escalation: A Library Response." *Library Journal* 113 (May 15, 1988): 27-29.

Dyl, Edward A. "A Note on Price Discrimination by Academic Journals." *Library Quarterly* 58 (1983): 161-168.

Faigel, M. "The Library as Marketplace in a Collection Management Environment." *Library Acquisitions* 12, no. 2 (1988): 191-195.

"Freeze on Journal Prices by Taylor & Francis." *Library Journal* 110 (September 15, 1985): 28.

Greene, Philip E.N. "Serials Prices: An Historical Perspective." *Serials Librarian* 11 (December 1986-January 1987): 19-29.

Hamaker, Charles. "Journal Pricing: A Modest Proposal." *Serials Librarian* 11 (December 1986-January 1987): 171-175.

———. "The Least Reading for the Smallest Number at the Highest Price." *American Libraries* 19, no. 9 (October 1988): 764-768.

———. "Library Serials Budgets: Publishers and the 20 Percent Effect." *Library Acquisitions* 12, no. 2 (1988): 211-219.

———. "Serials Costs and the Carrying Ability of Serials Budgets 1987." *Serials Librarian* 13 (October-November 1987): 129-134.

Heroux, M.S. "Anatomy and Physiology of the Publisher/Vendor/Librarian Relationship." *Library Acquisitions* 12, no. 2 (1988): 207-210.

Houbeck, Robert L. "British Journal Pricing: Enigma Variations, or What Will the U.S. Market Bear?" *Library Acquisitions* 10, no. 3 (1986): 183-197.

———. "If Present Trends Continue: Forecasting and Responding to Journal Price Increases." *Serials Librarian* 13 (October-November 1987): 113-127.

———. "If Present Trends Continue: Responding to

Journal Price Increases." *Journal of Academic Librarianship* 13 (September 1987): 214-220.

————. "Indignation Mounts over Questionable Marketing." *Library Journal* 111, no. 22 (June 15, 1986).

Ivins, O. "Serials Prices." *Serials Review 14*, no. 3 (1988): 61-66.

Joyce, Patrick, and Thomas E. Merz. "Price Discrimination in Academic Journals." *Library Quarterly* 55, no. 3 (July 1985): 273-283.

Lenzini, R.T. "The World Economic Condition: Its Impact on Serials and the Business of Scholarly Communications." *Serials Review* 14, no. 3 (1988): 91-92.

Leonhardt, T.W. "The Acquisitions Librarian as Informed Consumer: 'Mad as Hell and Not Going to Take It Any More!'" *Library Acquisitions* 12, no. 2 (1988): 149-154.

"Librarian Charges Publisher with Questionable Tactics." *Library Journal* 111 (June 15, 1986): 22.

Lopez. J.S. "The Great Leveler: the Library Budget." *Library Acquisitions* 12, no. 2 (1988): 229-234.

Lynden, Frederick C. "Prices of Foreign Library Materials: A Report." *College & Research Libraries* 49, no. 3 (May 1988): 217-231.

Maddox, J. "Exchange Rate and Inflation." *Library Acquisitions* 12, no. 2 (1988): 181-185.

"Medical Library Association Protests Differential Pricing." *Library Journal* 113 (November 15, 1988): 18.

Merriman, J.B. "Publisher, Vendor, Librarian—Uneasy Alliance." *Library Acquisitions* 12, no. 2 (1988): 155-158.

"MLA Protests Double Pricing." *Wilson Library Bulletin* 63 (November 1988): 14.

Okerson, A.L. "Periodical Prices: A History and Discussion." In *Advances in Serials Management*. Vol. 1. JAI Press, Greenwich, Conn. 1986. 101-134.

Presley, R.L. "The Rising Cost of Serials and Effective Collection Management." *Serials Librarian* 13 (October-November 1987): 155-158.

Ruschin, Siegfried. "Why Are Foreign Subscription Rates Higher for American Libraries Than They Are for Subscribers Elsewhere?" *Serials Librarian* 9 (Spring 1985): 7-17.

Secor, J.R. "A Growing Crisis of Business Ethics: The Gathering Stormclouds." *Serials Librarian* 13 (October-November 1987): 67-90.

Sexton, M. "SSP Meeting: Scholarly Publishing at Risk?" *Publishers Weekly* 234 (July 29, 1988), 129.

Somers, S.W. "The Exchange Rate and Inflation: A Study of Sacred Cows, Lemmings and Other Assorted Things." *Library Acquisitions* 12, no. 2 (1988): 177-180.

Szenberg, M. "Compensation for Journal Editors: A Major Cost Element." *Journal of Academic Librarianship* 14 (September 1988): 236.

Tagler, John. "Counterpoint: A Publisher's Perspective." *American Libraries* 19, no. 9 (October 1988): 767.

————. "A Peripatetic Dollar and Its Impact on Journal Prices." *Serials Review* 14, no. 3 (1988): 90-91.

Thompson, James C. "Guest Editorial—Journal Costs: Perception and Reality in the Dialogue." *College & Research Libraries* 46, no. 6 (November 1988): 481-482.

Thornton, S.A., and C.J. Bigger. "Periodicals, Prices and Policies." *ASLIB Proceedings* 37 (November-December 1985): 437-452.

Tuttle, Marcia. "Discriminatory Pricing of British Scholarly Journals for the North American Market: An Overview." *Serials Librarian* 11 (December 1986-January 1987): 157-161.

————. "North American Prices for British Scholarly Journals." *Library Acquisitions* 10, no. 2 (1986): 89-96.

————. "The Pricing of British Journals for the North American Market." *Library Resources & Technical Services* 30 (January 1986): 72-78.

Wall, R.A. "Publisher Pricing Policies and the Reprographic Copyright Controversy." *ASLIB Proceedings* 36 (July/August 1984): 325-332.

White, Herbert S. "Differential Pricing." *Library Journal* 111 (September 1, 1986): 170-171.

————. "The Journal That Ate the Library." *Library Journal* 113 (May 15, 1988): 62-63.

————. "The Management of Libraries and the Management of Money—Two Faces of the Same Job." *Serials Review* 14, no. 4 (1988): 66-67.

————. "Scholarly Publishers and Libraries: A Strained Marriage." *Scholarly Publishing* 19 (April 1988): 125-129.

SECTION IV

Resource Sharing

Collaborative Collection Development: Progress, Problems, and Potential

by David H. Stam

ibrary planning and collection building in the research libraries of the United States have long had to deal with two contradictory forces, autonomy and interdependence. The independence and autonomy of those libraries in providing for local self-sufficiency in information needs have been tested by a gradual but growing realization that local self-sufficiency is not possible for the programs of comprehensive university libraries or other large libraries. They continue to operate independently, making their own decisions for local needs, while routinely rejecting the "myth of the self-sufficient library" and paying lip-service to cooperation and resource sharing.

Some attempts to transcend these conflicting tensions by moving to the wider issue of assuring adequate national coverage of significant research resources have failed, foundered, or succeeded only partially. The Farmington Plan for distribution foundered for lack of careful monitoring of its implementation, though its importance for its time should not be underestimated. The Public Law 480 program, which used available foreign exchange funds for importing library materials from such countries as Egypt, India, Pakistan, and Sri Lanka, attempted to aid the local adequacy of many libraries, almost entirely in duplication of the Library of Congress. Although it successfully added to the research resources of the country, it was really a program of duplicative rather than

distributed responsibility. So was the National Program of Acquisitions and Cataloging (NPAC), which provided priority cataloging of foreign acquisitions usually duplicated by Library of Congress and member participants in the program. Without doubt, our most successful cooperative program has been the Center for Research Libraries in Chicago which has served the role of providing access to little-used resources which members preferred not to hold locally or could not afford to acquire. These are just a few examples of American attempts at collaborative collection development, but it is fair to say that none of them represents the true sharing of distributed collection responsibility that our rhetoric would suggest.

Since its founding in 1974 by four major research libraries (Harvard, Yale, Columbia, NYPL) in the northeastern part of the United Sates, the Research Libraries Group (RLG) has had these issues at the top of its agenda. Even with its strong starting base of four of the largest libraries in the country, its primary assumption was simply that no single library could do all it wanted to do and that collaborative programs had to be developed to address the major issues facing research libraries. That assumption operated for all its major programs including collection development, preservation, resource sharing, and bibliographical systems, and was also dominant in the work of subsidiary specialized programs of the consortium. Although all of those programs can be seen as interrelated, for example that collaborative collection development has direct implications for cooperation in preservation matters, the focus of this paper is mainly on the RLG collection development program itself.

COLLECTION MANAGEMENT AND DEVELOPMENT IN RLG

At the outset, from 1974 to 1978, the efforts of the founding members of RLG were devoted to three main areas: 1) the geographical distribution of collecting responsibilities, in which the members "divided the globe" and agreed mutually to take responsibility for particular countries; 2) collaboration in deciding who would purchase expensive sets to which all required some access; 3) agreement on a "master copy" concept for journals, whereby one member would agree to maintain a given title available to all, so that other members might discontinue it as they chose. I should stress that all actions were entirely voluntary, thereby recognizing the continued autonomy of each institution. The only coercion came from internal economic forces which required difficult choices to reduce the rate of growth in acquisitions and other budgets.

The experience of the four founding members with these programs proved extremely valuable in setting the context of discussion and showing possible pitfalls of such collaboration. The withdrawal of Harvard University from the group in 1978, for example, clearly undermined the continued application of the "master copy" concept and raised the question of what should happen when voluntary agreements are abrogated. The lack of a bibliographical system and its communication capabilities was an added problem. In addition, the initial experience of implementing these programs with manual files proved enormously onerous and illustrated the need for automated facilities to control the information about these programs.

With the withdrawal of Harvard and the selection of Stanford University's automated bibliographical system as the basis of RLG system development for bibliographical control, the stage was set for the expansion of RLG to other universities and libraries nationwide, and for expanded approaches to the collection development problem. From its original nucleus of four members, RLG grew by 1982 to twenty-six members, all actively engaged in collaborative collection development activities. Today the work has expanded beyond the RLG membership (now at thirty-four research libraries) to the North American Collection Inventory Project (NCIP), sponsored by the Association of Research Libraries, and the work of the Canadian Association of Research Libraries.

What has been the approach of the RLG Collection Management and Development Committee? When the Committee began its work in 1979 chaired by myself with Paul Mosher of Stanford University as Vice-Chair, its aims were both modest and ambitious. On the modest side, we merely wanted to understand more fully what actually was going on in collection development in our then limited membership, in order to get a better picture of what we were actually doing. More ambitiously, we were asked to succeed, where many had previously fallen short, in creating a system and climate to assure our collective capacity to support the nation's research needs. The tool developed to meet these objectives was the *RLG Conspectus.*[1]

In brief, the *Conspectus* was designed by the Committee as a collection assessment instrument to aid coordinated collecting activities. It attempts to present a composite picture of collection strengths and current collection practices in participating libraries. To provide this picture, the *Conspectus* is arranged by Library of Congress subject fields (now numbering over 5,000 subdivisions) for which each library provides an assessment of its own collection strength in each of these subdivisions, using a carefully defined range of numerical designators from 0 to 5. These levels are: 0) Out of scope; 1) Minimal Level; 2) Basic Information Level; 3) Instructional Support Level; 4)Research Level; and 5) Comprehensive Level.

In addition, for each subject each library also provides a second number to describe the current collecting intensity (i.e., what level they are attempting to achieve for that subject), and a language designator to describe the language coverage of that subject collection. The language code letters are: E: primarily English; F: selected foreign language material plus English; W: selection in all applicable languages; and Y: primarily in one language particular to that subject (e.g. Ukrainian as Yiddish literature). One example would be a 2E/4 W collection in computer science, indicating that an institution is attempting to move from its basic information collection, primarily in English, to a research level collection in a wide variety of languages. Another example would be a 4/3 F collection in anthropology signifying that the institution is deemphasizing its collecting in that field. A 4/4 Y research level collection of Ukrainian literature would include works mostly in Ukrainian. Finally, to illustrate further, a 5/5 E collection in German linguistics would be impossible, since a comprehensive collection level would require works in all applicable languages.

The compilation of these data for all contributing libraries provides the composite map which shows the various collection strengths and collecting policies for a given subject among the members. With that information we can determine whether there are adequate research resources within the consortium for that subject, whether there are endangered or neglected areas of concern to scholarship, and whether any member is willing to assume "primary collecting responsibility" (PCR) for the subject. Thus far, 315 primary collecting responsibilities have been assigned and accepted by member libraries, admittedly a relatively small number and often in narrow subject fields. These assignments have built on existing strengths in the consortium and in most cases required only the assurance that the member would maintain its present commitment to that field.

In order to test the validity of the assumptions and the data of the *Conspectus*, the Committee has engaged in a number of verification and overlap studies in such diverse fields as Russian literature, Swiss history, agricultural economics, Renaissance and Baroque art, and mathematics[2]. These studies have been helpful in improving the accuracy of reporting for the *Conspectus*, but in the vast majority of cases have confirmed the original evaluations made by the members about their collections. They have also illustrated in a concrete way not only the overlap and duplication among collections, but also the ways in which collections supplement each other to reach desired levels of research coverage.

As the data began to accumulate from the expanding membership and as more and more subject sections of the consepctus were developed, it became clear that the manual manipulation of the data would soon become very unwieldy, if not impossible. Thus, in 1980 we began work to program the *RLG Conspectus Online*, now a successful interactive database which can be searched by subject, classification, collection level, or institution. It is mounted as a special database within the Research Libraries Information Network (RLIN), and can best be regarded as the macro-bibliographic guide to the RLIN database (now containing over fourteen million records). Stated differently, the *Conspectus* is the guide map to the individual bibliographical records in the RLIN database as well as to member holdings not yet included in the database. As massive retrospective conversion projects proceed, extending the coverage of the RLIN database, the link between the map and the database will become closer.

The work on the *Conspectus* has now covered all Library of Congress subject categories except A (general) G (anthropology; U and V (military and naval science), and Z (bibliography), and has been completed in most of its parts by about twenty-five RLG members plus the Library of Congress. Three university libraries in Indiana (Indiana University, University of Notre Dame and Purdue University) have also completed certain segments of the *Conspectus*, and their data have been added to the online version as an initial step in the North American Collection Inventory Project.

One clear drawback of the original RLG attempt to create a composite picture of national collections and collecting practices was the fact that RLG membership did not include many of the most important library collections in the country. Even today its membership comprises only thirty-four of the 117 members of the Association of Research Libraries (ARL).

Concurrent with RLG efforts, that Association in 1980 also recognized the need to identify collection strengths nationally, and began to seek a way to realize that goal. It saw the desirability of building on existing work and in 1981 undertook a test of the *Conspectus* methodology in five non-RLG members (including one Canadian research library). The test clearly illustrated some of the same problems that RLG participants had encountered, but showed sufficient promise for the ARL to adopt the methodology as its national program, thus bridging the gap between RLG and other research libraries.

The second phase of ARL's work was the Indiana application noted above, all three participants being non-RLG libraries. That phase also included the preparation and publication of a *Manual for the North American Inventory of Research Library Collections*, published in January 1985, essentially a guide to *Conspectus* development for participating libraries. The *Manual* answered a long-felt need of RLG members and represents a model of interorganizational cooperation, aided of course by funding from outside sources.

A third phase of NCIP expansion has just been funded to aid further participation in the project by up to sixty libraries. In addition, the Canadian Association of Research Libraries is undertaking its own *Conspectus* development, including the difficult task of preparing a French translation of the worksheets (the reporting forms for *Conspectus* data). Other regional applications in the southeastern United States, in California, in the Pacific northwest, and even in Alaska, are proceeding apace. European library colleagues have also expressed interest in the approach and are watching our progress and problems with an appropriate critical detachment.

ISSUES AND PROBLEMS RELATED TO *CONSPECTUS* DEVELOPMENT

With all of the surprising and growing interest in this admittedly immature and evolving instrument, it would be well to share with you some of the difficulties we have encountered in attempting to develop a uniform (or at least unified) approach to national collection development.

1. *Subjectivity and Quantification:* From what I have said already, it should be obvious that the *Conspectus* data are an accumulation of thousands of subjective assessments by a diverse group of individuals (primarily selection officers), with a diversity of background and experience. The collections being described were often organized on varying principles of classification which could make comparison difficult and overemphasize or conceal strengths and weaknesses. To reduce the subjective element, some of our members argued for use of a shelflist measurement for each subject division to provide a precise count of the number of titles in that area. Others contended that a shelflist count would provide a measure of relative size, but could not indicate the strengths, quality, or cohesiveness of a given collection; in fact, it would represent the sum total of subjective judgements which went into the building of that subject collection.

The issue has not and probably cannot be fully resolved. Verification studies have helped to confirm or modify some *Conspectus* data. Current work of the RLG Task Force on Conspectus Analysis, a subcommittee which is charged with analysis of the data and which has overseen the distribution of primary collecting resonsibilities (PCRs), has been devoted to the development of benchmarks, or broad quantitative standards, for determining levels of strength in given areas. For example, a 4-level collection in the medical conspectus calls for "an extensive collection of periodicals, including at least 65 percent of the titles pertinent to the subject in the *List of Journals Indexed in Index Medicus*," while a 3-level collection would call for only 25 percent of the English titles listed there. A comprehensive collection in entomology would require 95 percent of the journals covered by *Entomology Abstracts*.

Such guidelines are still being developed and we believe will be helpful in substantiating conspectus assessments, but frankly they are unlikely to remove all doubts about the accuracy of conspectus information. I would merely emphasize that the tool is intended not as a precise representation but rather as a descriptive map.

2. *Arrangement:* The choice of Library of Congress classification as the organizing principle for the *Conspectus* did not come easily. In some areas there seemed to be excessive detail requiring such fine distinctions as to be meaningless. In others, especially in recently developing fields such as computer science, there were insufficient subcategories. Some members felt that in the latter case the data could not truly represent their real strengths in various subfields. Furthermore, not all of our libraries use the Library of Congress classification system (including The New York Public Library which like many European libraries, classifies its books by size). Many libraries have split collections with more recent books in LC classification, with older collections in Dewey Decimal classification or other schemes. Obviously the assessments for each library had to incorporate both elements of those split collections or translate the Dewey or other sections into the LC arrangement.

In the end we made a pragmatic decision to remain with Library of Congress classification through the *Conspectus* (although medicine is an exception). It is the most widely recognized standard nationally, especially among the research libraries in RLG and ARL. To compensate for the deficiencies noted, we have encouraged participants to add to individual section special "scope notes," revealing special characteristics of their collections which the LC arrangement might conceal. Nonetheless, I suspect there will always be individual specialists approaching the *Conspectus* and finding it wanting in the detail they desire.[3]

Curiously, one of our first debates was over how many subject divisions would be necessary to provide the broad picture we wanted to achieve. The estimate in 1980 was 1,500 to 2,000. We now show over 5,800 categories in the *Conspectus* and it continues to grow. Even with that large a number, the representation of specialized rare book and manuscript collections in the *Conspectus* is still far from adequate.

3. *Area Studies:* Allied to these questions was the desire of area studies librarians, those engaged in providing research resources concerning specific geographical regions such as East Asia, Africa, or Latin America, to create their own separate *Conspectus* to cover the whole universe of knowledge as applied in their own particular regions. How, for example, does the topic of the Shinto religion in Japan, relate to Shintoism in the Religion section of the *Conspectus*? What has emerged is a hybrid "two-track" configuration which allows the major area studies collections, embracing all classes of knowledge to convey their data individually. The indexing of the *Conspectus* online then enables us to retrieve data

lines from the various disciplines into a product which approximates an *Area Studies Conspectus*. Inconsistencies do occur and the system is far from perfect or comprehensive.

4. *Format Collections:* Another problem we encountered was the question of how to incorporate collections which were mainly determined by format rather than subject. Microform collections tend to reflect general collecting patterns, and maps usually involve geography and cartography, but other formats present unique problems. Government documents, recorded sound archives, manuscript and archival sections tend to be separately administered parts of our collections, unrelated to Library of Congress or other local classification schemes, and yet covering a myriad of subject fields.

Sometimes this separation can aid cooperative planning, as in the RLG program which has distributed cataloging responsibility for sound recordings by record company label. In other instances, both description and planning are more difficult. For example, subject disciplines which are mainly supported by journal and serial publications may be more difficult to evaluate and describe than are monograph collections. Distribution of responsibilities in these fields, mainly in scientific disciplines, is also more problematical. Again, scope-notes and cross references can help but the problems are not yet resolved and work on them continues.

5. *Language Codes:* Agreement on and use of the langauge codes, simple as they seem, has also presented difficulties for conspectus constructors. In the early stages of our work they were used sporadically and inconsistently, even though their value in distinguishing collection strength was commonly agreed upon. Moreover, the language code is normally only attached to the current collecting intensity, even though in the early work it was sometimes unclear whether it described the collection strength as well. This is an element of the *Conspectus* which has improved over the years and some degree of greater consistency has been achieved.

As interest in the *Conspectus* spreads, the issue of language codes will become more crucial, since the Anglophonic orientation will have to shift if the methodology is to be applied in other nations and language cultures. As the work of the Canadian Association of Research Libraries continues on the translation into French of the *Conspectus* and its worksheets, we hope to learn a great deal from their experience.

6. *Current Collecting Intensity:* For any given participant in the *Conspectus*, the sum total of all of its claims of current collecting intensity (CCI's) constitutes its de facto collection development policy. The question here is whether those claims are the desire (i.e., goals) of the library, or are, in fact, the actuality. Without a great deal of ongoing analysis in each separate area it is difficult to assess these claims and we are again dependent upon ultimately subjective and impressionistic criteria. The RLIN system is capable of generating management information from acquisitions and cataloging transactions which could help in this respect, but most of us have not been in a position to take full advantage of those possibilities. The true test will eventually be the level of user satisfaction of those who will use the distributed resources of the consortium as represented in the *Conspectus*.

7. *Logistics:* Obviously, the work which has already gone into the *Conspectus* represents a substantial investment of time and effort, and indirectly of money. The costs are not easily quantifiable; the process involves part-time work of most of the participants, extensive meetings and training sessions are often involved, and a great amount of paper work is generated before the data reach the online database. Questions therefore persist as to whether all this effort is worth it. I hope to provide some of the answer to that question in the conclusion of this paper, but at this point I would only note that most of that work—the analysis of the institutional collection development policies—involves not a new responsibility but a new element of traditional duties, engaging our bibliographers and selection officers in a realignment of duties with few additional costs. I should also note that the costs at RLG headquarters of programming the *RLG Conspectus Online*, of staff input of the data, and of program admininstration have been modest and partially covered by external funding.

Further work is required for refinement and expansion of the online *Conspectus*. Some reprogramming is needed to make the tool more user-friendly. We all agree that its present access and search strategies are somewhat unwieldly and cumbersome. We also need to develop transportable software for application of the methodology elsewhere. There are apparent limits to growth and effectiveness and we believe it may prove advantageous to mount other regional or national databases, such as the Canadian or California efforts, separately.

There is a further question of whether the eventual national *Conspectus* should include all collection data or be restricted to research and comprehensive level (4s and 5s) collections. That issue also awaits resolution as we gain more experience with this evolving tool.

8. *Local Political Considerations:* Given the tensions of independence and interdependence

emphasized at the outset of this paper, one must note that the *Conspectus* has been seen by some as a threat to the independent growth of collections. There are some fears that it will create restraints on individual collecting activities within participating institutions. Teaching faculty and researchers in universities may not wish to see primary responsibility in their areas of expertise assigned to other institutions, and may exert great pressure to avoid any reductions in collecting in their fields. Subject specialists and selection officers may not want to desist from their efforts to build competing collections.

Although we have consistently emphasized that assignments of primary collecting responsibility were not intended to inhibit or end collecting elsewhere—in fact, that continued collecting in other institutions was essential in achieving strong national coverage—these fears persist and are unlikely to disappear. Indeed, they may become more widespread as the program develops.

9. *Related Issues:* All of the foregoing deals directly with collection development practices and expanded approaches to them in a collaborative environment. Changing our collective behavior in collection development will, however, have wider implications for all library operations and raise related issues:

A. Document Delivery: In order to assure the widest possible access to research resources, especially when those resources are widely scattered, improvement in our document delivery system is required. Recently, the National Endowment for the Humanities, a federal agency supporting research in the humanities, has inaugurated a program to help scholars go to collections by providing small travel grants for specific research projects. Nonetheless, distribution of collections and collecting responsibilities still implies the need for rapid remote access. We believe that eventually electronic information transfer will answer part of this need in some areas of current research.

The RLG Shared Resources Program, in effect a priority interlibrary loan system, has placed a premium on rapid turn-around time in document delivery, by giving priority to member requests, but much remains to be done. Especially important are rare and less commonly held materials which owning institutions may not wish to lend, whether because of value, security, fragility, or local need. Surrogates or alternate copies are then required, but often take an unacceptable length of time to prepare. This is a key question of resource sharing and crucial for Universal Access to Publications (UAP).

B. Preservation. While the distribution of responsibilities in collecting can also be complemented by distribution of responsibilities in preservation, distribution may also threaten rather than enhance the survival of materials. The concerntration of use on a given collection, when the number of duplicative collections elsewhere is diminishing, would take its toll on those collections. Here we have to rely on the responsible collections to develop surrogate collections, for now primarily as master microfilms, from which working copies can be provided to users elsewhere. One thing is very clear: the preservation problem in the United States, with its 140-year history of bad paper and overheated libraries, is too big for any one library to address and there is no alternative to collaborative approaches. In fact, we believe it too great a problem for any one nation to handle and that international programs are required. In recent years we have seen some encouraging signs that movement in that direction can occur.

C. Bibliographical Control and Communication: In essence, a system of bibliographical control is a device for communicating information about collections. The RLIN database conveys information about specific holdings, additions, and changes. The *Conspectus* is also a commmunication tool which not only describes collection strengths and policies but enables members to convey changes in those policies as the individual (and autonomous) members make those changes. Current development of the Linked System Project, designed to allow different computer systems to communicate with one another, is another building block toward a truly national program of shared scholarly resources, a program which we again hope can spread beyond the boundaries of this country, improving document delivery, and eventually taking advantage of the potentials of full-text transmission.

D. Other problems of cooperation, nationally and internationally, are well-known to all of you and can be mentioned briefly. Language differences, the lack of agreed-upon standards, the speed of technological growth, the costs of cooperation and the relatively low level of library funding, problems of copyright, and the concomitant tendency toward charging fees for information are impediments to universal access and to the sharing of resources which we seek. But if we believe that scholarship matters, and that we have a vital role in the provision of adequate resources for research, we have to ask continually what are the alternatives to collaboration and the constant work of overcoming these barriers. Surely it is not the return to isolation—automation has effectively eliminated that choice, at least for libraries.

CONCLUSION

Since the focus of this paper has been on issues and problems of collaborative collection development, especially as seen in the RLG program, I will deal more briefly in conclusion with the more positive elements and byproducts of our work which give us some optimism that the problems can be overcome or at least minimized, and that our efforts have been worthwhile.

Although RLG was founded in a time of relative financial austerity in United States libraries, and although the initial motivation of the RLG collection development program was to reduce costs or at least to reduce the rate of cost increase in acquisitions, that, in fact, has not occurred. Apart from some substantial programs of serial cancellations (which were likely to occur independently in any case), to my knowledge no drastic cuts in collecting have yet been made by our members on the basis of *Conspectus* data, though there is no doubt that mutual reliance has increased. "The reality," as Scott Bennett, one of our Committee members, has recently said, "is that librarians are pursuing cooperative collection management (just as they have pursued automation) not to reduce costs but to improve services."[4]

Let me conclude with a brief description of some of the results of our work which have helped improve services while providing a framework for collaborative resource development. First, the *Conspectus* is an important reference tool, supplementing the RLIN database by enabling librarians to identify strong collections and likely locations for their users. The inclusion of NCIP participants, and others, will create the map of North American research collection strengths which we need for both collection development and public service referral purposes.

The engagement of hundreds of bibliographers and selection officers in the process of *Conspectus* building has been helpful in gaining a better understanding of their own collections and policies, and in greater awareness of supporting collections elsewhere. For many of our members it has provided a collection development policy (the aggregate of all the institution's *Conspectus* data), where none existed previously. Collectively, it has identified and addressed dozens of neglected and endangered areas of research not adequately covered by the member libraries.

The *Conspectus* has also provided a framework and capacity to relate collection development strengths to shared cataloging, retrospective conversion and preservation needs, and to serve as a basis for cooperative cataloging and national preservation planning.

For universities, the *Conspectus* has been used to enhance the library's role in institutional planning processes by providing better information on collections as they relate to changing academic programs. It has also helped establish a process to involve faculty more closely in collection development, while serving faculty more effectively by improved access to materials located elsewhere. It has also identified local deficiencies which have to be addressed locally, thus demonstrating to administrative officers the need for additional support, as well as suggesting fundraising opportunities.

Perhaps most importantly, the Conspectus constitutes an insurance policy against reduced budgets, the framework for redistribution of our own financial resources, and the groundwork for wide access. It is no panacea for budget woes. Richard DeGennaro expressed the issue recently in these words:

We must husband [our] existing resources and increase them in the future. It would be a tragedy if those who fund our libraries were to misunderstand the purpose of resource sharing and use it as a rationale for further reducing library appropriations. Resource sharing will permit us to do more with less by pooling our resources, but only if we keep the pool replenished.[5]

Notes

1. For a history and description of the *Conspectus*, see Nancy E. Gwinn and Paul H. Mosher, "Coordinating Collection Development: The RLG Conspectus," *College & Research Libraries*, March 1983. A manual on use of the *Conspectus* for the National Collection Inventory Project has been prepared by Jutta Scott-Reed and was published in January 1985 by the Association of Research Libraries, Washington, D.C.
2. RLG's verification studies have used a variety of statistical techniques to test the claims of its members concerning their collection strengths in given areas. The overlap studies are designed to test the redundancy or uniqueness of holdings within the membership.
3. We should emphasize that in our work the subject headings rather than the class numbers were the significant factor for analysis. For a recent analysis of the problems connected with the LC classes, see Thomas E. Nisonger, "Editing the RLG Conspectus...," *Library Resources and Technical Services* (Oct.-Dec. 1985): pp.309-27.
4. Scott Bennett, "Current Initiatives and Issues in Collection Management," *Journal of Academic Librarianship*, vol. 10, no. 5, pp. 257-61.
5. "Resource Sharing in a Network Environment," *Library Journal* 105 (1980): p. 355.

Think Globally— Collection Development

David H. Stam

... I use these more dramatic literary examples to illustrate one of the illusions associated with cooperative collection development, namely the notion that with adequate distribution of responsibilities we can reintroduce the notion of complete coverage of all material.

Some of you may be familiar with the music of a somewhat offbeat rock group called *The Police,* and specifically their song called "Too Much Information." The most qualified teenagers I know are unable to decode all of the words, but for the uninitiated, it goes something like this with a fair amount of repetition:

Too much information
Running through my brain
Too much information
Driving me insane

Seen the whole world six times over
Seen the passage. . . .

Overkill, overkill, over my dead body,
Over me, over you, over everybody

Too much information
Running through my brain
Too much information
Driving me insane

Stop. . . .

That song may seem an odd point of departure for a discussion of resource sharing, but it does, as far as I can judge, illustrate one of the two major concerns of resource sharing: the sheer quantity of information with which we have to cope. The other, quality, might best be seen in "The Sixth Sally" of Stanislaw Lem's Fables for the Cybernetic Age called *The Cyberiad*.[2] In that story, Lem's two hero-constructors venture into the wastelands of extra-galactic space to find an insatiable robot named Pugg whose Faustian dream was to know everything. Pugg was rusting out his mechanistic life collecting "precious facts, priceless knowledge, and in general all information of value." When Pugg encounters the invaders he holds them captive until they promise to construct a machine, with a printout tape which would select out of all the possibilities of jostling atoms only that information which has meaning.

The story suffers in my summary, but what Pugg eventually gets from this Metainformationator is a wonderful litany of golden fleece awards. The constructors manage to escape while "poor Pugg, crushed beneath that avalanche of facts, learns no end of things about rickshaws, rents and roaches, and about his own fate, which has been related here, for that too is included in some section of the tape—as are the histories, accounts and prophecies of all things in creation, up until the day the stars burn out; and there is no hope for him, since this is the harsh sentence the constructors passed upon him for his pirately assault—unless of course the tape runs out, for lack of paper." But before that happens Pugg realizes that "all this information, entirely true and

208

Act Locally:
and Resource Sharing

meaningful in every particular, was absolutely useless, producing such an ungodly confusion that his head ached terribly and his legs trembled."

That may be a good description of how research librarians often feel in facing what's now known as The Glut, but few of us are able to take refuge or comfort in the other extreme, the library of *Walden Two:*[3]

> As to a library, we pride ourselves on having the best books, if not the most. Have you ever spent much time in a large college library? What trash the librarian has saved up in order to report a million volumes in the college catalogue! Bound pamphlets, old journals, ancient junk that even the shoddiest secondhand bookstore would clear from its shelves—all saved on the flimsy pretext that some day someone will want to study the "history of a field." Here we have the heart of a great library—not much to please the scholar or specialist, perhaps, but enough to interest the intelligent reader for life. Two or three thousand volumes will do it.

The novel does refer elsewhere to an old barn where all the weeded books are kept for the insatiably curious, but obviously there are few in *Walden Two.* Skinner's hero gives, to the best of my knowledge, a unique fictional accolade to the collection development librarian, based solely on good choices.

There are of course more serious arguments for selectivity in collection development policies, such as Margit Kraft's landmark article in the *Library Quarterly* in 1967 and the more recent

work sponsored by the Rockefeller Foundation on *Coping with the Biomedical Literature.* But I use these more dramatic literary examples to illustrate one of the illusions associated with cooperative collection development, namely the notion that with adequate distribution of responsibilities we can reintroduce the notion of complete coverage of all material. Even in a wide sharing environment such a goal remains chimerical and is in any case not a desirable objective—one of the elements of sharing has to be the expertise needed for the right filtration devices or the quality control on what goes into our collections.

In considering collection development in a resource sharing environment, we have to ask at the outset whether that environment in fact exists. We do of course hear a good deal of lip service to the ideals of cooperation, often tinged with a sense of desperation at our inability to keep up even with our past performance or to meet the local demands placed on us. But we also hear considerable argument against the notion, including charges of a communistic conspiracy to defraud publishers of their captive markets and accusations that we are selling out on individual responsibilities which we ought to fight harder to honor without jumping on some cooperative band wagon. Apropos of costs, it is often argued that cooperation won't save money, that access to shared materials may be as expensive as purchasing them, that prices will rise as orders decline, and that it will be even more expensive, if not impossible, to fill gaps if sharing agreements fail.

In terms of service, some argue that "con-

Despite the alleged aloofness and elitism of large research libraries, you must all realize . . . that all libraries are linked in a great chain of access and that what each has and does will have importance for the whole universe of libraries and their users.

209

ventional resource sharing is cumbersome, un-reliable, and frustrating" (Downes) and a disservice to users who want material at hand as soon as they need it. Others contend that cooperative agreements create inevitable hardships for larger institutions which must always place the interests of their own constituents above those of outsiders. Nor can those large institutions rely on the agreements made by other institutions where resources may be reallocated as priorities and programs change. Others fear that the distribution of collection responsibilities will lead to the decline of the collection and quality of all participating libraries.

In considering collection development in a resource sharing environment, we have to ask at the outset whether that environment in fact exists.

As a believer, I don't intend to comment on these doubts, except to note that among the many cogent arguments remains an ostrich-like case against change and for business as usual. Unfortunately, in collection development matters, business as usual no longer works for any of us. Over the past three years, the Collection Management and Development Committee of the Research Libraries Group has attempted to face these problems with the clear purpose of assuring adequate coverage of the research materials needed within the membership in particular, and for scholarship in general. Although our membership, especially in the early days, represented a small fraction of the research libraries of the nation, we did hope to form the basis of a shared national collection development plan, identifying areas of strength and neglect, and to see what we could do about them.

From the beginning we made certain assumptions which have been tested along the way. One assumption was the voluntary nature of our association—that there would be no central authority reducing the autonomy of individual members, but that their own enlightened self-interest would be adequate for participation. We also assumed that a prime requirement for the national scheme we envisioned was an effective means of communication of the intentions, decisions, and alterations in policy which members might make. We believed that the failure of the Farmington Plan was largely due to the lack of such communication. For the most part we put aside or left to others the questions of access, sharing of resources, and delivery systems on the assumption that there could be no access without coverage. We also took seriously the term collection management in our name, especially in seeing a close relationship between collection building and collection maintenance or preservation.

The RLG Conspectus

Our first order of business and our most difficult task was and is to assess what the current collection development policies and practices of the participants are. Building on much of the work of this Committee, we developed a device now known as the RLG *conspectus*. The conspectus is intended to provide a composite picture of collection strengths and current collecting intensities by Library of Congress subject fields, using a numerical range of designators from zero (out of scope for that collection) to five (a comprehensive collection). Literally hundreds of selection officers in individual libraries have been involved in describing collection strengths and collection policies on worksheets used to submit the raw data to RLG central staff. The Library of Congress has participated in this work from the beginning and more recently five non-RLG members of ARL have been testing selected subject areas of the conspectus with a view to adoption of this methodology of collection analysis by other members of ARL. Concurrently, we have been pursuing the development work for putting the conspectus online as a special database, thus answering our original desideratum for an efficient communication device to indicate changes in policy throughout the network.

I won't dwell on the various problems we have encountered in the development of this tool, the recurrent concern for the problem of excessive subjectivity, the arguments over language codes, the detail or lack of detail in L. C. subject breakdowns, the need for uniformity of approach among diverse bibliographers, the peculiar problems presented by area studies. We do believe that the most critical stage in conspectus building is in very careful review of the comparative data after it is first tabulated. Reasonable assessments can sometimes look quite different when compared to other known collections. We have a great deal more work to do in that respect, though we have put together a remarkable amount of raw data about our collections and collecting policies.

While our original purpose in developing the conspectus was for communication and for the assignment of primary collection responsibilities (known as PCRs), we were somewhat surprised to find that our work also yielded a number of by-products. It has and will be useful in identifying regional as well as national strengths. It has already indicated a number of fields uncovered by RLG librarians; although these may be covered in non-member libraries it has been helpful for us to know of these weaknesses.

For the public service librarians the conspectus is already useful in referring readers to strong collections elsewhere and for general questions of interlibrary loan sources. For members who had no formal collection development policy the conspectus has in effect created one, without all the agony that many of us experienced. In a few cases the conspectus analysis has pointed out funding possibilities for specific areas of weaknesses in our collections. To many of us it has been an important training device in introducing collection evaluation issues to many staff. The most important advantage, it seems to me, for staff at all levels, is that in getting to know something about other collections, our staffs have also learned more about their own. I don't want to underestimate the problems and the uncertainties involved, or the need for more quantitative measures to confirm or change the subjective judgments that we have made. All in all the work of this Committee has been a very positive experience from which I hope many will eventually benefit.

That brings me to my final point and at last to the title I've chosen for this article. Despite the alleged aloofness and elitism of large research libraries, you must all realize, no matter what the nature of your own institution, that all libraries are linked in a great chain of access and that what each has and does will have importance for the whole universe of libraries and their users.

Research libraries are dependent on a whole range of libraries to provide services which large libraries can't provide well or which they couldn't afford to pick up if the smaller libraries didn't exist. In turn, the libraries of *Walden Two* can rely on us as the over-grown barns which even the apostles of selectivity recognize as a necessity. What I want to emphasize is that resource sharing does not remove in any way the obligation for any institution to fulfill its local mission.

In Rene Dubos' last book, *Celebrations of Life*,[4] there is a lengthy section from which I've taken my title: Think Globally but Act Locally. His story behind that phrase is that in lecturing at universities on environmental matters he often met faculty and students who were concerned, if not outraged, about environmental pollution, oil spills, atomic waste disposal etc., but left their own dormitories, cafeterias, and campuses a mess, and their social relationships in disorder. I find the analogy to libraries apt. Resource sharing is a necessity and it will continue to grow. But it has to grow from a strong local base, one which defines the individual institution's mission clearly and carries it out well.

I want to end with a brief passage from the final section of the Dubos book, appropriately called "Optimism Despite it All," and as you read it you can substitute library terms for the human ones he uses:

> This is not the best of times, but it is nevertheless a time for celebration because, even though we realize our insignificance as part of the cosmos and as individual members of the human family, we know that each one of us can develop a persona which is unique, yet remains part of the cosmic and human order of things. Human beings have been and remain uniquely creative because they are able to integrate the pessimism of intelligence with the optimism of Will.

Properly translated that represents the challenge of resource sharing.

References

1. The Police. "Too Much Information," from *Ghost in the Machine*. (Hollywood, Calif.: A & M Records, 1981.) (A&M SP3730).

2. Stanislaw Lem. *The Cyberiad: Fables for the Cybernetic Age*. (New York: Avon Books, 1980), pp. 119-134. First English edition, 1974.

3. B. F. Skinner. *Walden Two*. (New York: Macmillan, 1948), p. 121.

4. Rene Dubos. *Celebrations of Life*. (New York: McGraw Hill, 1981), Sections 3 and 6, p. 251.

Resource sharing is a necessity and it will continue to grow. But it has to grow from a strong local base, one which defines the individual institution's mission clearly and carries it out well.

Regional Cooperation for Research Collections

Medea Ionesco

With the dramatic expansion of information and of library users' need to access that information, cooperative collection development has become an increasingly attractive option. Debate in this area has recently been enriched by the simultaneous publication of articles by Ross Atkinson[1] and David H. Stam.[2] Against a vast background of literature already accumulated, we now have what might be considered a state-of-the-art basis for further discussions.

A related major development is the Research Libraries Group's Conspectus. Originating as a project among four major research libraries (Harvard, Yale, Columbia, and the New York Public Library), the RLG Conspectus soon emerged as a national system, responding to basic needs which in the past had been met by the Farmington Plan.

"The need to identify collection strength nationally"[3] is the logical first step of a project for cooperative collection development; it is a consequence of the idea of providing collective resources for research libraries nationwide. Practically, however, cooperation in collection development is going to be conducted on a regional, rather than on a national basis. The RLG program included among its objectives "rationalization and standardization of format and terminology of local collection development policies." These are, of course, preconditions for an effective collaboration at a regional level. And indeed, Conspectus makes possible and facilitates such cooperation. This result is a derivative one, a by-product of a program conceived and developed on a national basis.

The purpose of collaboration in collection development at a regional level is to ensure the necessary resources for research through an interdisciplinary approach. The Conspectus analysis of the collections is based on the extant Library of Congress class divisions, which are then broken down into specific categories.

The core of the standard collection development policies, writes Atkinson, "consists of a series of subject categories." That is "the heart of the policy," and it consists of "the segmentation of the collection into subjects, and the rating of the quality of each subject segment according to the system of collection levels."[4]

Undoubtedly, this statement describes the existing situation. The implicit premise for the development of a research collection is to develop all its component parts in corresponding proportion. The transition in this case is from particular to general, from the elementary subdivision of the collection to its multidisciplinary character. It follows that as collaboration on a regional basis is derived from a national plan, so the creation of a multilateral collection is derived from a presumed harmonious development of the constituent parts of the collection. This secondary status of efforts directed towards creating research resources at a regional level entails the risk that they might not be fully realized.

It is tempting to concentrate on developing various subdivisions of the collection, and imagine them to be "the heart of the policy." Traditionally, librarians have had to be subject-oriented. The cataloging system, the bibliographic expertise, the system of budgetary allocations to a large extent continue to be based on subject divisions. More than any other professional group, librarians live in what Magoroh Maruyama calls "the classificational universe." It is a static universe, consisting of substances classifiable into mutually exclusive categories, organized into a hierarchical structure of superdivisions and subdivisions. This universe, according to Maruyama's definition, generates "classificational information." The purpose of this type of information is to specify "categories as narrowly as possible."

EVENT-ORIENTED CLASSIFICATION

In the classificational universe, knowledge "is primarily knowledge about *something*." The division into subject matter "aims to answer the question *what* the study is about." The classificational universe and its corresponding type of information are contrasted with the relational universe and relational information. Instead of substance-oriented, they are event-oriented. The basic question is no more "What is it?" but "How is it related to others?" A dog sitting on a chair, to use Maruyama's plastic example, is purely "accidental" in the classificational universe, since there is no connection between the dog and the chair. "But in the relational universe, the relationship between the dog and the chair is not only obvious, but it is more important than the fact that the chair belongs to the plant kingdom and the dog to the animal kingdom."

Maruyama's ideas about a "meta-organization of information"[5] are still as valid for libraries' current activities as they were two decades ago. In substance they advocate a recognition of the relational universe in comparison with the classificational one, and of corresponding types of information.

The concept of relational information is making its way into libraries, not so much as theory, but as practice. The RLG Conspectus project contributed a great deal in this respect. In evaluating a research collection of French literature, Jeffrey Larson arrived at the following conclusion: "The methodology reinforced the fact that French literature is more than French literature." He goes on to explain, "It is impossible to limit titles to the PC or

PQ classes of the Library of Congress and still pretend to a research collection in French: this is not a shelf-list assessment project."[6] Indeed, boundaries have eroded in the past decade. French literature is not studied as a separate phenomenon. In current research, several other important fields are included: history, politics, philosophy, sociology, demography, and linguistics. Comparisons among cultures are also necessary. Other subjects are equally interrelated—social sciences, humanities and even the so-called exact sciences.

What then constitutes a level-four research collection? Conventionally, it is a collection containing 75-85 percent of titles that are considered important in a specific subject. The Center for Research of Air and Space Law at McGill University has a vast collection on its subject. Even if the Center had 100 percent of titles considered important, however, it would still not be enough to confer on the collection a research character in its full significance.

The idea of a relational universe and the corresponding need for relational information emerges clearly from one of the Center's scientific reports: "The space era now requires an osmosis of interchange of information of various sciences in order to avoid diversity [uncoordinated information] in a field which may—through lack of coordination—lead to erroneous results if not catastrophes that, by their very nature, could be fatal to world existence. Therefore, the manner in which society might find it useful to try to survive in the future would be by a periodical, if not constant, interchange of information and cooperation within various domains—political, legal, economic and technical—and from this approach should be inspired studies such as the one that we are projecting. It therefore follows that this study should be essentially interdisciplinary in nature, and it was thus conceived." Sources of information for the project supplementing the specific law literature include: rocket and space transportation systems, direct broadcast satellites, remote sensing technology, the use of solar energy, cultural, political and military implications, and so on.

Trying to demonstrate the interdisciplinary character of law research institute is so obvious that it is like forcing an open door. But sometimes it is necessary to remember that the interdisciplinary approach is valid for all areas of knowledge. New scientific disciplines continuously emerge. Edward E. Edwards made a comprehensive analysis of this process at the International Conference on Interdisciplinarity in 1983 at Dubrovnik. He dealt in detail with the way in which interaction stimulates the process of increasing specialized innovation.

New disciplines appear through a process of fusion under the influence of an external discipline (biochemistry, economic history, aerodynamics) or through the application of a common technique (thermodynamics, cristallography, spectroscopy, etc.). Some new disciplines appear under the stimulus of practical or professional needs. According to Edwards, "In the broader fields of social practice, environmental and ecological studies arise from a broad marriage of chemical, physical, technological, social and ethical sciences." At the same time we witnessed the proliferation of new area studies of an ethical nature: peace studies, community studies, liberation studies, etc. Edwards' conclusion deserves close examination: "These interdisciplinary innovations arose spontaneously rather [than] from any deliberate policy. They arose very largely in research and in application rather than primarily in teaching."[7]

INTERDISCIPLINARY COLLECTIONS

Keep in mind that the needs for teaching--undergraduate and graduate--are covered basically by a level-three collection. The qualitative difference of a level-four collection is that it must necessarily be interdisciplinary in character. In fact, we can hardly speak about a level-four collection in any particular subject unless it is supported by all the interrelated disciplines. For practical purposes, the research resources should be available in a given geographical area. This idea is basic to collaboration in regional collection development. As we have seen, such collaboration, although facilitated by the Conspectus project, has not yet been achieved. The process of collection development parallels the process of interdisciplinary innovations in its spontaneous character. Conclusion: the most that can be done is "an advocacy of perfect freedom and unlimited resources to the highly talented individual."[8]

Libraries to parallel must create a regional collection development strategy. Such a strategy, even if it didn't achieve the dream of unlimited resources for research, could still optimize the supply of research materials within a given geographic area. Cooperation in regional collection development does not need to be debated. No one needs convincing that an academic library cannot be a self-sufficient unit. Regional cooperation should result in more efficient use of common resources. We can envision such cooperation on a multi-tier level. For example, assuming a plan for cooperation in collection development originated in Montreal, the primary level of coopera-

tion would be among the four local universities (McGill, Concordia, Université de Montréal, I'UQAM) supported by a secondary level within a 200-mile radius (Québec City, Ottawa, Kingston), and a third level composed of libraries beyond this limit (Toronto, New York, Boston, Washington, D.C., etc.).

Similar groupings for cooperative collection development could be formed elsewhere. Physical access to resources is one of the major factors affecting cooperation on different levels. To a certain extent, an informal, unstructured cooperation has always been in place. For libraries in the Montréal area, for example, no agreement was necessary to establish that, for studies of French-Canadian civilization, one can rely on the resources of the Bibliothéque Nationale du Québec. A strong collection on the history of economic thought at Concordia University, in French linguistics an Université de Montréal, or in East European studies at McGill can also be relied upon by the local universities, even in the absence of a formal agreement. This is a kind of cooperation in collection development that has arisen spontaneously. While it is, of course, useful, it is also likely that a conscious, planned effort would uncover many untapped reserves.

Some of the obstacles to such cooperation are described by David Stam as local political considerations: the fear that it will be "a threat to the independent growth of collections" and that "it will create restraints on individual collecting activities." These are psychological impediments, which might eventually be overcome. There are also objective impediments: the lack of detailed knowledge about the contents of the collections and the acquisition processes of the libraries which are the potential partners in cooperation.

The conditions are not yet ripe for planned regional collection development, but they are on their way. Fiels recently observed that "a formal plan is the last key element"[9] in coordinating resource development. Participation in the Conspectus and the retrospective conversion projects are going to create the conditions still missing.

In anticipation, it might be useful to develop a strategy for regional cooperation. How can this be achieved? The answer could only be found through collective efforts. The aim of cooperative collection development should be to create an optimum regional basis for research. It goes without saying that it must be interdisciplinary in character. The methodology for evaluating such a program exists: it is the Conspectus methodology, extended from individual libraries to a regional profile.

The reason for such an extension derives from the very nature of a research collection. A collection at level four in any subject goes beyond the subject itself and exceeds the needs of the current teaching process. It is therefore unreasonable to duplicate the collection within the same geographic region, especially at a local level. This idea is in the background of the Conspectus itself. What else could be the ultimate purpose of trying to determine the current collecting intensity (CCI) of various libraries? We are interested in knowing not just the claims of the CCI but also the way in which they are brought into reality. David Stam expressed a legitimate skepticism regarding the concordance between claims and reality and concluded, "The true test will eventually be the...satisfaction of those who will use the distributed resources of the consortium as represented in the Conspectus."[10] The level of user satisfaction is incontestably the final test, but it can be known only *post-factum*. The question is—is it possible to plan in advance for user satisfaction?

A regional collection development plan should be based on the same methodology used for individual libraries. It would have to determine:

The region's current collection strength.

The planned collection intensity of the region.

The effective current collecting intensity of the region.

CURRENT COLLECTION STRENGTH

A precondition for determining current collection strength is completing the RECON project in all participant libraries. This yields the number of titles in each subject by eliminating the effect of duplication. The level of collection strength of the region can be defined as a percentage of the total extant literature, or by comparing it to the combined resources of a number of research libraries.

In assessing current collection strength, it should be kept in mind that the necessity for retrospective materials varies from one discipline to another. It might be useful to take as a standard of comparison not the total volume of literature in various disciplines, but the volume of important titles. Although it would be an enormous task to determine which are "important titles," it could be done if librarians and subject specialists collaborate.

PLANNED COLLECTION INTENSITY

The planned collecting intensity for a region is expressed by the level of collecting stated in the selection profiles for various disciplines at the participating libraries. Once a detailed knowledge of the region's collection strength becomes available, desirable levels of collecting in various libraries may be rationally determined. The problem is a complex one as it must project teaching and research evolution at the participating universities. Yet, knowing the strengths of various collections permits a realistic basis for dividing primary collecting responsibilities (PCR).

EFFECTIVE CURRENT COLLECTING INTENSITY

The effective current collecting intensity can be determined by comparing the number of titles acquired in various disciplines with the total publishing output, or preferably with the quantity of "important titles" published. As in evaluating current collection strength, "important titles" will have to be determined through the combined efforts of librarians and subject experts. Knowing the number of titles acquired by each library cannot be sufficient for this purpose. One reason is that subject assignment cannot always be properly determined at the moment of acquisition. Also, the most important titles often cannot be judged immediately after publication. Statistics for annual cataloged titles by each library in various disciplines can better serve this purpose. One should, of course, take into consideration the problem of cataloging backlog, but differences from one year to another should cancel this out. Participating libraries should adhere to a homogeneous statistical standard, thus creating a basis for comparing claims of current collecting intensity with reality.

These steps would, in fact, constitute a plan for user satisfaction. If budgetary shortfalls caused gaps to develop, the system would at least reveal where the gaps are, making it possible to mobilize efforts to solve problems and minimize user dissatisfaction.

Regional planning is necessary to give users access to a greater wealth of research resources. Technological advances in electronic information transfer will eventually solve some of the problems of physical access to resources. In the meanwhile, the commitment to cooperate and the readiness to share resources is essential to the success of regional collection development. It is not a panacea, but it is certainly a better alternative to lack of coordination in collection development.

Notes

1. Atkinson, Ross. "The Language of the Levels: Reflections on the Communication of Collec-

tion Development Policy." *College and Research Libraries* v. 47 (March 1986): pp. 140-149.

2. Stam, David H. "Collaborative Collection Development: Progress, Problems and Potential." *Collection Building* VII:3 (1986) pp. 3-9.

3. Gwin, Nancy E. and Mosher, Paul H. "Coordinating Collection Development: The RLG Conspectus." *College and Research Libraries* v. 44, no. 2 (March 1983), p. 130.

4. Atkinson, Ross, p. 142.

5. Maruyama, Magoroh. "Metaorganization of Information." *General Systems* v.Xi (1966): pp. 55-60.

6. Larson, Jeffry. "The RLG French Literature Collection Assessment Project." *Collection Management* 1/2 (spring/summer 1984), p. 108.

7. Edwards, E.G. "Interdisciplinarity. The Relation Between Objective Knowledge, Moral Purpose and Social Practice." *Bulletin of the Inter-University Centre of Postgraduate Studies (IUC) Dubrovnik, V.I.:* Hamburg, Inter-University Centre for Postgraduate Studies, Dubrovnik, 1983, pp. 42-43.

8. Stam, David H., p. 8.

9. Fiels, Keith Michael. "Edwin Beckerman: Administrator's Viewpoint. Coordinated Collection Development in a Multitype Environment: Promise and Challenge." *Collection Building XII:2 (Summer 1985), p. 29.*

10. Stam, David H., p. 7.

Managing Collections in an Automated Network Environment

Anne Marie Allison

The goals of cooperation and collection management in academic libraries may sometimes seem mutually exclusive. Individual institutional objectives may compete and conflict with the objectives of networking partners. The political and financial forces driving a college affect its librarians' commitments to cooperative resource sharing. Today's librarians face problems analogous to those of counselors in social service organizations. A mental health agency's counselors have obligations to society, to their profession, to clients, and to the specific agency unit where they practice (comparable in a university setting to the library). Further, they have ethical ties to a large parent organization (which would be comparable in the academic library model to the university or college itself).

In 1953, there were only three state universities in Florida: The University of Florida, founded in 1853; Florida State, founded in 1857; and Florida Agricultural and Mechanical University, founded in 1887. Today, nine universities make up the State University System (SUS). They are all full-service institutions. In 1953, 100 years after its founding, UF enrolled 11,000 students. In contrast, the University of Central Florida (UCF) (typical of the newer state universities) accepted its first enrollment of 17,500 students. As might be expected, the growth of library collections was affected by the life experience of their parent institutions.

The SUS universities are not as independent as their counterparts in Ohio or Michigan, but they do not follow the single-institution model found in North Carolina or California. The SUS is made up of nine separate universities in one system. The two most senior institutions are in Tallahassee and Gainesville, at considerable distances from the major population centers, while the newer universities are close to the concentrations of business and industry. A single Board of Regents (BOR) headed by one chancellor oversees the system. Florida's legislature is involved, at a significant level of detail through the budget process, in the operations of state-supported higher education. A member of the National Council for Accreditation of Teacher Education (NCATE), during a recent visit, noted the specificity of this legislative oversight of the university system and characterized the relationship as intrusive. Collections in the newer schools hold a greater proportion of microform than is typical of universities of similar size in other states. During their relatively brief existence, the newer libraries were energized by the focus on audiovisual media that characterized the sixties; and they lived through the introduction of library automation, the copyright anxiety of the 1970's, the Florida Union List of Serials (FULS), OCLC, AACRII, the trauma of LC's catalog closing, and finally, networking. Each of these events must be considered in analyzing collections and the management of those collections, as well as planning for resource sharing. UF and FSU, the two senior libraries, are members of the Association of Research Libraries (ARL) and (since the 1984-1985 academic year) of the Research Libraries Group (RLG). These two institutions, as well as the University of South Florida (USF), are members of the Association of Southeastern Research Libraries (ASERL). What follows is the author's subjective—not official—study.

FUNDING STRATEGIES

The SUS libraries are funded directly by the legislature through the BOR in an annual budget process. The question "How much money should the library receive?" is not answered on-campus. Library salaries and operations and materials budgets are determined at the state level. Individual institutions may provide additional dollars for their own libraries, an option that is sometimes exercised, but such internal allocation takes place at the expense of other institutional priorities.

After the system identifies the amount to be spent for the university libraries as a whole, it divides these funds among the nine institutions by using the Washington Formula. Before 1983, Florida's SUS libraries used the original Washington Formula, which applied variables such as number of programs, number of graduate and undergraduate students, and number of faculty. Since 1983, Florida has relied on the New Washington Formula, which is inventory-driven. It has been summed up as: "The more you have, the more you get." Some attempt is made to counteract the influence of size on its application, but the Formula has nevertheless tended to increase disproportions, awarding additional resources to those libraries with greater basic inventories.

The choice of the Formula to distribute funds among the SUS Libraries was well intentioned. The BOR and the legislature were committed to use an objective measure that would respond to needs rather than to politics. However, most Florida librarians now agree that the Formula does not equitably share funds among the nine universities. They do not agree on just what alternate distribution model would be more acceptable.

The New Formula was put into place in 1983-1984, when the legislature decreed that steady funding for libraries would be continued each year. Before that time, support for the libraries had fluctuated. There was a period, during the late 1970's, when significant added monies were made available for purchase of books, *without* a parallel increase in staffing. As a result, some of

the libraries held books unprocessed for several years. There were lean years, notably 1982-1983, when funding was so low that most of the SUS libraries could do no more than maintain subscriptions, with zero funding available for new monographs.

Some of the difficulty with the Formula is caused by the fact that the state universities in Washington were founded during the late nineteenth century and the early 20th century. Their libraries are relatively mature. The Formula was designed as a means of distributing resources among such a group, and it might be effective with another group of schools, comparable to those in Washington. It might also be used effectively with a group of newer institutions in areas with steady or declining demographics. In Florida, however, the Formula is applied in a situation where several institutions are experiencing rapid growth. This causes unfortunate results, especially in the SUS libraries at Miami, Tampa, and Orlando. They are Florida International University (FIU), USF, and UCF.

Application of the Formula produces a "resource unit entitlement" for each library. This entitlement forecasts a number of units, i.e., volumes required to move the library forward at an appropriate rate in a particular year. Having identified the number of resource units needed for each library, the Formula then multiplies that number by a per-volume average cost, based on the latest *Bowker Annual* estimated cost of a U.S. tradebook. The SUS university library directors object to use of the *Bowker* figure, pointing out that the average includes prices for popular fiction and children's books. This skews results and does not fit the profile of university libraries, where per-volume costs are affected by fugitive, esoteric, and society publications; the out-of-print market; materials published outside the U.S.; and fluctuations in international currencies. Relying on this figure has been especially unsatisfactory for institutions whose academic programs demand significant purchasing in the scientific and technical areas and whose literatures depend heavily on journals and monographs with a short half-life. Notwithstanding these difficulties, the directors finally agreed that having convinced the legislature to provide a sustained pattern of funding, they might be ill-advised to second-guess the Formula. Such a challenge could result in changes even less satisfactory.

The choice of the Washington Formula is an example of well meaning assistance that proved disappointing. It is also an example of poor transferability from one situation to another—the formula may have worked in Washington, but did not meet Florida's needs. It is interesting to note that the state of Washington no longer uses the Formula.

EXPLORING INNER SPACE

During the late 1970 s, several of the SUS libraries faced serious space problems related to services as well as collections. Some of them were contemplating new construction. The state considered building a remote storage facility to gather less-used items from all of the SUS libraries to a central location. Instead, in the spring of 1980, Richard Boss was chosen from a list of consultants and invited by the BOR to provide background for decision making. With Deanna Marcum, he visited the nine main campuses and their library facilities. Their report, *A Comprehensive Review of Library Facilities and Technological Changes for Improving Libraries in the SUS,*[1] recommended, among other things, that the libraries consider incorporating a weeding factor of ten percent of current annual acquisitions, change their planning horizon from five to ten years, and explore ways of making major capital equipment funds available as an alternative to construction funds. Boxx and Marcum pointed out that the SUS libraries lacked incentives to use technology to save space (surely a form of collection management). They suggested electro-mechanical compact storage, substitution of microform for binding back issues of journals, and development of a cost model for retrospective conversion of serials to microform. One of their most interesting suggestions, from the point of view of collection management, was that the existing courier service be improved, to upgrade the interlibrary loan process. The report acknowledged the advent of telefacsimile transmission, but speculated that it would probably not be cost effective to reproduce and transmit the text of entire books in hard copy. In this, the 1981 report was clearly on target.

JOINT VENTURES

Resource sharing, on a formal and informal basis, has existed in Florida for some time. One extraordinarily successful joint venture is the Florida Library Information Network (FLIN). It is a Library Service and Construction Act (LSCA)-assisted interlibrary loan cooperative, and has operated under the leadership of the State Librarian since 1968. The State Library's Bureau of Interlibrary Cooperation is the unit responsible for FLIN coordination. FLIN operates with a policy board, consisting of librarians from publicly and privately funded libraries of all sizes and types. It relies heavily on the SUS libraries, the University of Miami, and a group of major public libraries, designated resource libraries. Nevertheless, one of its notable strengths is the fact that small libraries regularly assist and support their larger neighbors.

Two model regional networks are currently active in the state. The oldest is the Southeast Florida Library Information Network (SEFLIN). It includes the University of Miami as well as two of the SUS libraries: Florida Atlantic University (FAU) and FIU. It also includes two significant public library systems, headquartered in Miami and Fort Lauderdale. By fall of 1988, 11 libraries will participate as members. Founded with an LSCA grant in 1984, SEFLIN is a multi-type cooperative, providing interlibrary loan, telefacsimile, and a courier service. A SEFLIN reference librarian, resident at the University of Miami's main facility, provided on-demand reference service to all the member institutions on a contract through the 1987-1988 academic year. The participating libraries recently decided that the demand for this special service was not great enough to continue the contract. Originally, the Broward County Public Library underwrote the salary of a SEFLIN Coordinator, who had responsibilities to the Broward system in addition to her work with the network. In the 1988-1989 fiscal year, the network's LSCA grant funds will have been exhausted and the network is currently in the process of becoming an independent corporation. It has announced a $210,000 budget for 1988-1989. During the summer of 1988, the network will appoint a new full time Director. The $210,000 is expected to be raised through assessment of all participating libraries, using a contribution schedule based on their annual materials budgets and the number of courier stops they require.

Another cooperative network is the 60 member Tampa Bay Library Cooperative (TBLC). It was founded in 1979, on the west coast, in the Tampa-Hillsborough County area. For the last few years it has operated under the leadership of a paid director. The annual operating budget is forecast as $178,992 for 1988-1989. TBLC is developing an automated system called SUNLINE, while the SELFIN cooperative calls its system SEFLINK. (Neither one of these terms is an acronym.)

At the end of the 1970's, the SUS libraries cooperated on an automation planning project, and they developed a set of demanding specifications that were let out for bid in 1977-1978. Only one organization responded with a quote, and that was CLSI. When the CLSI hardware and software were installed in some of the libraries, it became apparent there were significant gaps between reality and expectations. Two of the libraries withdrew from the plan, although one of them, the University of North Florida (UNF), later became a CLSI participant. The combined effort required to develop the specifications and implement the CLSI program paid off handsomely. UF was a CLSI participant for a time, and then terminated the relationship. After considerable investigation of alternatives, the senior SUS library eventually chose Northwestern University's automated system as the best. It was UF's successful experience with the Northwestern software that contributed to that system's selection as the basis for the Florida Center for Library Automation.

COLLABORATION AND AUTONOMY

Clearly, the most impressive cooperative effort to date has been the Florida Center for Library Automation (FCLA), with a database of over 4.5 million records, the largest such database in the Southeast. By late spring of 1988, the network was handling up to nine million transactions a month. The origins of the FCLA can be traced to late fall of 1983. The state had formed an Information Resources Council (IRC), a Cabinet level group, charged with overseeing the compatibility and appropriateness of automation purchases in all state agencies. In 1983, the organizations within the agencies were asked to prepare an Information Resource Plan (IRP). Like other units, the university libraries made forecasts and estimated costs for their automation needs. These were reviewed and considered as a whole. It was obvious that the collective cost of nine automated library systems was prohibitive, although the concept was appealing. The SUS libraries seemed a logical environment for pooling automation resources as well as technical expertise.

The potential of building a database that would multiply state-supplied resources and make collections in state-supported libraries available to all Floridians was attractive. It could be presented to the legislators as cost-effective management of state resources. An automation collective for the SUS had the added appeal of an initiative that could potentially assist public libraries, community colleges, and other organizations. In early 1984, the directors of the nine state university libraries were called together to formally address the problem. Their work was initially coordinated by a BOR associate vice chancellor for academic affairs. One of his assignments was oversight of library affairs in the SUS. This man invited Richard

Dougherty, of the University of Michigan, to testify before the Florida legislature on the positive aspects of library automation. In the months that followed, nine plans became one plan for library automation and the FCLA was established as a Type I Center: an independent unit, attached to a single university for payroll, personnel, and other administrative processing functions, but with responsibilities to more than one institution.

During the spring and summer of 1984, the nine directors continued to meet. They worked closely with UF staff who had been responsible for that institution's automated operation, based on its three-year-old association with the Northwestern Online Total Information System (NOTIS). Each institution was starting from a different point. One library had very little automation except OCLC; others were working with various CLSI releases. UCF was totally automated, using INNOVAQ for acquisitions and serials, and CLSI for circulation and as an online catalog that served campus and community. UF had adapted the NOTIS software and called it the Florida Online Catalog User System (FOCUS). FCLA members used the term FOCUS until they learned the acronym was a proprietary name.

The deliberations of the Board were marked by compromise and consensus. Members debated the benefits of centralized versus decentralized operations, considering a model with three or four centers scattered throughout the state, as well as the option of one principal site. They finally agreed the NOTIS operating system should be based at the massive Northeast Regional Data Center (NERDC) in Gainesville. They also agreed the Center itself should be located in the same city and attached administratively, as a Type I Center, to UF. They decided the advantages of one location with a central staff outweighed any possible convenience of decentralization, even though the single site configuration would potentially increase telecommunication costs. The UF staff, led by Max Willocks, played a critical role. He and his colleagues drafted the initial proposals and first five-year plan for review and editing by the entire Board.[2] Charles Miller of FSU accepted the diplomatically taxing assignment of Board Chair, a responsibility he has carried to date. A search committee was formed to recruit a suitable director, and James Corey of the University of Missouri was chosen from an impressive list of candidates. He brought the FCLA an unparalleled combination of technical and management skills. He has been especially successful in building a network staff whose abilities match his own and who work harmoniously together, and with the libraries. Table I shows the FCLA's activity in the fall of 1984 and 1987.[3]

Table 1

FCLA Activity Profile

Fall 1984-Fall 1987

Activity	Fall 1984	Fall 1987
Records Loaded		
Bibliographic	500,000	4,100,000
Authority	0	2,500,000
Item	0	2,240,000
Order	50,000	150,000
Online transactions (per month)	600,000	7,500,000
Terminals installed	65	900

When classes began in the fall of 1985, the libraries introduced the Library User Information Service (LUIS) public catalogs to their campus communities. They held special events and receptions and released balloons. Some distributed pins and stickers marked "Meet me at the library—LUIS." At UCF, where the patrons had used CLSI as an online public access catalog since 1983, the library created a special insert for the university house organ. It featured campus notables, from the Provost to the football coach with players in uniform, all using LUIS at terminals. Table 2 shows FCLA's operational status in fall of 1984, and again in 1987. Initially, the database held only 500,000 bibliographic records (those of the UF library). By fall of 1987, most of the SUS libraries' records had been converted through processing of the OCLC archival tapes.

The FCLA Director is advised by a Board that includes the Directors of the SUS libraries, the State Librarian of Florida, and a representative of the Board of Regents. In 1986, a representative of the State Board of Community Colleges was added to the membership. The Board is counseled on operational matters by a Technical Services Committee and a Public Services Committee. The Board itself has standing Priorities and Budget and Equipment Committees. The Technical Services Committee is made up of practitioners who represent the nine universities and their various processing centers, including the medical and law facilities. These working committee members interact regularly with the FCLA technical staff,

and they make recommendations to the Center's director and the board. The Public Services Committee, with appropriate subgroups as needed for specific functional concerns, plays a similar role. The Priorities and Budget Committee is an elected subgroup of the full board. Its members interact with the Equipment Committee and the director. They usually meet prior to a full board meeting, reviewing recommendations from the Equipment Committee, as well as the Public and Technical Services Committees. They consider detailed reports and proposals from the center's director, and finally, they prepare recommendations for the full board. These overlapping interactive processes seem cumbersome, but they work, and while local needs are sometimes deferred, they are eventually met through consensus.

DIFFERENCES

The initial proviso language in FCLA's enabling legislation included terms that were open to more than one interpretation. During the early years, the state librarian, the SUS librarians, other librarians, and some legislators saw different meanings in the proviso language. It called for a plan that would include services to community college, private academic, and public libraries. The charge was unclear on the precise extent and nature of such services, the timeline for when these services would be made available, the priority (among other tasks assigned to the FCLA) for extending

Table 2

FCLA Operational Status

Fall 1984 and Fall 1987

Functions operational	Fall 1984	Fall 1987
Online catalog	University of Florida	All state universities
		Santa Fe Comm. College
		Edison Comm. College
Catalog maintenance	University of Florida	All state universities
		Santa Fe Comm. College
		Edison Comm. College
Acquisitions	University of Florida	Univ. of Florida
		Univ. of South Florida
		Fl. International Univ.
Circulation	None	Univ. of Florida
		Univ. of South Florida
		Univ. of North Florida
		Santa Fe Comm. College
Serials	University of Florida	Univ. of Florida
		Univ. of South Florida

these services, or the types of libraries to which such services might be provided.

Some members of the library community, notably the community college representatives, believed the proviso language mandated full and early FCLA involvement for all community college libraries as part of the Center's original resource sharing commitment. The SUS Directors were convinced the proviso language intended that the FCLA database should be readily available to libraries throughout the state. They believed the proviso's intent was that the FCLA's planning and implementation activities would be models for possible later use by community colleges and others. They agreed that full access to the database from search only terminals was a right of all Florida libraries. These polarized opinions called for resolution. The state decided to solve this by asking the Post Secondary Education Planning Commission (PEPC) to study the FCLA organization.

The study concluded in spring of 1988. PEPC's final report suggested that community colleges would be better served by developing their own automation plans. It concluded that "the voiced desire of many community colleges to become affiliates of the FCLA is in reality an expression of a desire to enjoy the benefits made possible by library automation."[14] The PEPC authors agreed with the SUS library Directors (and the FCLA Director) that overextending the NOTIS software would be neither technically feasible nor cost beneficial.

CURRENT SERVICES

The FCLA was established to provide essential systems needed by the SUS libraries to support their necessary operations: Catalog Maintenance; Authority Control; an Online Catalog; Remote Access to the Online Catalog; Acquisitions; Serials Control; and Circulation. In addition to these bread-and-butter functions, the FCLA members share text electronically, and thus enhance their interlibrary loan potential through use of telefacsimile. The FCLA telefacsimile transmission

Table 3

Estimated FCLA Budget Required to Support
NOTIS Related Services

Category	FY 89-90	FY 90-91	FY 91-92	FY 92-93	FY 93-94
Salaries	596,843	626,685	658,020	690,920	725,467
Hourly Wages	23,060	24,213(1)	25,424	26,695	28,030
Expense	558,843	586,785	616,124	646,930	679,277
Data Processing	2,183,509	2,292,684(1)	2,407,318	2,527,684	2,654,068
Capital Equipment	200,000(2)	200,000	300,000(3)	300,000	300,000
TOTAL	3,562,254	3,730,367	4,006,886	4,192,230	4,386,841

(1) Includes one new Librarian FTE

(2) 5% annual increase: FY 90-91 through FY 93-94

program uses IBM ScanMaster equipment housed in each of the nine university libraries for flexibility in resource sharing. It is processed through the NERDC mainframe in Gainesville. Unfortunately, the current equipment does not accept transmission from originals. Text from books or journals must first be photoduplicated and then fed into the ScanMaster. As with any new technology, initial enthusiasm was followed by skepticism as problems arose. The resolution of transmitted text is often imperfect. In the receiving library the copies are printed on a coated paper that is not aesthetically pleasing. Small print and articles with scientific formulas are not always legible. One patron commented that the telefacsimile copies looked as if they had been printed in chocolate syrup. Nevertheless, ScanMaster technology has provided the SUS libraries with a service not possible before. It can clearly be identified as resource sharing, and hence part of collection management.

One very recent development is a joint application for a grant prepared by the SUS libraries, under the leadership of Carol Turner of UF. It asks for funds to replace the ScanMasters with state-of-the-art telefacsimile equipment for the SUS *and* the University of Miami. The inclusion of a private institution in the telefacsimile circle is in itself noteworthy.

Along with its basic services just described, the FCLA also provides affiliation with the Research Libraries Group (RLG). The two largest libraries are full RLG members, while the others participate in (CLASS), the Cooperative Library Agency for Systems and Services, allowing them access to the Research Libraries Information Network (RLIN). The RLG opportunity has proven especially useful in the smaller libraries for interlibrary loan verification and for cataloging items that cannot be found on OCLC. Reference librarians in some of the SUS libraries are enthusiastic about the subject search capability.

ON THE DRAWING BOARD

The Center recently presented its second five-year plan, submitting it to the legislature during spring of 1988. This document forecasts continuation of the current services described above. It also confirms a commitment to continue telefacsimile and to provide RGL services needed by the SUS libraries, giving these costs a place in the FCLA budget. In addition, the new plan identifies at least six new incentives: Key-Word and Boolean Searching; Cross Database Circulation; Exploration and Possible Development of New Cataloging Opportunities; Linking to Other Systems; and

Table 4

Estimated FCLA Budget Required to Support NOTIS Related Services Plus Proposed New Activities

Category	FY 89-90	FY 90-91	FY 91-92	FY 92-93	FY 93-94
Salaries	631,843	700,185	773,782	852,371	894,990
Hourly Wages	23,060	24,213	25,424	26,695	28,030
Expense	950,293	1,141,167	1,081,708	1,247,275	1,400,196
Data Processing Expense	2,686,629	2,876,960	3,304,508	3,644,834	4,081,163
Capital Equipment	206,000	206,600	476,600	571,000	300,000
TOTAL	4,497,824	4,949,126	5,662,021	6,342,175	6,704,378

Access to the Journal Article Databases and Document Delivery.

Table 3 shows five-year projections of the costs to continue present NOTIS-related operations. Table 4 shows budget projections from 1989/1990 through 1993/1994 for the continued projects (current NOTIS-linked operations, the RLG service relationship, and telefacsimile), as well as introduction of the new services just described.

The philosophic ideals of resource sharing and cooperative collection management are intellectually seductive. The advantages are obvious, but there are significant barriers. In fiscal year 1987/1988, Florida allocated $17,384,899 in a funding category called Other Capital Outlay for Library Materials popularly known as "Book OCO." In the SUS, libraries can use Book OCO funds for their OCLC membership fees and for binding, but its chief purpose is for purchase of books and journals. The $17,000,000 was distributed unevenly. The largest institution, UF, received about $4,000,000, while the smallest, UNF, received about $900,000. The typical amount was approximately $1.5 million. This distribution of funds is in itself a form of resource sharing.

The large, mature universities must offer library materials and services appropriate for a wide range of academic programs, including law schools; while newer institutions must respond to rapid growth, a focus on technology, and the reality of libraries' starting life as upper division universities. In the SUS, resources are shared through significant interlibrary loan traffic. Collectively, 68 percent of the interlibrary loan borrowing and lending in the SUS libraries is reciprocal within the state. There has been a significant increase in interlibrary loans since the advent of the FCLA. However, interlibrary loans seem to be rising nationally. It is not clear whether (or to what extent) the SUS increase is caused by, or merely simultaneous with, the FCLA experience. The relatively quick acceptance of the NOTIS system was not the typical experience found in most other automation collectives, where an extended planning period is usually followed by specification development, a bid process, and choice of vendor. The Florida corporation surely was and is a model. However, it is important to remember that to agree was virtually mandated by a single purse-holding authority, the Board of Regents. The same results might not have been possible among another group of libraries. The true measure of the network as a factor in collection management cannot be gauged accurately at this time.

Notes

1. *A Comprehensive Review of Library Facilities and Technological Changes for Improving Libraries in the SUS: Final Report* (Bethesda, Md.: Information Systems Consultants, Inc., 1981), p. 92-7.

2. University of Florida, A Proposal for the Establishment of the Center for Library Automation (Gainesville, Fla.: University of Florida, 1984).

3. Information based on materials distributed to the FCLA Priorities and Budget Committee, and the full FCLA Board, by the Center's Director and staff between January and May 1988.

4. Florida Center for Library Automation, *Five Year Plan for 1989-1994* (Gainesville, Fla.: FCLA Staff and Priorities and Budget Committee, 1988), pp. ii-iv, 5-14, 23.

Assessing "Readiness for Resource Sharing" in an Academic Library

by Judith M. Feller

In the last ten years, an abundance of writing has appeared on the need for cooperation, resource sharing, and networking. The terms themselves are not always well defined, although *networking* usually implies the use of computers and other telecommunication links. The consensus is that cooperation (resource sharing, networking) is an economic necessity. Resource sharing and cooperation are based on the assumption that academic libraries can no longer afford to be self-sufficient—they cannot purchase all materials required to meet the needs of their curricula and related faculty research.

This study was prompted by what seemed to be two very simple questions: When is an academic library ready to engage in resource sharing? What data should a library collect and analyze in order to decide what cooperative arrangements would be most advantageous? In short, are there measurements of *readiness for resource sharing*?

A survey of the last five years of the literature and study of the most pertinent earlier publications indicated that no such measures existed. Although three national conferences have convened to consider the state of resource sharing in its various forms, the subject of *evaluating* the need, then planning for resource sharing, was given scant attention.[1] Conference proceedings offered few concrete suggestions for the academic library trying to assess its need to engage in resource sharing:

> Before we develop grandiose networking schemes, at great expense, perhaps we should have a better idea as to what needs are not being met by traditional programs.[2]

One of the earliest reports to specifically address the problem of planning resource sharing for academic libraries was published in 1967 by Ralph Blasingame, former State Librarian of Pennsylvania. His study was full of useful insights and was of particular importance because its author pinpointed the analysis of interlibrary loan—the granddaddy of all cooperation—as an important basis for decisions involving resource sharing.[3]

McGrath's "pragmatic book allocation formula" (1975) was designed to determine the strength of relationships (correlations) which existed between a library's circulation and shelf list, circulation and current acquisitions, and shelf list and current acquisitions.[4] Could the intercorrelation of circulation, current acquisitions, and interlibrary loan be a productive measure of *readiness for resource sharing*?

The technique applied in McGrath's book allocation formula depended upon the construction of a *profile*.[5] McGrath and Durand proposed that an institution's catalog of courses most accurately "reflects the current, changing curriculum," and suggested, "Why not recognize the university catalog . . . as a selection tool and guide to the collection?"[6] With that objective, they assigned classification numbers to each course in their institution's catalog and produced a profile by academic department.[7]

NEED FOR THE STUDY

The Director of Libraries at Lehigh University was interested in exploring the feasibility of resource sharing with East Stroudsburg State College. Lehigh already belonged to the Lehigh Valley Association

Special thanks to Dr. Betty Turock, Rutgers University Graduate School of Library & Information Studies, for her advice and encouragement throughout the project and preparation of this article; to Berry Richards, Director of Libraries, Lehigh University, and her staff for their invaluable help with data collection.

of Independent Colleges, a local consortium. In spite of Lehigh's resource-sharing activities, access to additional library materials was thought to be needed to support some programs which could not be adequately funded.

East Stroudsburg State College (Now East Stroudsburg University) is one of 14 state-owned institutions comprising Pennsylvania's State System of Higher Education. In the last ten years, East Stroudsburg has instituted new programs in response to changing demands for "marketable" skills for its graduates. Although some of the librarians predicted that the library would not be able to fully support all of the new programs without jeopardizing the quality of materials for the established programs, no attempt at formal evaluation was made. New programs included nursing, computer science, environmental studies, and hotel and resource management. Most of the new programs required greater resources in science and technology: emphasis in collection building had previously centered on the social sciences and the humanities.

East Stroudsburg did not belong to local library consortia and had not previously considered formal cooperative arrangements; therefore, the questions, from the library's point of view were:

1. Was the library ready for resource sharing?
2. How could the library measure or judge its readiness?
3. What library materials could be shared?

Lehigh wanted to know if they could benefit from cooperation with the library at East Stroudsburg. They were particularly interested in access to more materials in education. They wanted to consider coordinated selection of U.S. government documents, since both libraries are depositories.

METHODOLOGY

The work of William E. McGrath and Norma Durand provided the foundation for this study.[8,9] The investigator hoped that adding the collection and analysis of interlibrary loan borrowing data to the procedures they developed would provide a useful measure of resource-sharing readiness or effectiveness.

The major premise is that interlibrary loan activity represents the first significant manifestation of a library's need to go beyond its own resources. By continuously monitoring it, coupled with measurement of other library functions, essential information about the degree to which a local collection is able to support its institution's curricula could be gathered.

There are three basic reasons why a library has to borrow or request photocopy, and analysis of those reasons is extremely important in building a foundation for resource sharing.

1. *Lost book or periodicals.* A circulating item is lost when a borrower reports that it cannot be found and returned. Articles torn from publications have been lost. Library materials are lost when they are not charged out but cannot be accounted for. It may be difficult to determine whether such losses are due to inadequate security or to poor stack management. Libraries cannot completely eliminate loss due to human error in shelving, but since availability is an important measure of effectiveness, a library should have some idea of the magnitude of the problem. If study reveals that a large percentage of items are requested through interlibrary loan because they are missing at the borrowing library, there are problems in the library which will not be alleviated by resource sharing.

2. *Owned—not identified.* Libraries do sometimes borrow materials they already own. This can occur if an item requested is not correctly verified or if a correctly verified item is included in an unanalyzed special collection, such as the ERIC microfiche. Items in this category also indicate management problems, e.g., the need for improved training of interlibrary loan staff.

3. *Not owned.* Materials in this category represent potential areas for resource sharing.

DATA COLLECTION

Data were collected from the libraries at Lehigh University and East Stroudsburg State College. All data were from the 1980–81 academic year. The same tables were constructed for each library, but only the tables and analyses for East Stroudsburg are presented here. Random samples of 400 were used to provide the information on acquisitions and interlibrary loan borrowing.

1. Profiles were created for each institution;
2. Circulation figures, including totals and detailed breakdowns by classification numbers, were compiled;
3. Book allocation formulas were calculated;
4. Information was collected from a sample of interlibrary loan borrowing records;
5. Data collected in the first four steps were intercorrelated and analyzed.

Step One—Institutional profile

A profile was drawn for each institution by classifying the courses in the current catalog by Dewey number, a technique described in detail by McGrath and Durand.[10]

Step Two—Circulation figures

The total number of volumes circulated, broken down by classification number, was collected for each institution. Using information given in the profiles, the classification totals were listed under the appropriate departments.[11]

Step Three—Book allocation formula

This phase of the study was designed to indicate what percent of its budget each library should spend for books, by department, in relation to what was actually used (circulation) during the academic year.[12] A random sample of 400 titles (individual orders) was taken from each library's current acquisitions file. For each order, data were collected on the department of the person who ordered the book, or classification number of the book if the department of the requestor could not be determined; and the price listed on the order form. The

availability of OCLC cataloging information made it easy to find classification numbers for most books in the sample when a requestor's department could not be identified.

The work forms were arranged by department. The prices on each group of department forms were added, and the total was divided by the number of orders to arrive at the average cost. Cost-use and percent cost-use were calculated, but actual budget allocations were not determined.[13] The result is shown in Table 1.

Step Four—Sample from interlibrary loan borrowing

Data were taken from 400 randomly selected records of books borrowed by each library. For each record, the following information was collected: reason for borrowing (lost/missing, not owned); subject of book (Dewey/LC no.); class of borrower (undergrad, grad, faculty, other); department or major of borrower (profile dept. code); institution(s) owning book (OCLC symbols); institution which lent book (OCLC symbol). Since

Table 1
Use-Cost Percentage Allocation
East Stroudsburg State College

Department	Total Use	Average Cost	Cost-Use	Percent Cost-Use
Art	1,053	$16.00	$ 16,848	2.8
Biology	1,717	24.00	41,208	6.86
Chemistry	638	34.00	21,692	3.61
Elementary & Early Childhood Education	795	9.00	7,155	1.19
Economics	729	16.00	11,664	1.94
Educational Communications	299	14.00	4,186	.69
English	3,226	13.00	41,938	6.98
Foreign Language	541	18.00	9,738	1.62
Geography	1,198	20.00	23,960	3.99
History	2,675	19.00	50,825	8.46
Health	615	17.00	10,455	1.74
Hotel & Resort Management	346	26.00	8,996	1.49
Mathematics	679	22.00	14,938	2.48
Music	380	10.00	3,800	.63
Nursing	413	17.00	7,021	1.16
Philosophy	1,384	14.00	19,376	3.22
Physics	474	18.00	8,532	1.42
Political Science	1,295	22.00	28,490	4.74
Professional Physical Education	2,414	14.00	33,796	5.62
Professional & Secondary Education	144	13.00	1,872	.31
Psychology	1,085	33.00	35,805	5.96
Recreation	329	7.00	2,303	.38
Reading	177	20.00	3,540	.58
Safety	0	0	0	0
Sociology	2,959	18.00	53,262	8.87
Special Education	146	7.00	1,022	.17
Speech	72	0	0	0
Speech Pathology & Audiology	19	0	0	0
Theatre	444	14.00	6,216	1.03
Miscellaneous	6,271	21.00	131,691	21.93
Totals	32,517		$600,329	99.87

Table 2
Number and Ranking:
Circulation, Acquisitions, Interlibrary Loan
East Stroudsburg State College

n = 30 Dept.	Circ. X		Acquis. Y		Intlib. Loan Z	
	Vols.	Rank	Vols.	Rank	Vols.	Rank
Art	1,053	20	27	15	6	7
Biol	1,717	25	27	15	20	13
Chem	638	16	9	8	6	7
Eced	795	19	12	9	8	9
Econ	729	18	18	11	6	7
Edcm	299	7	4	5	1	2
Engl	3,226	29	20	13	2	3
Flng	541	14	5	6	0	1
Geog	1,198	22	22	14	4	5
Hist	2,675	27	51	18	44	14
Hlth	615	15	3	4	7	8
H&rm	346	9	5	6	11	11
Math	679	17	13	10	3	4
Mus	380	10	4	5	0	1
Nurs	413	11	3	4	4	5
Phil	1,384	24	20	13	12	12
Phys	474	13	5	6	3	4
Pols	1,295	23	44	16	12	12
Prpe	2,414	26	19	12	5	6
Psed	144	4	1	2	2	3
Psy	1,085	21	7	7	12	12
Recr	329	8	4	5	1	2
Reed	177	6	1	2	1	2
Sfty	0	1	0	1	0	1
Soc	2,959	28	5	6	10	10
Spch	72	3	0	1	0	1
Sped	146	5	2	3	1	2
Sppa	19	2	0	1	1	2
Thtr	444	12	5	6	1	2
Misc	6,271	30	47	17	65	15

Rankings: 1 = lowest; 30 = highest

East Stroudsburg did not borrow 400 monographs, the alternative was to include requests for periodical articles and assign a Dewey number to each periodical title.

Work forms were first arranged by department to determine rankings, as shown in Table 2. Information from the forms was then keypunched, and two printouts were provided for each institution. One printout was by department, with reasons for borrowing, status of borrowers, and OCLC symbol for the library which filled each request. The other printout was by OCLC symbol and listed in descending order potential lenders with the number of times each was an actual lender.

In relation to resource sharing, it was important to determine patterns of use (what libraries lent books) and potential use (what libraries owned books but were not queried). Tables 3 and 4 were constructed to illustrate patterns of lending in relation to each institution. As a convenient frame of reference, service areas were designated using the 1979 Pennsylvania Higher Education Planning Regions.[14] The last relationship to be visualized was that of reason for borrowing to the institutional profile (Table 5).

Step Five—Analysis of data

Table 4 reflects the dependence of East Stroudsburg upon other institutions in the State System, with lenders scattered through all regions of the state. Table 3 shows that the greatest number of potential lenders was in Region 2, the Lehigh Valley, and Lehigh University led the list. One of the main reasons for not using most of the potential lenders in the Lehigh Valley is that they do not offer free photocopies, while libraries in the State System of Higher Education do provide each other with free photocopies.

The expected outcome was that the largest percentage of books borrowed—not less than 75 percent, for example—would fall in the "Not owned" category. A lower percentage would prompt ques-

Table 3
Potential Lenders in Service Area
East Stroudsburg State College

Service Area	Institution	No. Times potential lender	No. Times actual lender
1	Bryn Mawr College	10	0
	Bucks County C.C.	6	0
2	Lehigh University	46	7
	Lafayette College	33	4
	Moravian College	24	0
	Allentown College	23	0
	Cedar Crest-Muhlenberg	23	0
6	Dickinson College	10	1
	Franklin & Marshall	10	3

Table 4
Institutions in Service Area Which Lent the Most to East Stroudsburg State College

Institution	Service area	No. loans to ESSC
State Library of Pa	6	21
Kutztown State College	2	18
Millersville State College	6	15
West Chester State College	1	13
Bloomsburg State College	4	13
Mansfield State College	4	12
Lehigh University	2	7
Pennsylvania State Univ	4	7
Army War College	6	6
Lock Haven State College	4	6
Shippensburg State College	6	5

Table 5
Reason for Borrowing
East Stroudsburg State College

Department	Reason for Borrowing		
	Lost	Missing	Not Owned
Art	0	0	6
Biology	4	1	15
Chemistry	0	0	6
Elementary & early childhood ed	1	1	6
Economics	1	0	5
Educational communications	0	1	0
English	0	1	1
Foreign languages	0	0	0
Geography	0	1	3
History	1	2	41
Health	0	6	1
Hotel & resort management	1	0	10
Mathematics	0	0	3
Music	0	0	0
Nursing	1	0	3
Philosophy	0	0	12
Physics	0	1	2
Political science	0	1	11
Professional physical education	0	1	4
Professional & secondary education	0	1	1
Psychology	0	1	11
Recreation	0	1	0
Reading	0	0	1
Safety	0	0	0
Sociology	1	2	7
Speech	0	0	0
Special education	0	0	1
Speech pathology & audiology	0	0	1
Theatre	1	0	0
Miscellaneous	1	12	52
Total	12	33	203

Total transactions: 248
Percent of total Lost 4.83
Percent of total Missing 13.3
Percent of total not owned 81.85

tions about the adequacy of library security and stack management practices.

Of the materials borrowed, 81.8 percent were not owned by the library. Another 13.3 percent were designated "missing." "Missing" was used in cases where photocopy was requested to replace pages torn from periodicals. Considering the fact that the library has three self-service copiers and a change machine, the 13.3 percent appeared to be high. Unfortunately, the problem of vandalism is not unique to East Stroudsburg's library. A possible solution would be to acquire more back volumes in microform.

Spearman's *rho* was calculated for circulation, acquisitions, and interlibrary loan borrowing data. Hypotheses were: there should be no correlation between borrowing and circulation or between borrowing and acquisitons and there should be a high correlation between circulation and acquisitions.

Designations for correlation coefficients

.20	slight; almost negligible relationship
.20–.40	low correlation; definite but small relationship
.40–.70	moderate correlation: substantial relationship
.70–.90	high correlation; marked relationship
.90	very high correlation; very dependable relationship[15]

Table 6
Intercorrelation Matrix

	Y (Acquisitions)	Z (Interlibrary loan)
X (Circulation)	.891 (High)	.748 (High)
Y (Acquisitions)	—	.724 (High)

As shown in Table 6, the circulation-acquisitions correlation coefficient of .891 is considered high. It exceeds all critical values at a probability level less than 0.01 and indicates the presence of a desirably strong positive relationship between the two. The correlations between acquisitions and interlibrary loan and between circulation and interlibrary loan are also within the high positive range, indicating problems requiring closer examination. Such high positive correlations are not desirable, particularly between circulation and interlibrary loan.

By arranging circulation, acquisitions, and interlibrary loan as shown in Table 7, some of the discrepancies which might account for the high correlation coefficients became more apparent. Data from Table 3 provided additional criteria for analyzing the problem (Table 8).

In Table 7, locating the median for each group was the first step in identifying levels of activity. The

median was used because with ranked data, the difference between the highest and lowest numbers is so extreme that a *mean* would not be an accurate reflection of the distribution.

After medians were located, it was possible to designate magnitudes, such as "twice the median" (2Mdn) or "two less than the median" (Mdn – 2). This not only made it simpler to describe relationships, but provided a potential decision point; for example, after completing the analysis, a library might set an acceptable level of interlibrary loan at 2Mdn.

English had the second highest circulation, and at 20 volumes, the acquisitions rate was four times the median (4Mdn). Table 8 shows that although the percent cost-use was only 6.98, the sample percent cost-use was only 3.6. Coupled with the interlibrary loan rate below the median (Mdn – 2), indications are that supply is meeting demand, with no particular problems.

Table 7
East Stroudsburg State College
Circulation, Acquisitions, Interlibrary Loan Ranked in Descending Order

Circulation		Acquisitions		Interlibrary loan	
Dept.	No. vols. *	Dept.	No. vols. **	Dept.	No. vols. ***
Misc.	6,271	Hist.	51	Misc.	65
Eng.	3,226	Misc.	47	Hist.	44
Soc.	2,959	Poli. sci.	44	Bio.	20
Hist.	2,675	Art	27	Psych.	12
Prf. phys. ed.	2,414	Bio.	27	Poli. sci.	12
Bio.	1,717	Geog.	22	Philos.	12
Philos.	1,384	Eng.	20	Htl. & rst. mgt.	11
Poli. sci.	1,295	Philos.	20	Soc.	10
Geog.	1,198	Prf. phys. ed.	19	Elemen. ed.	8
Psych.	1,085	Econ.	18	Health	7
Art	1,053	Math.	13	Econ.	6
Elemen. ed.	795	Elemen. ed.	12	Chem.	6
Econ.	729	Chem.	9	Art	6
Math.	679	Psych.	7	Prf. phys. ed.	2
Chem.	638	Frgn. lang.	5	Nursing	4
Mdn = 626.5		Htl. & rst. mgt.	5	Geog.	4
Health	615	Physics	5	**Mdn = 4**	
Frgn. lang.	541	Soc.	5	Physics	3
Physics	474	Theatre	5	Math	3
Theatre	444	**Mdn = 5**		Prf. & sec. ed.	2
Nursing	413	Recreat.	4	Eng.	2
Music	380	Music	4	Theater	1
Htl. & rst. mgt.	346	Educ. com.	4	Spch. path.	1
Recreat.	329	Health	3	Special ed.	1
Educ. com.	299	Nursing	3	Reading	1
Reading	177	Special ed.	2	Recreat.	1
Special ed.	146	Prf. & sec. ed.	1	Educ. com.	1
Prf. & sec. ed.	144	Reading	1	Spch.	0
Spch.	72	Safety	0	Safety	0
Spch. path.	19	Spch. path.	0	Music	0
Safety	0	Spch.	0	Frgn. lang.	0

* Total volumes circulated during the 1980–81 academic yr.
** Based on sample of 400 orders
*** Based on sample of 248 interlibrary loan requests

Through further analysis of the data in Tables 7 and 8, it became evident that there were two basic categories.

Category I: Percent cost-use calculated in Table 1 is ≥ the sample percent cost-use, and, the interlibrary loan rate is ≥ 2Mdn.

Category II: Percent cost-use calculated in Table 1 is < the sample percent cost-use, and, the interlibrary loan rate is ≥ 2Mdn.

Category I subjects were Psychology and Sociology. Based on the high circulation of books in those subjects, the percent cost-use shown in Table 8 is also high; however, the sample cost-use figures indicate an acquisitions rate which is far *less* and may account for interlibrary loan rates two and three times greater than the median. A closer examination of materials being borrowed might give a clue as to how the funds could be effectively spent and the necessity of borrowing reduced.

With the exception of hotel and resort management, Category II subjects all fell above the circulation median. In all cases, the cost-use calculated from the acquisitions sample (Table 8) exceeded the cost-use calculated on the basis of circulation, but the interlibrary loan rate still ranged from two to ten times the median.

Hotel and resort management is one of East Stroudsburg's new programs, and another new program, the interdisciplinary environmenal studies, may account for the high use, heavy spending, heavy borrowing in biology. Category II prompted questions such as : Were funds being spent for materials which were really used? Should a sample of recently acquired books in those subjects be taken at intervals to see if they are circulating or are otherwise used? How does the level of materials being purchased compare with the level of materials being borrowed? How do the classification numbers of borrowed materials compare to the institution's profile? Are requests for interlibrary loans for materials which are in print or out-of-print?

IMPLICATIONS FOR RESOURCE SHARING

If resource sharing is to take the form of agreements on collection building, the Category II departments represent a logical point at which discussions between libraries might begin. Category I should also be included if libraries do not have the funds to increase the percent cost-use. Classification numbers from the profiles can be compared to determine how closely the department descriptions of each institution match each other and whether it would be possible for each institution to concentrate its acquisitions in specific classes.

Shelflist holdings could be estimated and used as additional decision points on where to continue building a collection and where to decrease or cut spending. The level of each institution's degree programs would have to be considered. Interlibrary loan borrowing should be analyzed in greater detail for information about language, level, format (books, reports, documents), in-print, out-of-print.

CONCLUSION

What appears to be missing in all of the literature on cooperation and resource sharing is the use of bench marks or indexes against which libraries can measure the degree to which they are succeeding in their efforts to provide library materials. Analysis of

Table 8
East Stroudsburg State College
Comparative Acquisitions Data

Dept.	Percent cost-use (Table 1)	Percent cost-use acquisitions sample*
Misc.	21.93	13.60
Soc.	8.87	1.20
Hist.	8.46	13.40
Eng.	6.98	3.60
Bio.	6.86	8.90
Psych.	5.96	3.20
Prof. phys. ed.	5.62	3.60
Poli. sci.	4.74	13.43
Geog.	3.99	6.10
Chem.	3.61	4.20
Philos.	3.22	3.80
Art	2.80	5.90
Math.	2.48	3.90
Econ.	1.94	3.90
Health	1.74	.70
Frgn. lang.	1.62	1.24
Hotel & rest. mgmt.	1.49	1.80
Physics	1.42	1.24
Elemen. ed.	1.19	1.40
Nursing	1.16	.70
Theatre	1.03	.97
Educ. comm.	.69	.77
Music	.63	.55
Reading	.58	.27
Prof. & sec. ed.	.31	.20
Recreat.	.38	.38
Special ed.	.17	.20
Safety	0.0	0.0
Speech	0.0	0.0
Speech path.	0.0	0.0

*This figure was arrived at by multiplying the average cost per volume in Table 1 by the number of volumes for each dept. in "Acquisitions" in Table 2, summing the results, and dividing each department total by the grand total.

Example Dept.	*from Table 1:* Average cost/vol.	*Table 2:* No. vols.	Total cost	%
History	$19.00	51	$969.00	13.40
Art	16.00	27	432.00	5.90
Psychology	33.00	7	231.00	3.20
		Grand total:	$7,207.00	

the data in this study suggests that the intercorrelation of circulation, acquisitions, and interlibrary loan might provide such bench marks. Even by using medians, a library would be able to establish reasonable or acceptable levels of borrowing in relation to the circulation and acquisition of materials.

Given the ubiquity of computers in libraries, the obvious extension of this study would be to design a management information system which would incorporate programs to routinely sample circulation, acquisitions, and interlibrary loan data and correlate it in periodic reports. Establishing such a system of ongoing measurement and evaluation would:

1. Give a library contemplating cooperative arrangements a means for determining areas of greatest need;
2. Give a library already engaged in resource sharing a measure of the effectiveness of its arrangements;
3. Identify internal problems which result in user frustration and under-utiliztion of the local collection;
4. Provide more effective allocation of funds for the acquisitions of both books and periodicals;
5. Provide objective data with which library managers can support their budget requests.

References

1. The three conferences were: Conferences on Interlibrary Communication and Information Networks, Airlie House, Warrenton, VA, Sept. 28–Oct. 2, 1970; Resource Sharing in Libraries, University of Pittsburgh, Sept. 29–Oct. 1, 1976; Conference on Networks for Networkers, Indianapolis, IN, May 30–June 1, 1979.
2. Richard E. Chapin, "Limits of local self-sufficiency," in *Conference on Interlibrary Communications and Information Networks*, Joseph Becker, ed. Chicago: American Library Association, 1971, pp. 54–58.
3. Ralph Blasingame, *Feasibility of Cooperation for Exchange of Resources Among Academic and Special Libraries in Pennsylvania*. University Park: Pennsylvania State University, Institute of Public Administration, 1967. (Pennsylvania State Library Monograph, 5) Also: ERIC document ED 016 495.
4. William E. McGrath, "A Pragmatic Book Allocation Formula for Academic and Public Libraries with a Test for Its Effectiveness," *Library Resources & Technical Services* 19 (Fall 1975): 356–69.
5. William E. McGrath and Norma Durand, "Classifying Courses in the University Catalog," *College & Research Libraries* 30 (November 1969): 533–39.
6. Ibid., p. 534.
7. Ibid.
8. McGrath.
9. McGrath and Durand.
10. Ibid.
11. McGrath.
12. Ibid.
13. Ibid.
14. *Design for Regionalization in Higher Education.* Harrisburg: Pennsylvania Department of Education, Office of Higher Education, 1973. (State Board of Education Higher Education Planning Regions map, p. 17, revised Jan., 1979.)
15. J.P. Guilford, *Fundamental Statistics in Psychology and Education.* New York: McGraw-Hill, 1956, p. 145.

Cooperative Collection Development Equals Collaborative Interdependence

by Paul H. Mosher

Resource sharing or cooperative collection development among American libraries is not new; history reveals waves of cooperative spirit over many decades. Librarians in the United States—at least since librarianship became a serious professional enterprise around the turn of the century—have exhibited a democratic altruism about information and its distribution that has resulted in the world's richest and most extensive library collections and a tradition of library service unmatched anywhere else on the globe. Cooperative collection development in one guise or another has long been a part of both that spirit and that enterprise.

Ruth Patrick reported in 1971 that at least ten library consortia established between 1931 and 1960 for resource sharing purposes were still operating 11 to 40 years later.[2] By early 1983, two-thirds of the libraries belonging to the Association of Research Libraries were involved in some kind of resource sharing collection development activity.[1] It has become part of the American library tradition.

MYTH OF SELF-SUFFICIENCY

Nevertheless, the spirit of altruism is not always paramount. Each institution's natural desire for academic self-sufficiency helps to foster competition among American university research libraries and a myth of the self-sufficient "comprehensive" collection necessary for any library with pretensions to greatness.

This myth has been punctured by collection overlap studies of libraries of all sizes and types.

Results show that there is a consistently large proportion of unique material distributed among libraries of a region, a state, or even a locality—whatever the mix of libraries: research libraries, multi-type libraries, or small academic libraries with different sets of programs. One surprising discovery was that it is even true of very small libraries in the same locality: in Juneau, Alaska, for example, the Capitol City Consortium of three libraries has only a 15 percent overlap in books, and 24 percent in serials in the field of education (the consortium includes one college, one public, and one state library). Unfortunately, the collections developed randomly rather than through planning, so the three institutions are missing many useful core titles desired by users of all of the institutions. Cooperation would have allowed collaborative development of core or basic collections as well as planned evolution of lesser-used materials, enlarging the pool of resources available to all. The literature describes similar patterns among libraries of all types and sizes in many configurations and in many parts of the country.[3]

REALITY OF COOPERATION

American librarians have come to recognize that circumstances call for cooperation—ways of optimizing service by joining in partnerships or consortia that will allow access to collective resources. Libraries can serve their patrons and programs better, as they become less collection-driven and more client- and program-oriented.

In 1980 the Research Libraries Group (RLG) began a program of mapping the research collections of member libraries using a common frame-

> Libraries can serve their patrons and programs better as they become less collection-driven and more client- and program-oriented

work (based on the Library of Congress classification system) and a set of standard codes representing collecting intensities, strength of existing collections, and characteristics of materials collected. This framework, called the *Conspectus,* gives a clearer understanding of collections, collecting efforts, and commitments by participating libraries, and improves local and cooperative collection planning and management options. The *Conspectus* has been adopted by all members of the Association of Research Libraries in the form of the North American Collections Inventory Project (NCIP), and the research libraries of Canada have joined in the effort as well. These new initiatives differ from earlier efforts, such as the Farmington Plan, in their focus on collection development and management rather than blanket acquisition. They are collectively supported by partner libraries rather than depending upon federal subsidies. NCIP and the data contained in its *Conspectus* provide the basis for cooperative efforts in the distribution, cataloging, and preservation of materials as well as for acquisition.

Comparative overlap or "verification" studies of the RLG Conspectus Project show that not even the largest libraries hold all of the significant books in any field of scholarly research. Distribution among libraries forms fascinating—and not always predictable—patterns. Even the Library of Congress with its 14,000,000 volumes, is exceeded by university libraries' holdings in a number of disciplines, such as agricultural economics. In French literature, no library—including the Library of Congress—holds more than 62 percent of the scholarly titles cited. On the other hand, four large university libraries together possessed 83 percent. This data supports Pat Battin's argument that "If we are to acknowledge openly our heretofore implicit acceptance of the responsibility for the health of national scholarship, we must channel our energies into the design and development of effective cooperative activities at the national level, which will then enable us to discharge our obligations to our regional and local colleagues."[4] And these cooperative efforts must involve collaboration and distribution of effort among libraries both within large consortia of research libraries, and among libraries of many types and sizes across the country.

A NEW APPROACH

A new and more useful mythology is called for. We need to go beyond "cooperative" collection development to "collaborative" collection development. Cooperation is the environment needed. The goal, fostered by the atmosphere of cooperation is *collaboration:* working, laboring, thinking, and planning together in new communities of enterprise which transcend the walls of local libraries—or even of large campus library complexes. Collaborative collection development requires communities of librarians who know their patrons and their programs well, and who are active rather than passive in their approach to collections. It requires librarians who act to produce change rather than react to random change.

When we begin to consider collaboration and collection development we enter into a realm seldom mentioned in the literature: the realm of attitudes. Attitudes form the context in which all human activities take place; they are an essential element of culture. In a recent survey of attitudes Hewitt and Shipman found four principal purposes for cooperative collection development programs: "1. To expand the range of research materials available to the community involved in the program. 2. To reduce duplication of expensive research materials. 3. To generally 'coordinate' development of collections and acquisition of materials. 4. To jointly acquire materials."[5]

Other viewpoints expressed in the recent literature also tend to focus on managerially determined outcomes (e.g. the bottom line), with little attention on how to achieve practical results:

- The collections, how inadequate they are and how we can collaborate to do something about it;
- The organizational structure (how should cooperative collection development be organized or structured?)
- The financial aspects (there are inadequate resources to maintain x, y, or z), and
- The "electronic imperative" ("thou shalt network, so shalt thou cooperate").

COOPERATION INVOLVES PEOPLE

Few studies have examined the human dimension of cooperation—collaboration. Few have emphasized the cultural rather than the structural aspects of cooperation, either locally or consortially; few have reflected on the communities of human beings who make the thousands of decisions that generate library collections, the communication between the individuals that form those communities, or the communication between communities that must be at the center of any process of cooperative collection development. Yet it is here—at the human level, and at the basic level of human communication—that cooperative collection development must succeed or fail.

Librarianship is often understood to be an applied social science, or a branch of organizational behavior; so it may be, but it is also a social enterprise, with culture rather than structure at its base, and with communication between humans rather than control by management as its operational routine.

Cooperation is reached by setting common goals rather than working out personal differences or organizational mandates. Cooperation is achieved by working ahead, planning, reflecting, and talking with both users and colleagues about the collections, the programs they serve, and about aspirations for the collections of the future. The accomplishment of a working collaboration among people doing selection and making collection management decisions is more central to effective cooperation within collection development than distribution of subject, language, discipline or format.

If working teams have a common purpose and function, have agreed upon goals and a set of objectives, a time frame, and the means they will use to achieve those goals, effective distribution of responsibility is likely to be a natural outcome along with other functionally desirable outcomes less readily perceived at the outset.

Psychologists' recent studies of cooperation in organizations support the view that effective cooperation is most readily achieved by forming small working teams. Workers should focus on sets of mutually desirable interdependencies and outcomes that link stakeholders, rather than emphasize the issues or problems of a single stakeholder. Such groups tend to foster cooperation rather than competition, and collaboration has been shown to strengthen such groups and encourage them to complete more challenging tasks. Collaboration—working together—on cooperative goals, fosters good work relationships, high morale, productivity and effective group integration.[6] Factors crucial to effective collaboration include: effective mutual communication; helpful attitudes; mutual sensitivity to needs, motives, and concerns; and a cooperative and supportive role by administrators.

Small groups generate more effective communication, shared influence, task orientation, friendliness and support. Studies of group performance have demonstrated that the highest verbal and arithmetical reasoning performance was observed during intergroup cooperation; shared attitudes fostered cooperation. It has also been shown that collaboration in groups engenders greater work-related learning by all participants. Various members of the group know various amounts about subjects discussed. Experts and novices must accommodate their differences, and evaluate, supply, and acquire more knowledge than they would acting independently.[7]

Such studies reveal the significance of the informal and social aspects of collection development and the importance of intergroup learning. They emphasize the benefits of both collaboration and interdependence in cooperative collection development—factors that are important at two levels: that of selectors or bibliographers, and that of the libraries themselves. Protocols, structures and guidelines, the Conspectus and policies, lay the foundation for the collaborative effort necessary to create cooperation, but it is people working in teams, that achieve cooperative collection development goals.

CONOCO STUDY

Since effective collaboration in the collection development sphere is the result of changes in the thousands of individual decisions made by many human beings, it must become habitual and customary to become effective. The potential benefits of collaboration among small groups of individuals were recently demonstrated by the Conoco Study. Members of the Collection Management and Development Committee of RLG (bibliographers from participating institutions and central staff) formed a project team, funded by Conoco, Inc. They surveyed groups of bibliographers from the humanities (German literature) and sciences (Geology) to examine the degree to which cooperative collection development could be effective, and whether goals could be internalized in ways that would affect long-term decision-making.[8] The findings in two areas are particularly relevant here: selector behavior in relation to identified resource sharing goals, and collection overlap.

It was found that German literature selectors were willing to change 40 percent of their selection decisions and rely on collections at other institutions if they could be reasonably sure of both bibliographic access and physical availability of items in those collections (maximum of seven days for delivery of materials). Geology selectors proved willing to change up to 50 percent of their selection decisions, if materials could be secured within three days. Selectors in both the humanities and sciences were more willing to focus cooperative action on materials they considered peripheral. They were reluctant to rely on other collections for materials important to the core of their work— usually curricular, instructional, or basic reference materials. In terms of overlap, the amount and distribution of uniquely held items was both greater and more widely spread than bibliographers had anticipated and, not surprisingly, geology collections proved more homogeneous than

Cooperation is achieved by working ahead, planning, reflecting, and talking with both users and colleagues about the collections, the programs, and aspirations for the collections of the future

German literature collections because of greater dependence on journals.

The results of the Conoco study are heartening. They show the benefit—perhaps the necessity—of personal collaboration in meetings, and team building and team work among bibliographers in realizing benefits of cooperative collection development. The study required collaborative effort among participating bibliographers, who were brought together to carry out the study and design the outcomes as well as prepare to achieve them. It may well be that this is an essential element in developing the collaborative interdependence necessary for effective results in cooperative collection development, and that such activity should be a part of the planning—and funding—for all cooperative collection development ventures.

References

1. Joe A. Hewitt and John S. Shipman, "Cooperative collection development among research libraries in the age of networking," *Advances in Library Automation and Networking*, I (1987), 225.

2. Ruth J. Patrick, *Guidelines for Library Cooperation: Development of Academic Library Consortia.* Santa Monica, 1972.

3. The results of the overlap studies are outlined in Paul H. Mosher, "A National scheme for collaboration in collection development: the RLG-NCIP effort," *Coordinating Cooperative Collection Development: A National Perspective." Resource Sharing and Information Networks*, II(1985) Numbers 3/4, pp. 22–23; and in Mosher, "Quality in library collections: New directions in research and practice in collection evaluation," *Advances in Librarianship,* 13 (1984), 227–230.

4. Patricia N. Battin, "Research libraries in the network environment: the case for cooperation," *Journal of Academic Librarianship,* 6 (1980), 70.

5. Hewitt and Shipman, 207.

6. (See, for example, Dean Tjosvold, "Cooperation theory and organizations," *Human Relations,* 37 (1984), 743–67; Barbara Gray, "Conditions facilitating interorganizational collaboration," *Human Relations,* 38 (1985), 911–36: Donald T. Tuler, "Professor-practitioner collaboration: an analysis of factors enhancing collaboration in education," (PhD dissertation, University of Wisconsin, Madison, 1983.) *Dissertation Abstracts International* Volume 44, No. 3, p. 640A.

7. Ellen A. Issacs, and Herbert H. Clark, "References in conversation between experts and novices," *Journal of Experimental Psychology: General,* 116 (1987), 26–37; Rupert Brown and Domino Adams "The effects of intergroup similarity and goal interdependence on intergroup attitudes and task performance," *Journal of Experimental Social Psychology,* 22 (1986), 78–92.

8. "Conoco Project: Executive Summary". An unpublished report. The Research Libraries Group, Stanford, Calif., May 13, 1987. Participating institutions in German were Columbia, Brigham Young, Cornell, N.Y.P.L., Stanford, Northwestern, Penn, Minnesota and Yale. Those in Geology were Colorado State, Columbia, Iowa, Minnesota, Stanton, N.Y.P.C. and Suny Stony Brook.

9. "Conoco Project: Executive Summary," pp. i–iv.

Coordinated Collection Development in a Multitype Environment: Promise and Challenge

by Keith Michael Fiels

magine, if you will, that the year 2010 has arrived, and that many of the wonderful things that librarians worked so hard for in the last half of the twentieth century have come to pass. Libraries of all types, large and small, are linked through a network of automated systems, providing total bibliographic access to the holdings of every library. Better still, patrons now receive items in hours or days through a combination of telefacsimile and ultrafast delivery. To the users, each library has become a gateway to all resources held by all libraries, and library information services are "location transparent," that is, the patron has little awareness of where a piece of information may in fact have come from—it may be from a library across the street or from one across the country.

Yet, despite the elimination of almost all location and delivery barriers, a number of problems still exist in this best of all possible worlds: books won't go away as a major source of information; expensive materials seem to be even more expensive; rare materials are even rarer; there are still never enough popular, high demand materials at the local level; the fill rate for information requests at the regional, state, and national level has stabilized, necessitating costly retrieval from outside sources.

Clearly, automated bibliographic access and ultrafast delivery alone are not going to resolve all existing problems in providing vastly improved library information services. Increasingly, coordinated collection development is being seen as the "missing link" in this process.

Coordinated collection development may be defined as the process by which a group of libraries develop individual and/or joint collections within an overall plan for the accomplishment of certain goals. Generally, these goals include increasing the total information resources available to the users of each library. In addition to thus guaranteeing that the whole is greater than the sum of the parts, coordinated collection development can also have as a goal insuring that each item within a network is placed where it will be most effective. As interlibrary loan is reactive, coordinated collection development is proactive —its goal is to have the item there *before* it is requested. Coordinated collection development may include a number of related activities, including coordinated planning; collection analysis; standardization of policies; establishment of shared databases; and coordinated or joint acquisitions, retentions, storage, and preservation.

Recently, a number of major efforts have refocused attention on coordinated collection development and its potential impact on library services. Concurrently, new technology has begun providing more powerful tools and methodologies in support of coordinated collection development. Most significantly, the number of efforts involving libraries of different types has grown markedly. The reasons for this are evident. The rationale for coordination in the development of collections is similar for every type of library—whether academic, institutional, public, school, or special.

First, the information explosion has led to a dramatic increase in the quantity and form of publication. In 1984 alone, Bowker reported an increase of 22 percent in new book and serial titles in the technical literature area. At the same time, the cost of purchasing, housing, and servicing these materials has more than doubled over the last ten years. Against these increases in publication output and cost must be placed the stable or decreasing materials budgets of most libraries.

To these factors must be added the increasingly sophisticated demands of users. As any one who has staffed a public service desk in any library is all too aware, the likelihood of owning a specific title requested by a patron is much lower than most of us would like to admit—some estimates place the average figure as low as 50 percent. This trend promises to continue unabated as the quantity and forms of publication multiply.

The impact of these trends has been generally acknowledged to be the end of self-sufficiency for the individual library. While automated bibliographic location and ultrafast delivery can and will help improve utilization of existing resources within a network, they alone cannot guarantee that materials are utilized as effectively as possible or expand the total resources available within the network. Coordinated collection development, however, offers real potential for both.

COORDINATED COLLECTION DEVELOPMENT NETWORK MODELS

Coordinated collection development efforts always occur within a network setting. A number of distinct types of coordinated resource networks may be identified, although most networks exhibit some combination of characteristics.

The first type of network is based on libraries of a similar type. Most notable and widespread have been efforts among academic librarires, but health science libraries have also developed coordinated collection plans in many states. Many public library systems have long practiced a form of coordination through specialized branch collections. Such groups often have the advantgae of beginning with a clear understanding of specializations within a discipline or field, an important prerequisite to coordination.

A second type is based on a geographical area—a county, region, or state. Geographically based networks are often multitype in nature. Such groups may also be more easily able to examine the respective roles of each participant in meeting the total information needs of a single community, and tailor services accordingly.

A third type is based on a particular resource or material format. Examples of this might include coordination among libraries in the development of serials, nonprint media, microform, or other such collections. Generally, the more expensive the material, the more likely coordination is.

A fourth type is based on a particular subject. In addition to obvious applications in technical fields, a group of libraries might, for instance, coordinate the development of resources in a specific foreign language, or a particular competency level.

The last type is based upon special communication linkage. In this model, a group of libraries sharing an automated system, a bibliographic utility, or compatible systems might seek to coordinate resource development. While such a group is normally based on ease of communication, it is important to remember that the communication system may or may not lend itself to optimal lending or to patterns of user need.

Within the network context, various degrees of intensity distinguish coordinated collection development. At its most fundamental level, coordination may mean only the development of stronger, more focused local collections within a framework of communication and resource sharing. Often, the first step in coordinated resource development is the cooperative acquisition of specialized or expensive materials, either housed in a central site or divided among libraries. In this instance, these acquisitions may have little impact on the collection policies of individual libraries. Often, the funding for these cooperative purchases comes from some outside source (such as the state), but shared purchase funds often support them as well.

On the other hand, libraries may cooperate in the division of in-depth collection responsibilities in certain subjects or format areas. In this instance, each library no longer attempts to maintain a comprehensive collection in every field, and begins instead to develop specific areas in depth. Only general works are purchased in other areas, the specialized collection of other cooperating libraries providing backup for those patrons with more specialized needs.

At its highest levels of development, coordinated resource development can allow the divesture of redundant collections by libraries and even the

> As any one who has staffed a public service desk in any library is all too aware, the likelihood of owning a specific title requested by a patron is much lower than most of us would like to admit—some estimates place the average figure as low as 50 percent.

transfer of existing collections in an attempt to insure that resources are physically located where they are most effective.

KEY ELEMENTS OF COORDINATED COLLECTION DEVELOPMENT

For any coordinated collection development project to succeed, a number of key elements must be present. The first of these elements is a firm *commitment to resource sharing*. When a library agrees to change its collection policies, it must be absolutely confident that it can depend on long-term access to other collections it now relies on.

The second element is interlibrary *communication*. Communication of three types is essential: libraries must be able to communicate management information on an ongoing basis to insure continued coordination; they must be able to quickly locate bibliographic holdings and status information on materials in other collections; they must be able to quickly and easily place interlibrary loan requests for those items once they are located. With the shared automated circulation system perhaps the closest to a total communication system available between libraries today, it is no surprise to learn that some form of subject specialization often follows close behind the implementation of a joint automated system. Even without formal effort, an increase in the title count often results as individual libraries begin checking the online database in order to avoid duplication of less desirable items.

Physical access to materials is a third element. While electronic communication systems speed up the location and requesting of materials enormously, studies indicate that the actual time required to get materials into patron hands has in fact changed very little. As a result, delivery speed is a critical issue in any coordinated resource network. While moving materials around more quickly is crucial, however, often little attention is paid to moving people around—direct access by patrons to other libraries in the coordinated resource network. Both must be taken into account, particularly on a regional level, in the design of a total system. Patterns of patron work and travel may have a substantial impact on the optimum placement of resources.

A fourth element is a *shared methodology for describing, evaluating, and analyzing collections*. A good deal of material is available on the techniques used by various groups of libraries to describe their physical collections. Perhaps the most significant efforts in this area have been the National Shelf List Count and the Research Librar-

ies Group (RLG) Conspectus Project. The conspectus is a comprehensive listing based on the Library of Congress classification system. Over 5,000 descriptors have been identified. A number of projects have developed Dewey conversion tables, a prerequisite to multitype coordinated collection development.

While this degree of specificity is necessary in a project involving the nation's major research libraries, most groups conducting collection analyses have sought to develop listings containing a smaller number of broader descriptors. In Illinois, three additional levels were developed, containing 20, 119, and 507 descriptors respectively. Others have utilized two additional levels. While the RLG conspectus promises to become the national standard, little consistency exists between those projects that have attempted to develop broader descriptors.

The evaluation of collections presents other challenges. In general, all evaluation techniques to date may be described as either collection- or user-centered. Collection-centered techniques depend on such factors as size of collection, age of collection, conformity with standard bibliographies, or the judgment of subject experts. While techniques such as shelf-list measurement are essentially quantitative, many evaluation techniques depend to a large degree on subjective, qualitative judgments. Both ALA and the RLG libraries use a standard series of levels to describe collections on a subject-by-subject basis. These levels are as follows:

A. Comprehensive level
B. Research level
C. Study level
D. Basic level
E. Minimal level
F. Out of scope

While much effort has gone into the development of detailed criteria for determining the level of a collection, additional subdivisions have proved necessary. Most recently, libraries in Alaska have developed a series of subdivisions for each of the levels. Other efforts have used delphi and other group techniques. In the end, however, use of such self-evaluation tools has proven to depend to a large degree on subjective assessments. These often vary from institution to institution and have proven to be of limited use in planning.

A second approach to evaluation is the client- or user-based. This approach derives quantitative information on collections through usage studies. These include circulation studies, document delivery tests, shelf availability studies, inhouse use studies, and citation studies. While both collection- and user-based techniques present advantages and disadvantages, each serves to suggest more clearly the strengths of collections in meeting local and network needs.

Analysis will normally follow description and evaluation. Often the analysis will be undertaken to identify uncovered or "endangered" fields and candidate areas for primary collection responsibility. Clearly, the use of computer analysis will increase the ability of libraries to make such decisions on a firmer statistical foundation in the future. In Illinois, a series of microcomputer software programs have been developed to allow standard analyses of local library and network performance.

A fifth element is accurate *statistical information* on collection usage and interlibrary loan activity. Interlibrary loan statistics have been used in Illinois and other places to determine the fill rate on a subject/collection basis. In New York, OCLC interlibrary loan statistics have been successfully used to provide an "objective" measure of collection strengths and overlaps between collections.

Ideally, decisions about coordinated resource development should be made on the basis of hard numbers, rather than conjecture or assumptions about usage not based on firm data. Were this not difficult enough, those attempting to conduct statistical analyses have discovered that even the most self-evident activities may be defined in different ways by different libraries. Until a clear picture of current use of materials is available, sound decisions cannot be made, nor can the impact of any coordinated resource development be evaluated. All too often, coordinated resource development plans are set up according to an intellectual model without a clear understanding of actual patron use.

A formal *plan* is the last key element. While some form of coordinated resource development on an informal level is relatively common, coordinated resource development on a regional level will require a formal, written plan. This plan requires a definition of the population to be served; a statement of needs, goals, objectives, activities; and the responsibilities of each library in the overall scheme.

COORDINATED COLLECTION DEVELOPMENT PROJECTS

In 1866, seven Chicago theological libraries undertook what is perhaps the first recorded example of coordinated collection development in this country when they agreed to specialize in an attempt to create a combined national research center for religious studies. Until relatively recently, most coordinated efforts have been based on groups of academic libraries. Generally, these groups have had as their goal an increase in the total number of titles available to researchers in each institution, the prevention of duplication, and the obtaining of rare or highly specialized resources. The most common method of achieving this goal has been through the assignment of subject specializations. Normally, publishing output has served as a standard measure of the comprehensiveness of these specialized collections.

An early example of such an arrangement is the libraries comprising the Triangle Research Libraries Network, which has been operating since 1934 between Duke University, The University of North Carolina at Chapel Hill, and the North Carolina State University. Under this arrangement, the participating institutions have agreed to mutual exclusivity in a number of subject and format areas, with faculty requests for specialized materials often referred to other participants for purchase. Similar in scope is the agreement between the five Massachusetts colleges which since 1951 have participated in the coordination of responsibilities for serials acquisitions in a number of research areas. Recently, this group abandoned a centralized collection in favor of a shared database and automated system, the first step toward cooperative acquisitions on a broader level.

Within the last five years, coordinated collection development among academic libraries has been given a new thrust by the Research Libraries Group (RLG) Conspectus Project. This project has attempted, among other goals, to create a framework for collaboration between RLG libraries on a national level and a standard series of collection descriptors. In Indiana, Purdue University, Notre Dame University, and Indiana University are participating in a related pilot project. Under the North American Collection Inventory Project (NACIP), the three research libraries will utilize the conspectus categories as a basis for the development of a coordinated collection development plan.

Other approaches to coordinated collection development among academic libraries have been initiated on a statewide level. In California, the nine University of California campus libraries have been involved in a state-funded shared-purpose program since 1976. Under this program, three percent of the total materials budget for the system has been devoted each year to the purchase of materials determined to be too costly for duplication, infrequently used, or of a unique nature. Decisions regarding placement of materials are made collectively. In New York State, legislation passed in 1981 now makes funding available each year to academic libraries for materials purchases determined in accordance with a cooperative, regional plan for coordinated collection develoment. While only academic libraries receive direct grants under the New York program, any library of any type may participate in the regional plan if it so wishes.

Within the last few years, multitype coordinated collection development projects have been undertaken in several states. In Colorado, six academic libraries and the Denver Public Library have identified classes of material for cooperative acquisitions. The goal of this group has been the creation of a single research collection to serve the residents of the state. In Alaska, eleven community colleges, three of the largest public library systems, and the University of Alaska have focused on the identification of research materials which are candidates for coordinated collection development.

Perhaps the most ambitious project on a multistate, multitype level to date has been the Pacific Northwest Collection Assessment Project, funded through a foundation grant. A total of 333 libraries are participating in this multi-year project, designed to establish cooperative methodologies for assessment and a regional approach to collection development.

Multitype coordinated collection development on a regional level has been undertaken in Missouri, Wisconsin, and Illinois. In Illinois, a series of manuals has been developed which allows local libraries to create collection development plans using standard methods of collection analysis. These individual library analyses may then serve as the basis for local and regional development of strategies for improving request fill rates at the local and interlibrary level. The Illinois process is based on voluntary groups sharing a subject-related concern and developing action plans based on response to identified needs rather than comprehensive coverage.

In Milwaukee, since 1976, the Library Council of Metropolitan Milwaukee (LCOMM) has undertaken to coordinate collection building through a Coordinated Collections Committee. This committee includes representatives from the Marquette University, Milwaukee Public, and University of Wisconsin-Milwaukee libraries. This committee has undertaken subject area assessments which involve libraries of various types collecting in a single field, followed by the designation of resource centers as appropriate. LCOMM has coordinated serials collections, developed a union list of newspapers, established a purchase clearinghouse for expensive materials, and made available

cataloging information cards which direct patrons to strong collections. In Missouri, a 1981 Conference launched a statewide effort at planning for coordinated collection development among libraries of all types.

PROMISE AND CHALLENGE

With the vast majority of multitype coordinated collection development efforts still in their initial stages, a number of observations may be made regarding their promise for the future. First, their concrete benefits are still largely in the future. While those libraries with long-standing arrangements are quick to caution that years or even decades are required before the impact of coordinated collection development is felt, a number of potential benefits can be predicted with some assurance. If successful, a coordinated collection develoment network can:

1. Provide all patrons with access to a wider range of materials and services.
2. Increase patron request fill rates at the local, regional, state, and national level.
3. Reduce the redundancy of less-used resources in a network.
4. Allow individual libraries increased specialization in meeting the primary needs of local clients/users.
5. Allow for expansion of resources without additional local expenditures through increased utilization of resources within a network

Not all coordinated collection development networks, however, are necessarily designed to provide all of these benefits. It is important to note that a fundamental difference between existing coordinated collection development networks and recent efforts at multitype groups lies in their objectives. Those groups which traditionally have been comprised of academic libraries have almost universally had as their objectives the development of comprehensive collections and an increase in the total number of titles available within the group. Multitype groups, on the other hand, are exploring objectives more closely related to increasing patron satisfaction levels at the local, regional, and state level. These groups must balance the demands of the research level for comprehensiveness with local needs for high demand materials.

Many projects currently underway are just beginning to develop initial goals and objectives for coordinated collection development, and they face the very difficult task of defining efforts in terms other than the development of comprehensive collections at the research level. While this must remain a key element of any coordinated collection development plan, the question of how to determine where other resources should be placed to increase system performance will be the subject of much study in the next few years. Libraries are beginning to collect and analyze standard data on collections and performance, but very little reliable data exist yet on how particular strategies relate to performance.

Happily, the attempt to analyze collections within a coordinated framework brings immediate benefits: libraries become aware of the strengths of other institutions, and more efficient referrals and requests as a result. In addition, the identification of collection gaps and areas of poor performance is almost always possible, and often remedied with minimal effort. Beyond the immediate benefits, the potential impact of coordinated collection development may in fact be as far-reaching as that of the new technology. In the end, it may have even more impact on the quality of service libraries offer.

Select Bibliography

Dorothy E. Christiansen, C. Roger Davis and Jutta Reed-Scott. "Guide to Collection Evaluation through Use and User Studies." *Library Resources and Technical Services,* October/December, 1983.

Collection Analysis in Research Libraries: An Interim Report on a Self-study Process. Washington, D.C., Association of Research Libraries, 1978.

Cooperative Collection Development in Multitype Library Networks: A Beginning—Goals and Methods. Proceedings of the 1980 Annual Conference of the Missouri Library Association. Ed. by Philip Tompkins. Columbia, Mo. Missouri Library Assn., 1981. Distributed by the Metropolitan Washington Library Council, 1875 Eve St., NW, Suite 200, Washington, DC 20006.

Guidelines for Collection Development. Chicago, American Library Association, 1979.

John Kaiser. "Resource Sharing in Collection Development," in *Collection Development in Libraries: A Treatise,* ed. by Robert D. Stueart and George B. Miller, Jr., p. 139–58. Foundations in Library and Information Science, V 10, pt. A. Greenwich, Conn. JAI Press, 1980.

Karen Krueger. *Coordinated Cooperative Collection Development for Illinois Libraries.* Springfield. Illinois State Library, 1983. 3 volumes.

New York State Library Conference on Planning for Collection Development, Albany, May 12–13, 1982. *Summary of Papers and Discussions.* Albany. New York State Library, 1982. Sponsored by the New York State Library; conducted by the Office of Management Studies, Association of Research Libraries.

RLG Collection Development Manual. 2nd ed. Stanford, California, RLG. Inc., 1981.

Toward Cooperative Collection Development in the Illinois Library and Information Network. Springfield. Illinois State Library, 1977.

Douglas L. Zweizig. *Test of Data Collection Approaches to Coordinated/Cooperative Collection Development.* Rockville, Md. King Research, Inc. 1982.

CONTRIBUTORS

Anne Marie Allison is Director of University Libraries at the University of Central Florida in Orlando.

Irena Bell is Assistant Chief of Multilingual Biblioservice at the National Library of Canada in Ottawa.

Joseph J. Branin is Associate University Librarian for Public Services at the University of Minnesota Libraries in Minneapolis.

Bonita Bryant is Assistant Director for Collection Development at the State University of New York, University at Albany University Libraries.

Carolyn Bucknall is Assistant Director for Collection Development at the University of Texas at Austin General Libraries.

Margaret M. Byrnes is Head of the Preservation Section at the National Library of Medicine in Bethesda, Maryland.

Cathy Carey is Adult Services Librarian at the Rochester Hills Public Library in Rochester, Michigan.

Cynthia H. Comer is Head of Reference at the Oberlin College Library in Oberlin, Ohio.

Ginnie Cooper is Director of Libraries for Multnomah County Library in Portland, Oregon.

Charles D'Aniello is Coordinator for Collection Development of the Lockwood Library, State University of New York at Buffalo.

Patricia E. Feehan is Instructor in the College of Library and Information Science, University of South Carolina in Columbia.

Judith M. Feller is Government Documents Librarian at East Stroudsburg University in East Stroudsburg, Pennsylvania.

Keith Michael Fiels is Executive Director of the Northwest Regional Library Cooperative in Chester, New Jersey.

Elizabeth Futas is Director of the Graduate School of Library and Information Science at the University of Rhode Island.

George C. Hammond is an Attorney with Dewey Ballantine in New York City.

Sara C. Heitshu is Assistant University Librarian for Technical Services at the University of Arizona in Tucson.

Ferne B. Hyman is Assistant University Librarian at Rice University in Houston.

Medea Ionesco is Librarian at the Richelieu Valley Regional High School in Montreal, Canada.

Bill Katz is Professor at the State University of New York at Albany, School of Library and Information Science and Policy.

J. Travis Leach is Serials Librarian at the University of Arizona in Tucson.

Paul Metz is Principal Bibliographer at Virginia Polytechnic Institute in Blacksburg, Virginia.

J. Wesley Miller is an artistic property lawyer in Springfield, Massachusetts. His companion essay on research library collections, "Thoughts on Endangered Book Librarianship" appeared in the *American Council* of *Learned Societies Newsletter*, 2nd Series, 3.1 (Winter 1991):7-8.

Marilyn L. Miller is Professor and Chair of the Department of Library and Information Studies at the University of North Carolina at Greensboro. She also is President-elect of the American Library Association for the 1992-93 term.

Anne C. Moore was formerly Humanities/Literature Catalog Librarian at the University of Arizona.

Paul H. Mosher is Vice Provost and Director of Libraries at the University of Pennsylvania in Philadelphia.

Mickey Moskowitz is Director of the Emerson College Library in Boston.

Lois Olsrud is Central Reference Librarian at the University of Arizona Library in Tucson.

Mark Sandler is Coordinator of Graduate Library Collections at the University of Michigan in Ann Arbor.

Patricia Glass Schuman is President of Neal-Schuman Publishers in New York City and President of the American Library Association for the 1991-92 term.

Mary Sellen is Library Director at Chapman College in Orange, California.

Judith Serebnick is Associate Professor in the School of Library and Information Science at Indiana University.

David H. Stam is University Librarian at Syracuse University in Syracuse, New York.

Richard Bruce Warr is Senior Consultant with FIND/SVP in New York City.

Marie Zielinska is Chief of Multilingual Biblioservice at the National Library of Canada in Ottawa.

INDEX